Converging Infrastructures

Converging Infrastructures

Intelligent Transportation and the National
Information Infrastructure

edited by Lewis M. Branscomb and James H. Keller

A Publication of the Harvard Information Infrastructure Project

The MIT Press, Cambridge, Massachusetts, and London, England

This book was printed and bound in the United States of America.

Library of Congress Cataloging-in-Publication Data

Converging infrastructures: intelligent transportation and the National
   Information Infrastructure / edited by Lewis M. Branscomb and James H. Keller.
      p.   cm.—(A Publication of the Information Infrastructure Project)
   Includes bibliographical references and index.
   ISBN 0-262-02407-1 (hc: alk. paper).—ISBN 0-262-52215-2 (pbk.: alk. paper)
   1. Intelligent Vehicle Highway Systems—United States.   2. Information
superhighway—United States.   I. Branscomb, Lewis M., 1926–   . II. Keller,
James H.   III. Harvard Information Infrastructure Project.   IV. Series.
TE228.3.C66   1996
388.3'12—dc20   96-15787
                                                                      CIP

Contents

Foreword   vii
Federico Peña

Preface   xi

Introduction: Converging Infrastructures   1
Lewis M. Branscomb and James H. Keller

Overview: Policy Frameworks for ITS and the NII

Assessing Federal Roles   23
David A. Whitney and Thomas O. Mottl

Common Policy Concerns   59
Stephen J. Lukasik

ITS Requirements in the Context of the NII

ITS Information Service Content   93
Elisabeth J. Carpenter

Metropolitan Communications Requirements   134
J. Bailey and G. Pruitt

Why Build a Dedicated ITS Communications System?:
A Private-Sector Perspective   148
Robert S. Arden and Padmanabhan Srinagesh

Technical Issues

Intelligent Agents and ITS   177
Su-Shing Chen

Global Interoperability for the NII and ITS:
Standards and Policy Challenges   191
Valerie Shuman and Richard Jay Solomon

Geospatial Data for ITS   209
Stephen J. Bespalko, John H. Ganter,
and Marsha D. Van Meter

Public and Private Roles

Shared Resources Policies and Highway Rights of Way   229
Thomas A. Horan and Susan Jakubiak

Public and Private Roles in Delivering Traveler
Information: Two Case Studies   251
Randolph W. Hall and Y. B. Yim

Market Deployment of Transportation Information
Infrastructure: Siemens' European Strategy   279
Hans K. Klein and Joseph M. Sussman

ITS Implementation Issues

Institutional Issues in Local Implementation   293
Douglas C. Melcher and Daniel Roos

Why Driver Privacy Must Be a Part of ITS   324
Simson L. Garfinkel

Problems of Success: Privacy, Property,
and Transactions   341
Marcus Wigan

Conclusion: Opportunities for Policy Convergence   355
Lewis M. Branscomb and James H. Keller

Glossary of Acronyms   371

Contributors   375

Index   379

Foreword

Federico Peña

The National Information Infrastructure (NII) will enhance our national well-being by providing increased access to information while protecting privacy and security. While much has been written about the NII's impact on education, the provision of government services, and the entertainment and shopping choices that will become available to us, the sector of the economy where better access to timely and reliable information may have the most immediate impact on our daily lives is transportation.

Unless improvements are made to the nation's transportation system, the projected growth in traffic will increase congestion, reduce mobility, lower business productivity, and adversely affect safety. The economic costs of increased congestion could be immense. New approaches are needed to address the imbalance between the capacity of our transportation infrastructure and the growing demand for transportation services. We need to make improvements to all components of the nation's transportation system. Simply stated, we need to find ways to use the existing transportation infrastructure much more efficiently.

Advances in communications and information technologies are critically important for improving the performance of the transportation system; a modern and efficient transportation system is essential for promoting economic development and raising our collective standard of living. Many of the improvements to the transportation system will rely on the ability of private firms and public agencies to gather, process, analyze, and disseminate information to travelers about the availability of different transportation services and the performance of the transportation system.

The Department of Transportation—in partnership with many private-sector companies and state and local governments—has been supporting a program to develop and implement Intelligent Transportation Systems (ITS). ITS integrates advanced communications, computers, sensors, satellites, and information processing technologies into transportation systems. Major advances in computer, communication, and electronics technologies are making it possible to implement ITS at a reasonable cost. No longer viewed as science fiction, ITS technologies are being adopted by communities throughout the nation to solve today's transportation problems.

New information technologies are already demonstrating an impressive ability to improve the safety and efficiency of highway operations. For example, advanced traffic control systems have cut travel time by 15 percent and vehicle stops by 35 percent in one travel corridor in California. Freeway management in Minneapolis has increased rush-hour speeds by 35 percent and capacity by 22 percent. Using automated toll collection, the State of Oklahoma has cut the cost of operating a toll lane by 91 percent. Remarkably, ITS technologies achieve these results at a cost as low as one-twentieth of what it would cost to construct new highways to achieve equivalent highway operating performance.

In another example, DOT has just finished a pilot program that successfully tested a computer system to allow 911 emergency dispatchers to receive information on shipments of hazardous materials directly from railroad dispatchers, greatly speeding up emergency response in the event of an accident. As one examines ITS, it becomes clear that although it appears to be about vehicles on roads, rails, and in the air, in fact it is primarily about information—and how travelers, shippers, and receivers use it. Indeed, information about transportation conditions and alternatives will be one of the major "products" distributed on the NII.

In addition to the U.S. DOT's research, development and implementation activities, one major aspect of our mission in the ITS area is to help create uniform standards to ensure the compatibility of ITS technologies and interoperatiblity among these systems.

The emerging national architecture is intended to allow ITS to be a user of NII distribution systems. Open system architecture will focus further research and development and will allow new information technologies to be introduced. The U.S. DOT has set a goal of having a core ITS infrastructure implemented in most metropolitan areas in the next decade. This core infrastructure will use the new products and services of the NII to deliver accurate, timely, and reliable travel information to people, whatever their location or mode of transportation.

In recognition of the importance of the information infrastructure to transportation, the U.S. DOT has initiated a series of research studies, workshops, and forums to begin to build appropriate bridges between the ITS and the NII communities and to assess the needs and opportunities for ITS applications on the NII. The potential scale, reliability, and security requirements needed to adopt ITS products and services make it one of the most challenging of all the potential NII applications.

The ITS/NII Workshop held at Harvard University in July 1995, upon which this book is based, represents an important step in understanding the vital relationship between ITS and the NII and developing a common bond between these two important national efforts. The workshop addressed fundamental questions about the role that ITS communications requirements can play in the definition of the NII. I offer my congratulations to the John F. Kennedy School of Government at Harvard University; The Massachusetts Institute of Technology's Center for Technology, Policy, and Industrial Development; and the DOT's Volpe National Transportation Systems Center, which, with sponsorship from DOT's Office of the Assistant Secretary for Transportation Policy, helped to make this workshop a success.

Preface

This volume explores Intelligent Transportation Systems (ITS) as a key area of public-sector activity in the development of advanced intelligent infrastructure. As Secretary of Transportation Federico Peña points out in his foreword, ITS has the potential to transform the transportation sector. This book is the result of a project undertaken at the request of the Secretary's Office to explore from a policy perspective the relationships between ITS and the general-purpose National Information Infrastructure. Most of the chapters were first presented as papers at a conference held at the John F. Kennedy School of Government on July 13, 1995, and subsequently revised and updated. The book does not attempt to present a set of consensus viewpoints (though the reader will find general agreement among the authors on larger issues). Instead, it offers a broad set of perspectives, intended to advance dialogue in this important area.

The book is presented in five sections. The first deals with federal policy issues, focusing on the ITS and NII program structures and especially on areas of common policy concern in the two programs. The second looks at ITS requirements in the context of the general-purpose National Information Infrastructure. The third turns to technological issues, analyzing ITS and NII requirements from the perspectives of information content, performance, standards policy, and technical solutions. The fourth examines the possibilities for collaboration between the public and private sectors in local implementation. The final section describes a variety of ITS implementation issues, including the question of privacy.

The conference and this volume were made possible by a grant from the Department of Transportation and the John A. Volpe National Transportation Systems Center. Additional support was provided from the operating funds of the Harvard Information Infrastructure Project, which during this period was supported by AT&T, Bellcore, Delphi Internet Services, GM Hughes Electronics, IBM, Microsoft, and MITRE Corporation. We want to thank the contributing authors, especially for their efforts to refine and update their work in a time of rapid change. We also thank those who helped in the production of the workshop and this volume, especially Liz Carpenter, Richard John, John O'Donnell, Ed Ramsdell, and Gary Ritter at the Volpe Center; Christine Johnson of the DOT Joint Program Office for ITS; the Office of the Secretary of Transportation; Lee McKnight at MIT; and Janet Abbate, Brian Kahin, Tim Leshan, and Beth Rosenberg at the Science, Technology, and Public Policy Program. We also express our appreciation to Larry Cohen and Bob Prior at the MIT Press.

This volume is the third in the Information Infrastructure Series, a collaboration between the Harvard Information Infrastructure Project and the MIT Press. The Harvard Information Infrastructure Project began six years ago with a small workshop on "Commercialization of the Internet" (summarized in the online document RFC 1192). Held right after the first commercial Internet services were announced, that workshop asked how the subsidized Internet should evolve toward commercialization. The Project's first book, *Building Information Infrastructure* (McGraw-Hill Primis, 1992) was an early effort to scope out the broader vision of a digital infrastructure. Subsequently, in September 1993, the National Information Infrastructure initiative was officially launched. Throughout this period, the Internet has continued its extraordinary growth, becoming accessible for the first time not only to universities and high-tech companies but also to the general public, and supporting an increasing array of new application areas.

This volume follows *Public Access to the Internet*, edited by Brian Kahin and James Keller, and *Standards Policy for Information Infrastructure*, edited by Brian Kahin and Janet Abbate. Future volumes will address the substantive areas where the Project is now involved—digital libraries, interoperability, the Global Information

Infrastructure, and intellectual property. It is our intention to create volumes that reflect the judgments and research of scholars and practitioners from a wide range of areas and fields. We hope that they will collectively make a contribution to both policy and practice.

Lewis M. Branscomb
Director, Science, Technology, and Public Policy Program

Introduction: Converging Infrastructures

Lewis M. Branscomb and James H. Keller

Just as the highway metaphor has driven the vision of advanced communications infrastructure, advances in communications are pushing the vision of our transportation systems future. How do these two systems interrelate? What policy issues does this relationship raise?

Over the past half century, the U.S. highway system has advanced regional and national economic development by enhancing access to markets for goods, services, and people. It has also provided direct quality-of-life benefits, by providing easier access to both work and leisure. Now, the traditional model for surface transportation is reaching its limit. In many areas systems are at or beyond capacity. Because of space and budget constraints and environmental concerns, building new or bigger roads is not the answer. Instead, transportation experts are now focusing on promoting more efficient use of existing capacity. The central theme of these efforts is more efficient integration of existing transportation components through the use of information technology.

The Department of Transportation's Intelligent Transportation Systems (ITS) Program is the focal point for coordinating the development of a national ITS system. The current program was funded in 1991 under the Intermodal Surface Transportation Efficiency Act of 1991 (ISTEA). Anticipated benefits of ITS include reduced travel time and pollution and increased traveler safety and convenience. While ITS services have clear public-interest benefits, the public sector's role in ITS development will in many respects be indirect. Consistent with activity in other elements of the National

Information Infrastructure, development will be a complex mix of public–private interactions.

The federal role in the development of ITS will primarily be one of enabler, just as it is for the NII. Thus ITS services and systems will not emerge in fulfillment of an agreed national plan, managed into place by the Department of Transportation, but will evolve under DOT leadership in response to the needs of states and communities and the investments of commercial firms pursuant to market demands. Nevertheless, a thoughtful projection of some of the most attractive and needed applications have been constructed for the ITS program. ITS user services are broken down into seven areas consisting of 29 applications. These applications are presented in detail in the chapter by Carpenter in this volume.

ITS systems involving fixed facilities will initially develop locally and regionally, while commercial products for use in vehicles and in trip planning will be sold nationally and internationally. The Department of Transportation will need to take a leadership role in a variety of system architecture and standards development, deployment, and coordination issues to ensure that all of these systems will coalesce into a coherent national system. Standards will be needed to address interoperability at different layers in the ITS architecture and issues of data compatibility across ITS systems. Data collected locally must integrate smoothly into national systems, which will require broad agreement on data definitions and coding. Local system developers will have to agree on what information is important, what it will be called, and how it will be recorded.

ITS standardization issues are complex relative to those in the traditional telecommunications environment because they span a broader array of technologies and systems. At the same time, however, the environment for standardization is relatively weak. Telecom standards evolved with a common platform and a stable— indeed regulated—competitive environment; ITS will consist of heterogeneous systems and a relatively independent set of players. In addition, many of the technologies for which standards will be most needed are nascent or immature at this time. As with other areas of computing and communications, players will face a conflicting set of incentives to seek standardization, including incentives to differentiate (for competitive advantage and to lock in market share) and to seek interoperability (to expand the market for services and to lower the costs for customers to migrate to their system).

Like standards development, many other aspects of ITS development and deployment will involve new and complex coordination issues. The technologies for many ITS applications have already been developed, but a variety of non-technical issues will determine how and when these applications become widely available. Liability, intellectual property, security, privacy, and data ownership issues will all influence private firms' commitment to deploying ITS services and the users' interests in adopting them (see the chapter by Wigan in this volume).

Those in government and industry responsible for planning and coordinating ITS developments recognize that some of its communications systems, such as those supporting traffic flow control and addressing emergency situations, will require real-time,[1] quick-response capability with very high reliability. Such systems will probably have to be dedicated to ITS applications. At the other extreme, trip planning and many other "off-line" applications can surely be supported by the nation's general purpose data networks and other communications services, which are collectively referred to as the National Information Infrastructure (NII).

Like ITS, the NII is a moving target. Today its digital network services consist largely of unregulated value-added services built on the largely digital national telecommunications infrastructure. The best-known and most ubiquitously interoperable set of those networks is referred to as the Internet, which was promulgated in research institutions in and out of government, with the universities playing an especially important role. The Internet is in transition from being an experimental platform for rapid innovation among research experts to being the basis for an international, commercially operated set of data, voice, and image services. This future will be realized in most dramatic form when telephone, cable TV, and wireless and satellite communication services reach homes and offices with broadband, interactive, digital capability. The providers of information content have started to make the investments needed to take advantage of these capabilities [1].

The boundaries between the NII and the ITS are unclear, however, and lie in what combination of architecture, commercial strategies, public services, and regulatory constraints will serve to define the NII/ITS relationship. In short, is the ITS a "domain-specific" application of the NII? Is ITS a special environment whose information systems support is specialized and only loosely coupled, through data sharing, with the NII? Or are ITS applications of such scale, diversity, and economic significance that ITS can shape the capabilities of the NII future?

Intelligent Transportation Systems

The mission of the ITS program is to improve the safety, efficiency, and capacity of the country's surface transportation system through the use of information technology. The ITS program is coordinated within DOT, bringing together each of the Department's major program areas. ITS systems integration and its real-time information requirements include not only managing the flow of real-time information to and from individual vehicles and the systems that control traffic flows, but also the seamless coupling of different modes of transportation. In addition, many ITS commercial applications for consumer motorists are anticipated. These include traffic management, vehicle navigation and tracking, electronic toll collection, augmentation of driver perception, automated emergency intervention, real-time traffic and travel information, trip planning, and eventually automation of at least parts of the driving process, such as collision avoidance.

Eventually ITS will call for a high-integrity, real-time network system. This system will take inputs from highway sensors, vehicle Global Positioning Satellite (GPS) systems, and other information-gathering systems.[2] This information will be continuously compiled in a system of databases with a dynamic model of the local, regional and national highway system, and will be used to provide real-time information on optimum routes, based on such factors as least-time and fuel economy. While there is a higher degree of homogeneity among ITS applications and data requirements than in the NII, the necessity for real-time information, the security issues, and the scale of some segments of ITS make it one of the most challenging NII applications.

There are many visions of the National Information Infrastructure. But the model that is emerging is that of a heterogeneous constellation of networks, services, and applications that are interconnected and, for many purposes, interoperating. Much of the popular dialogue on the NII has embraced the "information superhighway" metaphor. While this metaphor has successfully engaged the public, it conveys a limited vision of the makeup of information infrastructure. It evokes images of physical networks and switches, the lower level aspects of the infrastructure, and does not communicate the NII's higher-level content and processing elements.

The following elements provide a useful construct for thinking about information infrastructure [2]:

• *Telecommunications infrastructure.* The physical infrastructure (lines and switches). These are the elements that have traditionally been thought of as infrastructure.

• *Knowledge infrastructure.* The content—digitized information, organized for access and use.

• *Integration infrastructure.* The glue—the systems and processes that bring together heterogeneous networks, computers, databases, and applications. This will be a critical area for ITS, required to provide national-level information in an environment of local and regional implementations.

These three elements apply equally well to ITS. ITS will, of course, require a networking infrastructure. As described in later chapters, some ITS applications will require high bandwidth relative to today's telecommunications infrastructure, while others will run quite well on existing general purpose networks. A key question for planners is whether ITS requirements should influence NII network development. One example of direct interaction is the Shared Resources Policies currently being deployed in several states. In these programs state highway departments are providing right-of-way access to private telecommunications services companies to encourage the development of general purpose NII network capacity and help meet ITS infrastructure requirements (see the chapter by Horan and Jakubiak).

The integration infrastructure component of ITS has several aspects. The development of systems integration software, for integrating roadside cameras and other sensing elements with ITS networks and central management and monitoring facilities, will be market-driven. The more complex elements are the database structures and interfaces that will allow smooth integration of information across separately administered ITS systems.

Central to the development of ITS knowledge infrastructure will be the sorting out of public- and private-sector roles. The public sector will play an active and dominant role in collecting transportation information. How this information will be bundled with value-added services and distributed is less clear. What level of information services should be provided by state and local agencies? How should data be made available to private-sector information-service providers? Should a raw form of this publicly funded data be made available for free to anyone who would like to use or add value to it? Should it be sold to fund the cost of collection? Are there privacy issues that might limit these options? How these questions are sorted out will directly affect the quality and availability of information markets.

The Government Role

Like the NII initiative, ITS is at the forefront of changes in how the federal government will relate to the states and the private sector. In the post–Cold War economy, agency initiatives are being driven by a new set of requirements. These include: an active role for industry in project design, selection, and execution; reliance on private investment; mechanisms to ensure commercial adoption; complex management structures; and a federal role in consensus building [3]. ITS fits well into this model. The ITS program, and in particular the definition of ITS technical requirements, has been developed with active participation from ITS America, a broad-based consortium of industry, government and research interests, with the understanding that ITS will rely heavily on private investment and state and local deployment.

The ITS program was established by Congress through the Intelligent Vehicle Highway Systems Act (IVHS),[3] part of ISTEA. This legislation authorizes the Secretary of Transportation to conduct a program to research, develop, operationally test, and promote implementation of ITS systems.[4] While the Secretary is authorized in these areas, it is clearly indicated in the legislation that this role is intended to be cooperative and facilitory. The Secretary is directed to seek transfer of federally owned or patented technology to the states and the private sector. The Secretary is also directed to consult with the heads of the Commerce Department, EPA, National Science Foundation, and other agencies, as well as to maximize the role the private sector, universities, and state and local governments in all aspects of the program.[5]

The management of ITS is conducted by the Joint Program Office in the Office of the Secretary of Transportation. The JPO manages ITS activities in all areas of the Department, as well as working actively to coordinate and build consensus among ITS stakeholders. As directed by ISTEA, DOT has produced a planning document, the "IVHS Strategic Plan: Report to Congress" (December, 1992), outlining the program's activities, roles, and responsibilities. DOT is also funding the development of a national ITS architecture. This development is being conducted by private consortia under the direction of DOT, and is still in process. Currently, the architecture is loosely defined, identifying ITS system elements and estimating the communication and information requirements of each. It does not specify the technical characteristics of component interfaces that will be required for interoperability.

To examine federal policy in the development of ITS, it is perhaps easiest to break down the areas of federal activity. As ITS is broad in scope, applicable federal involvement will vary greatly between different ITS application areas. For example, in the case of emergency fleet management, technology development will occur under a more traditional procurement model. Many traveler information services may be offered by commercial information service providers, and on-board capabilities will require the participation of auto manufacturers and wireless telecommunications companies. This participation could, in principle, be achieved either through market incentives or by mandating compliance.

Opportunities for federal activity in the development of ITS can be broken down into the following areas:

• *Promoting the development and testing of ITS technologies and applications.* This is an area in which DOT has been actively engaged. A number of DOT-funded demonstration projects are now underway, most addressing multiple ITS applications. These projects should go beyond traditional R&D to include a diffusion component aimed at assisting future implementers. The projects should focus not only on feasibility, but also on measuring benefits and cost effectiveness, and identifying any dependencies on or needs for interoperability with other ITS systems.

• *Fostering an environment that will engage state and local agencies and private firms in the deployment of ITS services.* The availability of ITS services depends largely on the efforts of state and local agencies and private firms to implement them. Some ITS services will come about on their own, based on their commercial viability. In other cases, regulatory mandates or public sector procurement will be necessary to stimulate product development and availability. DOT must clearly articulate its ITS goals to allow systems developers time to anticipate these requirements.

• *Promoting the development and adoption of standards and a national ITS architecture that will both ensure that local and regional systems coalesce into a coherent national system and allow integration of U.S. components into international systems.* Facilitating the deployment of an interoperable set of ITS implementations will involve many challenges. ITS will likely be deployed as a set of semi-autonomous local implementations, and will involve stakeholders in many branches of the computing, communications, and transportation industries. For these systems to coalesce smoothly into a national system, early and broad consensus will need to be achieved among product and service developers and local implementors. It will also require a robust architecture that can expand in both scope and scale to accommodate unanticipated service requirements.

• *Identifying and supporting those ITS application areas that provide clear benefit to the public but would not otherwise be deployed by the private sector, and assuring equitable access to an appropriate set of essential services.* ITS represents a broad array of application areas. Some of these areas are consumer-oriented conveniences, while others are public goods that will extend transportation and non-transportation benefits to the public at large. Federal ITS investment should be made on application-by-application, based on the anticipated service benefits and the potential for private investment (with and without federal support). Equity issues are complex, many of the ITS applications are truly consumer options, unnecessary for using the roads. Furthermore, some applications, such as traffic flow management, can at least in principle use telemetry from a fraction of GPS equipped vehicles to infer the density and speed of unequipped cars. Nevertheless, the nation's streets cannot be reserved for only those people who can afford expensive add-on equipment.

• *Clarifying areas of law that may inhibit the adoption of ITS services, including product and service liability, data ownership, privacy, and security.* The move towards ITS services will raise issues in a number of yet-to-be-defined areas of law. Some of these issues are specific to transportation; others are more broadly relevant in the emerging information society.

One area is liability. As transportation systems become more complex and new systems, technologies, and organizations influence the movement of people and materials, liability concerns begin to touch a larger array of players, some of whom may be unwitting participants. It is currently unclear to what extent information services and systems providers, and the purchasers of such equipment for their vehicles, will be responsible for failures ranging from inconvenience to catastrophe.[6]

Do public-sector service providers risk liability? How will legal jurisdictions be defined in an ITS world? Must ITS systems located in one state conform to the traffic laws of every state into which their communications may reach? Such ambiguities are a potential deterent to the development and availability of ITS products.

ITS has also produced concerns about the abuse of personal privacy (see the chapter by Garfinkel). This is already a problem today, as many citizens object to their state governments selling motor vehicle registration records. The information-gathering potential of ITS is tremendous. ITS systems may be able to identify where individuals (or at least their vehicles) are, and where they have been. Who owns this information, and who will have access to it [4]? Will there be limits on its use? Will service providers be able to sell this information to marketers?

DOT's role in ITS differs fundamentally from its earlier direct role in developing the federal highway system, and anticipates future challenges federal policymakers will face in other sectors. Areas of federal activity administered by other agencies, such as environmental management, housing, health care, education, and social services, are also becoming more information-intensive. ITS offers a proving ground for federal efforts to coordinate the development of intelligent infrastructure. A critical factor in managing this effort will be to maximize the extent to which systems can be leveraged across sectors. If ITS can be leveraged in ways that will decrease the marginal cost of developing infrastructure for other areas, it can help to jump-start these efforts, and offset or reduce ITS costs.

ITS Architecture and System Coherence

While local and regional needs for ITS differ dramatically, and innovations based on local investment should be encouraged, cars, buses, trucks, trains, and aircraft must be able to operate across state and local jurisdictional lines, and indeed into other countries. Thus, in pursuit of compatibility between local and regional systems, DOT has initiated the National ITS Architecture Development Program. This program was established in September 1993 and is requirements-driven, based on the 29 ITS user services. The architecture seeks to define the systems components and component interactions of a national ITS. Given the breadth of interoperability issues related to ITS, such a high level of coordination will be necessary, but it is not without risk. Key challenges facing planners will be ensuring acceptance and conformance and designing a system that will be able to support unanticipated requirements and applications. To ensure flexibility, ITS architecture should be based on information requirements and interfaces, not specific technologies or the particular way in which a service is provided. For example, when placing a phone call, a user is typically indifferent whether the call goes over copper, fiber, or any other medium, as long as a basic set of performance parameters are met.

Fullfilling these architectural guidelines will require require political as well as technological prowess. It will be difficult to achieve consensus among diverse ITS developers and implementors. The most important means of achieving conformance will be to keep the process open and participatory. This has been DOT's approach so far, and private sector participation has been strong.

Another opportunity to acheive conformance will be in procurement. To some degree, DOT will also be able to tie conformance to federal funding. However, not all local and regional implementations will receive federal funds, and while it is possible to mandate conformance as a requirement for general DOT highway funding, these funds may be shrinking and yield less influence. Quite apart from congressional constraints on federal spending, ITS applications will always have to compete for funding with repair of potholes, bridges, and other basic needs of the physical transportation infrastructure.

The ITS top-down architecture approach is interesting to consider in contrast to other infrastructure development efforts. Some of the reasons for the Internet's success, for example, have been its ability to evolve from the middle out, to function over unanticipated types of networking technology, and support unplanned applications. The ITS application areas are highly defined at present, but technology planning is historically an inexact science, and much will rest on users' willingness to pay.

To the extent that the Highway Trust Fund constitutes a major source of federal investment that could be tied to ITS objectives, the ITS is different from the larger NII of which it is a part. However, the states have a much bigger role in ITS than in the NII; in fact, the states' NII roles, already largely confined to telecommunications regulations, are likely to be substantially curtailed in the future. Thus, while the NII requires more sensitive relations between the federal government and private industry, the development and deployment of ITS requires a three way collaboration between a federal department, which holds significant financial resources; states, which bear the major responsibility both for investment and operations; and private industry, without which neither level of government can realize its objectives.

ITS Infrastructure Requirements

Most ITS applications have an inherent communications component. In the minds of many, ITS evokes a vision of communications networks dedicated exclusively (or primarily) to transportation services. The assumption is often made that communication facilities to support ITS will have to be constructed by highway and traffic authorities, as are the roads themselves. The truth is that if ITS must have its own communications and database infrastructrure, its relationship to the NII becomes of marginal interest (except perhaps to the builders of the NII). However, the ITS communications element, while pervasive, is generally not beyond the scope of anticipated NII capabilities. Instead, it appears that ITS communications requirements could largely be met through general-purpose infrastructure.

To test this issue, two questions must be explored and each ITS application tested against them. First, does the application require a dedicated network and/or databases that are secure against interchange outside the ITS domain? There are three possible justifications for such dedication: (a) technical: the real-time response requirements may demand it; (b) operational: the reliability and security of the ITS application may demand it; and (c) financial: a dedicated system might cost less than market alternatives, although this seems unlikely.

The second question is, what is the meaning of "dedicated"? The level of government control required to assure the required response time, reliability, and security of an information system can range from ownership to contractual obligations by a commercial vendor, which may be sharing physical (rather than logical) network facilities with other clients. (For further discussion, see the chapter by Arden and Srinagesh.)

The communications requirements of ITS applications can be grouped into three categories. The first group includes autonomous, stand-alone systems that will not be part of a larger network; among these are intersection collision-avoidance systems, which will communicate between approaching vehicles and intersection-based sensors. The next category includes applications that will likely be supported by commercially available communications services, for example, low-bandwidth, bursty applications like pre-trip or en-route travel information, which will likely be served by otherwise-available circuit- or packet-based wireless or wireline services. Lastly, there are applications that will require the support of a dedicated, special-purpose network. The dedicated network requirement is not present in most ITS applications.

To proceed with this analysis we need to look at five elements of ITS that might call for special-purpose infrastructure:

Dedicated networks. This category is intended to identify those ITS applications that may not be supported by general-purpose NII infrastructure. Analysis may show that communications service companies cannot offer attractive commercial rates services with sufficient reliability to provide the extraordinarily high levels of safety the transportation system must support. In this case a dedicated network that meets those requirements would have to be developed and constructed. Similarly, if the network delay cannot be assuredly maintained under the limit dictated by a traffic control system's safety and effectiveness, a dedicated network might be needed.

Roadside element deployment. Sensors and broadcast devices will be required along roadways to sense or communicate with vehicles. Broadcast devices may signal vehicles about road conditions, speed limit, or other factors. Roadside elements may also communicate with central servers managing traffic or freight information, but this will not necessarily require a special-purpose network.

Information/database systems. These systems will be at the heart of ITS. Shared access will be provided to ITS databases that will manage information storage, retreival, and processing of ITS information. However, potentially serious issues of data integrity assurance (as well as privacy protection) could require robust gateway controls over data interchange with databases in the commercial domain. While these controls will probably be located in a secure ITS database and not in the network, this issue does suggest that the servers maintaining the critical data may require software with military levels of integrity assurance.

Service points. These are physical locations at which ITS services will be administered. Examples include electronic payment and emissions testing sites, and "weigh stations" for moving trucks.

Table 1   ITS User Services Infrastructure Requirements

User Service Area	Infrastructural Elements				
	DN	RED	I/D	SP	O-BV
Travel and Transportation Management					
En-route driver information		•	•		
Route guidance		•	•		•
Traveler services information			•		
Traffic control[a]	•	•	•		
Incident management		•	•		
Emissions testing and mitigation				•	•
Travel Demand Management					
Demand management and operations		•	•		
Pre-trip travel information		•	•		
Ride matching and reservation			•		
Public Transportation Operations					
Public transportation management			•		•
En-route transit information		•	•		•
Personalized public transit			•		
Public travel security			•		
Electronic Payment					
Electronic payment services				•	

On-board vehicle components. These include displays, sensors, and communication devices that will be installed in vehicles for the purpose of supporting ITS. This category encompasses both autonomous systems (route guidance using GPS and on-board CDROM maps) and communications-dependent systems (telemetry from the vehicle to traffic monitoring sensors, and information communicated back to the vehicle from the ITS databases, providing optimal routing and other information). Some applications, such as collision avoidance, may be supported by either autonomous or networked systems.

Table 1 maps the 29 ITS applications against the elements discussed above. This chart is not perfect. It does not, for example, recognize the changing requirements within application areas between early and advanced applications. Nor does it recognize that some applications may be enhanced by access to data gathered

User Service Area	Infrastructural Elements				
	DN	RED	I/D	SP	O-BV
Commercial Vehicle Operations					
Commercial vehicle electronic clearance			•	•	
Automated roadside safety inspection			•	•	
On-board safety monitoring					•
Commercial vehicle administrative processes			•		
Hazardous material incident response		•	•		•
Freight mobility			•		
Emergency Management					
Emergency notification and personal security			•		
Emergency vehicle management			•		
Advanced Vehicle Control and Safety Systems					
Longitudinal collision avoidance					•
Lateral collision avoidance					•
Intersection collision avoidance		•			•
Vision enhancement for crash avoidance					•
Safety readiness					•
Pre-crash restraint deployment					•
Automated vehicle operation	•		•		•

a. Traffic control can be considered a core application that will provide information available to enhance other ITS applications.

DN = dedicated network. RED = roadside element deployment. I/D = information/ database. SP = service points. O-BV = on-board vehicle

by the traffic control application. Despite this, the table does point out that a significant component of ITS services may be provided through general-purpose communications infrastructure. Only two applications, traffic control and automated vehicle operation, are identified as having a dedicated network requirement. While a dedicated ITS network will be needed for automated vehicle operation, this ITS application is furthest out on the time horizon. Traffic control is identified as requiring a dedicated network due to the multitude of sensors that will be needed in some areas as well as to anticipated video needs. Of course, these dedicated networks may be either owned or leased by transportation agencies.

One may conclude from looking at this table that most ITS services will not require a dedicated network; however, this conclusion is based on anticipated rather than available NII capabilites. For many applications there exist a variety of potential technological solutions, including public ATM, frame relay, or SMDS networks and the Internet. The Internet is a desirable solution from cost and ubiquity perspectives, but is currently lacking in speed, reliability, and security. It is presently a best-efforts network, with no guarantee of delivery. The Internet technical community recognizes the need to move beyond best-efforts service to provide a variety of quality-of-service levels consistent with the needs of different groups of users and applications [5]. Exploration of the development of quality of service parameters is now underway, including exploration of a reserved bandwidth service. Similarly, a variety of systems of encryption are now being developed and tested to ensure secure communications.

In terms of communications services available today, mobile communications are virtually ubiquitous. Today mobile phones are virtually free, given away to induce telephone service contracts, and it is reasonable to expect that they will soon be bundled with most new cars. Exploring the provision of basic ITS services through mobile cellular service may offer a low-cost means of developing and testing their marketability.

The trend so far in ITS service development has been dedicated private network solutions. Cost comparisons made by early implementors in state agencies have heavily favored the use of owned versus leased infrastructure. However, these estimates may not provide a balanced perspective. Analysis of owning versus outsourcing must consider customized rates available for multi-year contracts, as opposed to full tariffs, and anticipate the availability of advanced virtual network services. The price differential is also being driven by the lower cost of capital faced by public agencies. One means of leveling the playing field in this area is industrial bonding, which would allow private corporations to float tax-free bonds to raise money for public-sector projects.

It appears that there is considerable room for a larger open network role in the provision of ITS services. Realization of this role will require active dialogue between the telecommunications and ITS communities. A shared infrastructure approach can offer benefits beyond reduced cost. From the perspective of a national

ITS program, expanding the role of public communication service providers can provide a more stable and competitive environment for the deployment of ITS services. The case for owning versus outsourcing will of course vary from project to project, depending on the proximity of the site to existing infrastructure and its value as right of way. The debate between transportation officials and communications service providers has often painted a black-and-white picture of the ownership issue. Possible win-win solutions do exist; these recognize the value of roadside right-of-way, and explore options in trading access for bandwidth and sharing revenue from excess capacity (see the chapter by Bespalko et al. in this volume).

In most areas, ITS networks have been procured based on a predefined architecture. Alternatively, states could purchase services rather than networks. This would allow communcations services providers to determine what network architecture could most cost-effectively meet service requirements in the context of their overall business. It might also place expertise in ITS communications where it would more easily migrate to serve other areas. If the larger role in ITS network planning is undertaken by public sector officials, the resulting expertise and learning curve benefits may remain local. If this responsibility falls more heavily on the private sector, other regions may benefit from the provider's expertise. It may also permit services to roll out in a pattern that is consistent with underlying economics, rather than arbitrary, politically defined geographic areas.

Assuring the maximum public benefit from shared infrastructure opportunities will require an active role on the part of DOT and other ITS constituents in articulating ITS requirements and in participating in NII and Internet development activities. Quite apart from the demands of cross-jurisdictional operability, the states need to harmonize their requirements; this will aggregate their demand and thus obtain the lowest prices from telecommunications service and product vendors.

Referring back to Table 1, the information component is a dominant infrastructural element of both ITS and NII. People, vehicles, and freight will all move across regions and ITS deployment areas, and will require the integration of ITS information across these regions. Standardization of data structures will be a critical element in the success of ITS, and needs to be addressed in an anticipatory manner.

Opportunities and Barriers

Interest in advanced infrastructure is at an unprecedented level. The Internet and the NII have been embraced by both American political parties, and even more enthusiastically by the media. This interest is fertile ground for the advancement of ITS on both technical and programmatic fronts. To date, ITS activity has occured almost exclusively in the transportation domain. The conclusion that much if not most of the network communications needs of ITS can be met by the NII—if the NII develops into fully accessible, reliable services that can interoperate with all the specialized ITS subsystems—suggests that ITS depends on NII outcomes. Yet there is no formal mechanism connecting state and federal interests in ITS and the NII. In September 1995, a task force requested by the White House but sponsored by the Carnegie Commission on Science, Technology, and Government and the National Governors' Association recommended a number of policy principles and institutional changes at both state and federal levels; the goal of these recommendations is to address the growing interdependence of state and federal responsibilities in a number of areas of science and technology, including the NII and the ITS [6].

So far, ITS has been largely absent in reports coming out of the Clinton administration's Information Infrastructure Task Force, the focal point for federal coordination on NII activities. The IITF offers a high-level platform for DOT to articulate its ITS vision and seek integration with federal, state, and private-sector NII development activities. This type of federal leadership will be needed to promote the state and private-sector participation on which ITS relies.

Notes

1. "Real-time" is not a well-defined technical concept. It generally means "practically instantaneous"; that is, a sufficiently timely response that an interactive activity is not deleteriously affected by the actual time-delay. Thus a real-time

collision-avoidance system probably has to respond in less than 10 milliseconds (since two vehicles approaching one another at 60 miles per hour have a closing rate of 1.76 feet/10 msec). On the other hand, a real-time traffic-light control system might be adequate with a one or maybe 10 second response, since signal cycles will be computed from average vehicle density and speed. The opposite of "real-time" is "off-line," which applies to applications such as trip planning that can be done at the traveler's convenience and stored for later use.

2. A hand-held GPS receiver can be purchased today that will provide location to better accuracy than the width of an interstate highway.

3. In the fall of 1994 the IVHS Program was officially renamed Intelligent Transportation Systems Program in recognition of the program's multimodal scope.

4. Intermodal Surface Transporation Efficiency Act of 1991, Part B, Section 6051.

5. Ibid., Section 6053.

6. For example, suppose financially able auto owners purchase a vehicle locating system. This system communicates via telemetry with a database of road blockages and traffic congestion. In this way, information may be used to construct a model of the flow of unequipped cars in the same traffic stream. If one of those vehicles suffers damage attributable to a malfunction in traffic control, has the owner a right of action against the car with the GPS location equipment?

References

1. *Realizing the Information Future,* National Academy Press, 1994.

2. Kahin, Brian. "Information Technology and Information Infrastructure." In L. Branscomb, ed., *Empowering Technology,* MIT Press, 1993, pp. 135–143.

3. Branscomb, Lewis M. "New Policies, Old Bottles." In *Business and the Contemporary World,* 1995.

4. Branscomb, Anne. *Who Owns Information?* New York: Basic Books, 1994.

5. Computer Science and Telecommunications Board. *Realizing the Information Future,* National Academy Press, 1994, p. 66.

6. Thornburgh, Richard, and Celeste, Richard, chairs. *Report of the State Federal Partnership Task Force.* Columbus, OH: Battelle Memorial Institute, Sept. 1995.

Overview: Policy Frameworks for ITS and the NII

Assessing Federal Roles

David A. Whitney and Thomas O. Mottl

Introduction

This chapter examines government roles in the NII (National Information Infrastructure) and ITS (Intelligent Transportation Systems) national programs and how they can be synergized and focused to help foster development of the nation's Transportation Information Infrastructure (TII), the part of the NII that directly supports ITS users. We will review the surprisingly parallel development paths of the ITS and NII initiatives, including major technical and legislative milestones for each. Primary elements and objectives of current programs in each area will be reviewed from technical, organizational, and policy perspectives. Many technical synergies between the two program areas will be identified and program development philosophies compared. The various federal roles and policies adopted over time in each area will be reviewed and contrasted, and similarities identified. We will demonstrate that to date the NII program has enjoyed broad and consistent government support that has aided its progress and moved it further along than ITS down an evolutionary path towards privatization. We will also suggest that ITS is a less mature initiative that is not as far along this evolutionary path as the NII, for reasons to be discussed. We will highlight issues for discussion that are related to approaches by which the federal government can constructively steer the interaction of NII and ITS to accelerate ITS development and broaden the NII's customer base and societal impact.

The primary goal of this chapter is to highlight the different roles the federal government has played in the past, and more importantly can play in the future, in NII and ITS developments for the mutual benefit of both programs. We approach this task from the perspective of commercial-sector businessmen who have been involved in federally funded technology research and development programs for the NII and ITS over several years. This experience has exposed us to both the vision and the reality of the effects of federal policies in each of these largely independent areas.

This chapter presents a constructive mix of lessons and ideas related to future policy planning. The perspectives presented here are designed to set a foundation for continued discussion and debate. They are not prescriptions, but rather contributions to a developing understanding of the broader, fundamental issues that are critical to fostering improved efficiency and effectiveness of government action. We suggest that such improvements can be achieved by developing closer connections between NII and ITS initiatives.

Overview of NII and ITS Programs and Status

The NII and ITS have related missions from a broad perspective, but have significant differences in scope and structure. This section presents a brief overview of the scope and vision of the NII and ITS initiatives, their major focal points, and how they conceptually and functionally overlap.

Programs with National Scope

The NII and ITS initiatives are critical to the economic health and military security of the United States, and are likely to alter our cultural behavior and values in a variety of ways. In particular, advances in communications, computing, and information technologies addressed under the NII program make possible both the concept and the reality of universal access for virtually all forms of information. Both initiatives also offer potential solutions to many of the central problems and issues in freight and passenger transportation. Moreover, civilian freight transportation systems have a significant impact on military policy and capabilities; more than 80 percent of military supplies are moved by non-military carriers. The economic implications and other likely impacts of NII and ITS developments on institutions and citizens have far-reaching national significance.

The NII is continually highlighted in publications and public discussion as a critical and rapidly growing[1] new element of the economic and cultural milieu. NII-sponsored programs and spin-offs have already had a significant influence on the telecommunications industry, education, research, entertainment, and economic activities such as on-line and at-home shopping and electronic commerce. Similarly, ITS-sponsored programs have led to a growing number of technology developments, and a number of advanced technology field test demonstrations and prototype deployments are ongoing around the country. Table 1 summarizes some comparative statistics that indicate both the magnitude and growth rate of activities related to these two areas. Note, however, that there is no consistent way to directly measure or "size" the relative magnitude and importance of the nation's ITS and NII activities and needs directly.

Vision for the NII

The composite vision for the NII is to provide a nationwide assembly of systems that integrates five essential components: communications networks, computers and information appliances, information, applications, and people. These systems will use a wide variety of technologies to provide new ways for people to learn, work, be entertained, and interact with one another. The goal is to enable all citizens to access information and communicate with each other, reliably, securely, and cost-effectively in any medium—voice, data, image, or video—anytime, anywhere [10,11].

There are many different visions of the NII. This is due in part to the diffuseness of the NII development itself, which spans many agencies in government, with many different specific agendas. And while there are central steering and advisory groups, the authority to focus the NII's development does not lie with any single agency. In contrast, ITS, which has been developed as a highly structured program with an explicit evolutionary path—research, operational tests, development of National ITS and Automated Highway Sys-

Table 1   Snapshots of the NII and ITS

NII	ITS
Approximately 45 million PCs in home use in 1994, with 33% of new shipments going to homes [2]. 47% percent of U.S. homes with a PC also have a modem [3].	200 million motor vehicles; one million trolleys, locomotives, and passenger freight vehicles; 35,000 commercial vessels, ferries, barges; 300,000 civil aircraft in use in the U.S. in 1994 [9].
In 1993, about 14.8 million km of fiber-optic wire had been deployed in the U.S. Expected growth rate is currently about 13% per year [4].	6.4 million km of highways and roads; 400,000 km of rail and rapid transit lines; 42,000 km of navigable waterways; over 2000 commercial airports, seaports, and intermodal terminals in the U.S. in 1994 [9].
4,425 published references to the Internet or NII in the U.S. popular press in the first six months of 1995 [7].	44 published references to IVHS or ITS in the U.S. popular press in the first six months of 1995 [7].
13.5 million people are estimated to be able to use interactive services on the Internet [5]. 4.9 million estimated host sites on the Internet as of January 1995 [6].	Over 10 million freight containers were handled in U.S. ports in 1994 [36].
Consumer on-line business is estimated to have 3.1 million subscribers in 1994, who spent an average of $150 per year to go on-line [1].	Over $50 billion spent on U.S. tourism in 1994, in which transportation plays a central role [36].

tem architectures, and deployment planning—all of which are centralized under a single agency.

Examples of variations on the general NII vision statement are the following [12]:

• *Internet-based vision.* In this model, services spring up on the network without anyone directing or managing their development. These services are offered free to any user who asks. The system offers any-to-any connectivity of all kinds. The Internet "Newsgroup" model embodies a new type of social interaction.[2]

This vision is on its way to becoming feasible. Email and World Wide Web services are leading to rapid popularization of the Internet. Commercial carriers and other private investors are not only offering, but also demanding to be allowed, to develop and manage the infrastructure and provide information services.

• *Entertainment-based vision.* This model grows out of the video delivery services now provided by the cable TV industry. It is primarily concerned with residential customers and is linked to the notion of universal service. Whereas the Internet today serves approximately 4.9 million host computers, the entertainment, telephone and cable TV (ETC) networks will likely serve 50–100 million host computers, which will in many ways look more like cable TV set-top boxes than PCs. Cable TV networks will become interactive and telephone systems will have greater bandwidth to accommodate video. Movies, games, and home shopping will drive the ETC industry complex, which will be the source of major investment resources for NII.

• *Clinton–Gore Administration's vision.* The current Administration envisions an encompassing information infrastructure that integrates and rationalizes various ongoing network developments. This vision is motivated more by social and economic policy considerations than by technology advancement. It emphasizes universal access regardless of individual means or location, and use by industries and public institutions in support of national goals ranging from national and international competitiveness (including the Global Information Infrastructure [13]) to delivery of government services. For example, the Administration vision combines goals for universal access to broadband, interactive services with goals of connecting all classrooms, libraries, hospitals, and clinics by the year 2000.

All of these vision statements imply the notion of the integration of and extensions to a wide array of existing physical, electronic, information, and regulatory entities related to NII functionality but created for other purposes. The creation of *new* infrastructure elements through public sector involvement is not a highlighted need.

Vision for ITS

The Intermodal Surface Transportation Efficiency Act (ISTEA) of 1991 initiated the Intelligent-Vehicle Highway System (IVHS) Program, the forerunner of ITS. Strategic planning activities for IVHS have collectively provided a "vision" for ITS.

In substance, an intelligent transportation system is one that provides the information needed to enable informed decisions by transportation planners, managers, users, and operators. The primary focus of such a system, to be substantially developed over the next 20 years, is the creation of a truly balanced transportation system that improves safety, minimizes environmental damage, and provides a wide range of user-oriented services. The ITS vision entails a national system of travel-support technology, smoothly coordinated among air, transit, rail, marine, and highway operations, which provides safe, expeditious, and economical movement of goods and people. The system will provide universal access to guarantee mobility and accessibility for urban, suburban, and rural transportation users alike[8].

The ITS vision relies on the development of new transportation infrastructure with the functionality to realize ITS objectives. Some sectors of the telecommunications industry are debating whether such a specialized ITS information infrastructure should be built, or whether generic NII services will meet ITS functional needs and deployment schedules. The ITS initiative recognizes the need to foster new levels of cooperation between the public and private sectors in order to create the infrastructure required to realize the ITS vision. Stages along the way to realizing the ITS vision have been defined by U.S. DOT as the following: [8]

• *The Era of Travel Information and Fleet Management (1995–1999).* During this period, technologies and relationships among public agencies and private companies to share data and information from all modes of surface transportation will be built. State and local agencies will implement local traffic control and freeway operation systems. Also developed will be transit and emergency (e.g. hazardous materials spills) management systems, electronic tolls, mayday systems, in-vehicle route guidance, interactive intermodal kiosks, intelligent cruise control, and private information services. There will be support for commercial vehicle operations with improved computer-aided dispatch, EDI intermodal standards, electronic clearance, electronic safety inspections, and networked desktop paperwork processing.

• *The Era of Transportation Management (2000–2005).* During this period the vision of the "smart traveler" will become a reality. Institutional mechanisms and transportation infrastructure will provide a steady stream of reliable travel information for the individual. Public/private information dissemination procedures will be determined. More capable roadside-to-vehicle infrastructure and real-time jurisdictional sharing of information will enable the wide-area adaptive traffic control and up-to-the-minute information needed to support real-time dynamic route guidance systems. In addition, park-and-ride information, warnings, tourist information Yellow Pages, road geometry condition warnings, and integrated smart-card payments will be available. National, intermodal fleet management will improve safety and productivity, and toll/road pricing will help manage demand.

• *The Era of the Enhanced Vehicle (2010).* At this time, research and testing will have brought ITS to a stage of reliability and accuracy that will support the use of new, more sophisticated vehicle safety and control services, such as in-vehicle signing and more advanced collision avoidance systems. These systems will include lateral and longitudinal spacing control, driver vision enhancement, and assisted braking and steering. The data collection and dissemination systems established in preceding years will provide a foundation for the early stages of the deployment of automated highway systems. Work in this area has already begun in the form of the National Automated Highway Systems Consortium (NAHSC), a public/private partnership for the assessment, design, and prototyping of automated highway system technologies and implementations.

The Intersection of the NII and ITS: the TII

In economic or business terms, the NII can be viewed as a "horizontal market," that is, a set of basic technologies and services that cut across a wide range of application areas. The "National Challenges" designated under the High Performance Computing and Communications (HPCC) Program, which includes substantial research in NII technologies, are just such applications. These challenges, which require a combination of multidisciplinary skills on very large scales, address the following application areas: digital libraries, crisis and emergency management, education and lifelong learning, electronic commerce, energy management, environmental monitoring and waste minimization, health care, manufacturing processes and products, and public access to government information [32]. The NII architecture[3] will provide three component functional layers that build upon each other [14]: a *physical infrastructure* containing basic processing and communications components; *enabling services*, which are the building blocks that provide generic, low-level functionality for applications of the physical infrastructure, such as distributed computing services or secure transaction services; and *applications*, or information processing tools that deliver a service to the end user, such as sending mail. This framework is illustrated in Figure 1.

ITS, with an architecture built upon the concept of *user services* such as route guidance, electronic toll collection, and mayday emergency service, is a "vertical market" in economic or business terms. Currently, 29 ITS user services have been specified and grouped into seven *user service bundles* [15]. As a vertical market offering domain-specific applications, ITS can make use of the technologies, enabling services, and physical infrastructure of the NII's "horizontal" resource layers. Conceptually, the "intersection" of ITS user service requirements with NII resources and services defines a Transportation Information Infrastructure (TII) [16], as illustrated in Figure 2.

The overlapping of the services NII and ITS aim to provide further motivate the vertical and horizontal market perspectives adopted above. Representative NII enabling services [17] include:

Data and Knowledge Management

- Knowledge-based search and retrieval
- Distributed transaction management
- Information resource self-description
- Bulletin board and directory services

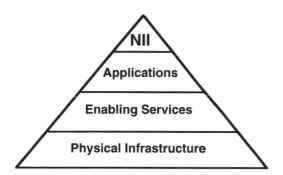

Figure 1 NII Functional Service Layers Framework.

Translation/Interchange
• Data format conversion services (including multimedia)
• Electronic Data Interchange (EDI)
• Electronic currency exchange

Core Network Management
• Identification (namespace and address management)
• Finding/network resource location
• Core communications services (transport/encoding; internetworking; rate adoption)

Security/Protection
• Authentication
• Information authentication
• Confidentiality and encryption
• Access control
• Digital signature

Billing, Capacity Management, and Policy-Based Routing

The ITS program has defined the collection of user services and service bundles [8] that describe the functions that ITS will provide to the public. These applications will be described in depth in the chapter by Carpenter in this volume:

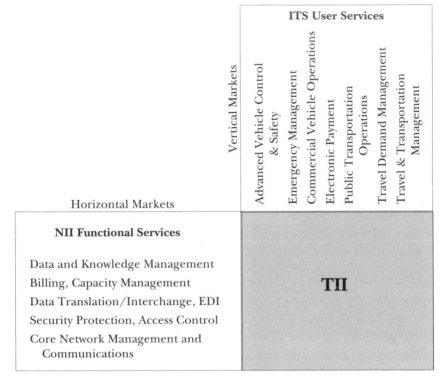

Figure 2 A Common Transportation Information Infrastructure.

Travel and Transportation Management Bundle
• En-route driver information
• Route guidance
• Traveler services information
• Traffic control
• Incident management
• Emissions testing and mitigation

Travel Demand Management Bundle
• Demand management and operations
• Pre-trip travel information
• Ride matching and reservation

Public Transportation Operations Bundle
• Public transportation management
• En-route transit information
• Personalized public transit
• Public travel security

Electronic Payment Bundle
• Electronic payment services

Commercial Vehicle Operations Bundle
• Commercial vehicle electronic clearance
• Automated roadside safety inspection
• On-board safety monitoring
• Commercial vehicle administrative processes
• Hazardous material incident response
• Freight mobility

Emergency Management Bundle
• Emergency notification and personal security
• Emergency vehicle management

Advanced Vehicle Control and Safety Systems Bundle
• Longitudinal collision avoidance
• Lateral collision avoidance
• Intersection collision avoidance
• Vision enhancement for crash avoidance
• Safety readiness
• Pre-crash restraint deployment
• Automated Highway System.

Many of the NII enabling services are those needed to implement ITS user services. For example, commercial vehicle operations will be a primary user of Electronic Data Interchange (EDI), while automated highway systems with platoons of coordinated, communicating vehicles will require reliable security and protection services. Market assessments of ITS performed in early 1995 segment the industry into four component areas—communications, control, sensors, and displays—and project that 51% of the ITS component market will be communications-related [34].

Preliminary results from the U.S. DOT's ITS Architecture Program have identified many specific existing and evolving NII infrastructure elements that support the TII, such as cellular telephony, FM subcarrier broadcasts, 900 KHz-range radio broadcasts, and fiber-optic backbones [18]. In addition, most of the ITS standards and protocols development work is being coordinated with ongoing standards activities for the NII "information highway" [20]. The function of such National Architecture design work is discussed in more detail below.

The TII is already under development through the natural evolution of market and technology forces. For example, by the late 1990s, the U.S. cellular telephone market is expected to grow to 30–35 million subscribers [20]. The "cellular phone force" of volunteers reporting traffic incidents or delays has already become a staple of today's traffic condition broadcast reports, and is one of the most effective and economical "sensors" for highway incident detection.

ITS programs have begun several operational tests of electronic toll collection systems using debit cards that can be read "on the fly." Large growth in debit card use (mainly for non-ITS applications today) is occurring already. The number of electronic devices accepting on-line debit cards at the point of sale was estimated to be nearly 400,000 by the end of 1994. This is nearly 122% growth in just one year, while on-line and debit transactions were up 59% in 1994, with more than 8 billion transactions logged [21]. With the proper concern to functionality requirements and standards adoption, a variety of industries could significantly benefit from coordination of such NII- and ITS-related development programs.

While the TII concept is not formally recognized by either the NII or ITS bodies, we believe its coordinated development through proactive federal influence and/or cross-industry private sector organizations is an important issue for enhancing the public value of both the NII and the ITS enterprises. In particular, gaining recognition for and exploiting the applications at the intersection of NII and ITS is essential for joining and making use of these two national initiatives. Redundant development of expensive national infrastructure is clearly not cost-effective, and will be detrimental to U.S. competition in the world economy.

Program Evolutions and Federal Roles

NII and ITS projects share a history of federally funded program development. Today, the federal roles in each program are significantly different in emphasis. These differences can be attributed to several factors.

One such factor is the genesis of each program. The concept of a NII was first articulated in the early 1990's. The technological basis for the NII grew out of DOD work in the 1960s on the development of individual technologies, such as packet switching for communication networks, to meet defense needs. This work, which quickly gave rise to the fledgling Internet (then known as ARPANET), was focused on developing networks for military communication and research needs. There was no coordinated, broad vision of the NII. The NII evolved as a collection of individual technologies that led to the growth of the common infrastructure. The federal role was a traditional one of funding technology R&D for defense objectives, with hoped-for spin-offs into commercial applications.

ITS, on the other hand, springs from the federal government's role in the development of the interstate highway system, which involved direct funding and control of the entire life cycle of development and deployment of a public sector technology. This was partly due to the scale of the project, and partly due to the public good served by enhanced national mobility.

Today, the federal government, especially the U.S. DOT, recognizes the need for public/private partnerships and full privatization of initiatives such as NII and ITS. However, the federal role in stimulating the development of ITS is much more direct and central than it is for the NII; again, this difference is based on the program development philosophies in which the two initiatives are rooted.

However, specific differences between the federal roles today in these two initiatives are not due solely to the historical origins of each program. Differences are also due in part to the different evolutionary stages of each program. While the NII has had a more diffuse funding and organizational structure, it has nevertheless benefited from a more consistent, uninterrupted, multi-agency (e.g., DOC, DOE, ARPA, NSF) funding history, due in part to its strong roots in defense programs. In addition, the NII horizontal technology base is fairly well-developed; there is significant competition within private industry to provide a variety of related services; and the media and public are intrigued with the idea of the "Infobahn." Given this environment, and given the fact that large amounts of required infrastructure are in place commercially, federal involvement is now focused on the regulatory and policy areas. However, significant federal R&D for the NII continues in programs such as the High Performance Computing and Communications (HPCC) Program.

ITS and its forerunner programs have had a more irregular funding history, due in part to the lower priority given "public works" budgets as they competed with military needs during the Cold War and the defense buildup of the 1980's. Table 2 presents a historical timeline summarizing NII and ITS evolution [22, 23] from the early 1960s up through the "formalization" of the programs in the HPCC and ISTEA Acts in the early 1990s.

Today, having been formalized and elevated in priority by the ISTEA legislation, ITS is focused on development and deployment of a broad range of vertical-market user services. Deployment of highway ITS infrastructure is dependent on state and local Metropolitan Planning Organizations (MPOs) that do not have adequate technical capabilities to evaluate, deploy, and maintain these new systems and often approach them with extreme caution. Standards issues have restricted progress in integration and market efficiencies on a national level (e.g., several largely incompatible electronic tagging systems for automatic vehicle identification are competing for the market, and databases that are developed in geographical, political, or institutional isolation are often incompatible), even though the private freight industry has deployed considerable ITS infrastructure. Figure 3 depicts both the parallel

Table 2   Major Milestones in the Evolution of the NII and ITS Programs (1956–1991)

Time Period	NII	ITS
1956		Federal Highway Act
1960's		Bureau of Public Roads R&D develops many key communications and control
1969	First ARPANET node	technologies (UTCS, ERGS, PAS)
1971	20 ARPANET nodes in place, 30 universities funded for research	Northeast Corridor plan for ATIS and AHS; a "Post–Interstate Highway Program" rejected by Congress
1972	TCP research begun	
1975	ARPANET management transferred to Defense Information Services Agency	Modest research, UMTA Automatic Vehicle Location program, video, wide-area detection, highway advisory
1980's	The Internet begins to take shape from programs such as DOE's MFEnet and HEPnet	radio (HAR)
1981	and NASA's SPAN	Interstate Highway System still under construction
1982	BITNET initiated	
		Further downturn in IVHS research
1983	AT&T consent decree leading to its breakup	
1986	TCP adopted (a few hundred computers on the early "net")	TRB begins National Cooperative Highway Research Program (NCHRP)
1987	NSF CSNET, NSFNET	Project 2020 (IVHS concept being informally developed)
1988	Expanding regional networks: SURA net, NYSERnet, BARRnet, Midnet, PSCnet, Sesquinet, Westnet; NREN emerging	
1989		Mobility 2000 formed (IVHS concept refined and broadened)
1990	ARPANET decommissioned, replaced by NSFnet as backbone; NREN activities of NSF, NASA, DOE, and ARPA will become components of Internet. High Performance Computing Program emerging.	Interstate Highway System substantially completed
1991	Commercial development of Internet proceeds	IVHS America (now ITS America) formed
	High Performance Computing (HPC) Act	Intermodal Surface Transportation Efficiency Act (ISTEA)

and competing forces that have acted on both the NII and ITS, and how the programs have evolved as a result.

With respect to public transportation, little ITS infrastructure exists today. As a result of this environment, timely progress in ITS appears to rely on a stronger federal R&D role. In particular, initiatives such as the National ITS Architecture Program are designed to promote and facilitate rapid, efficient development of the required infrastructure and services by both the public and private sectors, and to optimize system deployment nationwide.

Federal Roles Today

The historical trends and circumstances described above strongly influence the way federal roles are defined today for ITS and NII. The Department of Transportation sees its role in ITS as [15]:

• Facilitating and leading in early stages of development

• Providing a national perspective and emphasis on safety, congestion relief, mobility enhancement, environmental impact, energy conservation, productivity improvements, and system standards

• Funding high-risk research

• Participating in major operational field tests

• Playing a key role in ITS cost–benefits evaluations.

Corresponding key elements of the federal role in NII are [24, 32]:

• Helping to develop technologies underlying the NII, including advanced information services, software development environments, and user interfaces, in order to address HPCC National Challenge problems

• Creating a focus on the critical issues of information and telecommunications policy

• Encouraging simultaneous private sector development of new information and communications technologies

• Protecting citizens' rights of access and privacy, balanced with law enforcement and national security concerns.

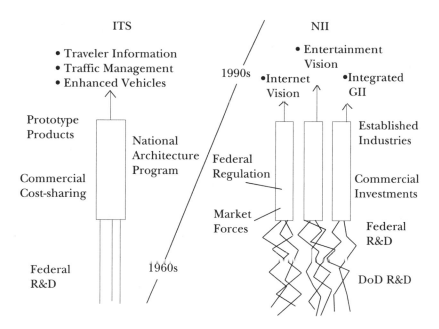

Figure 3 Program Evolution and Federal Activity.

The following section will discuss how these differences in objectives have mapped into differences in federal roles for each program.

Federal Involvement

National Information Infrastructure. The federal government is deeply involved in both NII and ITS activities. On the NII side, a variety of federal agencies are involved in NII itself and/or its connections to the High Performance Computing and Communications (HPCC) program. The Information Infrastructure Task Force (IITF) is a primary way that HPCC connects to the NII. The IITF was formed by the Clinton White House, operates out of the Office of Science and Technology Policy, and is chaired by the Secretary of Commerce. It is an interagency coordinating body for information infrastructure issues, whose goal is to articulate and implement the administration's vision for NII.

The IITF's membership is composed of high-level representatives of those federal agencies that play a major role in the development and application of information and telecommunications technologies. IITF research focuses heavily on technology-base issues for the NII, such as promoting technological innovation and new applications; seamless, interactive operation; information security and network reliability; and improving management of the radio frequency spectrum [26].

Domestic and international telecommunications and policy making is the focus of the National Telecommunications and Information Administration (NTIA). NTIA is an agency of the U.S. Department of Commerce, headed by an Assistant Secretary for Communications and Information. It focuses on such issues as pro-investment and pro-competitive policies, managing and allocation of all federal use of the electromagnetic spectrum, and universal-access advocacy.

The National Information Infrastructure Advisory Council (NIIAC) is an advisory committee to the Secretary of Commerce. Its focus is on defining the roles of the public and private sectors in technology development, maintaining the balance of protection of intellectual property rights with the needs of users, generating national strategies for applications, conceiving approaches to maximize interoperability of networks, and addressing the issues of privacy and security [27]. In addition to these primary policy and technology management organizations, there are a large number of government organizations that have prominent roles in various NII research activities funded through HPCC or other sources. A major NII funding element is the Information Infrastructure Technology and Applications (IITA) portion of the HPCC, funded at a level of approximately $280 million in 1995 [25]. Additional sources include:

- Advanced Research Project Agency (ARPA)
- Agency for Health Care Policy and Research (AHCPR)
- Department of Energy (DOE)
- Environmental Protection Agency (EPA)
- National Aeronautics and Space Administration (NASA)
- National Institute of Health (NIH)

- National Institute of Standards and Technology(NIST)
- National Oceanic and Atmospheric Agency (NOAA)
- National Security Agency (NSA)
- National Science Foundation (NSF)
- Department of Veterans Affairs (VA)

The federal web of NII activities is clearly diverse and distributed. This list of participants reflects the importance and diversity of information and telecommunications requirements for a wide variety of programs and missions. It is also clear that the annual IITA budget cited above is only a fraction of the total annual federal expenditures that can be linked to the NII.

Intelligent Transportation Systems. In comparison to the NII, federal agency involvement in ITS is on a smaller budgetary scale, and focused in only a few agencies. The Department of Transportation's Federal Highway Administration[4] (FHWA) has been and continues to be the lead agency for ITS research and advocacy. The FHWA proposed an annual budget of approximately $240 million for ITS activities for fiscal year 1996[5]

Within the last two years, DOT has established an ITS Joint Program Office (JPO) within FHWA. The JPO reports to the DOT ITS Management Council, which is chaired by the Deputy Secretary of Transportation. The JPO's mission is to coordinate interagency intermodal technology development, foster and catalyze deployment of ITS technologies, and take on an increased advocacy and policy role within the government for intermodalism and ITS.

After FHWA, the National Highway Traffic Safety Administration (NHTSA) has been the next-largest participant in ITS research to date, with a strong emphasis on the study of the human-machine interface and crash-avoidance aspects of new technologies. The Federal Transit Administration (FTA) has established an Advanced Public Transportation Systems Program. The Federal Railroad Administration (FRA) is interested in technological systems related to road–rail-grade crossing safety, advanced train control systems, and high-speed passenger transportation. The Research and Special Projects Administration (RSPA) is involved in system approaches and technologies with intermodal impacts, including the development of telecommunications and radio navigation policy. The National Academy of Sciences, through the Transportation Research Board, sponsors a program called ITS-IDEA (Ideas Deserving Exploratory Analysis) which is designed to provide research and development "seed money" to foster the transfer of new technologies into the ITS realm.

ITS America, a non-profit organization chartered in 1990 as a federal Advisory Committee to the U.S. DOT, has shown a strong influence on the development direction of ITS. ITS America members are drawn from the federal, state, and local public sectors, from private businesses and agencies, from associations, from academic institutions and private individuals. ITS America has been a key technical and policy advisor to FHWA, especially in the conception and initiation of the National ITS Architecture Program, and has been active in promoting linkages with international ITS programs and activities.

DOT's ITS Program has recently shifted its perspective to emphasize multi-modal (car, rail, air, marine) and intermodal (coordinated modal) transportation. Indicative of this change, the program's name was recently changed to the ITS Program from the "Intelligent Vehicle Highway System (IVHS)" Program. The ITS Program involves public transit and commercial vehicle activities, in addition to private motor vehicle systems, but the majority of the research effort to date has been focused on highways and privately owned vehicles.

The contrast in federal involvement in ITS as compared to NII is particularly evident in the fairly limited participation from various agencies that would stand to benefit from an improved intermodal transportation system. For example, there is no formal participation in ITS by such non-highway modalities as the Federal Aviation Administration (FAA) and the Coast Guard (USCG), and very modest involvement by the Federal Transit Authority (FTA) and Federal Railroad Administration (FRA). This may in part be attributable to ITS' former emphasis on highway travel. However, the program's recent refocusing towards an intermodal ITS perspective should encourage broadened participation from all the modal agencies. Such participation is vital since there is significant technology and policy experience that can be transferred from areas such as aviation, commercial rail, and the marine container freight business to ITS.

In recognition of the need for broad participation from modal agencies, state and local governments, private industry, and consumers, the ITS program has initiated some innovative approaches to redefining the federal role in the area of technology development and deployment. FHWA has established a consistent and highly successful emphasis on public-private partnerships for ITS developments. Significant (almost 50%) private sector "cost-sharing" has been the norm in most operational field tests of new technologies, as well as in the more modest cost sharing in selected ITS research projects. FHWA last year joined in the formation of an eight-member consortium for the development and demonstration of concepts for an automated highway system, called the National Automated Highway Systems Consortium (NAHSC) [28]. Private-sector consortium members are providing 20% of the program costs, and FHWA has explicitly taken the role of a co-equal consortium participant, rather than the consortium leader. The NAHSC is spearheaded by General Motors Corporation.

Congressional Actions and Mandates

The information, communications, and computing elements that comprise the NII have been the subject of a variety of legislation, especially in the 1990s. Major Congressional actions related to the NII include:

• 1982 AT&T Consent Decree
• High Performance Computing Act of 1991 (PL 102-1 94)
• Information and Technology Act of 1992 (S.2937)
• National Competitiveness Act of 1993
• National Information Infrastructure Act (H.R.1757)
• Telecommunications Bill
• Digital Telephony Act

While the High Performance Computing Act of 1991 enabled significant research and development spending for NII, the emphasis for many of the other legislative actions has been on regulatory policy for the commercial telecommunications and computing industries.

There are fewer major federal legislative actions directly related to ITS. Those that have been enacted have primarily provided federal funds for public works or research and development programs:

• Federal Highway Act of 1956

• Clean Air Act Amendments of 1990

• Intermodal Surface Transportation Efficiency Act of 1991 (ISTEA)

The Clean Air Act Amendments have been related to ISTEA through an explicit linking of federal funding for ITS projects to demonstrated compliance with specified provisions of the Amendments.

These legislative histories reflect a central difference between the state of federal involvements in ITS and NII today: Federal agencies seek to influence NII development through regulation and deregulation of the private sector. On the other hand, their influence on ITS evolution is primarily through federal investment to achieve private-sector research and development.

NII and ITS Today

For both the NII and ITS initiatives, the federal government's objective is to promote development of services that will support the public interest, enhance the U.S. economic competitive position in world markets, and promote national security. Simultaneously, however, is the ongoing political tug-of-war between those who advocate an active, direct federal role in such developments, and those who believe in pushing public roles down to the state and local level, creating legislative incentives to private industry in lieu of government spending programs, and strong restraint on any form of direct federal intervention or sponsorship of initiatives such as NII or ITS. The "public mandate" of the 1994 Congressional elections appears to strongly reflect sentiments for this latter approach. Proposed recissions to planned ITS budgets and government R&D in general will likely change the course of both the NII and ITS initiatives over coming years.

Recent federal spending on ITS, both in DOT and DOD (e.g. ARPA's new TransTech initiative), could be characterized as focusing on "jump-starting" ITS—either in technology development, system deployment, or system design—in order to achieve a critical mass of infrastructure and services to sustain ITS growth and address defense policy needs.[6]

The current federal role in NII is primarily regulatory/ deregulatory, as discussed above. Although there is still significant government spending in related research and development, infrastructure and technology investment in NII is expected to come from private industry. In the NII arena, there is also considerable debate on the nature of the regulations that should be imposed, for example in defining the roles of cable television operators and telephone services in providing in-home video and interactive services. In contrast to the reduced federal (spending) role some have proposed for ITS, there is as much or more attention being given to what aspects of the emerging NII should be (federally) regulated or deregulated.

For example, the area of security and privacy regulations is currently receiving some publicized government attention. An analog of the automobile highway patrol has been proposed for the Internet: a National I-Way patrol. This proposal reflects growing government concern that escalating attacks by external hackers and disgruntled insiders could undermine the public's faith in electronic information systems, as well as its ability to use the systems effectively and safely. The I-Way proposal would also direct the government to work with industry to develop alternative ways of implementing both a reliable encoding system and adequate law enforcement that at the same time protects individual freedoms, in response to the controversy surrounding the government's "Clipper" chip encryption system [29]. Other fundamental issues of free speech and privacy are involved in current proposals for criminal penalties for the transmission or viewing of certain types of information on the Internet.

The Programs Today: Contrasts and Synergies

If one recognizes the TII as integral to ITS, the technology linkages between ITS and NII become apparent and significant. The horizontal and vertical market perspectives described earlier might suggest that these linkages are one-way flows, i.e., from NII to ITS. However, NII horizontal market technologies can be driven by new vertical market needs that highlight requirements for technology growth in established or new areas. For example, ITS market requirements are likely to have such an effect on NII development due to the much more demanding speed, precision, and integrity needs of real-time transportation applications. High-bandwidth video transmission for mobile systems, and security and reliability requirements for real-time "mission-critical" ITS systems, are examples of such potential technology needs.

Federal Programmatic Elements

Table 3 summarizes the emphasis on different programmatic areas within each federal program. Inspection of this table shows what might be characterized as a technology development and testing emphasis for ITS, and more of a regulation and standardization emphasis for NII. These observed differences support the perspective that the federal role in ITS is one of "seeding" technologies, while its role in the more mature NII has already moved to the control and management of an expanding technology base. One can conjecture that the early "seeding" phase for NII occurred in the period from the late 1960's to about 1980, when DOD was spending heavily for command, control, communication, computing and intelligence (C^4I) technology development.

Critical NII Implementation Issues

The perception at the federal level of areas and issues critical to NII development and implementation are reflected in the roles the federal government plays in NII. The following are some examples of areas and issues that have been identified by the federal government [30]:

• *People:* Equitable access, user acceptance, privacy, user training, organizational learning, private-sector acceptance

• *Information:* Intellectual property, security, access, information and data standards, information conversion

Table 3   Federal Emphasis on Areas of NII and ITS

Activity Areas	ITS	NII
Research and Development	G	M
Operational Tests	G	S
National Architecture	G	S
Deployment Support	G	S
Regulations and Legislation	S	G
Private Sector Development	G	G
Security and Privacy	S	G
Standards and Guidelines	M	G

G=Great emphasis. M=Moderate emphasis. S=Slight emphasis

• *Software, Hardware, and Networks:* User-friendliness, interoperability, reliability, scalability

• *NII Architecture:* Standards, public and private roles

• *Other:* Cost and pricing, funding

The need for a national architecture for NII infrastructure and enabling services has only recently been addressed by several groups. With the unprecedented growth in computing and communications technologies and services over the last decade, both governmental and commercial stakeholders have recognized that there is a growing chance the NII may develop in a manner that allows developers to create multiple systems and applications that are not interoperable.

The IITF Working Group has concluded that given the distributed nature of NII development, no single authority (including government) has either the knowledge or the span of control to develop, mandate, or legislate a services architecture [17]. On addressing the same issue of an NII architecture, the Cross-Industry Working Group (XIWT) takes a slightly stronger stand. It has concluded the following: An enduring, public body and process is necessary to allow for a logical evolution toward interoperability. Such a body must work under a sufficiently broad substantive and legal charter; and this body must have a sufficiently broad resource base to ensure that it is removed from the short-term motivators that beset present attempts at collaboration within and between industry and government [14].

Critical ITS Implementation Issues

The following areas and issues are those generally recognized as critical to the success of ITS. While these items parallel those identified for NII, there are several distinct differences in emphasis and meaning within the identified categories:

• *People:* Equitable access, user acceptance, privacy, user training, organizational learning, stakeholder acceptance

• *Information:* Security, private-sector access to data, information and data standards

• *Software, Hardware, and Networks:* User-friendliness, interoperability standards, scalability to large regional transportation systems

• *Commercialization:* Private-sector investment, addressing liability issues

• *Deployment:* Proving technologies, demonstrating benefits, educating state and local agencies and MPOs

• *ITS Architecture:* Definition, stakeholder acceptance, mechanisms for deployment

A major implementation planning issue for ITS today is the definition and promulgation of a consensus National ITS Architecture, which is being developed by competitive private sector teams. This architecture development is directed by DOT, although it strives to involve a range of stakeholders and develop a consensus architecture and associated 20-year deployment plan. U.S. DOT's recent highlighting of the intermodal perspective in ITS brings to the fore another critical issue for implementation: a lack of significant involvement from many of the non-highway modes, such as the freight industry, with federal ITS programs. This problem is due in part to the historical highway-side emphasis of U.S. DOT programs. The advanced stage of development and application of many ITS technologies in industries such as freight makes this private-sector involvement vital to capturing the operational experience and lessons-learned that can be leveraged for more rapid ITS implementation.

Finally, there are two particularly critical areas that will impact ITS implementation. The first is the currently inadequate level of understanding, knowledge, and experience within state and local agencies for planning and managing the projects that will create the required ITS infrastructure. Most of these agencies are insufficiently trained for and culturally mismatched with ITS. The second area is that of achieving public acceptance of and participation in ITS operational processes and procedures. The key issue in this latter area is probably cultural, indicating the need for long-range planning and outreach initiatives, some of which are already underway.

Models for Alternative Federal Roles

Supporters of the ITS initiative are devoting considerable effort to determining the best way for the federal government to continue its participation in ITS development and deployment, and the ITS Architecture Program is formally addressing this issue as part of its work. Figure 4, adapted from the ITS National Program Plan [15], provides a qualitative construct for considering the space of alternative models for federal and private sector involvement in either NII or ITS.

The quadrants in Figure 4 represent the roles being played by public and private sector participants in the NII and ITS initiatives today. The assertive federal role in ITS is partly driven by historical factors (ARPA, DOD, etc., as discussed earlier in this chapter), coupled with the view that ITS also requires a large technology and infrastructure investment to provide a broad public benefit in the areas of congestion relief, environmental improvement, consumer safety, and national productivity. On the other hand, the NII arena is characterized by a set of existing prototype architectures and technologies grown out of earlier federal investments. This foundation, in cooperation with the exponential growth of computing and telecommunications technology, has enabled a highly proactive

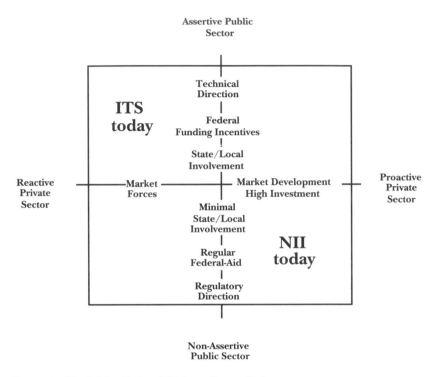

Figure 4   Model for Federal/Private Sector Roles.

private sector to develop with regulatory direction from the federal government. If public and private sector roles could be synergized and harmonized, the second quadrant (upper right) would represent an environment in which dynamic, constructive, and efficient development of these initiatives would occur.

The development or deployment environment defined by any specific "quadrant" in Figure 4 involves organizational dynamics and conflicting agendas, conceptualized by labels used in this figure. Issues inherent to these environments often correspond to political camps and basic issues of public/private domain rights and responsibilities, which can overshadow the use of this model to define federal roles. Nonetheless, one can use/expand on this model to frame discussions of the potential federal roles and approaches to development and implementation issues.

Barriers to Success

The NII and ITS initiatives face several common barriers to success that involve people, technology, or regulatory issues. These barriers differ in severity and nature within and between the two initiatives. Table 4 lists the principal barriers and identifies issues involved with each of the NII and ITS initiatives.

In the authors' opinion, the key barriers to success for both NII and ITS are cultural issues, interoperability, and privacy/security concerns, in that order. The cultural barriers impact the NII through issues related to learning requirements and user-friendliness, which can arise from the potential flood of information that a user faces, and those related to economic and class differences. In the case of ITS, the cultural barrier relates to the ability of state and local agencies to deal effectively with their responsibilities to create and manage the required infrastructure, and to the traveling public, especially drivers, who must accept and be integrated with planned operational procedures for them to be successful.

The interoperability issue is similar for NII and ITS: success in developing, deploying, and gaining acceptance of standards and open architecture systems to speed deployment and provide universal access. The privacy/security issue involves all three barrier areas: people, technology, and regulations. While the application specifics are different for NII and ITS, the problem is the same: gaining agreement on the breadth and depth of privacy and/or security that can and must be guaranteed to individuals and organizations.

In addition to the barriers listed in Table 4, there are procedural and philosophical impediments to processes critical to the development of NII and ITS. One example impacting both NII and ITS is the discrepancy between how technology develops and how standards are set. Standards setting has typically taken place over-time spans during which technology, especially information technology, can evolve through many product generations.

New standards-setting processes are striving to reduce these delays, but such work must be accelerated to match the pace of information technology development. This expedition will be

Table 4 NII and ITS Barriers to Success

General Barrier Type	NII Issues	ITS Issues
Application Penetration	Small but growing number, primarily for Internet services	Very few
Cultural	Reluctance to collaborate; tight control of information	Issues of personal control, changes in roles, seeing future problems
Regulatory and Legal Environments	Few legal precedents; complex evolving regulations	Potential liabilities for developers; no legal precedents
Cost-Benefit Tradeoffs	Many short-term benefits will be in the intangible entertainment area	Not yet demonstrated clearly; not clear how uniform
Interoperability	Improving and evolving, but rapidly changing technologies complicate standards setting	National Architecture being developed and needs to be effectively deployed by the stakeholders
Intellectual Property	No effective control of software piracy, copyright violations	Traditional patent procedures can address hardware protection
Privacy and Security	Technology is being developed; personal freedom issues are being debated	Privacy threatened by electronic vehicle tracking, electronic toll collection
International Cooperation	Standards must be coordinated and information must be exchanged freely for GII	Interoperability an issue as it affects world markets for ITS products

particularly difficult in the international standards-setting arena in which the U.S. must operate.

There is also a potential philosophical discrepancy between the fundamental nature of certain programs and the policy style chosen to implement them. In particular, the NII initiative has used a top-down approach to developing an infrastructure and associated standards to create bottom-up vertical applications. ITS, on the other hand, is a bottom-up program that will be deployed by local agencies, but is being handled top-down, on both the technical and policy sides. Progress in efficiently, effectively, and rapidly developing the TII, which represents the intersection of these two initiatives, could suffer from this procedural difference in development philosophy.

Steering NII/ITS Linkages through Federal Action

This section will suggest a range of activities through which the federal government might seek to support, foster, intensify, and structure the interaction between NII and ITS; it will also identify the potential benefits to each program that will result from governmental activity. While benefits can accrue to NII and ITS individually, the short-term benefits passing *from* NII *to* ITS are probably larger. The following sections present several options for action as starting points for further discussions.

NII Support for ITS

The ITS Program can benefit from NII development by being designated as one of its prominent vertical applications and focusing on broadening its technology base to support the unique requirements of the TII. This initiative can be supported in a number of ways:

• Add ITS to the list of HPCC/NII National Challenge Application focus areas. This will accelerate directly related research, foster relevant and timely standards, and address security and privacy issues.

• Capitalize on NII progress in standards and technologies to assure interoperability of information systems on the desktop and within the vehicle

• Leverage existing large private-sector information infrastructure and services developments, such as cellular telephony, to speed development and deployment of TII communication elements

• Employ broad-based NII organizational and political support to promote understanding and acceptance of ITS.

ITS Support for NII

The NII Program can benefit from ITS development by creating an environment conducive to deploying NII services today into the nation's 200 million "dashboard desktops" (vs. today's 3–4 million computers on the Internet). Such action would accelerate the visibility of NII, demonstrate NII's significant public good and "end-user" value, and quickly create a large community of motivated users (travelers and freight operators) to begin the process of cultural adaptation to an "information society." Actions to be taken at the federal level could include:

• Broadening the NII research agenda to include issues that are uniquely motivated by ITS user services and those in which ITS pushes the edge of NII technology (operationally critical systems technologies; difficult safety and reliability issues; packaging, cost, and technology issues for in-vehicle systems)

• Promoting commercial development of new information delivery services such as personalized traffic, weather, and entertainment data for motorists

• Spurring development of "high-end technologies" not required for typical NII applications, such as real-time, full-motion video transmission, fail-safe reliability in a real-time control system; and high-speed transmission of image and map data over radio or microwaves

• Applying ITS' extremely successful model for public/private partnering in research and development (almost 50%) within the NII community.

Common Benefits

In addition to the area-specific benefits listed above, there are several activities that the federal government might undertake to facilitate complementary NII and ITS development for both public good and private economic interests:

• Accelerate the pace of liability and regulatory legislation to remove barriers to commercial development of NII and ITS technologies and systems. Technology and markets are moving much more quickly than legal policy, especially in the area of the nation's non-wireless communications law.

• Apply managed deregulation by eliminating barriers to all players at about the same time [31]

• Develop national consensus architecture(s) for both NII and ITS. Recognize and support the technical and political value of such an architecture. Seek to maximize stakeholder, grass-roots development of the architecture, using federal involvement and funding only as a catalyst. This approach reflects the view that "When people disagree on where we should be going, asking government to draw the road map is dangerous" [31].

• Promote the stability of markets to encourage long-term private-sector investment and commitment. This can be achieved by stable federal policies and actions in such areas as regulation and architecture and the "seeding" of technology developments.

• Promote industry competitiveness and participation in international markets. While the NII standards-setting involvements are laying some groundwork for this, ITS has, to date, focused on domestic perspectives. Asian markets are particularly suitable for ITS because much of their modern highway infrastructure is being built "from scratch."[7]

• Create mechanisms for Congressional cross-committee coordination and cooperation regarding NII and ITS legislation and budget actions, especially with respect to research programs

• Pursue mechanisms for privatization of services, especially for ITS, such as private infrastructure ownership and demand/service use-pricing, which is widespread in Europe and Asia.[8]

• Continue to look for opportunities for convergence between NII and ITS that can fundamentally impact our way of life. For example, NII technologies such as video transmission, groupware, and interactive financial transactions have the potential to develop telecommuting and telepresence into a widespread new "mode of transportation." Such revolutions will also impact traditional travel patterns and infrastructure needs, resulting in increased commercial delivery traffic associated with electronic shopping, and increased use of transportation for leisure and more localized travel as byproducts of telecommuting.

Conclusions

This review of the programmatic and technology evolutions of the NII and ITS identifies past, current, and potential commonalities and divergences between these two national initiatives. A Transportation Information Infrastructure (TII) is identified as the conceptual and technological intersection of these two activities. Our purpose has been to further the understanding and appreciation of action that can be taken at the federal level to enhance the national effectiveness and benefits derived from synergies between the NII and ITS. An understanding of the concept of a TII is central to this purpose, and to defining detailed actions in terms of technology and policy evolution that achieve these ends. Coordinated federal action can constructively steer the interaction of NII and ITS to accelerate ITS development and broaden the NII's customer base and societal impact. This posture will help assure the successful development and convergence of ITS and NII.

Notes

1. While NII components like the Internet are currently experiencing explosive growth, predictions can be overenthusiastic. For example, if we simply extrapolate the current growth rate of Internet usership, we find that every person on the planet will be on the Internet by the year 2003 [33]!

2. For a provocative alternative view of the desirability of the types of interactions and educational paradigms developing under the Internet model, see Stephen L. Talbott's *The Future Does Not Compute* (O'Reilly & Associates, Inc., 1995).

3. The Cross-Industry Working Team (XIWT), which is studying NII architecture issues, is a membership organization consisting of a diverse group of over 40 communications, computer system, information, and service providers that have joined together to develop a common technical vision of the NII.

4. These discussions are based on the current U.S. DOT structure, and do not reflect recently proposed reorganization of the DOT along modal lines, designed to streamline operations and better support an intermodal perspective on the national transportation system.

5. This is the FY96 proposed budget, including appropriations from the Intermodal Surface Transportation Efficiency Act (ISTEA) and appropriations for NHTSA. Significant recissions to this budget are currently being debated in Congress.

6. Current DOD policy objectives conclude that adequate transportation infrastructure does not exist to support two simultaneous conflicts anywhere in the world.

7. Road and bridge construction is projected to consume close to half of Asia's transportation infrastructure spending during the 1990s, with China alone expected to build 250,000 km of new roads by the year 2000 [35].

8. For example, the Malaysian government recently (1994) granted a private firm a 30-year concession to design, operate, and maintain 850 km of expressways [35].

References

1. *Information Industry Bulletin*, Vol. 10, No. 28, September 8, 1994.

2. *U.S. Industrial Outlook 1994—Computer Equipment*, pp. 26–21 and Dataquest, 1994.

3. *EDGE: Work-Group Computing Report*, Vol. 6, No. 251, p. 13, March 13, 1995.

4. *U.S. Industrial Outlook 1994—Telecommunications and Navigation Equipment*, p. 30 17, 1994.

5. *The Internet Index*. Compiled by W. Treese, February 1995.

6. *Internet Domain Survey*. Compiled by Network Wizards (http://www.nw.com), February 1995.

7. U.S. Magazine Index and U.S. Newspaper Index searches, June 1995.

8. Euler, G.W. and Robertson, H.D., eds. *National ITS Program Plan Synopsis*, March 1995.

9. U.S. Department of Transportation, 1994.

10. *Perspectives on Competition and Deployment of the NII*, The Computer Systems Policy Project and the Information Technology Industry Council, December 1994.

11. *Breaking the Barriers to the National Information Infrastructure*, Conference Report by the Council on Competitiveness, December 1994.

12. *Realizing the Information Future: The Internet and Beyond*. National Research Council of the National Academy of Sciences, 1994.

13. Brown, R.H., Irving, L., Prabhakar, A., and Katzen, S. *The Global Information Infrastructure: Agenda for Cooperation*, February 1995.

14. *An Architectural Framework for the National Information Infrastructure*. Cross-Industry Working Team, September 1994.

15. Euler, G.W. and Robertson, H.D., eds. *National ITS Program Plan Vols. 1 and 2*, March 1995.

16. Ritter, G. *Improving Transportation: The National Information Infrastructure and Intelligent Transportation Systems—Draft for Comment*, September 1994.

17. *Services and the National Information Infrastructure*. Technology Policy Working Group, Committee on Applications and Technology, Information Infrastructure Task Force, December 1994.

18. *ITS Architecture Development Program Phase I Report Summary.* U.S. Department of Transportation and ITS America, November 1994.

19. *Intelligent Transportation Systems Architecture Development Standards and Protocols Catalog.* U.S. Department of Transportation Federal Highway Administration, March 1995.

20. *U.S. Industrial Outlook 1994—Telecommunications and Navigation Equipment,* p. 30-9, 1994.

21. *Electronic Funds Transfer Association Debit Card Directory* 1994.

22. Saxton, L. *Mobility 2000 and the Roots of IVHS,* Appendix D in French et al, *A Comparison of IVHS Progress in the Unites States, Japan, and Europe Through 1993,* March 1994.

23. *Federal Networking: The Path to the Internet.* Appendix A in *Realizing the Information Future: The Internet and Beyond,* National Research Council of the National Academy of Sciences, January 1995.

24. *Information Infrastructure Technology and Applications.* National Coordination Office for HPCC, Office of Science and Technology Policy, February 1994.

25. *HPCC Funding Program Components.* National Coordination Office for HPCC, March 1994.

26. *Fact Sheet.* Information Infrastructure Task Force (IITF), March 1995.

27. *Common Ground: Fundamental Principles of the National Information Infrastructure.* National Infrastructure Advisory Council, March 1995.

28. *National Automated Highway System Cooperative Program.* NAHSC Opportunities Workshop, April 1995.

29. Fialka, J. "U.S. to Propose Data-Highway Agency", *The Wall Street Journal,* June 14, 1995.

30. *What It Takes to Make It Happen: Key Issues for the Application of the National Information Infrastructure.* Committee on Applications and Technology of the Information Infrastructure Task Force, January 1994.

31. Obuchowski, J. *The National Information Infrastructure: Communications and Computing—Converging or Colliding?.* The Annenberg Washington Program, November 1993.

32. *HPCC: Technology for the National Information Infrastructure.* Supplement to the President's 1995 Budget, National Science and Technology Council, 1994.

33. *The Internet Index..* Compiled by W. Treese, November 1994.

34. *Moving Transportation into the Information Age.* ITS America, May 1995.

35. *The Private Sector in Highways, Roads, and Bridges in Asia.* AIC Conferences, July 1995.

36. John, R. R. *Remarks on the Occasion of the 25th Anniversary of the Volpe Center.* September 1995.

Common Policy Concerns

Stephen J. Lukasik

Two Perspectives

In seeking the intersection between the Department of Transportation's (DOT) Intelligent Transportation Systems (ITS) initiative and the National Information Infrastructure (NII), it will be helpful to contrast the two with respect to their perspective on travelers and traveling.

The two activities start from different bases. ITS derives from a systematic national effort to define future surface transportation systems across a broad set of users: private, public, commercial, urban, rural, intermodal, etc. The ITS program has brought to bear, through a variety of committees, demonstration projects, system studies, conferences, and government-industry joint ventures, a wide range of stakeholders who participate in the development and execution of the program. Despite the many successful cooperative efforts at planning and experimentation, however, it is important to note that there is a major separation between ITS national planning and its local implementation. As one follows the transportation hierarchy from the federal level through state, regional, county, local, and even neighborhood levels, one recognizes that there will inevitably be increasing degrees of heterogeneity introduced in response to specific local needs and the local availability of resources.

The NII lacks, to some extent, the organizational focus the Department of Transportation has given ITS. The NII is the result of the private investments in the computer, consumer electronics, and communication industries as a result of the opportunities provided by advances in the underlying technologies. It has as its conceptual base several loose confederations with very different historical precedents. One of these confederations is the value-added information providers operating on the Internet, augmented by alliances between communication facility and content providers, computer and consumer electronics equipment manufacturers, software creators, academics, and regulators. Another confederation is the communication common carriers themselves, who are experiencing a significant reduction in the regulatory oversight that governs their local and long-distance service offerings. A third set of participants is the broadcasting, motion picture, and cable entertainment industries. All NII participants are subject to a variety of governmental policy arms, including the Department of Commerce, Federal Communications Commission, Department of Justice, Federal Trade Commission, and state and local regulatory agencies.

A fundamental ITS paradigm is the collection and distribution of traffic information for the purpose of traffic capacity supply-and-demand management. Figure 1 illustrates this ITS perspective. Traffic information is collected by various local public agencies using a number of systems and techniques to expedite the flow of traffic. The collected information allows traffic signals to be adaptively managed, lanes reallocated, and emergency vehicles dispatched to accident sites. In a growing number of cities, public data is merged with data from privately owned collection systems, such as those from airborne platforms, and delivered "free" to consumers through advertiser-supported news utilizing radio and TV broadcast spectrum; in these cases, broadcast traffic information is not delivered as quantitative data but as newsworthy traffic reports. Value can be added to publicly and privately collected traffic information by data fusion organizations that may include map references, turn-restriction data, route guidance, or do analysis and formatting for specific user needs. These organizations may supply custom information to users on either a transaction- or a subscription-fee basis. Alternatively, traffic information can bundled with other communication services such as paging, cellular tele-

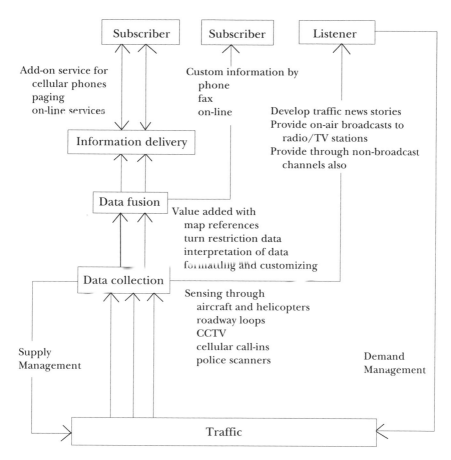

Figure 1   Use of Information to Manage Traffic Capacity Supply and Demand.

phony, or on-line data and delivered through the organizations that provide those services. These various communication paths for delivering current traffic information to travelers ultimately serve to manage traffic demand by enabling users to alter their destination, departure time, transportation mode, or route in response to current traffic conditions.

The NII view of travel, to the extent that this diverse community of information providers identifies travel as a market segment, is shown in Figure 2. The paradigm here is that users and systems will be connected through a variety of ubiquitous information paths between various information sources and receivers and that the

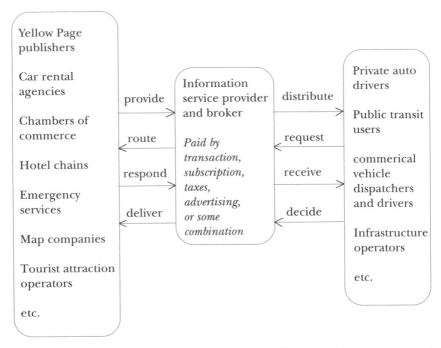

Figure 2 Use of Infrastructure to Increase the Size and Competitiveness of Information Markets.

size and quality of information markets will thereby be increased. On the left of the diagram are examples of current businesses that provide services to travelers. On the right are examples of the customers for these services. A key role in this view is played by information service-providers and brokers who create the market between travel service providers and their customers. Within the context of the NII they will do this by enabling interaction, distributing traveler information made available by travel service providers, receiving and routing traveler requests for information on available services, receiving and routing responses from travelers to providers, and delivering the traveler's choices to the providers. In addition to making available information on services and prices, they may provide evaluations of quality, assemble packages of services, and handle payment.

Thus, while *traffic* and *vehicles* are a central concern of ITS, *information* is the central concern of the NII. The overlap of ITS and

NII arises because traffic, in and of itself, constitutes a form of information, and information of a wide variety is needed by travelers. As their names imply, ITS is a set of transportation *systems* while the NII refers to an information system *infrastructure* within which those transportation systems operate.

In what follows, the central communications and information policy issues that are being considered by NII participants are outlined independently of what might be undertaken as part of ITS initiatives. Using the same policy structure for the discussion, comparable issues for ITS are noted, without particular reference to NII. From these two sets of issues, areas of common policy concern can be identified and then discussed in more detail. These, in turn, suggest some proposals for possible government initiatives to exploit synergies between the transportation and information domains.

NII Policy Issues

The issues of concern for the NII are by and large those of communication policy as it has evolved since the invention of telegraphy, radio transmission, and the application of the principles of common carriage to communication regulation. What are these central concerns of communication policy and how do they relate to transportation information policy?

• *Universal connectivity and interoperability.* Since the earliest recognition that a governmentally appointed Postmaster General would insure that all citizens should be able to communicate with each other and thereby encourage commerce, the principles of universal connectivity and interoperability have been key to government initiatives. Originally this meant a uniform system of postal rates, standards of service, post offices, and a national distribution system. Later, it meant encouraging technical standards for the encoding of telegraphic information and for offering such service nationally and internationally. Still later these principles were extended to encourage national systems for telegraphy, telephony, and radio and television networks.

• *Universal basic service.* An important communication policy principle calls for the provision of a minimum level of service to all citizens by cross-subsidizing, where necessary, uneconomical low-density routes with high-density profitable routes.

• *User rate regulation.* In return for allowing communication service monopolies, which were seen as necessary for the economical provision of national service, rates of return for interstate service were regulated by the federal government and by state governments for intrastate service.

• *Spectrum resource management.* Where communication depended on the efficient use of the limited electromagnetic spectrum resource, the domestic allocation of spectrum to types of service, the technical standards for the use of that spectrum, and the assignment of licenses became a federal responsibility.

• *Cross-ownership of communication facilities.* Broadcast, cable, common carrier, and other media facilities are privately owned. But a goal of communication regulation has been to avoid concentrations of ownership of information channels in market areas; this encourages open discussion of all aspects of public-concern issues. Hence, restrictions have been placed on the degree of cross-ownership of those facilities.

• *Rights of privacy and ownership of information.* As specified in the Communications Act of 1934 (Section 605), communications are private and ownership of information communicated is retained by its creator. Thus, limits are placed on the use of intercepted information and on its redistribution.

• *Content regulation.* The use of scarce communication resources implied a degree of public sanction and trust in their users. Consequently, various principles governing public service content, equal time for opposing views, and other regulations were applied in the licensing and operation of communication channels.

Current advances in information technology have enabled us to reduce our dependence on some of these communication policy prescriptions. The availability of communication channels has increased to the point where they are no longer seen as a scarce commodity and thus subject to strict oversight and regulation. We are less concerned about *cross-ownership* of local concentrations of radio, TV, and print media; indeed, draft legislation seeks to reduce restrictions in this area. *Universal connectivity and inter-*

operability require less government mandate because the computer, communication, and consumer electronics industries are moving toward that goal for reasons of market access and growth. *Rate regulation* is now less critical. This is a result of an increasing degree of competition in the common carrier industry, and has been a foundation for some of the changes in communication policy over the past 10–15 years. Views on *content regulation* are also changing, not as a result of technology advances, but rather in response to the view that content regulation imposes unnecessary burdens on operators. However, this trend is less clear, as current debate about content regulation on the Internet has increased and as obscenity and violence issues and the need for quality children's TV continue to receive attention.

Three of the above principles of communication policy remain of central importance in the NII era. We continue to focus on the need for *universal basic service.* State public utility commissions will still require at least a minimum level of local service at a price that is widely affordable. Discussions of the NII include concerns about "information have-nots," although the means of addressing their needs has not yet been established. Schools, libraries, and other community services are likely to play a role, and public-access kiosks are a potentially useful approach. Interactive TV and cable can also provide a means of layering broader information access on the already pervasive television entertainment structure. Some degree of *spectrum resource management* will continue to be necessary to prevent interference among users of the electromagnetic spectrum. And the *right of privacy and ownership of information* remains an NII issue. This has been evidenced recently by government actions to strengthen the protection of intellectual property in international commerce, though weakened by proposals to enable the government to decrypt intercepted digital communications for reasons of public order.

ITS Policy Issues

While the movement of people and material goods is quite different from the movement of information, from a regulatory standpoint there are nevertheless some similarities between the two domains that lead to common information policy concerns.

• *Universal connectivity and interoperability.* Roadways are nationwide, with the Interstate Highway System a model for uniform technical standards. This is because federal funding provides a major part of its capital cost. Other aspects of highway systems are uniform because vehicles are sold and operate in a national market. Thus, market forces encourage connectivity and interoperability of vehicles, their subsystems, and related infrastructures.

• *Universal basic service.* To the extent that the transportation infrastructure occupies public land and is user- or tax-supported, there is the expectation of universal access. The tax rates and user fees are established, directly or indirectly, through a political process and thus are subject to the judgment of those impacted that access is fair and reasonable. It is also recognized, both as a matter of social policy as well as a necessity for economic development, that some level of public transit be provided.

• *User rate regulation.* Freight rates and other regulations are approved by the Interstate Commerce Commission. However, there has been a substantial move in recent years toward deregulation and a dependence on market, rather than administrative, mechanisms as is the case in communication. Vehicle costs and other service and operating costs are almost totally market-determined, but are influenced by fuel, license, and vehicle taxes and by import regulations on vehicles and spare parts. While tolls for some roads and water crossings have existed for a long time, there is growing discussion of road and congestion pricing. The efficiency with which tolls and use-charges can be collected will be significantly enhanced if vehicles can be rapidly identified and facility use and billing handled automatically.

• *Spectrum resource management.* While much traveler information is available through conventional distribution means, real-time links to mobile users or users in areas not well-served by wireline service will be dependent on adequate spectrum for wireless transmission. These links to mobile users will become increasingly important as information technology decreases in cost, as it becomes increasingly ubiquitous, and as the demand for more and higher-quality information and for computer-mediated transactions continues to increase.

• *Ownership of transportation facilities.* Most road infrastructure is publicly funded through taxes and is publicly owned, although there is increasing interest in privately financed toll roads. If private roads become more common, the frequency of toll transactions and the use of automated techniques for toll collection arc likely to be favored to reduce operating costs and to reduce the delay in the collection process. To the extent that tax jurisdictions seek to derive revenues from road user charges, even publicly supported road facilities could make greater demands on the NII. Thus, an issue emerges as transportation systems become increasingly dependent on information and its efficient transmission: the degree to which transportation communication facilities should continue to be embedded within the transportation system or whether they could more effectively utilize available NII capacity

• *Privacy.* Privacy is emerging as a new issue in view of the interest in automatic vehicle identification and toll collection. There is legitimate concern that the conventional near-anonymity of private vehicle travel will be compromised as services based on the automated recording of vehicle location and identity become widespread.

• *Content regulation.* Content-related transportation regulation is illustrated by the transport of hazardous or environmentally dangerous materials or the movement of people across international borders. Other issues include protection of high-value cargoes, the reduction of transportation targets of crime, and the use of motor vehicles for illegal activity. Local jurisdictions need to be aware of such movements and to be able to maintain order in the transportation infrastructure. Facilitating the exchange of information between vehicles and operating facilities, both public and private, will assist in meeting such requirements.

Additional transportation policy issues relate to safety and environmental impact. While by far the largest impact of these considerations is on the design of vehicles and their propulsion systems, there are some secondary implications related to information and communication. These include minimizing vehicle emissions under congested traffic conditions, and the ability to signal hazardous and emergency circumstances with enough warning time for the traveler to take effective action.

Areas of Common Policy Concern

Comparing the above outlines of policy and regulatory issues for the NII and ITS, one can identify a number of points of commonality between the two. It is important to appreciate the ways in which the NII and the information components of the ITS relate to each other if we are to benefit most from the advances in technology and suffer the fewest unexpected consequences.

National ITS system architecture descriptions imply that ITS is an integrated system with an embedded "communication subsystem." The view taken in this paper is that this need not be the case; in fact, an embedded subsystem would be an inefficient use of resources. For the most part, many of the functionalities of ITS will be achieved more quickly and at lower cost if ITS shares the nation's information and communication infrastructure with other uses and users to the greatest extent possible. The traditional ITS domains of travel and transportation are, in this view, logical subsets and submarkets of the larger NII national information and communication enterprise.

What is this NII, the totality of the nation's rapidly evolving information and communication enterprise? The current view has several central features:

1. Virtually all current information will be stored, and hence retrieved, manipulated, and distributed, in *digital form*.

2. *Interface devices*, and the *skill* to use them, will be common—as common as cars and the ability to operate them are today.

3. Information will be accessible through *interconnected information networks*, probably a conceptual descendent of the current Internet, global in extent but with significantly greater bandwidth and ubiquity.

4. *Ownership rights* to information will be maintained, with market-derived prices and mechanisms enabling owners of information to be compensated for its use. This also implies that means to deny access, for reasons of privacy or other reasons, will be adequate, much as we currently protect other forms of private property against theft.

5. Information, as used here, refers to a *broad range of enterprises,* including publishing, entertainment, education, commerce, medicine, and information- intensive services such as financial services.

Support for this view comes from observation of the Internet's evolution over the past 25 years, especially in its recent adoption by commercial organizations for communication and advertising— and as the World Wide Web, wide-scale commercially available electronic mail, and graphic interfaces to online services have simplified its operational intricacies.

What are the policy areas whose satisfactory resolution are important for the effective pursuit of the travel and transportation "user services" envisaged as part of the ITS [1]? There are six that are of major significance within the context of this discussion: (1) demand management, (2) spectrum management, (3) universal connectivity and interoperability, (4) universal basic service, (5) privacy, and (6) funding of infrastructure facilities.

Demand Management

Both the NII and ITS must address a virtually unlimited demand for service. While most information infrastructure and services are market-driven, over-the-air broadcasting is generally perceived as an entitlement by providers and recipients. Mobile services, currently limited by the availability of spectrum, could consume large amounts of spectrum especially were there to be a large demand for wireless transmission of multimedia images. The road infrastructure is also seen as an entitlement, currently with only limited toll payments for premier service. But roads and accommodations for vehicles have practical limits.

A fundamental premise of ITS is that traffic congestion can be eased and construction of additional road capacity reduced through the application of presumably less-costly information technology. This is only partly realistic. Certainly increasingly sophisticated traffic engineering has resulted in improved travel conditions, and there is reason to believe that additional efficiencies can be achieved through the application of more technology. The flaw in the premise is that every improvement that provides additional effective capacity is quickly negated by increased vehicular traffic due either to general population growth, even more intensive land use, or the increased attractiveness of the road system. Greater reliance on pricing mechanisms in transportation are likely to be required after traffic management technology has exhausted feasible increases in road throughput. By reducing transaction costs, ITS information technologies are likely to enable increased application of market mechanisms to road transportation.

This is not to say that there is not currently a market for traveler information. A survey of commuters in Seattle [2] showed that 77% would use current traffic information to improve the quality of their traveling experience. The survey further showed that 16% would change their departure time, route, and even mode of transportation if given information adequate to make such decisions. Another 40% would be willing to change their departure time and route, but would not change the mode of transportation. And 21% would at least change their route. The rest could or would make no use of real-time traffic information were it available.

Another survey [3] showed that commuters would be interested in knowing, and would be willing to pay to know, the length of travel delays, the travel time for a particular trip, the best route for a particular trip, and the location of traffic congestion. Peak-period public-transit users indicated their interest in knowing the arrival time of the next public transit vehicle and how close to schedule the system was running.

These are, of course, limited surveys. But the results are plausible and are probably roughly representative of travelers broadly. However, what neither of these surveys tell us is the amount of money that people would be willing to pay for such information. Various ITS demonstration projects and commercial traveler information service companies are presently trying to determine this. Assuming that there is some price at which travelers will purchase real-time traffic information and that such information can be collected and distributed profitably, there exists the potential for some redistribution of traffic demand to make more efficient use of available road capacity.

Other measures directed to demand management are implicit in some of the ITS discussions. For example, automatic toll collection and automatic vehicle identification would make technically feasible pricing facility use on the basis of demand. A different approach to demand management is represented by the Commuter Choice Initiative, a partnership of the Federal Highway Administration, the Federal Transit Administration, the Environmental Protection Agency, and the Association for Commuter Transportation. The initiative's intent is to examine ways of shifting commuters from singly occupied vehicles to other modes of transportation; for example, implicitly subsided employee parking could be eliminated by changing the U.S. Tax Code.

But the major impact on transportation will come from the degree to which an effective NII can reduce the demand for physical travel by providing equivalent functionality through telecommunication. Perhaps the most obvious example is the impact of telecommuting the on home–work trips that are a central feature of urban transportation patterns. Current estimates [4] are that 10 million workers in the U.S. out of a work force of 125 million telecommute either full- or part-time. These estimates suggest that by the year 2000 this will grow to 25 million people. Increasing numbers of "knowledge workers" will be able to utilize powerful, low-cost information technology and information-distribution networks, either from home or from dispersed regional support locations.

Other, longer term, impacts will result from home shopping, telemedicine, and changes in the way some education might be provided. This change has already been demonstrated in the entertainment industry, as replacement of travel to performances has been superseded by at-home consumption. But beyond the consequent reduction in demand for physical travel is the increase in the market for goods or services that will be enabled by easy electronic delivery. In essence, new products and new markets will develop around electronic commerce, and some physical travel to browse or purchase physical goods will be eliminated.

Spectrum Management

In the past, computing was based on the requirements of large central processors, data servers, displays, and fixed facilities that utilized the results of computation. But the evolution to client/

server architectures and the availability of low-cost portable computing devices are driving the current demand for mobile computing. Through a number of new technologies, including satellite paging, cellular telephony, the newly allocated Personal Communication Service, and wireless local area networks (LANs) based on either radio frequencies or on infrared technology, the computer has been disconnected from wall plugs. Adding to this need for mobile connectivity is the large amount of information available from public and private networks. Interaction with information regardless of the user's location and state of motion is, of course, exactly what a traveler requires. The technologies of spectrum-sharing, signal compression, and data compaction will be critical if the supply of wireless service is to keep up with demand. But how to best meet the needs of large numbers of mobile users is unclear.

Some parts of the ITS communication requirement will be satisfied through common carrier wireline facilities and thus place no additional demand on the electromagnetic spectrum. These include links between parts of traffic management systems such as sensors, traffic signs and signals, controllers, and operations centers. They also include access facilities to online services in homes, offices, hotels, transportation terminals, and parking facilities for downloading information and for interactive queries. Vehicle electronics will be designed around onboard local area networks connecting the many sensing, receiving, processing, storing, and actuator devices on vehicles.

The crucial link is that between the fixed transportation–communication infrastructure and the vehicle. While short-range links can use infrared signaling, by and large, use of electromagnetic spectrum will be required.

The most attractive spectrum for mobile use is in the 100-MHz to 2-GHz region. Below these frequencies antennas are awkwardly large for portability and above them antenna directivity effects become a factor. These are not firm limits, and there will, of course, be differences in communication requirements between a person with a cellular phone in a subway and a driver in a tractor-trailer. Nevertheless, there is likely to be considerable pressure from mobile service providers and users to convert spectrum in the 100-MHz–2-GHz range that is currently allocated to broadcasting and fixed service to mobile uses [5].

The adequacy of existing spectrum allocations for mobile service is difficult to assess. There are two limiting scenarios. At one extreme, technology developments could be such that pressure for increased allocations will be minimal. Such developments would include highly efficient modulation techniques; powerful algorithms for data compression; architectures based on large amounts of data storage on the vehicle with only modest amounts of updating information required; highly customized data transmissions to vehicles; mini-cell systems allowing a high degree of frequency reuse; minimal requirements for the transmission of voice, graphics, images, and video; preferential use of higher frequencies having greater information-handling capability, including satellite-based systems; and other possible advances. All of these developments are possible to some extent , but achieving them will require resources for R&D, infrastructure investment, and user-owned devices. Still unknown are they total costs, the prices users will be willing to pay, and how attractive private investors will find these markets.

The scenario at the other extreme is one in which the required technologies do not develop as favorably as one might hope and at the same time ITS services turn out to be very popular, with data requirements larger than expected. The pressure on existing spectrum allocations for cellular telephony, paging, FM subcarrier authorizations, and other existing services would in this scenario be heavy. Organizations dependent on these allocations would seek spectrum allocated to broadcasting and fixed services.

One of the most obvious places to turn, in terms of amount and quality of spectrum, is the spectrum currently allocated for broadcasting. One possibility is the use of additional spectrum proposed for high definition television (HDTV). While welcoming additional spectrum, broadcasters are not convinced that, were additional spectrum to be made available, HDTV would be their choice for its use. Broadcasters instead have proposed that they have flexibility in the use of new spectrum, and cite data transmissions as one possible service offering.

An important new element in the dynamics of spectrum management has recently been added by the FCC: the spectrum auction.

While contrary to the original idea that the electromagnetic spectrum is a public good whose use for a specified purpose is decided through public processes of allocation and authorization, auctions are based on the sale of the right to use the spectrum to the highest bidder. Once an entrepreneur has purchased such a right, the service provided and the standards to be met are less a matter for the regulator. In this way the auction of licenses could assist in the conversion of spectrum to new uses, such as, in this case, mobile services. Under such a licensing regime entrepreneurs have far greater flexibility in seeking the most valuable use of the spectrum, measured by what consumers want and by what they are willing to pay. In this manner, use of the spectrum is more directly decided by the consumer than by the government regulator acting as a proxy for the consumer.

Interoperability and Technical Standards

The communication industry has long recognized the benefits of technical standards for system interoperability, from its earliest needs for telegraphy across political boundaries. As nationwide communication networks developed at the end of the 19th century, the need for open industry standards for interconnection became clear. The computer industry came to this understanding more recently, and has moved away from proprietary systems for all but the smallest palmtop and embedded computing devices. Much of the consumer electronics industry still thinks in terms of proprietary standards but is likely to bow to the inevitable pressure for open systems, as it already has for much content media. Vehicle manufacturers also must face the need for open systems, and to this end ITS can provide an important guiding hand. It is important that open systems for vehicle and transport-related devices be achieved at the earliest possible time, lest progress and the application of information technology to transportation be constrained by incompatible and market-limiting technical standards. This can come about by a combination of market pressures on the computer, software, and consumer electronics industries; by voluntary industry standards to enlarge product markets and to improve the delivery and maintenance of goods and services; and by government regulation, if necessary.

The size of the ITS market and hence the attractiveness of ITS services will depend on the degree to which users can be assured that purchases of terminal devices, software, and communication hardware will remain useful through the life of the product. Vehicle manufacturers will be less likely to move aggressively to incorporate new ITS services into their mass-market products if they are not convinced that such new services will be part of the transportation environment over the long term. Vehicle location techniques such as those utilizing the Global Positioning System (GPS) will only be available at low cost if there are portable devices that can utilize the information. Traffic management systems will not be designed to use real-time vehicle locations for adaptive control unless such data are available. Data providers will not produce products for a transportation market that does not exist. And communication companies will not be able to justify changes in spectrum allocations and technical standards without a convincing market pull.

These problems are little different from those facing the information industry generally. One result could be for the transportation segment of the market to be seen as too small, too splintered, or too high-risk to attract adequate investment. In such a case investors will elect lower-risk and potentially more lucrative opportunities instead.

There is an answer to this conundrum: the concept of open systems and voluntary standards reached through the cooperative efforts of the major stakeholders. This concept is proving its effectiveness in the computer and software industry, and is needed if ITS services are to find their place in the information markets seen by NII proponents.

There are no parts of these markets that are not seeking open standards, although the pace varies from market to market. The Internet, the World Wide Web, electronic mail, electronic data interchange (EDI), and other communication and application areas have seen major advances in enabling people and organizations to exchange information effectively. There is a great deal more to be done, and these technologies can be daunting to the average user, but progress is encouraging. Most importantly, these applications demonstrate that solutions exist for the transparent exchange of information between a wide range of people, systems, and platforms.

The existence of an open standard for GPS has also been effective. However, greater precision in location will be needed, through local differential GPS or other approaches, if vehicles are to be guided through complex lane structures in urban areas.

Voluntary industry-supported mapping organizations such as the Open GIS Consortium are working to make maps conform to open system specifications, so that nationwide electronic maps can be purchased and vehicle location information can be tied to local reference grids.

The traffic management system industry is currently split on the issue of standards. Some in this specialized market adhere to proprietary standards while others support open standards. Proprietary standards was the strategy originally adopted by the large computer companies; one can predict that proprietary standards will be no more successful for the traffic management industry than they have been for the computer industry.

Vehicle manufacturers are the remaining unknown for open ITS standards; however, the advantages of vehicle LANs for the flexible configuring of on-board sensing, control, display, communication, and navigation electronics are likely to be sufficiently attractive that the manufacturers will adopt industry standards. It is likely that these will be open standards so that manufacturers can avail themselves of the cost benefits that will come from the largest possible market of suppliers.

The adoption of open standards is a necessary, but not sufficient, condition for ITS services to develop and prosper under an NII umbrella. There will still be difficult problems that could prevent deployment of some of the more exotic ITS service proposals. Even with open standards, ITS services might end up resembling personal computing today. Users could be plagued with configuration management issues, incompatibilities between applications, limits on upward and downward compatibility between hardware, bugs in software, and obtaining technical support for hardware, software, communications, and data through third-party providers. Anyone who has attempted to configure a modem or get their anti-lock brakes debugged will appreciate the problems that could be encountered. Pessimists will see these concerns as indicative of flaws in the ITS grand vision. Optimists will see them as opportunities to excel.

Universal Basic Service

Systems for wide access to traffic and travel information will be effective to the degree they are ubiquitous and reasonably priced. In the U.S. today there is one telephone line per 1.3 people, 28 personal computers per 100 people, and TV in 98% of households. But the use of online services and the Internet is weighted heavily at upper income levels, and computer literacy, while increasing rapidly, is still limited. There is some concern that parts of the population will be disenfranchised from the benefits of the "information superhighway," or will be too slow in adopting its technologies.

On the basis of past experience, adoption of new technology can be quite rapid. This is especially the case where the technology undergoes substantial decreases in cost; when product cycles are short so that there is a large secondary market in used or older models; and when there is a clear value directly seen by the user of the technology. One can conclude that at the consumer level, it is important that ITS initiatives include public transit users as well as operators of private and commercial vehicles to address the broadest set of societal needs.

In deciding how to achieve universal access to a socially important service such as the NII or ITS, it is useful to ask first what will happen without government intervention. In the area of information, in addition to a large and vibrant market, society has taken steps to assure some level of protection for information and for some degree of subsidization of access to it. This takes the form of the licensing without fee of spectrum for broadcasters, public funding for schools and libraries, cross-ownership restrictions on public media channels, subsidization of local telephone rates by long distance service, and the like. But these are minimum protections intended to supplement the free market in information provided through print media, broadcasting, advertising, and other commercial goods and services.

In the area of transportation, a U.S. population of 246 million (in 1988) owned 140 million autos. In addition, the U.S. has extensive urban and national transportation facilities, the result of both public and private investment. The finite life of vehicles and an active resale market means that, as new information technology is introduced into vehicles, it will be substantially diffused into the national stock over the next decade. And if something approaching universal basic service is achieved by the NII, it is not unreasonable to expect that real-time travel information to be available to public transit users as well.

It is therefore instructive to examine how rapidly society has adopted new technology in the past in order to assess how we might achieve universal access solely through market action. A recent discussion of information technologies offers some insights [6].

The cost of the technology or service is critical for its adoption. If one uses as a metric of adoption rate the time for a technology to penetrate to 50% of households, and if one notes that product prices in the range of 1–2% of per capita income signal rapid market penetration, the data suggest the following: In the case of such consumer electronics products as black and white TV, color TV, and videocassette recorders, the period from market introduction to 50% penetration was 8–10 years. The cost levels for such products is $200–400, well within the cost regime for deep penetration.

Personal computers will have taken closer to 20 years to achieve similar penetration, for a number of reasons. Not only is their cost more like 10% of per capita income, but to the technology development and marketing time must be added the time to increase the level of computer literacy needed to cope with their complexities.

The penetration time of cable TV and telephones took even longer. Discounting 10–20 year periods of slow initial growth, cable TV took 25 years and the telephone 50 years to achieve similar market penetration. Telephone costs were originally quite high, and both technologies required large investments in network infrastructure to make them widely attractive to consumers. The Internet experience parallels this, with a 25-year period between its initial development and use by the computer science community in

1969 to its explosive commercial growth in the mid-1990s. What do these facts suggest about the likelihood of universal basic service in the NII and ITS through normal market behavior? The signs are promising. While computer prices will probably remain higher than 2% of per capita income, much of the market penetration of information technology will consist of portable personal wireless communication devices such as personal digital assistants, electronic organizers and other palmtops, games, and set-top boxes. It is critical to make affordable spectrum and wireless service in order to make this class of device the central element of "social" as opposed to "specialist" technology. Pagers cost only $50 and cellular phones less than $100, but communication costs are considerably in excess of these prices. One may conclude that the rapid decrease in technology prices due to the automatic fabrica tion of microelectronic chips and the growth in the market that enables producers to share development, marketing, distribution, and support costs over larger number of units will go a long way to making these technologies widely available without government intervention.

Nevertheless, there remain questions of equity. If the market penetration of information technology tops out at 75%, leaving 25% of the population disenfranchised, there is still cause for concern. While "universal" means something less than 100%, substantial elements of society still may be excluded. An appropriate role of government is to examine patterns of use to identify where new information technologies and/or their applications to transportation have not penetrated. Increasing computer literacy is a logical role for education, and while this requires at least a generation to see a significant effect, it must not be delayed. Federal support of specific programs, or through local tax revenues or tax incentives, may be considered. In urban areas this could take the form of encouraging applications of technology to public transit, such as displays in stations and for kiosks in public areas, much like telephones. Payment schemes could be established for full or partial recovery of operating costs. Finally, some services, such as emergency communication, can be mandated under existing vehicle safety programs just as occupant restraint systems have.

Privacy

Organizations that have made information networks the basis of their operations soon reach the point where they become concerned about the protection of their private or proprietary data and with preventing unauthorized entry into their internal information systems. Various approaches that can be taken to secure information systems include audits, personnel security measures, educational programs, the erection of "firewalls," and encryption of stored and transmitted information. But such protection is effective only to the extent that it limits the distribution of information, which is contrary to the primary purpose of its broad use within the organization. Concerns about privacy in connection with ITS arise when one considers the amount of information about a vehicle's movements implicit in various ITS services, such as automatic vehicle identification, toll collection, route guidance, and the like. There exists the potential for significant loss of privacy, and for overly intrusive monitoring of employee activities, in some of the proposed ITS "services."

Negative views of ITS based on this "Big Brother" image of its intrusiveness are common. Similar concerns are increasingly being expressed about the fragility of parts of the NII to penetration, disruption, and misuse. To some, the broader the access to information and the wider its distribution the better, as in cooperative group activities. But to others this leads to violations of personal privacy and of ownership rights to information.

There is an implied notion that a significant degree of privacy exists today, and that this privacy should not be thoughtlessly abandoned. This is, unfortunately, not the case. Credit cards and identification for automated access to facilities and systems leave a trail of space- and time-data that record our activities. License plate readers similarly record entry into parking structures, and cellular phone operations record a user's location cell by cell. Computer system access, telephone logs, and records of financial transactions further add to the detailed picture of one's daily activities.

Each person must make tradeoffs with respect to the degree to which NII and ITS technology provides benefits commensurate with its cost in loss of privacy. An individual must also reckon with privacy concerns in dealing with an employer, where the terms and conditions of employment often imply the surrender of some rights of privacy.

An architectural principle that should be adopted in the design of automated information systems is that a user be able to select a level of service with both an attached financial cost and a privacy-loss cost in mind. There are numerous options where the benefits of information technology can be achieved with minimum loss of privacy. A person can pay cash for purchases and tolls, at a cost of using cash and waiting in service lines; that person can also rely on paper maps and other on-board information assets only, or rely on broadcast information at the cost of lack of timeliness and non-specific content.

Beyond "roughing it" in the Information Age, technology does exist that can be implemented to minimize loss of privacy. Anonymous smart cards can represent cash that can be used in lieu of identifiable credit transactions. Vehicles can be identified by an arbitrarily assigned or user-defined identity for the purpose of negotiating with traveler support systems. Public key encryption can protect the content of transactions while they are being transmitted and processed. Vehicles should have the ability to turn off all transmissions and operate under conditions of radio silence. Public agencies should make known their monitoring activities so that travelers can be aware of them, in much the same way that one is warned that baggage and vehicles are subject to search or that a public place harbors hazardous substances.

If large numbers of people "vote with their feet" or with their wallets with respect to user privacy, will the potential utility of ITS technology be sufficiently undermined as to make its deployment valueless? There are two answers to this. First, the presumed benefits of information technology *must* be such that, on balance, they outweigh the privacy-loss cost, and this must be a clear requirement in the design of such systems. Second, even if only a few choose to use the system, for example commercial and public transit system operators and high-end luxury users, then some reduction in peak congestion will occur, thereby improving the transportation environment for all users.

Funding of Infrastructure Facilities

Capital improvements to address the traffic needs of a local juris-diction are designed as part of an integrated project covering design and installation of roadway, signaling, and communications. From the standpoint of engineering and management this increases the likelihood of achieving the desired goal. As traffic management systems become increasingly sophisticated, operations centers and their supporting communications become an ever-greater fraction of the total cost. The increase of these costs this will accelerate as ITS-derived technology is introduced into the transportation infrastructure.

A factor contributing to the cost of local traffic management facilities is the use of closed-circuit television to enhance traffic managers' ability to assess traffic characteristics immediately, make responsive changes in traffic signals, or to be able to decide when to summon emergency personnel to the site of an accident or other disruption. As camera costs decrease, the ability of traffic managers to have on-scene presence at virtually all locations under their control seems desirable, despite the fact that it leads to adding large amounts of dedicated cable to the municipal infrastructure. Much of the cost of these dedicated communication facilities is not met by local taxpayers but from federal funding, including from the Federal Highway Fund, so the public has the sense of receiving the benefit of a free good.

Prior to deregulation in the 1970s and 1980s, communication common carriers acted similarly. In return for being granted a local monopoly to encourage private investment, carriers were required to deliver an adequate level of service and were assured a return on their investment. Rates to users were cost-based, determined by operating costs and a guaranteed rate of return on invested capital. System costs were met by the ratepayer. Local rates were kept within bounds by cross-subsidization from long distance revenues.

With the introduction of competition into the communication industry, carriers must now keep rates as low as possible. They do this in a variety of ways: aggressive pricing plans; new product and service offerings to attract customers; joint ventures with suppliers and users; and by increasing the size of their market to enable them to spread the cost of their transmission and switching capacity across the largest number of users. This last is done through multiplexing large numbers of circuits and through resale via value-added carriers.

The issue for ITS planners is how to get the greatest value from public investments in transportation infrastructure. Single-user, single-use communication facilities that are redundant with those in the NII would seem to be an inefficient use of public funding. Using NII facilities that are provided through private sources not only reduces the capital investment required from public funds, but fixed operating costs can then be spread over a larger set of users.

An argument against this idea is the fact that exchanging capital costs for operating costs leads to a net financial loss for the local jurisdiction. The capital costs are heavily subsidized by the federal government, while operating costs are not. But using less efficient transportation infrastructure investment strategies would seem to be poorly justified by artifacts in federal funding formulas.

Proposals for Government Initiatives

Neither the NII nor the ITS lack for ideas from a large number of constituencies. Proposed here are several initiatives that link the information and transportation domains. For each proposal, federal government facilitation or coordination could be useful in promoting synergies between the two domains.

• *Access to public real-time traffic data.* Information from traffic sensors, responses of public service agencies to incidents, warnings of hazardous conditions, and the like are commonly available in local traffic management centers. Information about the status of public transit operations is available in the control centers of those systems. Such information, in near-real-time and in open digital formats, should to be made available to transportation users and to value-added traveler information providers. Local jurisdictions should be encouraged by the U.S. DOT and its constituent agencies to make available real-time traffic information. It is suggested that:

(1) The public right to such data, in a timely manner and at reasonable cost, be assured.

(2) Federal action should encourage the adoption of open system data formats.

(3) Ownership rights to traffic information should be clarified and resale of that information should be encouraged by arrangements with public agency collectors.

(4) Reasonable compensation to the public provider for the cost of access to the data should be provided. Congressional Public Law 104-13 has established pricing guidelines for such transactions. The requirement in the legislation is that information be provided for a price no greater than the cost of dissemination. This legislation could serve as a starting point for state legislation as required.

(5) Modernizing and reconfiguring traffic and other public transit system operation centers to allow public access to real-time traffic information should be encouraged. Costs can be covered through partnerships between public agencies and value-added information suppliers. The local cost share could be eligible for federal assistance under existing DOT programs.

• *Historical traffic data and models.* Substantial sums are expended at the federal level on programs to collect and distribute comprehensive, high-quality transportation data. These programs should be encouraged and expanded where appropriate. Detailed local traffic data at the street-intersection and freeway-interchange level tends to be collected to meet particular needs and are not easily available for purposes beyond those for which they were collected. Such detailed historical data are of value to calibrate traffic flow models for use in real-time route guidance and for assessing the size and structure of markets for value-added traffic information products. While this is clearly a local responsibility, private investment in the development of information on a national scale can be encouraged if guidelines exist for the collection, storage, and retrieval of such information.

There is an important federal role in encouraging states and local jurisdictions to establish standards for the collection and formatting of data and the underlying models for its analysis, and for implementing systems based on them. The DOT could assist, for example, by:

(1) Supporting the compilation and publication of representative collections of local intersection-level data in standard formats. This data could be used in market analysis and information product design.

(2) Assisting local jurisdictions to provide access to this data and underlying models through public such means as local-jurisdiction WWW sites.

• *Regulation of "tele-activities."* Encouraging socially necessary activities while at the same time minimizing the need for physical travel is an important approach to reducing the rate of vehicular traffic growth. It is therefore important that unnecessary regulatory barriers not adversely impact such efforts.

(1) One of the most obvious tele-activities is commuting. The home as a workplace, while not a new idea, has a varied history. Abuse of workers in the early years of the industrial revolution, child labor laws, unsafe working conditions, local real estate zoning, and efficiencies of central capital investment and management supervision have limited its broad applicability. Many of these concerns are no longer relevant for information workers in an information society, but regulations from earlier eras remain. An interagency task force, led by DOT, should be convened to identify regulations that could inadvertently limit tele-activities. Helpful actions would include, for example, tax incentives to telecommuters, and modifications of government procurement regulations to recognize shared home environments for work performed under contract, for the allocation of liability, for fair overhead rates, and the like.

(2) Our social regulations governing education, the practice of medicine, and other activities with mandated standards of quality and professional performance, protection of public health and safety, and other forms of consumer protection, need to be reexamined in light of the potential for traffic-reducing tele-activities. Leadership for an interagency activity would be appropriate for the Office of Science and Technology Policy.

• *Mobile spectrum planning.* An in-depth dialogue with the FCC is needed for long-term planning. This planning would include the provision of adequate spectrum to meet the needs of mobile computing users and the support of transportation-related information and communication services.

(1) A joint FCC/DOT working group would provide user input to the FCC. It would also create an important forum for the joint consideration of future communication needs to support transportation-related initiatives.

(2) The DOT should play an active role in responding to FCC inquiries and rule-makings related to the allocation of spectrum and the establishment of technical standards for mobile services. This should take place both domestically and in international fora.

(3) Initiatives to make maximum possible use of broadcasting facilities and spectrum for real-time traffic data distribution should be encouraged. Not only could this provide additional revenue to broadcasters, but the existing nationwide system for broadcasting and spectrum management could be used to greater effectiveness.

(4) Two-way interactive broadcast services should be encouraged to help transportation users deal effectively with information service providers.

(5) Cross-ownership restrictions on communication facilities should be examined to ensure that they do not unnecessarily interfere with providing effective provision of traffic and traveler information.

(6) In recognition of the fact that the major funding for ITS programs will be at the state and local levels, it will be important to include communication planning as part of the dialogue with state transportation agencies. This will be particularly critical in the area of open system standards, in order to avoid a proliferation of incompatible standards by separate states and local jurisdictions.

• *Open information systems and software standards.* The DOT should play an active role in national standard-setting activities that will impact information distribution within and between vehicles and supporting infrastructure organizations. Of particular importance are the automotive, trucking, and traffic management equipment industries, where the DOT has the greatest leverage. Government actions should be directed toward facilitating private initiatives, rather than taking a primary role in setting information standards. The transportation industry and its regulators should, wherever possible, follow the lead of the computing and communication industries, in which open system standards are already well advanced in many areas of importance for transportation. These latter industries have strong incentives to address the greatest possible part of the information market.

(1) A first step would be for the DOT, in conjunction with industrial and professional standards organizations, to identify what standards are critical for the effective interaction of the NII and ITS and to identify where important standard-setting is lagging.

(2) The introduction of information technology into vehicles, especially software-dependent functionality, raises issues of product safety and market structure. For example, should vehicle software receive compatibility certification? Should software failure analysis be required before software is marketed? How should design, test, production, installation, and maintenance of vehicle software be accomplished? These issues will become increasingly important as vehicle software undergoes a transition from being embedded in hardware to being consumer options. The DOT, in conjunction with software standards organizations in government, industry, and academia, should consider the safety aspects of the future transportation systems' software in order to make recommendations for needed changes.

Conclusion

There are some similarities between the NII and ITS. Both appear to have the purpose and goal of increasing the capacity of the underlying infrastructure. However, in the case of urban transportation, substantial increases in capacity are difficult to achieve. Therefore, the ITS strategy must be a mix of increasing supply through information technology, but also of limiting demand, either by shifting demand paradigms or by replacing it with information-based alternatives to physical travel.

Both NII and ITS pose problems for rational system design. Optimum communication system design requires that the source, the transmission medium, and the terminal be considered as a whole, with appropriate cost and performance tradeoffs made to achieve the desired objective. In the case of information and transportation systems, the terminal end is under the control of both the consumer and terminal manufacturers such as the makers of computers, TV receivers, and vehicles. The transmission medium is controlled by the FCC, cable and telephone operating companies, or local traffic management jurisdictions. The underlying infrastructure is controlled by investors in space and terrestrial transmission facilities and by jurisdictions supported by federal, state, and local taxes. Both domains, consisting of separate and difficult-to-coordinate parts, display system pathologies: deficiencies in system throughput, congestion delays, saturation, accidents, and failures.

Thus, while efforts are made to apply formal system engineering discipline to the design of both the NII and ITS, both of these infrastructures also display characteristics of self-organizing systems. The "design" evolves by trial and error, and while no one is "in charge," the system "works," though not optimally. Lacking overall system managers who can use metrics to improve system performance, we are, in a bottom-up view, left with local solutions to local needs. In a top-down view, we take a best-practice approach, and hope that by working through the many levels of our political and economic structure we are able to maintain a rough match between supply and demand.

Overcoming these inherent system difficulties should be the joint goal for the responsible public agencies and private organizations if we are to improve the efficiency of transportation-impacted sectors of society. Automated highways and communication systems can improve safety by reducing accidents and improving the timely provision of emergency medical care. Intermodal transportation's operating efficiency can be improved by the automated tracking of vehicles and shipments across road, rail, air, and ship interfaces. Transportation targets of crime can receive protection, and transportation-dependent crime such as narcotics traffic, hit-and-run accidents, and car theft and hijacking, can be more easily monitored. These are but a few examples where society as a whole can benefit from an effective integration of transportation, information, and other social systems.

References

1. Carpenter, E.J. "Intelligent Transportation Systems (ITS) User Services: A Discussion of Information Service Content." Background paper provided for the ITS/NII workshop, Harvard University, John F. Kennedy School of Government, Cambridge, MA, July 13, 1995.

2. Haselkon, Mark, Barfield, Woodrow, Spyridakis, Jan, and Conquest, Loveday. "Improving Motorist Information Systems: Toward a User-Based Motorist Information System for the Puget Sound Area." University of Washington report WA–RD 187.1, April 1990. Also Haselkon, Mark, et al. "Real-Time Motorist Information for Reducing Urban Congestion: Commuter Behavior, Data Conversion and Display, and Transportation Policy." University of Washington report WA–RD 240.2, June 1992.

3. Peter Harris Research Group. "The Public's Interest in and Willingness to Pay for Enhanced Traveler Information as Provided by IVHS." A report prepared for TRANSCOM under contract with James H. Kell & Associates, June 1994.

4. Nilles, Jack. "Telecommuting Trends June 1995." JALA International, Inc. Los Angeles, CA.

5. Detailed information on spectrum allocations can be obtained from the *Manual of Regulations and Procedures for Federal Radio Frequency Management,* available from the Superintendent of Documents, Washington, D.C. 20402; from the National Telecommunications and Information Administration, Department of Commerce, 14th Street and Constitution Avenue, N.W., Washington, D.C. 20230; and from the Federal Communication Commission, 1919 M Street, N.W., Washington, D.C. 20554.

6. Stix, Gary. "Domesticating Cyberspace." in *The Computer in the 21st Century,* special issue of *Scientific American,* 1995.

ITS Requirements in the Context of the NII

ITS Information Service Content

Elisabeth J. Carpenter

Introduction

Intelligent Transportation Systems (ITS) are based upon the concept of using advanced communications, computers, sensors, and information processing, storage, and display techniques to improve the efficiency and safety of the surface transportation system and to reduce its harmful environmental effects. ITS goals will be realized through public and private partnerships involving the U.S. Department of Transportation (DOT); state, regional, and local transportation authorities; industry organizations, private firms, and academia. The national ITS program has five major elements: research and development, operational tests, development of a national ITS architecture, development of appropriate standards and guidelines to facilitate interoperability, and ITS deployment planning support.

The DOT and ITS America, in the National ITS Program Plan, have defined twenty-nine user services as the basic building blocks of ITS implementation. These user services will employ a variety of technologies in the areas of sensors, computers, information processing, data storage and retrieval, and data and voice communications. Depending upon the particular service, the user can be a private individual in a vehicle, a common carrier, a transit authority, an emergency response unit, or a regional, state, or federal transportation agency. Some elements of ITS user services exist and are in use today; many others are in the development and test stages; others, such as completely automated highway systems, are further out on the horizon. These user services are evolutionary in nature, with a preliminary near-term application for most. Their development path relies on increasingly advanced technology and interaction with other user services, and potentially with services outside of the ITS domain. Implementation of the user services will involve both the public and private sectors.

For program planning purposes, the twenty-nine user services have been divided into seven groups, or bundles, that share common institutional or technological parameters. It should be noted that many of the requirements for these user services are still in the development phase; results of operational tests currently underway by the ITS partnerships will refine requirements.

The national architecture activity will define the framework within which the ITS user services will be implemented. The architecture will not specify design details or implementation paths, however, but will define how components interact to ensure nationwide compatibility and interchangeability while allowing for flexibility at the local and regional levels.

In this paper, the twenty-nine ITS user services will be defined and an overview of information service content for each user service also will be provided. Information service commonalties among the user services also will be defined, and potential near-term and far-term areas of relevance for the National Information Infrastructure (NII) will be discussed.

ITS in the Framework of the NII

The NII will use emerging technology to revolutionize the exchange of information. It will integrate and build upon many different existing and emerging physical components, including communications networks (such as cable, telephone, radio communications, Internet, and satellite systems); computers and information appliances (smart televisions, computers, and supercomputers); and information in the form of databases, information services, government documents, bulletin boards, and libraries. The NII must be built on the principle of open interfaces, as interoperability is the key to the NII's success. The NII will be built, owned, and operated primarily by the private sector, which will most likely have the lead role in developing industry standards.

However, as in the case of ITS, successful implementation will depend on government and industry cooperation. The government has a major role in promoting a competitive market, ensuring broad access to and ease of use of the NII nationwide, and funding testbeds and demonstration projects.

ITS can be viewed as an application or subset of the NII or as a specific domain that will utilize some or all of the capabilities of the emerging NII. Some ITS user services are obviously self-contained applications, using in-vehicle sensors and warnings, for example. Some will share information with other ITS services or with information services and databases outside of the transportation domain. The NII has the potential to more efficiently provide real-time information on transportation systems; it can also provide access to services and workplaces without the need to travel, particularly in today's environment of ubiquitous personal computers.

ITS User Services and Their Information Service Content

Travel and Transportation Management

The first ITS bundle, Travel and Transportation Management, includes the following six user services:

• En-Route Driver Information

• Route Guidance

• Traveler Services Information

• Traffic Control

• Incident Management

• Emissions Testing and Mitigation

These services all collect, process, and use information about the surface transportation system. They are of great interest to both public and private service operators and providers. Many end-user products and services will be developed by the private sector, but they will often rely on information and infrastructure provided by the public sector.

Travel and Transportation Management services share requirements for surveillance, communications, multiple user interfaces, and database processing. For all services in this bundle, the major technical information management issues will involve gathering and integrating static and dynamic information from multiple sources; maintaining the resulting databases so that they contain current, accurate, and reliable information; transmitting the desired portions of the information to users in each service and among services in this bundle; and presenting information to users in a useful form.

En-Route Driver Information

The En-Route Driver Information service provides travel-related information to drivers after their trips are underway. This user service includes two subservices: *driver advisory*, which provides real-time information on traffic, transit, and roadway conditions; and *in-vehicle signing*, which provides in-vehicle displays of roadway signs and warnings of hazards, traffic controls, or special roadway conditions.

The *driver advisory* subservice conveys real-time information to drivers about traffic conditions, incidents, construction activities, transit schedules, weather conditions, and other occurrences relevant to drivers of personal, commercial, and public-transit vehicles. This information could be transferred to the driver by a number of communications techniques and presented via voice, text, or map displays. Each vehicle would need to have the appropriate equipment for receiving and displaying messages. Methods currently available for transmitting information to mobile users include auditory messages using FM sideband, data on the FM subcarrier, two-way radio, cellular telephone service, microwave or infrared beacon, and transponder-based vehicle-to-roadside communications. None of these systems has true nationwide coverage; however, at the time of this writing, nationwide mobile satellite telephone service from geostationary satellites was planned to be operational within the next few years, and several other mobile satellite communications systems were in the planning stage.

Information in this subservice potentially could come to the driver from a control center or from multiple sources. A control center could collect information on the transportation system by means of some of the other user services. It could then analyze the information, develop an integrated output, and transmit the results to drivers. A traffic management center could obtain congestion information from various sources, and broadcast advisory information to vehicles over commercially available radio or by other means to suitably equipped vehicles. Driver advisories also could be provided to vehicles through roadside displays or from electronic devices that would provide information at stationary sources.

In-vehicle signing provides information directly in the vehicle that is currently found on physical road signs. In the short term, in-vehicle signing may be limited to drivers with special requirements, such as those with impaired vision. As the technology matures, this service could be extended to provide warnings of road conditions and safe speeds for specific types of vehicles. In the future, in-vehicle signing could be integrated with other ITS user services, using in-vehicle heads-up displays, video monitors, and other audio or visual presentation methods could be used. Terminology conventions, consistent data formats, communications standards, and resolution of spectrum issues would be needed for a comprehensive service.

Initial definition of performance requirements indicates that in-vehicle signing must support real-time communications to transfer current information to the driver. The service should be capable of transferring information between advisory sources and appropriately equipped vehicles, and between signs and in-vehicle signing equipment with a round-trip transmission time of less than five seconds. In-vehicle signing should be provided within a range of 100 to 1,500 feet in the lanes of travel from the external sign, and should be presented in an audible or visible form consistent with safety and human factors.

Route Guidance

The Route Guidance user service provides travelers with a suggested route and instructions on how to reach selected destinations. Users might include private vehicle drivers, drivers of commercial vehicles, transit operators, and eventually pedestrians using hand-held units.

Route Guidance is closely related to the En-Route Driver Information service. It relies on the same real-time transportation information, but requires further processing into route guidance instructions. Early implementations of this service will provide static information (e.g., roadway networks and transit schedules) to the user. A fully deployed user service will provide route directions based on real-time traffic information and will have access to public transit data to facilitate the transfer of intermodal information.

A position determination system, such as the Global Positioning System (GPS), is required to permit a route guidance function to locate itself on a map, and may need to be supplemented by dead reckoning or map-matching to provide the required accuracies. Digital map databases and common spatial information/map database standards are required for an interoperable, nationwide route guidance service.

Many methods are available for communicating information from and providing information to vehicles. Route determination can be processed either in the vehicle or by processors installed in the transportation system infrastructure; mobile, autonomous guidance systems can operate independent of the infrastructure. Real-time information would be obtained by adding the capability to receive and integrate communications from the infrastructure.

Performance requirements defined to date for Route Guidance provide for real-time two-way communications between the transportation infrastructure and appropriately equipped vehicles, with a round-trip transmission time of less than five seconds. The service is also required to support autonomous route guidance in the absence of two-way communications. Vehicle location must be provided with a position accuracy ranging from 20 to 300 feet, velocity accuracy within five mph, and directional accuracy within 15 degrees. Route guidance and transit scheduling information should be provided within 60 seconds of request.

Traveler Services Information

Traveler Services Information provides travelers with a business directory of service information that could include hotels, restaurants, events, and facility locations. This information could be available at fixed locations such as homes, offices, or public locations (kiosks), or it can be provided en-route in the vehicle (although it may be necessary to have the vehicle stationary for safety reasons). Future expansion of this service may allow for interactive connections between users and service providers and also possibly financial transactions. This service is related to the Pre-Trip Travel Information user service, which will be discussed later.

Traveler Services Information includes the ability to access travel aid information from many different sources. This information is likely to come primarily from private-sector sources, but could also include public service information. Traveler Services Information overlaps with other electronic traveler services and possibly with other consumer options not directly related to travel or transportation. The service would be useful for both the private traveler and common carrier operators.

Traveler Services Information uses two-way communications for interactive request and access to directories and databases of services, perhaps stored on CD-ROM. User-friendly query languages, procedures, and user interfaces for presentation and display of service information are essential for the success of this service, which could be provided as an additional capability on personal, portable traveler information systems. Prerecorded verbal information could be broadcast on a special radio channel or accessed through dial-up telephone lines. It is also possible that in less congested areas a common ITS channel could accommodate provision of these services.

In its mature implementation phase, Traveler Services Information could connect users and providers interactively. A future integrated service could support reservation and confirmation services, and financial transactions such as automatic billing.

Performance requirements developed to date indicate that Traveler Services Information should be capable of supporting two-way interactive communications between traveler service providers and users, with a round-trip transmission time of less than fifteen seconds. It should support data collection, management, and access to current database information on traveler services within thirty seconds, and should provide traveler service information within sixty seconds of inquiry. A goal of deploying this service is to have a nationally interlinked traveler services information system that is accessible from any location in the United States and is able to provide information about any location in the United States.

Traffic Control

The Traffic Control user service manages the movement of traffic on streets and highways. Integrated and adaptive control of freeway and surface street systems will improve traffic flow and give priority to certain types of traffic. This service will minimize congestion while maximizing movement of traffic and improving pedestrian safety. The real-time traffic information required for this service will also provide the foundation for many other user services.

The Traffic Control service collects surveillance data from the transportation network, fuses the data into usable information, and adaptively applies traffic controls to reduce congestion. Many different information technologies are required to support this user service, including traffic surveillance sensors, data and voice communications, data processing and automation, control technology, and the means for human interface.

Surveillance of traffic conditions is an essential first step in this service. There are many surveillance techniques available, ranging from loop detectors and video cameras at specific locations to aerial surveillance for wider-area applications. Surveillance using position information from in-vehicle radio navigation receivers can only be done when individual vehicles are equipped with both GPS or other positioning technology and a communications link to the central surveillance facility. These vehicles will then function as probes in traffic. A combination of the most appropriate surveillance methods will most likely be used.

The diverse forms of data resulting from infrastructure surveillance will be received at the traffic control center for processing, analysis, and fusion. This procedure will be supported by incident reports, traffic models, and the use of historical patterns for traffic prediction. An appropriate area-wide traffic control strategy will be developed and controls will be implemented by communicating control data to devices such as street traffic signals, information signs, and freeway ramp meters, and by various procedural mechanisms. The Traffic Control service could be implemented for a local area by a single traffic management center, or for regional traffic control by multiple traffic-management centers linked together by a regional traffic-control communications network.

With respect to performance requirements defined to date, the Traffic Control system should support immediate two-way communications between control devices, traffic control and management centers, and surveillance equipment, with a round-trip transmission time of less than five seconds. It should be capable of supporting real-time collection and management of and access to current traffic surveillance and control parameters. The system should be able to process areawide surveillance data, incident reports, and historical time-of-day patterns, and it will need a hierarchical control system to provide accurate and reliable feedback. Real-time traffic adaptive control will require major advances in software integration and automation.

Incident Management

The Incident Management user service will help public and private organizations quickly identify incidents and implement a response to minimize effects of incidents on traffic. This service will enhance existing incident response capabilities with new ITS technologies. Incidents can include accidents, road and building construction and maintenance, activities such as parades and sporting events, impacts of adverse weather conditions, and many other situations that could affect the flow of traffic. Because incidents can be scheduled, forecast, or unplanned, a major focus of this service is improving response to unpredicted incidents. There are many potential users of this service, including transportation and public safety officials, other government organizations, and private firms involved in incident response.

Many diverse information technologies are used for incident management detection, verification, and response. This service uses advanced sensors, data processing, and communications technologies to improve the incident-management and -response capabilities of responsible organizations.

The Incident Management service will be activated by the report of an incident to a traffic management or other control center. Incidents can be detected and reported in a number of ways: from advanced sensors monitoring conditions in the infrastructure; from reports by individuals using freeway call boxes, cellular or fixed telephone 911 service, or other communications systems; or from reporting by law enforcement or other roving patrols using dedicated communications systems. Advanced computer-based decision support systems, artificial intelligence, and traffic modeling systems will be used to verify the incident at the control center and aid in developing a response. Computer-based incident detection algorithms will be used to monitor all incoming data for unusual conditions or reported incidents. Input from different surveillance technologies will be correlated, integrated, and analyzed, and algorithms will verify locations, characteristics, and impacts.

A response plan for each incident will be developed at the control center, using dynamic and static databases that can store and retrieve all incident management information. Data processing technologies can help to automate the selection of the appropriate response, and responses can be linked into dispatch systems. Resulting traffic control would be managed by the Traffic Control user service. Eventually, it may be possible to link emergency vehicle management services and other resource management systems directly to the Incident Management service.

Incident verification, response, and management might take place at a single location, such as an area-wide traffic management center. Various centers might also be connected by a communications network to share information. Extensive communications and institutional coordination will be required for effective incident management, with continuous contact among organizations needed during the incident. Coordination and information dissemination might be handled by a regional coordinating committee.

A variety of communications technologies will be used to communicate video, voice, and data from traffic flow monitoring locations to the central processing locations and to share information among organizations participating in incident response. Most of the connections between fixed points will be handled by dial-up landlines.

Conventional mobile radio systems, cellular systems, or the emerging mobile satellite services could be used where landlines are not feasible, both at the incident site and in transit to and from it.

In a fully developed Incident Management service, responses, organizations, and incident status will be tracked, coordinated, and archived by the system, with an eventual goal of full automation.

Preliminary work on performance requirements for the Incident Management service indicates that real-time, two-way communications among information sources, responding agencies, and traffic management centers is required, with a round-trip transmission time of less than one second. The system should support real-time collection, management, and access of current traffic surveillance information; incident information statistics; and the status of responding agencies, resources, response actions, and traffic networks. It should detect incidents within two minutes of initial congestion indications, with detection rates up to 90% and maximum false alarm rates of 0.1%. The system should also provide real-time incident verification capabilities for control, presentation, and verification by system operators, and should facilitate incident response formulation and execution upon system operator command. Potential response options will include notification of appropriate agencies (law enforcement, emergency medical services, etc.). The system should accept system operator inputs for incident recordkeeping and collect incident response status for subsequent evaluation. Many of the necessary decision support tools currently exist or are being developed; advanced surveillance techniques are expected to come to maturity within a few years; and automated incident management will be implemented beyond the year 2000.

Emissions Testing and Mitigation

The Emissions Testing and Mitigation user service provides information for monitoring air quality and developing air quality improvement strategies. The resulting information can be provided to the driver or fleet operator as an alert or to transportation planning and operating agencies for pollution control.

This service is based on the use of advanced vehicle emissions testing systems. These systems can be in the vehicle (as on-board diagnostic equipment) or installed at the roadside (using fixed or mobile sensing and testing equipment). Roadside-installed detectors with computer diagnostics may evaluate and identify passing vehicles instantaneously and notify drivers if there is a problem. The equipment installed in the infrastructure (roadside) could, depending on the density of the sites, detect air quality problems on a wide- (such as a metropolitan) area. A central data collection and analysis point would be needed; the information could then be provided to a regional pollution-control authority.

These systems can also provide monitoring and guidance, using the Traffic Control service, for rerouting traffic away from and controlling access to problem areas. Various communications systems can provide alerts to owners and operators of vehicles and fleets that are exceeding emissions standards. However, there may be a personal privacy issue involving identification and reporting of vehicles that are allegedly exceeding emissions standards.

Travel Demand Management

The Travel Demand Management bundle consists of three user services:

• Pre-Trip Travel Information
• Ride Matching and Reservation
• Demand Management and Operations

The services in this bundle promote the common goal of encouraging modes of travel other than the single-occupancy vehicle in order to decrease congestion and improve environmental quality. Elimination of single-occupancy vehicle trips is a major objective of this bundle. These services attempt to change travel behavior by providing alternatives, arrangements, and incentives for the traveler, and conveying this information in a convenient and timely manner. They rely on information collected and processed by the Travel and Transportation Management bundle and the Public Transportation Operations bundle (which will be discussed below).

Pre-Trip Travel Information

This service provides travelers with information prior to a trip. Travelers will be able to access a complete range of real-time intermodal transportation information at home, work, or other fixed sites where trips originate. This service should encourage alternatives to the use of single-occupancy vehicles. Users will include not only travelers but also providers who will develop and market pre-trip information services.

The Pre-Trip Travel Information service integrates information from various transport modes and presents it to the user through electronic communications or public information centers. The service provides real-time highway condition information as well as public transportation information, including routes, schedules, fares, and ride matching information. The traveler can make decisions, such as whether to take a private vehicle or use the public transportation system, based on this information.

Information on highway conditions will come from the Traffic Control and Incident Management services and should be processed by and resident in the control centers, as discussed previously. Information on transit systems will then be integrated with this information to provide the traveler with comprehensive information on all transit modes. This information could be geocoded and combined with map data. It could then be presented to the user as part of a wider information network through personal computers with modems, cable television, or videotext terminals connected to telephone lines. Personal communications devices might also be used. At public locations, more complex video systems might include elaborate interactive map presentations.

Performance requirements developed to date for Pre-Trip Travel Information indicate that the system must support two-way interactive communications between data-collection systems and data-processing systems and between data processing systems and users. The round-trip transmission time should be less than 15 seconds. The system should support collection and management of, and access to, current information on available services, traffic conditions, and trip planning within 30 seconds, and should provide travel information within 60 seconds of inquiry.

Ride Matching and Reservation

Ride Matching and Reservation provides specialized ride matching information for the user at home, work, or other locations, and assists transportation providers with vehicle assignments and scheduling. This service is intended to encourage ride-sharing options (such as carpools and vanpools) and can provide transportation services for those with special needs. The goal of this service is to match user preferences and demands with providers as quickly as possible, and to coordinate all travel modes and special services.

A wide variety of information technologies will be brought into play to make Ride Matching and Reservation a reality. Low-cost, high-performance computer hardware, generic relational databases with dynamic multimodal information, moderately priced scheduling and dispatching software, smart cards and inexpensive card readers, and off-the-shelf vehicle location and navigation technology will all be used. User-interactive technologies will include touch-tone and cellular phones, voice synthesis techniques, interactive video displays, personal communications systems, and roadside or transit center monitors.

The intent of this service is to provide information to the traveler through a single point of contact. The traveler would initiate the request via telephone, for example, by providing an itinerary and any other pertinent information. He or she would then receive ride-sharing options from the services database of transportation providers and traffic information. This central service will also provide electronic billing for ride-sharing services. This means that there must be electronic safeguards against fraud and abuse of the system, as well as automatic generation of necessary reports and financial documentation.

Information from Ride Matching and Reservation will likely be provided in conjunction with the dissemination of other transportation information, such as Pre-Trip Travel Information. However, this service will rely on an information infrastructure developed primarily for non-transportation applications. Existing computer network services could be supplemented with ride-matching information; public service channels on cable TV could provide information; and ride-sharing information could be included as part of a privately provided information service. For example, a large company with many employees might institute its own ride-sharing service.

Performance requirements for Ride Matching and Reservation include two-way communications between traffic information sources, ride matching and reservation services, billing services, and ride-sharing personnel. Round-trip transmission time should be less than 15 seconds. The system should support collection, management, and access to current information on riders, transportation providers, and billing within 30 seconds, and ride matching and reservation services should be provided within 60 seconds of inquiry.

Demand Management and Operations

The Demand Management and Operations service—which is actually more of a management strategy—supports policies and regulations designed to promote operational, environmental, and social efficiencies in the transportation system. Strategic use of advanced technologies will result in improved transportation alternatives, provision of economic incentives and disincentives, and allowance for flexible, alternative work arrangements. Use of services in the Travel Demand Management bundle, as well as many other ITS services, will support effective application of the Demand Management and Operations user service.

This service will function as an areawide traffic management system using interactive computer operations and communications centers to implement travel demand management and control strategies. Information will be received from transportation operators (state, local, and private) and users on the current status, needs, and levels of activity. Operational information and commands will be disseminated to operators and users on how to control or manage activity to conform to travel demand management programs, policies, or regulations.

Demand Management and Operations will be based upon management plans that support current government policies (e.g., reduction of single-occupancy vehicle use, improvement of environmental quality). Strategies could include facilitation of high occupancy vehicles; lane, ramp, or parking area management and control; highway tolls based on periods of congestion; support for changing transportation modes; telecommuting and alternative work schedules; and public awareness programs. The above strategies will be implemented by making use of many of the other ITS services.

Performance requirements defined to date for Demand Management and Operations indicate that the system must support real-time, two-way communications between transportation operators, traffic management centers, traffic surveillance equipment, parking areas, travelers, and virtually all other players in this service. Round-trip transmission time should be less than five seconds. The system should support the collection, management, and access of current database information on travel services, traffic conditions, roadway and weather status, and trip planning within 30 seconds. The system should present the latest travel demand computation and management activity.

Public Transportation Operations

The Public Transportation Operations bundle includes four user services:

- Public Transportation Management
- En-Route Transit Information
- Personalized Public Transit
- Public Travel Security

Every service in this bundle will share a common public transit database; each user service will customize that data as appropriate for its function. A common architecture with standardized interfaces and databases that allow for frequent, high-speed user access is essential for the services in this bundle. The public transit data will also support services in the Travel and Transportation Management and the Travel Demand Management bundles. Public Transit Operations should be adaptable to urban, suburban, and rural environments. They will be provided by public transit authorities.

Public Transportation Management

The Public Transportation Management user service applies advanced vehicle electronic systems to various public transportation modes and uses the data generated by these modes to improve public transportation service. The public transportation provider is the user of this service. Some of the information it generates can be used by the Pre-Trip Travel Information, En Route Transit Information, Personalized Public Transit, and Public Travel Security user services. This service includes three subservices: operation of vehicles and facilities, planning and scheduling, and personnel management.

Public Transportation Management involves integration of multiple databases (some of which have been developed over the years by transit agencies), with subsystems for vehicle location, communications, in-vehicle data gathering, and data processing. For operation of vehicles and facilities, real-time information from both is communicated over a digital data link and is compared with schedule information and other predetermined parameters. A computer with appropriate software in the transit facility identifies deviations, displays them to the dispatcher or controller, and determines the optimum scenario for returning to the schedule. Corrective instructions are transmitted to the transit driver using voice or data communications.

Operation of vehicles and facilities might also be used in coordinating connections and transfers. Information transmitted from the transit vehicle could include vehicle location, passenger loading, mileage, and running time. This could be gathered using such technologies as advanced passenger counters, smart cards, and in-vehicle navigation equipment. It may be necessary to transfer data among various devices in the vehicle. Systems in the vehicle may be polled, or information may be automatically sent on a timed basis to a central repository (central or regional control facility) for real-time operations or storage for off-line analysis.

The *planning and scheduling* subservice will use the above data for off-line analysis. This information will be used for activities such as schedule adjustment, maintenance planning, and status reporting. The *personnel management* subservice will assign and schedule transit personnel (e.g., drivers and maintenance and service workers). This subservice has the potential to improve automation, with features such as automated timekeeping and updates of inventory and maintenance databases.

As in any large fleet-management operation that uses two-way communications, implementation of Public Transportation Management involves many technical issues. Communications protocols for large vehicle fleets are needed so that messages do not conflict. Radio frequency spectrum needs to be conserved, so the length of messages must be minimized. Common data formats are needed. Industry-accepted standards for reliability, performance, and system compatibility should be used.

Performance requirements defined to date for Public Transportation Management include real-time communications among appropriately equipped public transportation vehicles, public transportation facilities, and emergency assistance facilities, with a round trip transmission time of less than five seconds. The system should provide vehicle identification with accuracy of 99.9% within one minute of initiation, and vehicle location with position accuracy in the range of twenty to 300 feet. It also should provide public transportation drivers and dispatchers with current optimum routing information in response to schedule delays; this will include planned route connection coordination. Public Transportation Management should include an integrated traffic-control capability that provides traffic signal preemption (when required for schedule adjustment) for transit vehicles at traffic signals. Current data collection for planning and scheduling of public transit operations and driver and maintenance personnel management should be supported.

En-Route Transit Information

The En-Route Transit Information user service provides transportation information to transit users after their trips have begun, which enables user decision-making while the trip is underway. This service is related to En-Route Driver Information, but focuses on public transportation. In the future, this service and others could be combined to form an integrated service information bureau.

Much of the information used in this service will come from the common public transit database developed for the Public Transportation Operations bundle, particularly for the Public Transportation Management service. Data will be collected from transit systems, traffic management systems, and rideshare programs, and integrated, maintained, and stored on-line for interactive access from a wide variety of locations. This interactive service could be provided through kiosks at travel information centers and other transfer points, enabling passengers to view their public transportation options for completing a trip. Interactive displays could also be on-board buses for passenger queries en route to a destination. In the future, passengers could use personal communications devices to access this information. Financial transactions for transit services would be supported.

En-Route Transit Information will eventually require an on-line, interactive system similar to ATMs. Arrangements might be made with local ATM providers to tie into their communications networks. This would help to provide an integrated financial-transportation service.

Performance requirements developed for En Route Transit Information to date indicate that this service should support real-time communications between transit advisory sources and appropriately equipped vehicles, with a round-trip transmission time of less than five seconds. The system should provide for collection, management, and access to current transportation and trip planning information within 30 seconds, and should provide transit advisories within 60 seconds of inquiry.

Personalized Public Transit

Personalized Public Transit will provide users with access to more convenient ride-sharing services (such as vanpools and carpools) that are more sensitive to their transit requirements. This service can be randomly routed (such as dial-a-ride) or flexibly routed from a somewhat fixed network of operation. It can be publicly or privately operated.

Personalized Public Transit requires that close track be kept of vehicles, passengers, and the amount of time vehicles spend in transit. Sensors on board the transit vehicle will monitor vehicle location, passenger loading, fare collection, and other activities. This system requires that vehicles be located with respect to the existing road network. Data must be transferred between geographically dispersed points (vehicles and potential riders) and a central base. The data may be processed on board the vehicle before being transmitted to a computer at the central base; this computer, with the aid of a geographic information system (GIS), will then automatically determine vehicle assignments and routing.

The central data facility will also process subscriber services and real-time billing for them. Advanced fare payment systems eventually will be a part of this service as it transitions from cash-based transactions to electronic smart cards. For random route service, a reservation system will be used; instantaneous service will be provided only if it can be accommodated. A goal of Personalized Public Transit is to allow reservations and vehicle and scheduling assignments to be made in real time.

For full implementation of Personalized Public Transit, real-time communications between appropriately equipped transportation vehicles, facilities, and passengers are required, with a round trip transmission time of less than five seconds. Vehicle identification should be provided with an accuracy of 99.9% within one minute of initiation, and vehicle location should be provided with position accuracy in the range of 20 to 300 feet. The system should provide transportation drivers and dispatchers with current routing information in response to passenger reservations and offer passengers near-real-time reservation confirmation and imminent arrival notification. It should also offer continuous 24-hour access to service. Ideally, Personalized Public Transit should provide vehicle assignment to pick up passengers within a four-block radius of all trip origination sites in the area.

Public Travel Security

The Public Travel Security service creates a secure environment for public transportation patrons and operators. The environment in transit stations, public parking lots, bus stops, and possibly transit vehicles is monitored; security incidents are detected, identified, and processed; and alarms and notification are given if appropriate. Actions taken in response to notification are not part of this service.

This service relies on the use of advanced sensors to monitor the designated environment and transmit the information and alarms to central dispatch or police stations. Many technologies could be applied: closed-circuit television, image processing, and microphones for surveillance; and radio, telephone, cellular service, or personal communications devices for communication of the alarm. Vehicles could also be monitored by central dispatch if requested by the driver.

Preliminary work on performance requirements indicates that real-time communications are required from equipped facilities and vehicles to central dispatch or the local police, with a round-trip transmission time of less than one second. The system should provide continuous surveillance. It should also provide real-time traveler-activated alarms to encompass all physical areas related to public travel, as well as silent driver-activated alarms on board public transit vehicles. The system should provide passenger identification, location, and incident status information within five minutes of message receipt.

Electronic Payment

The Electronic Payment bundle has one user service, Electronic Payment Services. This service will support other ITS services, and is similar to other electronic payment services outside the transportation domain.

Electronic Payment Services

Electronic Payment Services will allow travelers to pay for transportation services directly, and will eventually provide a common electronic payment medium for all modes and functions of transportation, including fares, tolls, and parking. This service could eventually be expanded to accommodate many personal financial transactions that are currently made with bank or credit cards.

Electronic Payment Services includes electronic toll collection, fare collection, and parking payment. These three technologies are being developed separately because they are not currently at a point where they can be integrated. A goal of this user service is integrated electronic payment for the above three functions; it also can facilitate the implementation of Travel Demand Management strategies.

Electronic funds management systems will be used in Electronic Payment Services in conjunction with various types of smart cards with embedded computer chips. However, a general-purpose card could be created that does not need to be transportation-specific. Use of electronic funds management systems will require coordination of the electronic financial systems of all participating agencies and firms, which implies national compatibility. Much of the technology necessary for this system is already in place. Remote sensing and identification (for example, using radio frequency interrogation of an electronic tag) of a specific transit vehicle will be required for billing.

Performance requirements developed to date indicate that Electronic Payment Services should support real-time communications between appropriately equipped vehicles, electronic payment services, and electronic payment facilities. Round-trip transmission time for toll collection should be a small fraction of a second; round-trip transmission time for other transactions should be less than five seconds. The system should support collection and management of, and access to, current information on driver and rider eligibility within 30 seconds. It should support off-line storage of the driver and ridership levels on specific routes for transit operator scheduling and route planning. The system should verify electronic payment authorization with greater than 99.99% accuracy, and present confirmation of transactions within ten seconds.

Commercial Vehicle Operations

The Commercial Vehicle Operations bundle includes six user services:

- Commercial Vehicle Electronic Clearance
- Automated Roadside Safety Inspection
- On-Board Safety Monitoring
- Commercial Vehicle Administrative Processes

- Hazardous Material Incident Response
- Freight Mobility

A common goal of this bundle is to improve commercial fleet productivity and highway safety through the application of advanced technology.

Commercial Vehicle Electronic Clearance

This user service will allow transponder-equipped commercial carriers to have their safety status, credentials, and weight checked at mainline speeds without having to stop when entering each state. Nationwide availability is critical for the successful deployment of this service, which could eventually be used for international border clearance.

Information used for clearance may reside in the vehicle or may come from centralized or distributed databases located at agency facilities or carrier headquarters. This service will require technologies to support the electronic exchange of information, including vehicle identification, safety, credentials, and weight. Vehicle-to-roadside communications will be used to transmit the information to the infrastructure checkpoint facility.

An on-site computer at the infrastructure facility may be part of a LAN supporting several workstations; the computer may also be linked to remote information systems to access the necessary historical information on carriers and vehicles. Information under the jurisdiction of national, regional, and state agencies may be involved. International border crossing applications will require the use of additional non-DOT federal databases and information systems. Linking these systems with the checkpoints will require a standard protocol for data linkage and will most likely exploit the latest in open system networking.

Performance requirements for Commercial Vehicle Electronic Clearance include two-way real-time communication between appropriately equipped commercial vehicles and the infrastructure facility, with a round-trip transmission time of less than five seconds. The system should support interstate and intrastate commercial vehicles traveling at speeds up to 100 mph. It should provide carrier vehicle identification with 99.99% accuracy and vehicle weighing of 95% accuracy, up to one mile before the roadside inspection facility. The system should support collection, management, access, and coordination of current information at roadside inspection facilities within 30 seconds.

Automated Roadside Safety Inspection

Automated Roadside Safety Inspection will facilitate roadside safety inspections with the use of increasingly automated diagnostic equipment. It will eventually be integrated with the On-Board Safety Monitoring service.

While the focus of Automated Roadside Safety Inspection is on devices and techniques to automate the inspection process at the roadside facility, access will be needed to the historical safety performance records of carriers, vehicles, and drivers to determine which vehicles or drivers should be stopped for inspection and to ensure that problems have been corrected. Thus, the system must have access to the appropriate state and federal information systems. Using historical information from a database—or in the future, information derived from on-board sensing devices—a vehicle will be selected for inspection at a fixed or mobile inspection site.

A goal of this service is automation of the inspection and diagnostic process, and reduction of manual techniques. The first phase in achieving this goal is likely to be automated brake inspection. Performance requirements for this service are the same as those described above for Commercial Vehicle Electronic Clearance, with the addition of performance requirements for the timeliness of output of automated inspection and diagnostic equipment.

On-Board Safety Monitoring

On-Board Safety Monitoring senses the safety status of a commercial vehicle, cargo, or driver, and reports warnings of unsafe conditions to the driver and, if appropriate, to the carrier company and roadside inspection officials. The intent of this service is to minimize accidents for participating carriers. This service will be most effective when integrated with Commercial Vehicle Electronic Clearance and Automated Roadside Safety Inspection, as all three are safety-related.

The focus of On-Board Safety Monitoring is the development of in-vehicle sensing and monitoring technology, but warning of an unsafe condition may require access to historical safety information in state or federal systems. On-board systems and sensors developed for this service would sense and collect data on the condition of critical vehicle components. This equipment will determine thresholds for warnings and countermeasures, sense cargo shifts or other unsafe cargo conditions, monitor driving time and time-on-task, monitor driver alertness using non-intrusive technology, and provide warnings to the driver, carrier company, or enforcement officials if appropriate. Most of this technology is not yet mature.

Eventually, safety data will be compiled on board the vehicle, integrated with Electronic Clearance service information, transformed into a comprehensive output, and transmitted to the roadside facility for computer processing via the same vehicle-to-roadside communications used for the Electronic Clearance user service. Identification of the vehicle and driver is critical for this service, as it is for the preceding two services.

Preliminary performance requirements for On-Board Safety Monitoring indicate that two-way real-time communications are necessary between appropriately equipped vehicles and infrastructure, with a round-trip transmission time of less than five seconds. Vehicle speeds of up to 100 m.p.h. should be supported. The system should support real-time on-board sensor monitoring and warning control, monitoring of vehicle components and driver conditions from on board the vehicle, and providing data storage every few minutes. The system should provide safety problem information or potential warnings to the driver in near-real-time, to fleet managers on an exception basis or at one-minute intervals, and to the inspection facility within five seconds of query receipt. Driver and vehicle identification should be provided to the inspection facility with 99.9% accuracy within five seconds of on-board sensor query. The system should support collection, management, and access of current information at roadside inspection facilities within 30 seconds.

Commercial Vehicle Administrative Processes

This user service will provide commercial carriers with the ability to purchase credentials electronically, and with automated mileage and fuel reporting and auditing. This automation helps the commercial carrier by reducing burdensome paperwork.

With Commercial Vehicle Administrative Processes, commercial carriers will be able to electronically select and purchase annual credentials via computer link to the base state, and temporary credentials via computer link to individual states. Payment for these credentials could be handled through electronic funds transfer. In addition, participating carriers can electronically capture mileage, fuel purchase, trip, and vehicle data by state. Mileage and fuel purchase within each state would be automatically calculated.

The electronic funds transfer function would require electronic forms for licenses and permits, and software for electronically transferring funds from the carrier account to the appropriate base state. Communications software would be required to send information from carriers to the states and information and credentials from the states back to the carriers. Security must be built into this service. If communications were to be provided directly to the vehicle, a read-write transponder, smart card, or some other technology that would permit an authorized source to put the data on the vehicle would be necessary. Information capture would require electronic collection, calculation, and reporting of mileage and fuel data by state. Mileage information at state borders could use satellite (GPS) positioning technology; mileage data could also be captured by a network of beacon sites at state border crossings. Data received by states would be used in the Commercial Vehicle Electronic Clearance service.

Hazardous Material Incident Response

Hazardous Material Incident Response will locate vehicles carrying hazardous material cargoes when they are involved in incidents, and will electronically provide, at the site, accurate identification of and information on the hazardous material cargo to law enforcement officials and other emergency responders. (It is not cost-effective to track all hazardous cargo from origin to destination.) This will aid in developing the appropriate response for handling the material. A universal, integrated, low-cost system is desired.

Hazardous material cargo identification, description, and information at the incident site could be provided by vehicle-based systems such as the transponders used for Electronic Clearance, or electronic tags, which would require readers of some kind at the scene. For example, a recently initiated test will use police radar guns to read tags on barrels of hazardous materials. Alternatively, identifying information could exist in infrastructure-based systems such as carrier databases, state systems, or other Commercial Vehicle Operation user service systems. This would require that emergency responders at the incident site be able to remotely access these databases.

Freight Mobility

Freight Mobility provides commercial fleet operators with both real-time information on the location of their fleet and real-time communications with the vehicles, allowing for more efficient dispatching and freight mobility operations. This service will provide commercial drivers and dispatchers with real-time routing information in response to congestion and incidents. It could also allow for intermodal freight tracking. Aspects of this service are already deployed by many carriers.

Freight Mobility uses onboard computers, vehicle location systems, and communication systems. Vehicle location and identification are transmitted to the central dispatch facility to allow for vehicle tracking and dynamic re-routing. Additional information on driver hours, cargo location, delivery times, fuel consumption, and general trip condition information may be provided to the freight or dispatch headquarters. Dispatchers could also make use of real-time traffic information from the public sector, but there is an issue of compatibility between public and carrier information. For example, most companies do not currently see a need for real-time traffic information (beyond radio broadcasting) or for a technology to facilitate intermodalism.

With respect to performance requirements, Freight Mobility should provide two-way interactive communication between commercial vehicles, commercial vehicle drivers, dispatchers, freight mobility centers, and intermodal transportation providers, with a round-trip transmission time of less than 15 seconds. This service should provide commercial drivers and dispatchers with current routing information in response to congestion or incidents. Vehicle identification should be provided with accuracy of 99.9% within five minutes after initiation, and vehicle location should be provided with position accuracy in the range of 20–300 feet.

Emergency Management

The Emergency Management bundle consists of two user services: Emergency Notification and Personal Security, and Emergency Vehicle Management.

Emergency Notification and Personal Security

This user service includes two subservices: Driver and Personal Security (user-initiated distress signals) and Automated Collision Notification (automated notification of emergency personnel of the location, nature, and severity of serious crashes).

In the *Driver and Personal Security* subservice, requests for assistance, accompanied by automatic transmission of vehicle location, can be directed to law enforcement, emergency personnel, or private towing and repair services. This service relies on appropriate communications links and vehicle location sensors. Similar services exist today that use cellular telephone service and GPS receivers. In the future, notification may be automatic, rather than user-initiated. This subservice can tie into existing public safety and emergency services.

For the *Automated Collision Notification* subservice, crashes will be automatically detected and notification messages, including the location of the crash and indication of its severity, will be automatically relayed to an emergency medical service dispatcher. Additional information may include vehicle identification and condition. This subservice requires crash-sensing and vehicle location capabilities, and at least one-way crash-survivable communications equipment. Communications for this service could take advantage of many existing and planned voice and data services, including terrestrial mobile and fixed radio systems, cellular telephone, and planned mobile satellite services that will cover the entire country. Automated Collision Notification must be capable of interfacing with incident response or EMS dispatch facilities. Services should take advantage of existing communications networks as much as possible. A desired capability of the system is to travel nationwide without having to change equipment or procedures.

Performance requirements for Emergency Notification and Personal Security include continuous real-time communications from appropriately equipped vehicles to at least one response unit from any location in the United States; this should take place with a round-trip transmission time of less than one second. Vehicle location should be provided with position accuracy in the range of 20–300 feet. Manual and automatic initiation of emergency notification should be provided within one minute. The system should monitor vehicle component conditions from inside the vehicle every few seconds and, for critical emergency condition cases, automatically send the appropriate distress signal.

An example of technologies that could be used with this service is an emergency notification operational test planned for 1995 in central Colorado under FHWA funding. Elements of this operational test include an in-vehicle GPS unit for vehicle position location; a two-way communications link between the vehicle and the control center using commercially available cellular telephone service; and control-center equipment for processing vehicle location, type of assistance required, and routing of the request to the appropriate response agency. The motorist will be notified of the action taken and the anticipated response time.

Emergency Vehicle Management (Public Safety Services)

The Emergency Vehicle Management service will provide for more efficient management and assignment of emergency response vehicles. Its intent is to reduce the amount of time between a public safety operator's notification of an incident and the arrival of emergency personnel on the scene. The service will provide public safety agencies with fleet-management capabilities, route guidance, and signal priority and preemption for emergency vehicles. This service consists of three subservices: Emergency Vehicle Fleet Management (improves the display of emergency vehicle locations to aid dispatchers in sending vehicles efficiently); Route Guidance (directs vehicles to the incident location); and Signal Priority (optimizes traffic signal timing in the emergency vehicle route). The primary users of this service are police, fire, and emergency medical units.

Real-time reliable transportation and traffic information is required by this service in order to provide travel alternatives for the arrival of the emergency vehicle at the emergency site; location of the incident and of emergency vehicles in the fleet is essential at the dispatch center. Emergency Vehicle Management will identify the closest and most appropriate response vehicle, and transfer complete, accurate information on the nature and location of the incident to it.

Emergency Vehicle Management will make use of the variety of telecommunications systems used by other ITS services. With changes in frequency spectrum and development of digital voice and new modulation schemes, there may be a need to develop a new public-safety service communications infrastructure as an integral part of ITS requirements.

Systems providing traffic signal priority for emergency vehicles are part of the traffic management infrastructure. The emergency dispatcher and the traffic signal could communicate directly; the emergency vehicle could communicate with the traffic signal to control right-of-way; or there could be direct communication between the emergency vehicle and other objects, such as private vehicles within the radius of the immediate area, in order to warn drivers that an emergency vehicle is approaching.

Performance requirements developed to date indicate that Emergency Vehicle Management should provide real-time emergency vehicle fleet management, offer vehicle identification with 99.9% accuracy within one minute of initiation, and vehicle location with position accuracy within the range of 20–50 feet. The system should also provide real-time traffic signal prioritization by maintaining current information on signal timing, emergency vehicle locations, and emergency vehicle routing.

Advanced Vehicle Control and Safety Systems

The Advanced Vehicle Control and Safety Systems bundle consists of the following seven user services:

• Longitudinal Collision Avoidance

• Lateral Collision Avoidance

• Intersection Collision Avoidance

• Vision Enhancement for Crash Avoidance

• Safety Readiness

• Pre-Crash Restraint Deployment

• Automated Highway Systems

The user services in this bundle have a common focus on increasing the safety and efficiency of vehicle operations through application of advanced technologies. With the exception of Automated Highway Systems, every service relies on self-contained systems within the vehicle, although functionality can be enhanced by supplementing on-board systems with additional sensors deployed in the infrastructure. As these systems are mostly self-contained and rely on in-vehicle sensing, warning, and control, there is little application for the NII in this bundle.

Longitudinal Collision Avoidance

This service helps prevent longitudinal (head-on or rear-end) collisions. The individual driver is the user of this service, which is completely contained within the vehicle.

Longitudinal Collision Avoidance will sense potential or impending collisions, provide instructions to the driver, and possibly take partial or complete control of the vehicle. Technologies involved are sensors, processors, and driver/vehicle interfaces. Sensor technologies include headway detection systems based on radar and video image processing, and lidar. Ultrasonic and infrared sensing might also be used. Processors will differentiate and interpret the data. The driver interface may be audible or visual, and can provide updates continuously, periodically, or only when there is a threat. Preliminary requirements indicate that this service should support vehicles traveling at speeds of up to 100 mph, provide sensing of impending collisions within a range of 1,000 feet from the front or rear of the vehicle, and warn the driver within three seconds of determining a potential incident.

Lateral Collision Avoidance

The user of Lateral Collision Avoidance is the vehicle driver. The service helps prevent collisions by providing crash warnings and controls for lane changes and vehicles leaving the roadway. This system is completely contained within the vehicle.

As in Longitudinal Collision Avoidance, this service will provide the driver with information on potential collision threats, provide warnings and instructions to the driver, and possibly take automatic control of the vehicle. This service also depends on various types of sensors (in this case, specific to sides of the vehicle and the road edge), processors, and driver/vehicle interfaces. Lateral Collision Avoidance and Longitudinal Collision Avoidance will be most useful when integrated. Preliminary requirements indicate that this latter service, like the former, should support vehicles traveling at speeds of up to 100 mph, provide sensing of vehicles within 100 feet of a driver's blind spot, and provide warning to the driver within three seconds of sensing of a potential incident.

Intersection Collision Avoidance

The user of Intersection Collision Avoidance is the driver. This service helps prevent collisions at intersections that have traffic controls by alerting the driver when collisions are imminent or when right of way is unclear or ambiguous.

The Intersection Collision Avoidance system could function autonomously inside the vehicle, or could interact with equipment in the roadway in the vicinity of intersections. Differential GPS or other technology could determine vehicle location relative to intersections. The system could track the position and state of vehicles within a defined area surrounding an intersection using communications infrastructure at the intersection. Again, radar, lidar, or video image processing could be used. Advanced processors, perhaps using artificial intelligence, would determine the collision threat and appropriate response strategies. Vehicle-to-vehicle communications could be employed for cooperative intersection collision avoidance systems.

Preliminary requirements indicate that this service should support vehicles traveling at speeds up to 60 m.p.h., provide detection of vehicles at a range of up to 400 feet, and provide warning to the driver within three seconds of sensing of a potential incident.

Vision Enhancement for Crash Avoidance

Vision Enhancement for Crash Avoidance will augment the driver's ability to see the roadway and objects in the vicinity of the roadway when visibility is low. This service will be entirely contained within the vehicle.

This service will use in-vehicle equipment for sensing potential hazards (possibly using infrared technology), processing the information, and displaying the processed information to the driver. Performance requirements for this system include real-time in-vehicle sensing for outside scene imaging, and real-time visual display of imagery. The system should also be capable of providing warnings in case of system malfunction.

Safety Readiness

The user of the Safety Readiness service is the driver. Safety Readiness provides driver warnings about driver, vehicle, and road conditions based on information obtained from in-vehicle monitoring equipment. (Warnings from outside the vehicle are provided by the In-Vehicle Signing or En-Route Driver Information services.) This service may eventually be capable of rendering the vehicle inoperable when conditions are unsafe.

Safety Readiness has three subservices: impaired driver warning and control override; vehicle condition warning; and in-vehicle infrastructure condition warning.

Safety Readiness uses sensors to gather data on the vehicle, driver, and roadway; processors to generate information on driver condition, status of vehicle components, and roadway condition; and driver interfaces for presentation of the information and warning to the driver. Vehicle-condition warning systems could be expanded to alert other nearby vehicles or to transmit a message to a nearby emergency service center through other user services such as Emergency Notification and Personal Security.

Some in-vehicle infrastructure warning systems may include one- or two-way communications to obtain warnings from infrastructure-based components outside of the vehicle. This function may possibly overlap with functions in the En-Route Driver Information service.

Pre-Crash Restraint Deployment

In this service, collisions are anticipated and passenger safety systems are activated prior to impact. This service is contained entirely in the vehicle. Users are the vehicle driver and passengers.

Pre-Crash Restraint Deployment determines mass, velocity, and direction of vehicles or objects involved in the potential crash. Response is based on number, location, and major physical characteristics of any occupants. Some of the longitudinal and lateral collision avoidance technologies can help in developing this system. Despite the efficacy of air bags, there is no currently available system that can anticipate a crash.

Automated Highway Systems (AHS)

This service provides a fully automated highway system. Automated Highway Systems will be vehicle–roadway coordinated to move suitably equipped vehicles under fully automated control along dedicated highway lanes. Implementation of this service is a long-term goal. Longitudinal Collision Avoidance, Lateral Collision Avoidance, and Safety Readiness services will all contribute to eventual implementation of AHS.

AHS is viewed as an evolutionary service; there will be a transition period in which AHS will operate next to lanes of traditional traffic. The goal is to be able to integrate passenger and commercial vehicles and transit systems to function in urban, suburban, and rural settings as part of a community's transportation system.

The range of technologies is quite broad for AHS and there are many different visions of how it will be implemented. AHS may be a cooperative system, integrating vehicle–infrastructure and vehicle–vehicle communications for various functions, including check-in. Preliminary performance requirements developed for the AHS indicate that automated AHS-access check-in should take five seconds or less; round-trip transmission for messages to and from the infrastructure to request and authorize use should take less than two seconds. Vehicle diagnostics to determine qualifications for access to AHS should have an accuracy of 99.99%. Controls of appropriately equipped vehicles on the AHS should be provided, with closing velocity accuracy within three to five mph. Monitoring should provide updates of both critical in-vehicle components and the driver every few seconds.

AHS should accommodate speeds up to 100 mph and real-time two-way communications among vehicles and between vehicles and the infrastructure. Automated check out for egress from AHS at designated points should take place within three seconds. Prior to automated check-out, driver alertness should be tested in real time, with an accuracy of 99.99%. Institutional issues may include a requirement for a special electronic drivers permit. Although AHS systems are self-contained, checking of driver and vehicle credentials at entry points may require access to information outside of the AHS domain.

Discussion

Many of the twenty-nine user services described in the above sections will interact with or use the National Information Infrastructure in some way. Some of the services, however, are obviously self-contained and are closed systems operating for a unique ITS function. A third group of ITS user services does not yet have an obvious interaction defined.

Some of the issues that would determine a service's interaction with the NII include:

• What is the geographic coverage or extent of the service? Is it intended to be nationwide, implying national standards and compatibility, or local and independent?

• Is the service heavily dependent on sensor technology or information system technology? The latter would require a greater degree of interaction with the NII.

• What is the public-/private-sector mix for providing ITS services? ITS services range from privately provided consumer services to public safety activities.

Many ITS services will be developed and implemented using public/private partnerships. For example, both sectors must cooperate in planning for the use of RF spectrum for communications. The federal governments role is primarily in research and development, national architecture definition, tests and demonstrations, and fostering the development of standards and guidelines. Where driver and public safety standards and regulations are concerned, the federal government will continue to be involved. State and local transportation agencies will play key roles in services that involve traffic and transit management and incident response; these services will often require coordination among regional and local agencies. Private sector involvement will be high for consumer-oriented services such as traveler information and self-contained in-vehicle equipment, and commercial activities such as freight mobility. Major issues in the public/private mix are how to integrate public and private information for the seamless provision of services, who is to provide this service, and how will it be priced and paid for.

The following sections put each of the twenty-nine user services in one of four categories (see Table 1): high potential for NII interface, potential for physical infrastructure sharing, unique ITS applications, and possible NII applications.

High Potential for NII Interface

The user services in this category have a relatively high potential for interactions with or use of the NII. A high degree of common data use and sharing of the physical information systems infrastructure is implied. The ITS services in this category may involve nationwide applications requiring access to information systems resident in different agencies and organizations (some of them not transportation-related). They may be obvious candidates for consumer pay-for-access over existing information networks as an addition to existing services; or they may require integration into a nationwide financial-transaction and electronic-billing service.

Table 1 ITS User Service/NII Interface

ITS User Service	
Travel and Transportation Management	
En-Route Driver Information	High potential for NII interface
Route Guidance	Possible NII application
Traveler Services Information	High potential for NII interface
Traffic Control	Potential for physical infrastructure sharing
Incident Management	Possible NII application
Emissions Testing and Mitigation	Possible NII application
Travel Demand Management	
Demand Management and Operations	Possible NII application
Pre-Trip Travel Information	High potential for NII interface
Ride Matching and Reservation	High potential for NII interface
Public Transportation Operations	
Public Transportation Management	Potential for physical infrastructure sharing
En-Route Transit Information	High potential for NII interface
Personalized Public Transit	Possible NII application
Public Travel Security	Potential for physical infrastructure sharing
Electronic Payment	
Electronic Payment Services	High potential for NII interface
Commercial Vehicle Operations	
Commercial Vehicle Electronic Clearance	High potential for NII interface
Automated Roadside Safety Inspection	Possible NII application
On-Board Safety Monitoring	Possible NII application
Commercial Vehicle Administrative Processes	Possible NII application
Hazardous Material Incident Response	Possible NII application
Freight Mobility	Potential for physical infrastructure sharing
Emergency Management	
Emergency Notification and Personal Security	Potential for physical infrastructure sharing
Emergency Vehicle Management	Potential for physical infrastructure sharing
Advanced Vehicle Control and Safety Systems	
Longitudinal Collision Avoidance	Unique ITS application
Lateral Collision Avoidance	Unique ITS application
Intersection Collision Avoidance	Unique ITS application
Vision Enhancement for Crash Avoidance	Unique ITS application
Safety Readiness	Unique ITS application
Pre-Crash Restraint Deployment	Unique ITS application
Automated Highway Systems	Possible NII application

• *En-Route Driver Information.* The driver advisory component of this service has a high potential to include non-transportation information and has potential for interstate or nationwide use by travelers.

• *Traveler Services Information.* This system could be a component of commercially provided consumer services. Most of the information in this service will be privately provided, but some could be public. This service will involve financial transactions and will have nationwide applications for travelers.

• *Pre-Trip Travel Information.* This service will provide information on all transit modes, and may have regional or nationwide applications.

• *Ride Matching and Reservation.* This system could be a privately provided service in a local area. It might operate as a bulletin board coordinated by, for example, several large employers in the area. Electronic billing will be part of this service, requiring interaction with financial transaction systems.

• *En-Route Transit Information.* This service will offer driver information on all modes of public transportation. It will provide financial transactions and may have nationwide applications.

• *Electronic Payment Services.* This service involves billing transactions for all modes of transportation, and will include billing for privately provided services such as parking. It could be integrated with financial transaction systems not related to transportation.

• *Commercial Vehicle Electronic Clearance.* This service will be used in interstate and nationwide applications and will require interaction between state and carrier information systems. International border clearance will require access to federal, non-transportation information systems and possibly to international information sources.

Potential for Physical Infrastructure Sharing

The following services focus on specific ITS applications with data unique to ITS, but potentially can share some physical components of the NII infrastructure (e.g., fiber-optic cable, privately operated mobile wireless services) at a lower level.

- *Traffic Control*
- *Public Transportation Management*
- *Public Travel Security*
- *Freight Mobility*
- *Emergency Notification and Personal Security*
- *Emergency Vehicle Management*

Unique ITS Applications

The services in this group have a low potential for interface with or use of the NII. They are largely self-contained systems focusing on a specific area of application.

- *Longitudinal Collision Avoidance*
- *Lateral Collision Avoidance*
- *Intersection Collision Avoidance*
- *Vision Enhancement for Crash Avoidance*
- *Safety Readiness*
- *Pre-Crash Restraint Deployment*

Possible NII Applications

This group includes the user services that may have some overlap with the NII, but the connections are not clearly discernible at this time.

- *Route Guidance.* This service could potentially be used nationwide.
- *Incident Management.* This service may require use of non-transportation information and may need to link many different organizations, albeit in a local area.
- *Emissions Testing and Mitigation.* Interaction with EPA or regional/ state pollution-control authorities may be necessary.
- *Demand Management and Operations.* This service is very broadly defined and appears to have interactions with many of the other services.

• *Personalized Public Transit.* This service may need to support financial transactions in a local area.

• *Automated Roadside Safety Inspection.* Access to state or possibly federal records on vehicles, drivers, or companies may be needed.

• *On-Board Safety Monitoring.* As above, access to state or possibly federal records on vehicles, drivers, or companies may be needed.

• *Commercial Vehicle Administrative Processes.* This service will require interaction with carrier and state information systems, and may involve financial transactions.

• *Hazardous Material Incident Response.* Identification of hazardous cargo in an incident may involve access to company, state, or federal information.

• *Automated Highway Systems.* Clearance procedures for access onto AHS may require interaction with other information systems to check vehicle or driver qualifications.

The twenty-nine ITS services, as they are currently developing, offer differing degrees of overlap or interface with the NII. The ultimate correlation between these systems, however, will depend on the public and private-sector roles in each service. While the NII will be developed primarily by the private sector, ITS services will be implemented by public/private partnerships. The public role in ITS is primarily concerned with ensuring availability and safety of transportation, supporting current government policies (e.g., environmental quality, resource conservation, or aid for the disadvantaged), and providing seed dollars and incentives for the private sector. The private role in ITS is concerned mainly with provision of feed services and development of marketable technology.

ITS and NII share issues about the security and privacy of information. Some ITS services will involve electronic financial transactions between individuals and service providers. Others will supply access to information on driver and vehicle records; company information on fleets, cargoes, and operational history; law-enforcement information, including criminal records; and possibly to driver medical records for safety and emergency response personnel. Both ITS and NII need to deal with the issue of how to protect this information.

ITS and NII will both be affected by the continuing integration of information technologies. Telecommunications services providers will be able to deliver many different services to the end user by voice or data transfer; these might include positioning and navigation information, public service and safety information, consumer services information, and personal communications. What were once considered separate services, such as navigation information and paging, may eventually be provided as service options in a single package. Service providers for the ITS and NII need to consider the implications of integrating public and private information in a single service.

Finally, the Department of Transportation's ongoing national ITS architecture definition project is chartered with defining the framework within which the ITS services will operate. An examination of the interplay between ITS and the NII at the *architecture level*, as the ITS architecture definition matures, may clarify areas of interface between the two.

Bibliography

Brown, A., J. Kiljan, and J. Siviter. "An Operational Test of a Vehicle Emergency Location Service in Colorado." *NAVIGATION: Journal of the Institute of Navigation*, Vol. 41, No. 4, pp. 451–462, Winter 1994-1995.

Computer Systems Policy Project. "Perspectives on the National Information Infrastructure: Ensuring Interoperability." Washington, D.C., February 1994.

Inside ITS. May 8, 1995, Vol. 5, No. 10, pp. 11–12.

Krakiwsky, E.J., and C. Harris. "Communications for AVLN Systems." *GPS World*, November 1994.

Loral Federal Systems. *IVHS Architecture Phase One Final Report, Vol. 1.* Prepared for the Federal Highway Administration, Washington, D.C., October 3, 1994.

Rockwell International Corporation. *IVHS Architecture Phase One Final Report, Vols. 1 and 2.* Prepared for the Federal Highway Administration, Washington, D.C., October 3, 1994.

U.S. Department of Transportation and ITS America. *National Program Plan for Intelligent Transportation Systems (ITS).* Final Draft, November 1994.

Metropolitan Communications Requirements

J. Bailey and G. Pruitt

This chapter explores the communications requirements of ITS from the perspective of a moderately large (3–5 million population) metropolitan area such as Baltimore or Boston. Analysis is based on the architectures advanced during the first phase of the Department of Transportation's ITS National Architecture Development Program, and examines ITS information flows from the perspective of vehicles, individuals, and fixed facilities (including their supporting sensors).

Three Viewpoints

Vehicle Views

Private vehicles (i.e., your car) will use route guidance information (which might be in many different forms, including GPS corrections); travel information such as the location of the nearest hotel or Thai restaurant; electronic payment information for tolls, parking, and the like; and traffic/situational information. This information may be presented either in the form such that the vehicle can make intelligent (autonomous) routing decisions, or as local condition information such as speed limits, hazards, or incident advisories. Vehicles are also producers of information, in the form of information requests, condition reports ("probes," in the ITS vernacular), and incident reports.

Transit vehicles (primarily buses, but also rapid transit) will use ITS information in a slightly different way. Route guidance is less of a factor than with private vehicles, as the route is fixed for most transit vehicles (individual "paratransit" vehicles such as vanpools are a potential exception). However, the passengers of the transit vehicle may wish to know "real time" (as opposed to published) schedule information. Obtaining this information may involve a two-way information exchange—the transit vehicle will receive other vehicle schedule adherence data, and send its own vehicle schedule adherence reports. In addition, the transit vehicle may report certain operating data periodically, such as vehicle condition data and/or various types of revenue-related information. Another potential information flow for a transit vehicle is requests for traffic signal priority.

Emergency vehicles (police, fire, rescue/ambulance) need priority routing information, both in order to set favorable signals along the route from its current location to the incident, and to expedite route guidance as necessary. (Anyone who remembers the brouhaha in Washington, D.C. over ambulances getting lost en route to 911 responses will appreciate the importance of that function.) Finally, these vehicles are both sources and consumers of information on the status of incidents.

Commercial fleet operators are consumers of service routing and schedule information, as well as various other aspects of fleet management. For interstate fleets, this can include credential verification and clearances.

For the most part, vehicles will communicate with service providers or (traffic, fleet, and emergency) management facilities to obtain the information described above.

User-Level Views

The primary information flows at the user level (either vehicles or pedestrians) are requests for information and the resultant response. Typical requests are pre-trip planning information, route guidance, traffic information, and advance reservation requests. Venues for these transactions might include home or office PCs, telephones, interactive cable TV, information kiosks, or perhaps personal digital assistants or messaging units.

Traffic Management Center Views

The traffic management center (TMC) is a key component of ITS. It gathers data from various sensors and produces information. Some of this information is used by the TMC to determine appropriate commands for traffic signals and variable and changeable message signs, and to coordinate incident responses.

Other TMC information is made available externally, either to traffic information service providers or directly to the public, perhaps through broadcast media. However, this process is not without controversy. An ongoing policy debate is whether or not a publicly funded TMC can "sell" traffic information exclusively to service providers, thereby isolating public information from the segment of the population that cannot purchase traffic information from service providers.

TMCs also provide coordination of traffic information with adjacent TMCs to permit more widespread benefits from their combined actions. A prime example of this is the I-95 Corridor Project, which plans to share traffic data along the path from Richmond, VA, to Maine with major "nodes" at Richmond, Washington, D.C., New York City, and Boston. Emergency and Fleet Management centers also are "customers" of the TMC information for incident coordination.

It is conceivable that TMCs might obtain information from service providers. These entities might have their own traffic data sources (such as the probe vehicles mentioned earlier), which a TMC might use to augment its resources.

Potential Roles of Information Service Providers

Information Service Providers (ISPs) are private commercial companies that most likely will provide many ITS value-added services, including traffic and traveler information. The evolving ITS National Architecture is based on the assumption that ISPs will provide many of the more advanced ITS information services, particularly those that do not directly involve traffic control. Examples of the types of services that ISPs provide include:

• Traffic updates to travelers and fleet operators

• "Yellow Pages" of information on businesses, restaurants, hotels, and other travel-related services

• Incident detection and mayday services to intercept distress signals and direct emergency service or roadside assistance

• Interfaces to roadside assistance services

• Route guidance data, particularly for more sophisticated dynamic route guidance or link impedance functions

• Distribution of electronic map and traveler information data to support in-vehicle navigation systems, traveler information kiosks, and traveler information services provided on computer networks and cable and broadcast TV systems

• In-vehicle signing of traffic and commercial information

• Ride matching services

• Public transit information such as schedules, adherence to schedule, access information, and other static and dynamic data on transit services

• Electronic payment services, such as toll collection, fare usage information, and distribution of revenues to the appropriate agencies

• Commercial Vehicle Operations (CVO) services such as electronic clearance, vehicle tracking, distribution of data from weigh-in-motion systems, and calculation of road use taxes

• Private transportation operations, including toll collection, private highways, and custom transportation services such as handicap pickup.

Information service providers will use a variety of wireless and wireline NII communications services and systems to provide these ITS-related services. The communications services used will include computer networks, and cable, telco, and commercial wireless services. They may also require interface to public communications systems to gain access to traffic sensors such as traffic surveillance systems and cameras. Further, they may be able to use information directly from next-generation traffic control systems that use standard messages and protocols.[1] Alternatively,

ISPs may deploy their own traffic surveillance, probe, and camera systems. Many of these information services could also be provided by public agencies; however, the mix of public and private provision of these services may vary from region to region.

Estimates of ITS Information/Data Volumes

Table 1 presents an estimate of the daily traffic (in kilobits, not vehicles) for the ITS service bundles and services that appear in the National Program Plan. In addition, the table determines the potential provider of each service as Government or ISP, based upon the assessment of whether the service will be offered commercially or by the public sector (in some instances, services could be provided by both). There are some caveats that need to be made when looking at the table.

These figures represent the communications load levels based on the results of Phase 1 of the National Architecture Development contracts. Phase 2 (which is a merging and further refinement of the two Phase 1 selected architectures) is well underway, and there will be changes to these estimates, although the changes probably will not be as large as an order of magnitude. Note that Advanced Vehicle Control Systems are not included; Phase 1 teams did not address that service in any detail, and its deployment is far off. Also, several other services have no loading associated with them, because no messages could be identified as contributing to that service.

The numbers in Table 1 were derived by assuming typical driving patterns in a moderately large urban market (3–5 million population) and market penetration of roughly 20 percent[2] (a fairly high level for early deployment). There is a rather large "wild card" not included in the loading: Neither existing nor possible future video surveillance services are included, since the loading due to video surveillance varies so widely with implementation and operating philosophy. Video data loading will be discussed in greater detail later in this chapter. The table presents the data volume for a full traffic cycle (one day). While there is a maximum data rate implicit in these numbers, the National Architecture does not specify time budgets for the ITS applications. Without these requirements, it is

Table 1 Estimated Daily Traffic (in Kilobits) for ITS Service Bundles and Services in the National Program Plan (Urban region, Population 3–5 Million)

Services	Daily Load (Kb)	Possible Provider Govt.	ISP
Travel and Transportation Management			
En-Route Driver Information	5,470,000		X
Route Guidance	25,800,000		X
Traveler Services Information	25,800,000		X
Traffic Control	127,000	X	
Incident Management	55,300	X	
Emissions Testing and Mitigation	N/A	X	
Travel Demand Management			
Demand Management and Operations	N/A	X	
Pre-Trip Travel Information	35,400,000		X
Ride Matching and Reservation	N/A		X
Public Transportation Operations			
Public Transportation Management	841,000	X	
En-Route Transit Information	1,630,000	X	
Personalized Public Transit	1,630,000	X	
Public Travel Security	27	X	
Electronic Payment			
Electronic Payment Services	9,810,000	X	X
Commercial Vehicle Operations			
Commercial Vehicle Electronic Clearance	1,440,000		X
Automated Roadside Safety Inspection	2,570	X	
On-Board Safety Monitoring	98,900,000		X
Commercial Vehicle Administrative Processes	98,900,000		X
Hazardous Materials Incident Response	98,900,000	X	
Freight Mobility	5,130,000		X
Emergency Management			
Emergency Notification and Personal Security	1440		X
Emergency Vehicle Management	442,000	X	X

impossible to infer the required bandwidth. Time budgets could reasonably range from a fraction of a second, to several seconds. With this range, resulting data rates could vary up to an order of magnitude. As the National Architecture becomes further refined, and the experiences of early adopters are revealed, performance requirements for ITS will become better understood.

Underlying the data in Table 1, are two types of applications. Those in which the information requirements are universal, and those in which the data requirements are individualized. For applications such as route guidance, loading is a function of individual requests, and the load can be expected to increase linearly as market penetration increases. For generalized applications such as broadcast traffic information, the load will not vary with increased utilization. As a result, aggregate demand should be expected to increase at less than a linear rate, as utilization increases or with deployment in larger markets.

Figure 1 depicts the three generic nodes in an ITS communication infrastructure: Vehicles, Fixed Infrastructure, and Roadside Systems. The volume of communication flowing between them during a typical 24-hour period is shown next to the lines connecting the nodes. This figure represents a different "cut" of the data presented in Table 1; rather than examining the data transferred from the standpoint of the ITS service being provided, Figure 1 shows how much data is exchanged between the generic nodes for all the services. The numbers assume a typical Phase 1 Architecture deployed in a region of approximately 1,500 square miles with approximately two million vehicles.

Some Observations on Communications Loading

The relatively low fixed-infrastructure-to-roadside and roadside-to-fixed-infrastructure loadings shown above are a reflection of the fact that video surveillance is not included in the estimates. The impact of video surveillance is explored more fully below.

The numbers shown in both Table 1 and Figure 1 seem rather large, but when the vehicle loads are examined on a per-vehicle basis, they become manageable. With approximately two million vehicles in the scenario, the load represents 5–10 kilobits per

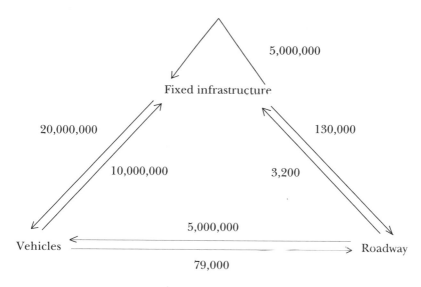

Figure 1   Generic ITS Communications Nodes and Link Loading (estimated daily information flow in kilobits).

vehicle. Most vehicles were assumed to be taking two trips per day, so on a per trip basis, the average load is in the area of 2.5–5 kilobits. Even if this information were required within a one-second window, the data rate is well within the capabilities of current mobile technology, such as Cellular Digital Packet Data, RAM Mobile Data, or enhanced ARDIS data networks. This implies that the ITS data requirements explored here are within the bounds of today's technology.

Many assumptions and parameters go into these loading analyses. By far, the largest impact on total vehicle loading (which is important from an infrastructure perspective) is market penetration. There is some debate about how great that market penetration will be and how it will affect the deployment economics and benefits of ITS. Suffice it to say that higher penetration places greater demands on the communications infrastructure, but also produces (potentially) greater benefits and presumably greater economic incentives for deployment.

Perhaps the most interesting variable is the effect that video surveillance can have on roadside-to-fixed-infrastructure loading and thus on the technologies appropriate for this segment of the communications infrastructure. A video camera generally creates a large amount of data. If the camera has a resolution similar to the video graphics adapter employed in many entry-level PC displays and uses a 16-level gray scale (not color), a frame of video generates on the order of 1.2 megabits. At 15 frames per second, 18 megabits of data per second are generated.

If this level of resolution is needed for a 24-hour continuous surveillance situation, the load is 381 megabits/day for a single camera, almost four orders of magnitude greater than the current estimates for roadside–fixed infrastructure. This is why many municipalities look to high-capacity services such as fiber-optic cable for surveillance applications.

Several things can be done to alleviate this huge service demand. For example, many surveillance applications do not need high resolution or "full motion." By sending a smaller number of frames per second, the loading can be significantly reduced. Loading is also reduced (on a total-volume but not an instantaneous basis) by viewing areas as needed, rather than continuously. Even more dramatic reductions in loading can be achieved by placing intelligence at the camera, and transmitting only the needed information, rather than the "raw" data, to a central facility. This may not be cost-effective in all situations, as intelligence at the camera can be very expensive. Finally, video compression technology can significantly reduce the volume of data from a camera; 10:1–20:1 compression is not unusual.

ITS Communications Issues

In addition to bandwidth, ITS applications will require the following features:

Data Integrity

Some ITS functions may be safety-critical; therefore, guaranteed data integrity will be essential. NII services will need to ensure that options for high data integrity are available, including protection from intrusion, spoofing, jamming, or other forms of corruption. This requirement is not unique to ITS; financial services is another market area with similar integrity concerns.

Coverage

Communications coverage for all rural as well as urban and suburban areas is required for ITS services. It is anticipated that rural areas will not be heavily covered by terrestrial-based services such as CDPD (Cellular Digital Packet Data), but instead will be covered by a number of satellite operations.

Service Reliability

Many ITS services require a high level of service reliability—24 hours a day, seven days a week. This implies responsive maintenance as well as system design features to achieve the required high level of reliability and availability. This factor has caused many transportation agencies to implement their own communications networks, where the service levels and reliability are under their control. NII services must have proven reliability to replace transportation-agency-owned services for safety and public security functions of ITS.

Market Penetration vs. Service Adequacy

Market penetration plays an important role in the decisions of private carriers to expand and enhance services. ITS implementation may be a "chicken and egg" problem and may go through incremental acceptance and deployment based on the availability of communications and information services to support individual ITS applications in specific geographic areas. As described earlier, market penetration will not affect communications requirements for those ITS applications that utilize broadcast technology to distribute non-individualized information.

Interestingly, the economic benefit of ITS is not necessarily a linear function of utilization. In those areas at the threshold of traffic saturation, modest changes in driver behavior (stimulated for example through the use of route guidance systems) can result in significant reductions in delay. With many applications, however, benefits will accrue as a linear function of adoption. In the case of traveler services information, such as the location of gas stations and hotels, impact on the network and benefit to users will both accrue linearly with increased utilization.

Latency of Data Processing and Delivery

Viability and acceptance of some ITS services will be affected by the latency of data processing and communications systems. These latency factors will be determined not only by the bandwidth of NII communications links, but also by overhead requirements for communications protocols, addressing, data coding, data integrity, security, and other delivery requirements, and by delays introduced by information processing in the ITS subsystems, or nodes.

Privacy

There are many potential privacy concerns in the deployment of ITS user services. Some individuals are concerned about the system's "Big Brother" attributes such as the potential to track the location of vehicles, determine planned travel destinations or routes, or track progress along a route. Information service providers may be concerned about theft of service, such as someone other than a service subscriber receiving travel or "Yellow Pages" information. Transportation operating agencies may be concerned about interference with the operation of ITS subsystems by hacker intrusion, jamming, or spoofing.

Spectrum Availability and Cost

Many ITS user services require wireless links to vehicles and individuals. However, spectrum availability for this technology is low, even for commercial services such as cellular, new satellite services, and personal communications systems (PCS). Much of the new spectrum being made available is subject to auction, resulting in high costs that could increase the price of wireless service, at least initially. For evidence of the cost of spectrum, one need only consider that the auctions of the first two blocks of frequencies for wideband PCS grossed a total of over $7 billion. Subsequent auctions have been delayed for various reasons and will not likely elicit the same response, because many licenses will be limited to smaller market areas.[3] ITS services will ultimately add to the market demand for NII wireless services, and must be considered in the evaluation of spectrum needs and utilization planning.

Addressing

ITS subsystems will require unique addresses, such as IP addresses or the equivalent. This is a potentially vexing issue given the multitude of vehicles and wireless applications that will need such addresses, and will require careful planning of addressing mechanisms. NII deployment planning must consider addressing requirements for mobile systems, particularly in roaming situations and in applications where national interoperability is required. For some applications such as toll collection, the addressing mechanism may be required to match up vehicle IDs with bank accounts, physical addresses, or other identification means to accommodate billing. This may in turn raise some privacy concerns.

General Mobile Communications Requirements

Mobile communications have a number of attributes that are considered in the design of NII wireless services. These include multi-path, fading, random channel error conditions, susceptibility to varying environmental conditions, signal path blockage, coverage and propagation patterns. Mobile communications are more expensive to provide than fixed communications, and this is reflected in the cost of service.

Fiber Optics Networks and ITS

Recently, there has been a great deal of attention focused on issues related to public agency implementation of fiber optics networks, particularly transportation agencies that have rights of way to facilitate fiber installation. Highways, subway tunnels, sewer and utility systems, light- and heavy-rail rights of way, and other public facilities provide the necessary locations to install fiber systems. In some cases, public agencies have installed fiber systems to achieve lower costs than by using commercial communications services. In other cases, control of costs and service factors such as reliability was a driving force. In still other cases, service was required where appropriate commercial service was not available, so that installation of new fiber was the only option.

Most of these justifications for public deployment of fiber systems are disputed by commercial communications service providers. The debate has reached the attention of Congress, sparked partially by the installation of fiber systems by public agencies using federal funds.

There are a number of issues related to the deployment of fiber networks on public rights of way and their use in ITS systems. Where the fiber is being installed primarily for use in ITS systems, one might ask whether fiber bandwidth is required to support ITS functions. The loading estimates discussed earlier do not seem to support the need for dedicated fiber-optic paths for ITS, unless extensive video surveillance installations are included. Even video applications may not need fiber bandwidth, depending on their resolution and update rate requirements. In some cases, ITS applications may be combined with a wider range of public agency requirements, and the need must be viewed on a broader basis and a total cost/benefit evaluation. Public agencies need to look at the total life-cycle costs of owning their own fiber networks, as well as the maintenance and support requirements of the network equipment and software. These considerations must be balanced against the desire to control costs relative to general market forces that affect commercial companies' pricing.

Conclusions

ITS deployment will require a wide range of communications and information services that provide new business opportunities for travel-related data. ITS subsystems will use both raw sensor data and processed information that may incorporate combinations of public and private processing systems. The NII is evolving at just the right time to facilitate this market. Options exist for both public and private communications infrastructure ownership and operation; debate on the viability of these options will center primarily on institutional decisions.

The data-loading requirements presented in this paper indicate that the necessary bandwidth and data rates to service ITS mobile functions are, in general, well within the capabilities of the currently available data services that will form the backbone of the mobile portion of the NII. With the exception of video monitoring of traffic, the same is true for the fixed infrastructure needed to support ITS. When video requirements are included, however, similar conclusions cannot be drawn without making assumptions about the operating concept used for video monitoring of highways. In some cases, ITS will require extremely large amounts of bandwidth to support video monitoring. While the technology exists to support this bandwidth, in many instances new communications infrastructure will be required, offering opportunities for new public/private partnerships, such as those described by Horan and Jakubiak in their chapter, "The Key Role for Shared Resources in Highway Rights of Way."

In many ways, ITS mirrors the NII in required communications functionality. ITS requirements (particularly for mobile access) need to be considered in NII backbone design and deployment plans. ITS data loading is not so large as to dominate or drive development of the NII. Nonetheless, there are some performance requirements such as latency and privacy that may be especially important to ITS, and it is crucial that the ITS and NII development and deployment communities continue to work together so that all requirements can be met.

Notes

1. One mechanism is the NTCIP, or National Transportation Communications for ITS Protocol. This protocol has been developed by the National Equipment Manufacturers Association with assistance from an FHA-sponsored steering committee of state and local government traffic officials, consultants, and equipment manufacturers.

2. Analysis assumes a 20 percent market penetraion rate for private users, and 100 percent for commercial users. Commercial users represent less than 10 percent of traffic during rush hour.

3. As of April 1996 the "Block C" auctions have netted bids totaling $9.7 billion. Readers interested in the FCC auctions should check the following web site: http://www.fcc.gov/wtb/aucres.html.

Why Build a Dedicated ITS Communications System?: A Private-Sector Perspective

Robert S. Arden and Padmanabhan Srinagesh

Introduction

State and local government transportation agencies are in the early stages of deploying core infrastructure elements for Intelligent Transportation Systems (ITS). These core elements are essential for providing ITS user services, including traffic control, incident management, public transportation management, public travel safety, and electronic payment services. A critical aspect of these deployments relates to the provision of wireline communications.

The fundamental question addressed in this chapter is the following: Should the public sector deploy its own dedicated wireline communications network for these core ITS infrastructure user services, rather than utilize the communications infrastructure that exists today and is being planned for the National Information Infrastructure (NII)? Our economic analysis of the benefits and costs of these options concludes that the latter option is decisively better. The ITS should be an application riding on the NII.

We will begin by briefly assessing the potential impact of dedicated ITS networks on the NII. We will then discuss wireline communications requirements, in particular bandwidth requirements, for the core ITS infrastructure elements. We will examine issues related to state and local governments building their own ITS wireline communications network rather than using general-purpose networks from private-sector communications companies, and discuss general theoretical and practical considerations of public- versus private-sector provision of communications services, including issues of highway rights-of-way resource sharing. We will identify several ITS procurement policy issues that might lead the public sector to choose a less than optimal approach to the provision of communications for ITS, and present conclusions drawn from our assessment of these issues.

The Relationship between ITS and the NII

The NII is viewed as a set of information applications that will help solve many problems facing the nation in the 21st century. In *The National Information Infrastructure: Agenda for Action*, the Clinton Administration describes a vision of "a seamless web of communications networks, computers, databases, and consumer electronics that will put vast amounts of information at users' fingertips." A central goal of the NII initiative is to "develop and apply high-performance computing and high-speed networking technologies for use in the fields of health care, education, libraries, manufacturing, and provision of government information" [1].

Different applications envisioned for the NII place very different requirements on the underlying communications infrastructure. The needs of educational institutions are characterized by applications that vary from narrowband to hybrid broadband/narrowband to broadband communications requirements. Other NII application areas such as health care, manufacturing, and electronic commerce will also place a wide range of requirements on the communications infrastructure. Because the NII must be designed as a flexible, multi-purpose system with a wide range of capabilities and options, it is ideally suited for the heterogeneous applications of ITS.

Some examples of heterogeneous NII applications, spanning a range of narrowband and broadband communications requirements, are described below. The range of communications requirements spanned by these examples can be compared to the range required by ITS applications. Much of the information made available by the NII can be supplied to the public using Internet protocols such as FTP (File Transfer Protocol) and SMTP (Simple

Mail Transfer Protocol), which do not require high bandwidth or real-time capability. For instance, "The 1992-1993 Science-by-Electronic-Mail Program reached 149 rural West Virginia students in five junior high school classes. Via the Internet, ten professional scientists and five resource specialists worked with students and their teachers" [2].

The National University Teleconference Network is a satellite-based, one-way (teacher to student), full-motion video teleconferencing service that uses the Internet to send questions from students to the lecturer. Other applications may require high-speed, two-way real-time capability. The North Carolina Information Highway, which is used to support education and other state activities, is an example of a high-bandwidth, fiber-based network that supports real-time two-way video [3]. The Highway utilizes the latest in communications technology, including Asynchronous Transfer Mode, which could also be used for ITS applications. Investment in the communications infrastructure will be based on the requirement that it be flexible enough to satisfy the needs of diverse applications. Both of these projects are successful examples of public-sector applications running on standard private-sector network infrastructure.

A decision to run ITS applications over a separate, dedicated network would be counterproductive to the NII initiative. First, it would reduce the range of users and uses over which the sunk costs of the NII communications networks could be shared, driving up the costs to all users of these networks. Second, it would add uncertainty to the policy environment in which important investment decisions are made. The Clinton Administration has promoted a limited role for the public sector in the NII; there is now a consensus that the private sector will build, maintain, and operate the communications infrastructure. The *Agenda for Action* states that "the private sector will lead the deployment of the NII" [1]. If this policy is set aside for one application area (ITS), providers of the communications infrastructure may be less confident that they will be able to compete on equal terms with the government for communications services in support of other NII applications, such as distance learning or digital libraries. A state interest in both highways and education, for example, may lead states to serve both these application areas on a single dedicated network. The private sector's incentive to invest in the communications infrastructure may thus be diminished, and prophecies that the infrastructure will not be built may well be self-fulfilling.

Wireline Communications for the Core ITS Infrastructure

This section briefly describes the wireline communications needed to support the core ITS infrastructure elements for metropolitan areas.[1] Of the 29 ITS user services,[2] near-term deployment of the core infrastructure is likely to focus on a subset of ITS user services. Our analysis concentrates on five of these: Traffic Control, Incident Management, Public Transportation Management, Public Travel Security, and Electronic Payment Services. We will also focus on the wireline communications that would likely be required to support the delivery of these ITS user services. This is not meant to suggest that this subset is the only role for wireline communications in ITS but rather to focus our discussion on the issues surrounding their deployment for these critical ITS services.

ITS Communications Endpoints and Characteristics

Figure 1 illustrates the wireline communications between endpoints for the five ITS user services identified above. The core infrastructure includes several key centers: the Regional Multimodal Traveler Information Center (RMTIC), Traffic and Freeway Management Centers, the Public Transit Management Center, and the Incident Management Center. Public transit stations and other government agencies are relatively minor centers. The other major endpoints are the roadside sensors and actuators and the toll plazas. Sensors detect the flow and volume of vehicle traffic and use cameras for video surveillance; actuators are traffic control devices such as traffic signals, ramp meters, and variable message signs. Toll plazas collect electronic toll payment and related information.

Below are illustrations of the type of wireline communications that will be needed for the core ITS infrastructure:

• *Traffic Control* manages the movement of traffic on highways and arterial roads by using data collected from various sensors, and

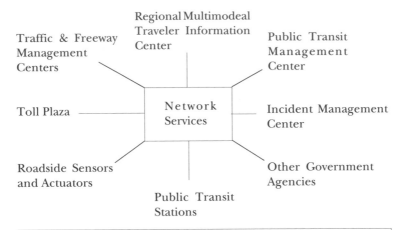

Traffic & Freeway Management Centers

Regional Multimodeal Traveler Information Center

Public Transit Management Center

Toll Plaza — Network Services — Incident Management Center

Roadside Sensors and Actuators

Public Transit Stations

Other Government Agencies

ITS User Services: Traffic Control, Incident Management, Public Transportation Management, Public Travel Security, and Electronic Payment Services.

Figure 1 Core ITS Infrastructure Elements: Wireline Communications.

controlling traffic signal systems, ramp meters, and variable message signs. Traffic Control requires communications links between Traffic and Freeway Management Centers (T&FMCs), roadside sensors and actuators, and the RMTIC. Data and video signals are sent from various sensors to T&FMCs, and T&FMCs communicate traffic control actions back to actuators. Information collected by local T&FMCs would be communicated to a RMTIC that would share relevant data among T&FMCs and coordinate Traffic Control on a region-wide basis.

• *Incident Management* rapidly identifies incidents and implements responses to minimize their effects on traffic. Incident Management requires communications links between the T&FMCs, the Incident Management Center, and other agencies such as police and fire departments. T&FMCs will detect incidents on highways and roads using sensors; this information, including video from surveillance cameras, will be transmitted to Incident Management Centers. The Incident Management Center will respond to the incident. T&FMCs will share information with each other, the RMTIC, and other government agencies to coordinate traffic control and rapid response to the situation.

• *Public Transportation Management* automates the operations, planning, and management functions of public transit systems. Wireline communications for transit functions will be needed between the various transit centers, including the Public Transit Management Center (PTMC), bus transfer stations, park-and-rides, and transit operations and maintenance. The PTMC and T&FMC would also share data to coordinate transit and traffic management functions.

• *Public Travel Safety* creates a secure environment for public transportation travelers and operators. Monitoring the safety of transit passengers and personnel might include video surveillance. The video might only be used locally—e.g., cameras at the bus station could be monitored by security personnel at the bus station rather than monitored remotely—but if remote video monitoring is employed, it would require higher bandwidth communications.

• *Electronic Payment Services* allow travelers to pay for transportation services electronically. Wireline communications would be used to transport electronic toll-collection data from the toll plaza to the T&FMC, other government agencies, and financial institutions. This data could likely be carried on the communications links for sensors and actuators along the interstates and toll roads.

Communications Bandwidth Requirements

Video requires the highest bandwidth for wireline communications, and is likely to dominate ITS communications requirements for the foreseeable future. Video would be transmitted from surveillance cameras on highways, arterial roads, and other facilities to the T&FMCs; to a lesser degree, video would be shared among government agencies. Figures 2 and 3 illustrate wireline communications between the sensors and the T&FMC. In Figure 2, sensors and actuators are connected to controllers or video controllers. Except for the cameras, the bandwidth requirements are very low, usually below 64 thousand bits per second (Kbps). The video bandwidth for each camera depends upon the desired quality of the video to be received at the T&FMC video monitor and the amount of compression of the video signal. For example, assuming high-quality video with very little compression of the video signal, each camera could transmit at 45 million bits per

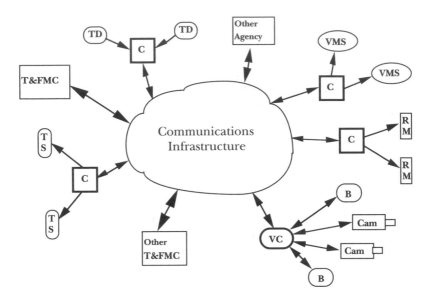

Figure 2 Wireline T&FMC and Sensor/Actuator Communications. C = Controller. VC = Video Controller. T&FMC = Traffic and Freeway Management Center. TS = Traffic Signal. TD = Traffic Detector. VMS = Variable Message Sign. RM = Ramp Meter. B = Beacon.

second (Mbps). Increased compression reduces the need for bandwidth—e.g., T1 (1.5 Mbps) could be used with MPEG2 compression—but increases the compression equipment costs.

Figure 3 illustrates the connection from the video cameras to the T&FMC. In this example, each video controller could handle three or more cameras, with any three capable of transmitting simultaneously from the controller to the controlled environment vault (CEV) by multiplexing the signals onto an OC-3 (155 Mbps) fiber path. The CEV could accommodate an input of 15 video controllers for a total of 15 OC-3 fibers, which could be multiplexed onto an OC-48 [2.5 billion bps (Gbps)] fiber path to carry the video signal to the T&FMC. In addition, the CEV could handle fifty other controllers that connect to traffic signals, traffic detectors, ramp meters, variable message signs, and beacons. Each of these controllers would handle multiple sensors and actuators, requiring a combined bandwidth of 64 Kbps. These controllers would be multiplexed at the CEV onto a 45-Mbps communications path and

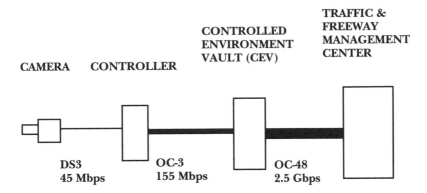

Figure 3 Video Bandwidth Requirements. Three cameras are connected to each controller. Fifteen video controllers (plus non-video controllers) are connected to each CEV.

added onto the OC-48 fiber path with the video signals. Each CEV could transmit 45 camera signals simultaneously to the T&FMC along with the other non-video data. Camera signals could be selected at the T&FMC for viewing.

This architecture would have multiple CEVs connected to the T&FMC in a star configuration. Other centers could be connected to the T&FMC and to each other via a fiber link that would likely be used for local area network interconnection and for the sharing of video. However, the bandwidths on these links would be well below those from the CEV to the T&FMC, since the data transmissions are individually low bandwidth and bursty. An exception might be the video requirements for Public Travel Safety, if the video monitoring is done remotely.

The above discussion illustrates a very high bandwidth requirement for video ITS applications, as it assumes very little compression and continuous transmission of the video signals back to the T&FMC. Use of video compression and transmission of the signal only when the video is to be viewed would greatly reduce the video bandwidth requirements.

The ITS Architecture Phase I studies provide considerable information on communications load analysis.[3] Estimates of aggregate daily bandwidth requirements for traffic control, traffic sensors, transit operations, and emergency services yield about 10 billion bits per day[4] or slightly above 100 Kbps. (This does not include video for the camera deployment discussed above.) For comparison, a T1 private line carries 1.5 Mbps; an OC-1, 51.8 Mbps; and an OC-48, 2.5 Gbps. Thus, current estimates of bandwidth requirements are not overwhelmingly large, except possibly for video, and communications traffic is not continuous. Though much work remains to be done on wireline communications load analysis, it appears that video dominates bandwidth requirements, and that bandwidth requirements will depend on the amount of compression (quality of video signal) and how frequently the signal is sent from the camera to the T&FMC.

Special-Purpose vs. General-Purpose Networks

In this section we will discuss whether government transportation or other public agencies should build their own ITS special-purpose networks or utilize general-purpose networks provided by private sector communications companies. We consider the factors favoring special-purpose networks and determine whether ITS meets these criteria.

Typically there are four reasons for an organization to implement a dedicated network: communications traffic characteristics, costs, special requirements, and strategic objectives.

• *Communications Traffic Characteristics*—Organizations that use dedicated networks generally have a fixed number of locations that they desire to connect, and a substantial amount of voice, data, or video communications. These dedicated networks tend not to require access to a large and varying number of locations, which would require greater switching capabilities in the network. Also, a large volume of traffic is necessary to justify a separate network. Corporations may not put their smaller locations on the dedicated network if the volume of traffic does not warrant it; these sites may gain access to the dedicated network through a private-sector communications service provider.

• *Costs*—An organization may decide on the basis of costs to set up its own dedicated network rather than use the general-purpose network and services of a communications company. In large part, this is because of telephone companies' traditionally regulated tariffs, and not because the corporation is more cost-efficient than telephone companies. Historically, regulated tariffs were not necessarily based on the costs of the services but may have included socially desirable subsidies. Some organizations had an incentive to set up dedicated networks to avoid paying the subsidies, thus lowering their costs.

The move to incentive-based regulation (such as price caps) may result in tariffs that better reflect the underlying costs of communications services.[5] In addition, telephone companies may provide customer solutions on an individual-case basis or customer-specific proposal, which typically cost less than a tariff-based solution.

In most cases, the organization will use the private-line special services of the telephone company to provide basic communications transport. The organization will recognize that it would likely be too expensive for it to deploy its own communications links because of the telephone company's advantage in economies of scale for basic communications transport. The corporation will then deploy its own higher level communications functions, including routing/switching and network management on top of the telephone company's private line services.

• *Special Requirements*—An organization may believe that the information on its networks is so sensitive and so critical that breaches in the security of its information might jeopardize the organization, its customers, or its mission. In other cases, an organization may require that its network be highly available and reliable because disruption to its network might result in sizable loss of business.

• *Strategic Objectives*—Communications may be a strategic asset affecting the corporation's ability to compete in its markets. In such cases, the corporation will desire to maintain control of its network and to implement the latest in communications technology. Network control and leading-edge communications innovations may give the organization an advantage over its competitors in delivering its products or services to customers.

An organization's evaluation of these factors against the resources necessary to develop its own communications expertise determines whether or not it develops its own communications capabilities. The outcome of this decision has shifted over time; in recent years, the pendulum has swung away from dedicated networks toward services offered by private sector communications companies. This is because organizations are placing more focus on their core business; outsourcing usually proves to be cheaper; and it is difficult and expensive to keep up with rapid technological change. This trend is evidenced by the decline in PBXs, as corporations migrate to switched Virtual Private Network services offered by communications carriers [8]. Further, as new technologies, such as Asynchronous Transfer Mode (ATM), are more widely deployed, the shift from dedicated networks to private sector communications company general-purpose networks may accelerate [9].

Based upon the four criteria discussed above, we offer an assessment of the ITS core infrastructure elements for utilization of a dedicated network. First, communications traffic characteristics for these elements involve a relatively fixed and small number of centers and many fixed end device locations. Communications traffic volume, with the potential exception of video use, is not large. The ITS communications requirements for the core infrastructure yield arguments both for and against a special-purpose ITS network. However, as discussed below, the volume of ITS data and video information is not sufficient to justify deployment of a dedicated government-owned ITS network.

The development of appropriate public policy requires an evaluation of the economic or opportunity costs of providing the communications services.[6] Can a government transportation agency provide communications services more efficiently than a private sector communications company? For a positive answer, we would need to demonstrate that there are no economies of scale or scope in the production of communications services,[7] and that the government could duplicate a communications company's workforce expertise and skills. This is most likely not the case. Studies comparing the efficiency of government and private sector provision of similar services find the private sector generally more efficient [10]. Hence, private sector communications services are most likely to be more efficient than government provision of those services. Moreover, the trend in foreign countries is to move telecommunications industries to a competitive market structure and away from government monopolies.

Nevertheless, traditional tariffing of communications services and government transportation agency use of capital-intensive/ operations-deficient funding may give the agency an incentive to build its own dedicated ITS communications network. Highway right-of-way resource-sharing may also affect the outlays incurred by government transportation agencies for communications services. (This is discussed below.)

Security and reliability/availability are always an issue for an organization's communications needs. Organizations responsible for ITS implementation must determine if ITS communications needs in these areas are different from those of the many organizations in the private sector that use communications services. While these requirements for ITS are important, they do not appear very different from those of many corporations in finance and other industries that utilize the network services of private sector communications companies. Hence, security and reliability/availability are not a justification for the deployment of special-purpose dedicated ITS communications networks for the core infrastructure.

Finally, communications is not a strategic resource for ITS managers, as it is for many information-intensive corporations. Given the state of the art of ITS applications and institutional issues, currently available and planned communications services from private sector communications corporations likely meet or exceed requirements of Traffic and Freeway Management Centers to share and utilize ITS information. The latest in communications technology does not appear to be critical to the success of ITS; in fact, the latest communications technologies may not be the most cost-effective and reliable approach for ITS user services. The costs of updating an ITS dedicated network for the latest technology are not likely to be offset by added benefits to ITS applications or users.

ITS communications traffic characteristics, requirements for security and reliability/availability, and strategic criteria do not provide a compelling argument for the deployment of special-purpose ITS networks. This is not to say that the wireline communications needs of the core ITS infrastructure elements are unimportant, but rather that these needs are consonant with the needs of medium and large private corporations that rely on the services of private-sector communications companies. Since security, reliability, and strategic importance are not critical issues, the key issue for a special purpose ITS network is cost.

Cost Considerations

State and local transportation agencies are typically deploying fiber-based communications systems for core ITS infrastructure elements. In this section, we will discuss the different cost components of an ITS communications network. Several components are considered: communications transport, higher-level communications services, and operations and support.

• *Communications Transport*—Deployment of wireline transport communications functions requires a physical medium such as copper, coaxial cable, or fiber to connect the end device to the controller, the controller to the hub, and the hub to the T&FMC. Key communications cost components include the highway right-of-way, the conduit for the cable, cable, and electronic equipment.

In a metropolitan area, an extensive communications network would need to be deployed to connect the end devices to the T&FMC. Such a network would be similar to and replicate networks that telecommunications companies have deployed and are deploying. Moreover, a dedicated ITS communications network would likely have substantial excess capacity, especially in the backbone part of the network. For example, fiber cables deployed by communications companies tend to have 12 to 36 fibers per cable. Four fibers are used per path between two points (one fiber each for receive and transmit and two fibers for protection against a fiber cut or equipment malfunction). Depending upon the electronic equipment deployed, a fiber path of up to OC-48 could be provided today. A cable of 12 fibers could provide three OC-48 paths; a 36-fiber cable could provide nine OC-48 paths. In the example illustrated by Figure 3, the connection from the Controlled Environment Vault (CEV) to the T&FMC utilized only one OC-48. This is about one-tenth of the available capacity, which assumed very high bandwidth for video, or 90% excess capacity. Video compression and noncontinuous transmission of the video signal could reduce bandwidth significantly and further increase excess capacity.

Because communications networks have economies of scale that exceed the likely bandwidth needs of ITS, private sector communications companies are likely to have lower costs for communications transport.[8] A government-deployed network would either have a higher cost than services from a private sector communications company or require the government to move other government communications applications onto the ITS communications network to utilize the ITS network's excess capacity.[9]

• *Higher-Level Communications Services*—Higher-level communications services run on top of the communications transport layer. For example, in the above discussion the communications transport layer might use SONET to provide dedicated private line service between the end device and the T&FMC or between T&FMCs and other agencies. Higher-level services, which include Cell Relay, Frame Relay, and Switched Multimegabit Data Service (SMDS), can run on top of SONET. These services provide more functionality than private line service; their implementation requires additional equipment in the network and in operations and support. For some ITS communications applications these services would be suitable; however, the volume of ITS communications traffic may not justify the expense of deploying these services in a special-purpose ITS network owned and operated by the government. Economies of scope for communications services favor provision of these services by a private sector communications company unless more government communications applications are added to the ITS network. Most of the ITS communications studies that favor building dedicated systems have focused only on private line services and have not considered newer communications services that are becoming available.

• *Operations and Support*—Cost studies of ITS communications systems tend to focus on the deployment of fiber and private line services with very little attention paid to operations and support. Examination of network costs suggests that this may be an oversight. Data reported by the Federal Communications Commission for local exchange and interexchange carriers indicates that a substantial portion of their costs are accounted for by expenses other than plant and equipment [12]. In addition, surveys of people in private industry and government who use dedicated networks show that communications transport costs are not the major portion of the network's costs [13]. Operations and support costs are likely to be much higher than those currently estimated in ITS communications design studies. Also, operations and support functions require both highly trained and experienced personnel and sophisticated operations support tools, which add to the overall operations and support costs. Private-sector communications companies are likely to have lower operation and support costs by virtue of their extensive experience and the ability to spread these costs over a larger base of users than would the public sector.

ITS applications and their underlying wireline communications represent a relatively new role for government transportation agencies. The new wireline communications needs far exceed the types of communications that these agencies have historically used. Given these new responsibilities, it is natural for them to have concerns about private sector communications companies' capabilities to meet their wireline communications needs (e.g., performance, reliability, integrity, and security) in a cost-effective manner.

These concerns may be misplaced. This section suggests that transportation agency wireline communications needs are similar to those of corporations that are serviced by private sector communications companies, and that the economic costs of private sector communications services are lower than those of government-owned dedicated ITS networks.

Theoretical Analysis

The roles of the public and private sectors in the provision of ITS services can be analyzed from both theoretical and practical viewpoints. From a theoretical perspective, it is widely recognized that there are at least three sets of circumstances in which markets fail to provide the optimal amount of a service: in the provision of public goods; when there are externalities; and when there is a natural monopoly. Some might argue that there are significant elements of public goods and externalities in the provision of ITS services and that an important input (communications) to ITS user services is still in transition from a regulated natural monopoly to unregulated competition. Below, we will provide a theoretical approach to the analysis of public and private roles in the provision of ITS services and the communications infrastructure they will ride on. Our conclusion is that the public provision of ITS services and the private provision of the communications infrastucture for ITS applications may be optimal from an economic point of view.

A *public good* is defined as one that is nonexcludable (no individual can be prevented from consuming the good) and nondepletable (one individual's consumption does not reduce the amount available for others to consume). Elements of national defense, such as the nuclear deterrent, are examples of public goods. Public goods are not well-provided by private markets. Individuals have an incentive to understate their willingness to pay for the service, resulting in underprovision by the market. Economists often recommend that public goods be provided by the government and be financed out of general revenue.

Traffic Control, a key ITS user service, may have significant public good aspects. For example, control of traffic signals systems may improve the flow of traffic for all vehicles, and therefore is nonexcludable. Variable messages displayed on digital signboards are nondepletable and nonexcludable. En-Route Driver Information, when it is provided through unencrypted/unscrambled radio broadcast, is also a nondepletable and nonexcludable public good. In these cases, a strong argument can be made for the public provision of ITS services.

Externalities arise when the private costs and benefits facing individual decision makers are not equal to true social costs and benefits. In these circumstances, individuals will make decisions that are not socially optimal. Congestion is one such externality: The private cost of using a congested highway or bridge is equal to the expected waiting time for the individual, but the social cost should include the additional delay imposed on other travelers by one person's decision to join the queue. In this case, a free market generates too much congestion.

There is a legitimate social purpose in providing public services that alleviate this problem. ITS services that can serve this function include variable message signs that route traffic around congested paths, efficient toll booths that allow individuals to pay with more money and less time than free but congested roads, and incident management that reduces the time required for the roadway to recover from accidents.

As with public goods, a strong case can be made for the public provision of those ITS services that help deal with congestion externalities while imposing small transaction costs on the public. However, the public provision of a service does not require the public provision of all or any of the inputs used to produce the service. For example, national defense, the quintessential public good, depends on a variety of goods and services produced by private companies and procured for use as inputs by the government. The deployment of ITS services should be based on an appropriate mix of inputs, some possibly provided by the public sector and others provided by the private sector. From a theoretical point of view the question is: Are the inputs themselves public goods or subject to externalities or other forms of market failure?

From a policy perspective, the most important features of communications services include the large investment in infrastructure that is required to support the underlying network, and the possibility of persistent excess capacity in important components of modern digital networks built with fiber optic technology.

The economics of communications service provision in the evolving environment is complex, and the determination of a detailed public policy framework is beyond the scope of this paper. However, two broad features of modern digital networks may serve as useful working hypotheses for guiding public policy:

(1) Given the large sunk costs associated with building a communications infrastructure, the market will likely consist of a very few facilities-based firms.

(2) Competition among service providers with large fixed (or sunk) costs and excess capacity may be unstable [14].

In modern networks, the cost of the fiber is a relatively small proportion of the total cost of construction and installation. It is therefore common practice to install "excess" fiber. According to the FCC, between forty and fifty percent of the fiber installed by the typical interexchange carrier is "dark." In other words, the lasers and electronics required for transmission are not in place [15]. The comparable amount of "dark" fiber for the major local operating companies is between fifty and eighty percent.[10] The presence of excess capacity in one important input can affect equilibrium prices and industry structure. The market could be unstable if firms provide an undifferentiated commodity and compete purely on price. In these circumstances, competition may drive price down to incremental cost, and the sunk costs of the infrastructure will not be recovered. The combination of a small number of facilities providers, potentially unstable competition, and entry by the government (which is not required to break even) into this sector will likely result in a reduced private sector incentive to invest in the communications infrastructure.

A key variable that influences the investment decision of network providers is the share of the revenue from communications-based services recoverable over the lifetime of the investment. A government's decision to deploy its own communications infrastructure will reduce the potential revenue available to the private sector. While the initial loss of potential private-sector revenue may be small both in absolute terms and as a proportion of current revenues,[11] history indicates that future impacts could be substantially higher. In early discussions of competition, the FCC argued that the new carriers would be authorized to provide limited services and that only three percent of AT&T's revenues would be at risk [17]. However, these projections were rapidly undone by economic forces. The new carriers realized that their investments would be more quickly and surely recovered if they spread their costs over more users and uses, and they quickly developed switched services (such as MCI's Execunet) that had not been authorized by the FCC. Networks built by the government will face the same economic incentives: The cost to any one department can be reduced by sharing the facilities with other departments, and the development of switched services may be necessary to accommodate the needs of different departments.

When firms undertake large investments in infrastructure, they may choose to phase in their deployment over time, beginning with demonstrated market demand by a few customers whose needs lead the rest of the market. The initial revenue forecasts for new services may be small. Lost opportunities, which appear small relative to traditional revenues of communications companies, may appear large relative to initial revenue forecasts.

While many regard as desirable increasing competition from new specialized carriers in the private sector, it is not clear that competition from the government would be viewed in the same light. Government departments do not pay taxes and can compete unfairly by operating at a loss that is covered by general revenues. The prospect of the government entering the market (either as a self supplier of network services or as a provider of facilities to new firms that will not have large sunk costs of network development and deployment) may be an additional disincentive to investment in infrastructure and an additional market destabilizer.

Cost and Efficiency

The theoretical analysis presented above suggests that competition will lead to reduced prices for communications services. The following evidence supports this analysis: In recent years there has been a strong downward trend in leased line prices in the long distance market. According to *Business Week*, private line prices fell by eighty percent between 1989 and 1994 [18]. There has also been a dramatic increase in the use of term and volume discounts. For example, one interexchange carrier offers customers a standard month-to-month tariff for T1 service and charges a nonrecurring fee, a fixed monthly fee, and a monthly rate per mile. Customers who are willing to sign a five-year contract and commit to spending one million dollars per month are offered a discount of 57% off the standard month-to-month rates. Published tariffs often understate the discounts available: "There are two types of tariffs: 'Front of the book' rates, which are paid by smaller and uninformed large customers; and 'back of the book rates,' which are offered to the customers who are ready to defect to another carrier and to customers who know enough to ask for them" [19]. In these circumstances, a forward-looking evaluation of the prices likely charged by telecommunications firms will probably be dramatically less than a backward-looking analysis of traditional tariffs. Moreover, regulated telephone companies offer services on individual-case bases, which cost less than standard tariff solutions.

In addition, the relative costs of the private and public sectors in managing and operating businesses on an ongoing basis should be considered. There is considerable evidence that the private sector is more cost-efficient than the public sector. Wolf [10] contains a survey of 48 studies comparing public- and private-sector companies in 19 industries ranging from airlines to weather forecasting. In two cases the public sector was more efficient (barely so in one case) and in five cases there were no significant differences in productivity. In the remaining forty-one cases the private sector was more efficient, often by very large margins. Supporting evidence for the greater efficiency of the private sector is also provided by Nellis [20], who reviews recent research on the effects of privatizing state-owned enterprises in a variety of countries. He asks, "Is privatization necessary?" and replies, "The answer is a decided yes."

The history of the federal government's decisions with regard to "make" versus "buy" is consistent with the arguments made above. Currently, the federal government purchases a mix of voice, data, and video services from the private sector as part of FTS 2000, a contract that replaced an earlier arrangement, FTS, under which the government owned its own switches and leased lines from private carriers. Datapro, a communications research company, estimates that the FTS 2000 contract saved the federal government about $1.2 billion over the life of the contract, compared with earlier FTS arrangements [21]. This example demonstrates the relative efficiency of the private sector in providing communications services.

In sum, government investment in a communications infrastructure has the potential to destabilize a market that is likely to be characterized by excess capacity and may be prone to unstable competition. As public sector enterprises can operate at a loss for long periods of time, the initial entry of the public sector into the telecommunications market may be viewed by private investors as a cause for some concern. Prices for commercially provided communications services are likely to fall, particularly for large customers (like government transportation and other agencies) who can negotiate customized packages, while the public sector will have higher ongoing costs of providing service. ITS will be less expensive if a dedicated network is not built. Other telecommunications services will also be less expensive as the common costs can be spread over more users and uses. In these circumstances, the case for building a large (initially dedicated) communications infrastructure for ITS services may be weak.

Highway Right-of-Way Issues

Highway right-of-way (HROW) is receiving substantial attention for ITS infrastructure deployment and also as a means to both introduce competition into the local exchange telecommunications market and to stimulate the information highway. (HROW refers here to all types of highways and roads, and in particular considers those in metropolitan areas.) However, it is not possible to cover all aspects of HROW in this paper; our comments focus on the role played by government transportation agencies with respect to communications.[12]

We begin with the assumption that state and local transportation authorities are granted permission to use the HROW to obtain wireline communications facilities or services for ITS core infrastructure elements.[13] Based on this assumption, we consider several approaches to exchanging or sharing the HROW:

(1) Government transportation agency sells the HROW to a private company and uses proceeds to buy ITS communications services.

(2) Government transportation agency trades HROW to a private company for conduit and fiber for ITS applications; the private company installs conduit and keeps the remaining conduit space and fiber for its own use or resale.

(3) Government transportation agency deploys conduit and fiber and sells excess space or fiber to private sector communications companies or uses the fiber for other government non-ITS applications.

Alternatives (1) and (2) differ only in the manner of compensation. Both limit the role of the government transportation agency to obtaining ITS communications services or facilities. The government transportation agency is not entering the communications arena or investing in communications beyond its own ITS needs. Furthermore, HROW resource sharing may facilitate entry of companies into the telecommunications market and hasten private sector investment in the NII. This would be likely to the extent that HROW sharing provides private companies with cheaper and more rapid access to HROW than obtaining their own private right-of-way.

In alternative (3), the government transportation agency owns the conduit and fiber and would need to dispose of the excess capacity in some manner. The government transportation agency could become a wholesaler of conduit or fiber to private sector communications companies. In this case, the government transportation agency has made an investment with some level of risk using taxpayers' resources and has entered the communications business. This raises serious issues about the role of the government in the communications industry, and it could be detrimental to private sector investment in the NII.

The HROW issue and these alternatives raise several ITS-related questions.

(1) Should government transportation or other agencies enter the conduit or fiber business? Clearly, this would put the government transportation agency into a traditional domain of the private sector. Before the government does this, the implications, impacts, and process should be carefully assessed.

(2) Who has access to conduit space that is put onto the HROW? All three alternatives provide new access to HROW that could be offered to one or more private sector companies. How the conduit space and fiber are made available and on what terms needs to be evaluated.

(3) Is sharing the HROW a requirement for providing the government transportation agency with communications services for ITS applications? Not all companies wishing to compete for the provision of ITS communications services/facilities for a government transportation agency may want to use the HROW. Instead they may choose to use alternative rights of way or may already have facilities in place, obviating the need for new HROW. Again, the process of HROW resource-sharing needs to be evaluated so as not to bias the process of bidding on ITS communications requirements.

ITS Communications Procurement Policy Assessment

The basis for some of the issues identified above may be found in traditional government transportation agency highway policies and their extension to ITS. ITS user services are a radical departure from the traditional business of providing highways and roads. Consequently, procedures that have served well for the construction and maintenance of highways and roads should be re-evaluated for their strengths and weaknesses vis a vis ITS deployment. ITS communications deployments may need to move away from the traditional government transportation agency design-and-build approach for highways, toward methods that more closely parallel processes used in both the private and federal government sectors for communications systems.

Two particular aspects of the design-and-build approach need to be reconsidered. The first is government transportation agencies' historical procurement procedures for building highways and roads, which have included a design phase and a low-bid phase. This process has two major problems when applied to ITS communications. First, it emphasizes building as opposed to purchasing services; the process focuses on construction of facilities and not the whole communications system. Second, the design is pre-set and then put out to bid for low-cost construction. This may not lead to the most cost-effective system. An alternative approach would be to determine the performance requirements for ITS communications systems and have communications companies provide systems and services that cost-effectively meet performance requirements. This would be similar to the processes used in private industry for its networks and by the federal government for FTS 2000.

The second aspect of procurement needing reconsideration is that federal funding for highways emphasizes capital expenditures. This creates two problems. First, it tends to encourage state and local governments to build their own ITS communications systems rather than outsourcing the communications function. Second, it de-emphasizes the ongoing expenses for maintenance, operations and support. This may not be a problem for highways, where maintenance can be postponed for short periods of time, but communications systems must be maintained and supported continuously if they are to function effectively [24]. Thus, federal funding for ITS communications and other technology-intensive services should be reexamined.

Conclusions

This chapter has considered two alternatives for providing wireline communications infrastructure for ITS services: government deployment of a communications infrastructure dedicated to ITS, and procurement of a mix of communications services from private sector communications companies. Our economic analysis concluded that procurement from the private sector is likely to be superior to deployment of a dedicated infrastructure. Two sets of arguments were used. First, a narrow comparison of the relevant costs of the two options suggested that procurement would be more cost-effective. The private sector can take advantage of greater economies of scope and scale, has a large employee pool with specialized skills in communications technology and has the ability to spread common costs over a wider variety of uses and users.

A more general analysis of the NII suggested several factors besides cost efficiency that should be considered in choosing which alternative to pursue. We argued that other NII applications require the same range of communications services (in terms of bandwidth, reliability, security, etc.) as ITS services. The NII applications will be carried by private sector communications networks, which will compete with one another for traffic and revenue. With low incremental costs of carrying traffic, and with excess capacity, the industry is unlikely to reach stability with many firms. An unstable equilibrium with a few more firms is likely to emerge.

If ITS applications are to ride over a dedicated network that will itself have substantial excess capacity (up to 90%), there is a strong likelihood that other NII applications controlled by the states, such as education and digital libraries, will migrate to the state-owned ITS network. Under these circumstances, the private sector may not be able to make a strong business case for investment in a communications infrastructure that will support the NII. If this becomes true, the Clinton Administration's vision of a NII that serves all people well into the 21st century may not be realized in the near future. On the other hand, if ITS applications use current and emerging NII networks, greater cost sharing will be possible and lower costs will result for all NII applications, including ITS services, and help realize the NII vision.

Notes

The views expressed in this paper are those of the authors and do not represent the views of Bellcore or its owners.

1. See reference [4], p. 11, for a description of the core ITS infrastructure.

2. See reference [5] for descriptions of the ITS user services.

3. The ITS Architecture Phase I studies focused on the communications load for ITS above and beyond communications that would be deployed in the baseline, or business-as-usual, scenario. The baseline assumed the deployment of most traffic sensors and actuators for traffic control; this included video. Consequently, some of the main drivers for ITS communications were in the baseline and not included in the architecture studies for Phase I.

4. See reference [6] for estimates of ITS communications loads.

5. See reference [7] for a discussion of regulatory mechanisms.

6. Opportunity costs are defined as the costs of all the resources used to provide the service. Opportunity costs may differ from accounting costs in a regulated environment.

7. Economies of scale mean, in this case, that a larger network has lower per unit communications transport costs than a smaller network. Economies of scope indicate that the costs of providing multiple communications services on one network are less than the costs of providing each service on its own network.

8. Because of the issues raised in this section, we believe that Carpenter's conclusion that traffic control, public transportation management, and public travel security have low potential for use of the NII (see her chapter in this volume) is incorrect from a communications network point of view. Government-owned dedicated ITS networks, especially in major metropolitan areas, would duplicate the fiber networks being deployed by the private sector.

9. In at least one case this is already planned. See reference [11].

10. The excess capacity is not evenly spread through the entire serving area of the telephone companies. Large urban business centers and routes with high-density traffic are more likely to possess excess capacity. These are also likely to be areas where many ITS services would be initially be deployed.

11. For instance, the lost revenue is estimated at less than $2.5 million for a state-owned fiber-based network in Iowa [16].

12. See references [22] and [23] for more detailed discussions of Highway Right-of-Way issues.

13. Potentially the revenues from private corporations that the government receives for HROW access could be used for any number of government purposes.

References

1. Information Infrastructure Task Force. *The National Information Infrastructure: Agenda for Action.* September 15, 1993.

2. Stone-Martin, Martha, and Breeden, Laura, eds. *51 Reasons: How we use the Internet and what it says about the Information Highway.* FARNET, Lexington, MA; 1994.

3. "Special Issue: North Carolina Information Highway." *IEEE NETWORK,* November/December 1994.

4. FHWA/HTV. *Core ITS Infrastructure Elements for Metropolitan Area ATMS/ATIS Deployment.* Version 1, March 9, 1995.

5. "Synopsis." in ITS America *National ITS Program Plan* First Edition. March 1995.

6. Pruitt, G. "Communications, Fiber Optic Cable, and ITS." ARINC, Inc., April 1995.

7. Baron, David P. "Design of Regulatory Mechanisms and Institutions." *Handbook of Industrial Organization,* Volume II, Edited by R. Schalensee and R. D. Willig. Elsevier Science Publishers B. V., 1989.

8. "'Negative Growth' to Come for PBX Manufactures." *Business Communications Review,* March 1995.

9. Passmore, David. "Choosing between Public and Private WANs," *Business Communications Review,* January 1995.

10. Wolf, Charles Jr. *Market or Governments: Choosing Between Imperfect Alternatives.* Cambridge: The MIT Press, 1988.

11. "MCI to Build Fiber-Optic Link for MD." *Baltimore Morning Sun,* August 28, 1994.

12. Federal Communications Commission. *Statistics of Communications Common Carriers.* 1992/1993 edition.

13. Lusa, John M. "Escaping the Budget Squeeze." 8th Annual Budget and Spending Survey, *Networking Management,* March 1992.

14. Gong, J. and Srinagesh, P. "The Economics of Layered Networks," Paper presented at NII 2000, Washington, D. C., May 23, 1995, Bellcore, 1995.

15. Kraushar, Johnathan. *Fiber Deployment Update.* Federal Communications Commission, May, 1994.

16. Ernst & Young. *Analysis of the Project to Establish a State Communications Network for Education.* March 15, 1991.

17. Temin, Peter. *The Fall of the Bell System.* Cambridge University Press, 1987.

18. "Dangerous Living in Telecom's Top Tier." *Business Week,* September 12, 1994.

19. Hills, Michael T. "Carrier Pricing Increases Continue." *Business Communications Review*, February 1995.

20. Nellis, John. "Is Privatization Necessary." In *Public Policy for the Private Sector*, The World Bank Group, March 1995.

21. "FTS 2000 Network." In *Communications Services: Communications Networking Services*. Datapro, May 1993.

22. Hess, Ronald W., Mitchell, Bridger M., River, Eleanor C., Jones, Don H., and Wolf, Barry M. *Feasibility of Using Interstate Highway Right-of-Way to Obtain a More Survivable Fiber-Optics Network*. The Rand Corporation R-3500-DOT/NCS, January 1988.

23. *Task "A" Report: Literature Review, Project Survey, and Identification of Issues* (Draft). Prepared for Federal Highway Administration, Shared Resources Project: Identification, Review and Analysis of Legal and Institutional Issues, November 30, 1994.

24. Patel, Raman K. "IVHS Operations and Maintenance Issues." Presented at the ITS America 1995, Annual Conference, March 15-17, 1995.

Technical Issues

Intelligent Agents and ITS

Su-Shing Chen

Introduction

Transportation is a complex domain that has traditionally been the realm of federal, state, and local governments and transportation industries. As transportation becomes increasingly information-dependent, examining Intelligent Transportation Systems (ITS) requirements from an information technology perspective becomes essential for policy makers, program managers, industry planners, and university researchers who are involved in ITS development and deployment.

This chapter will examine technical issues in the development of the transportation information infrastructure (TII), and will explore the relationship of ITS to the general purpose NII. Some of the critical questions are listed below:

• What are the key technical issues unique to ITS and how are they different from those of other NII domains?

• How will these issues place additional demands on the NII technological base?

• What are the key technical features of the NII that are sharable with ITS?

• How will ITS development push the boundaries of the NII technological base?

• What can we leverage from the lessons learned and results accomplished in other NII activities to benefit ITS deployment?

The TII, which encompasses the entirety of transportation enterprises, consists of wireline/wireless communications networks, sensors, laptops, computers, control systems, and databases of information about transportation enterprises. It supports various activities, including: (1) decision making to maximize the safety of travelers; (2) planning and control to assure the efficiency of the entire operation; (3) logistics of vehicles and monitoring systems to maximize the capacity of transportation and minimize the bottleneck of traffic jams; and (4) information archives and analysis tools to enable the continuous refinement of transportation management.

This chapter is organized as follows: First, we will describe general technical issues of the NII and the possibility of embedding ITS functions into the NII framework. Next, we will discuss ITS requirements, challenges, and opportunities, focusing on ITS' challenge to information management, which may push the boundaries of the NII. Intelligent software systems offer opportunities for handling this challenge; we will therefore outline a key technical approach to the deployment of ITS: intelligent agents. Intelligent agents are smart software systems that provide intelligent capabilities for the access, control, and management of information. They can handle uncertain circumstances and events, and can support interoperability of various components of the information infrastructure. Finally, we will discuss how many technical issues of ITS, such as interoperability, electronic payment, real-time control, decision making, and information access, can be addressed through the use of intelligent agents.

The National Information Infrastructure (NII)

The notion of a National Information Infrastructure (NII) has captured the attention of the general public as well as that of the computer and information technology communities. A vision for the future NII—including its objectives and strategies—is emerging from various efforts on the part of industry, government, and users [8, 10, 11, 12, 13].

This chapter relies on the high-level framework for information infrastructure presented in Chapter 1. As Branscomb and Keller point out, "integration infrastructure" will be a critical area for ITS because it will provide national-level information in an environment of local and regional implementations [1]. In the following sections, we shall discuss how intelligent agents may enable the development of the integration infrastructure component of ITS.

Deploying the Infrastructure

The deployment of an information infrastructure has the following components: (1) layout or utilization of telecommunications networks; (2) acquisition of computers and information peripherals; (3) capture and organization of information; (4) development of application software; (5) standards and content monitoring; and (6) establishment of government regulations and user supports. A brief assessment of the readiness and feasibility of this deployment is described as follows:

The capture and organization of ITS information will enhance the growth of the U.S. information industry. However, this activity requires significant investments and resources for converting existing media from non-digital to digital. The development of application software also requires significant investments and resources. The technical issue in this case is software interoperability and maintenance. Throughout the current process of technology diffusion, software interoperability and maintenance have proven to be costly, however, the software technology necessary for ITS deployment is maturing.

There are several NII frameworks (or reference models) for achieving software interoperability and maintenance (e.g., OLE and CORBA for distributed object-oriented systems [5]). However, the overall interoperability and maintenance of software, middleware, and content remains the most dominant technical issue of the NII. This issue will be covered in more detail, including a discussion of how the technical approach of intelligent agents will help solve it.

The key technical issues in the deployment of the NII and ITS depend on the development of intelligent, interoperable software and middleware, which will enable the access, manipulation, organization, and management of data. For example, intelligent browsing, navigating, retrieving, and searching systems for information access [6, 7, 9, 10] will all be required. Also, intelligent systems are needed to carry out problem-solving and decision-making tasks in various ITS/NII applications (e.g., traffic control and transportation management [2]).

The Mapping of ITS into the NII: Requirements, Challenges, and Opportunities

ITS systems are large, complex infrastructures of highways, vehicles, sensors, toll booths, administrations, organizations, information bases, and the like, which have both mechanical (physical) and informational (virtual) parts. The ITS information infrastructure contains pertinent information of all kinds: global weather, maps, local traffic, site emergency, and individual traveler plans. Thus, the TII requirements must include the following basic features:

1. Information access
2. Real-time control
3. Decision making
4. Active sensing and monitoring
5. Wireless communications
6. Confederated information bases

ITS America has formulated 29 user services for the ITS information infrastructure. As explained in previous chapters, the 29 user services are divided into seven groups, or bundles. As indicated in Carpenter's chapter, ITS can be viewed as an application or a subset of the NII, or as a specific domain that will utilize some or all of the capabilities of the emerging NII. The three fundamental technical areas of ITS issues are information access, real-time (i.e., quick response time) control, and decision making. Among these, real-time control and decision making have unique characteristics in ITS: they are sharable with NII, demand information access, and are mobile. These are features which may place additional demands on the NII technological base.

Information access is the basic feature of the seven ITS user-service bundles, and it is also common to other NII activities. For example, En-Route Driver Information and Traveler Services Information are information-access services. Information access is also a critical feature of the NII's digital libraries and government information services [6, 7].

Real-time control is the basic feature of traffic control in the Travel and Transportation Management bundle, and on-board safety inspection is a real-time control feature of commercial vehicle operations and collision avoidance. Real-time control is also needed in other information infrastructures, such as manufacturing [4], but is more critical in ITS situations, because of safety.

Decision making is the basic feature of incident management in the Travel and Transportation Management group, ride matching and reservation in the Travel Demand Management group, and public transportation management in the Public Transportation Operations group. Decision-making is also needed in manufacturing and health-care information infrastructures. However the degrees of intelligence and sophistication of decision making may differ in various application domains.

The ITS information infrastructure requires real-time information access. Transportation information, such as weather reports and traffic conditions, is time-sensitive. In addition, ITS services must control traffic efficiently and make decisions about situations quickly. For example, emergency-handling is a difficult decision-making process, covering areas ranging from traffic accidents to weather emergencies. The circumstances surrounding some emergencies may be complex. Moreover, the transition from human decision-making using local information exchange (e.g., local police emergency databases) to semi-automated decision making based on a large-scale ITS information infrastructure will be slow and perhaps difficult.

In metropolitan areas, sensors (e.g., video cameras) and monitoring systems are set up at key locations. These systems must have active information processing; i.e., they must be automated and intelligent (see the section on intelligent agents for more detail). As soon as sensory data are captured by the systems, they should be extracted into useful information and relevant portions collected remotely at regional offices for quick control and decision making.

Active sensing and monitoring requires intelligent information processing techniques, such as image processing, pattern recognition, and artificial intelligence. For example, electronic tolls and vehicular speed monitoring can become fully automated by implementing active sensing and monitoring systems. Furthermore, intelligent information processing will significantly reduce the bandwidth overload in telecommunications networks, because processed information, not raw data, is sent over them.

Wireless communications will play a major role in ITS. As the current cellular technology moves from analog to digital, the ITS information infrastructure will bring a significant impetus to the development of wireless communications technology. Wireless communications will be used in various NII applications, such as healthcare, manufacturing, and distance learning. However, the TII's requirements for wireless communications will be much more stringent than other wireless requirements due to high-mobility and real-time multimedia applications.

NII and ITS Challenges

The ITS information infrastructure is a complex hierarchy of heterogeneous, networked information systems. Federal, state, and local government and private-sector information systems will be implemented locally, regionally, and nationally, forming a confederated information system. Unlike federated information systems, these systems are loosely coupled with diverse formats, and often present large interoperability and integration issues.

ITS requirements are compatible with other NII activities, but do place additional demands on the NII technological base. The following outlines suggestions for meeting the requirements of ITS deployment:

1. *Further develop ITS system concepts.* The following features of ITS have yet to be developed fully: information access, real-time control, decision making, active sensing and monitoring, wireless communications, and confederated information bases. The challenge here is to develop innovative basic research results within the

context of ITS by funding ITS research and continuing to build prototype ITS systems [3, 6]. For example, although the technical approach of intelligent agents has been developed [3, 4, 5, 9], its relation to the ITS system has not been fully explored.

2. *Demonstrate new technological results.* The technological demonstration closely follows innovative research on system concepts. Technology transfer from basic research results to implementation will be crucial to the successful deployment of ITS. In turn, industry needs to demonstrate that ITS capabilities can capture the interest of the marketplace.

3. *Integrate government and private-sector efforts.* ITS services encompass the needs of both the public and private sectors; thus ITS deployment depends on the integrated efforts of all parties. What are the policy issues of integrated efforts? Should integration be bottom-up or top-down? What incentives should the federal government provide to state and local governments and the private sector? (Other chapters in this volume discuss these issues more thoroughly.)

4. *Develop international standards and protocols.* ITS products will compete in the global marketplace, and must incorporate international standards and protocols. A significant effort should be made to both participate in international standards development efforts—and coordinate these efforts with domestic technology planning and development.

ITS requirements place demands on the NII technological base, and can push the development of NII technologies and capabilities. In particular, the systems-level integration of diverse technological areas will push current system integration technology, which will be sharable with other NII activities. Similarly, advancing the wireless communications industry will lead to new markets for new technologies, and real-time control and decision making will become useful to other industries such as healthcare and manufacturing, to augment the expertise of physicians in hospitals and engineers on factory floors. Active sensing and monitoring and wireless communications will become essential to electronic commerce and other NII activities to facilitate flexible and dynamic fieldwork not bound by wireline communications.

Intelligent Agents: A Key Approach to the ITS Information Infrastructure

Users of the TII will access and navigate through the networked information space to collect information and to make decisions. Transportation systems staff will control and manage ITS information, including mechanical systems—toll collection, traffic control, emergency management, etc.—that rely on the ITS information infrastructure. Intelligent, interoperable software and middleware hold the key to ITS deployment. Their experimental implementation in an ITS testbed should be a top priority of federally funded research and development programs. Intelligent agents offer one possible approach.

Intelligent agents are smart software systems that serve as go-betweens for incompatible hardware, software, and data components (see [3]). sense, receive, and process data into useful information. Agents can also make decisions and execute them onto the external environment.

An intelligent agent can be thought of a suite of software components (see Figure 1). An intelligent agent understands and interacts with the external environment because it can reason, learn from experience, or make decisions. As a whole, intelligent agent suites can carry out each of the ITS requirements described in the last section.

Software components in an intelligent agent suite are modular and reusable. The *input and output components* are software elements that interact with physical data-acquisition devices, such as sensors. These devices are connected to mechanical equipment and systems in ITS. The input component monitors external events and transmits data packets to other components. The output component transmits processed data (e.g., control and decision data) to the external world. Because the volume of data packets will be huge, a software component, called the *feature extractor*, finds patterns in data packets and collects information based on data packet patterns.

Collected information needs to be organized into prioritized information for decision making. Thus, another software component, called the *classifier*, identifies functionalities and sets priori-

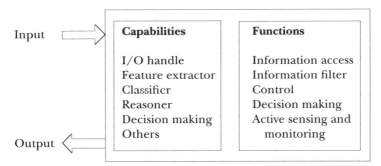

Figure 1 Intelligent Agents.

ties of collected information (prioritized information requires further processing in order for it to be used by ITS management systems). A software component, called the *reasoner*, understands prioritized information and follows rules set by transportation authorities to generate decisions. The decisions generated by this intelligent system could be executed to solve problems, control traffic, and manage situations.

ITS requires intelligent agents of many types. First, intelligent information-access agents will access various user services. These intelligent information-access agents will have the capabilities to help users retrieve answers to their questions, and filter in and out information from a large data pool. Second, intelligent control and decision-making agents will manage and make real-time informational decisions on vehicles, highways, and incidents in order to serve ITS users, operators, systems, and enterprises. Third, intelligent sensing and monitoring agents will gather information from ITS mechanical components and will communicate necessary information to ITS information components (e.g., regional offices) remotely.

Intelligent Agents and the ITS Information Space

The information space in the TII is made up of different multimedia information resources, including databases, knowledge bases, information repositories, and bulletin boards. Users of the TII may browse, navigate, and search through the information space to collect information and solve problems. Characteristics distinguishing the ITS information space from other NII information spaces include:

• Greater real-time information requirements

• Information is mostly spatial data (e.g., maps)

• Sensor-intensive

• Communications are mostly wireless and computing is mostly mobile

• Control and management require decision-making, rather than just access.

Consequently, ITS information processing requires richer information content (i.e., meanings or interpretations of information), not just organizational identifiers (i.e., names, types, and meta-information fields). This is because control and decision making are heavily content-based, and identifiers are not significant enough bits of information to process ITS data.

Intelligent Agents and Sensor Technology

ITS deployment depends on sensor and actuator technology. Actuators are mechanical devices, such as the automatic gate of a toll booth, that are controlled by humans or computers. Information processing for sensors and actuators will be bidirectionally linked to the TII. Information processing systems will collect the essential information from incoming data packets and transmit them to the intended ITS database .

For example, a monitoring video camera may acquire the speeds and license plates of passing cars at a particular highway location. However, information processing only extracts the information it needs; it can discriminate between speeding and nonspeeding cars, and will only send the critical information (which cars are speeding) to the remote ITS regional office. Thus, only essential information is transmitted along communications links, and communications bandwidth requirements are limited.

Intelligent sensing and monitoring agents can provide this information-processing capability through the use of signal and image processing, pattern recognition, artificial intelligence, and neural network techniques. Therefore, essential information rather than full video can be transmitted, and fiber-optic links to all the ITS communications routes may not be necessary.

Intelligent Agents and Interoperability

Interoperability is compatibility among subsystems at specified levels of interactions. This is achieved by a prescribed set of rules and protocols. Interoperability allows diverse subsystems to communicate with each other so that any service will be transparent to its users. However, interoperability means more than the (hardware or software) compatibility among different vendors; it also means the compatibility among different applications, services, and data environments.

ITS presents interoperability issues in each of these areas. Standardization is an obvious remedy, but a large number of legacy systems and formats still exist, and even new formats are being implemented with only local and regional requirements in mind. Achieving interoperability requires standardizing ITS system interfaces.

In an information infrastructure, there are four essential system interfaces: Information appliance-to-network, information appliance-to-application, application-to-application, and network-to-network [8]. Information appliances include such items as smart TVs; personal, palmtop, and laptop computers; high-end workstations; and supercomputers, many of which can be interfaced with one another.

A system interface is a software connection between two subsystems that can be specified in logical (message format and exchange procedure) terms. The interface specification provides system information and parameters for how subsystems communicate with each other. In particular, a data format system interface is a "transformation" (a computer parsing program) that reformats incoming information into the designated internal format. In ITS deployment, transformation will become a tedious problem. Diverse information bases of transportation products, federal, state, and local government information systems, and user groups may require interoperability.

There will be many data format interfaces needed in the ITS deployment. Standardization of each ITS system and its components will eliminate the number of different information formats. However, intelligent interface agents will still be needed to integrate standardized system components.

Intelligent Information Access, Control, and Decision-Making Agents

The traditional means of querying databases and information systems is through a menu-driven screen. This allows the user access to only a finite amount of information. Browsers and navigators, with their use of hypertext and links, allow users to obtain far more information, which accounts for the tremendous popularity of the Mosaic and Netscape browsers.

Intelligent agents have been constructed to conduct a search relying on pattern recognition and matching techniques [5, 9]. For example, a user's interests can be built into an agent that will filter incoming information and present only the kind of data that the user will find relevant or interesting.

Intelligent Electronic Payment Agents

Electronic payment agents must be developed to bill users for ITS services. Incorporated with sensors and computers, these agents will carry out the work of human operators at toll booths and elsewhere. There will be many new ITS functions executable by intelligent eletronic payment agents-these might include payments for travel and transportation management, public transportation, and other information services.

The security and privacy issues of ITS user services can be compared to those in electronic commerce. Although users may abuse ITS services in the same way they abuse long-distance telephone services, ITS applications have sensing and monitoring devices that can physically capture the abusers' license plate numbers, car types, and facial features.

A simple transactional identification card for ordinary users may help to alleviate the problems of ITS system abuse. This effort and others like it will establish an efficient billing system. However, implementors must continually consider user privacy when designing them.

Conclusions

The ITS information infrastructure offers excellent opportunities to push the NII technological envelope. Because ITS' impact on the U.S. economy and on the society as a whole can be significant, federal, state, and local governments and the private sector should collaboratively develop a long-term vision and policy to support the research and development of the ITS information infrastructure. Due to the potentially large investments and development involved in ITS deployment, the time frame, and a strong understanding of the technical issues is important at this planning stage.

The complex and dynamic nature of ITS will require intelligent software. One may ask whether ITS will be managed completely by intelligent agents. Of course, the answer is no. Intelligent agents will support human operators. Agents can limit the need for transportation personnel to monitor the several hundred simultaneous video images that may be captured on a given roadway, but human intervention will still be required to manage and respond to crucial situations that are identified by intelligent ITS technology.

References

1. L. M. Branscomb and J. H. Keller. "An NII Primer." Background paper, Workshop on ITS and the NII, Kennedy School of Government, Cambridge, MA, July 1995.

2. E. J. Carpenter. "Intelligent Transportation Systems (ITS) User Services." Preliminary Draft, Volpe National Transportation Systems Center, June 1995.

3. S. Chen. "Spatial Mental Models in Cognitive Systems." *Fundamenta Informaticae*, Vol. 18, 1993, pp.183–192.

4. S. Chen. "The Role of Information Infrastructure and Intelligent Agents in Manufacturing Enterprises." *Journal of Organizational Computing*, 1995, Vol. 5, pp. 53–67.

5. S. Chen. "Agents and Objects: Enterprise Integration and Representation." In preparation.

6. S. Chen. "Technologies for Digital Libraries." Proceedings Digital Libraries Conference: Moving Forward into the Information Era, Singapore, National Computer Board, March 1995.

7. S. Chen. "The NSF/ARPA/NASA Research on Digital Libraries Initiative." Proc. Digital Libraries Conference: Moving Forward into the Information Era, Singapore, National Computer Board, March 1995.

8. Computer Systems Policy Project. Perspective on the National Information Infrastructure: Ensuring Interoperability. Washington, D.C., Feb. 1994.

9. *Communications of the ACM*, Special Issue on Intelligent Agents, 1994, Vol. 37, pp. 18–149.

10. E. A. Fox, Ed. *Source Book on Digital Libraries*. December 1993.

11. "FCCSET/OSTP, HPCC: Toward a National Information Infrastructure." A report by the Committee on PMES, 1994.

12. B. Kahin and J. Abbate, Eds. *Standards Policy for Information Infrastructure*. MIT Press and Harvard Information Infrastructure Project, 1995.

13. B. Kahin and J. Keller, Eds. *Public Access to the Internet*. MIT Press and Harvard Information Infrastructure Project, 1995.

14. U.S. Department of Commerce, "Putting the Information Infrastructure to Work." Report of the Information Infrastructure Task Force Committee on Applications and Technology, 1994.

15. U.S. Department of Transportation and ITS America. National Program Plan for Intelligent Transportation Systems (ITS). Final Draft, Nov. 1994.

Global Interoperability for the NII and ITS: Standards and Policy Challenges

Valerie Shuman and Richard Jay Solomon

Introduction

The National Information Infrastructure (NII) today is a grab bag of technologies and organizations that have evolved for a myriad of different purposes over the last century and a half. From the first telegraphs, which began as adjuncts to the early, fragmented steam railroads, to today's mix of analog and digital public switched telephone systems, private data networks, and complex arrangements for use of radio spectrum, no master plans or national objectives have ever existed for a coordinated, optimized infrastructure to serve the population's electronic information needs—nor is it likely that this infrastructure will ever exist. Networks, by nature, are messy. Interfaces between differing transmission channels, capture and storage devices, and user appliances tend to depend more on optimizing the specific characteristics of a physical component than on applications or the needs of compatibility or anticipation of future technologies or uses.

The transportation system is a similarly messy set of networks, with different transportation modes, jurisdictions, and extensive existing infrastructure. The situation is becoming rapidly more complicated by the recognition that enhanced physical infrastructure is no longer the only key to solving transportation problems. This realization has led to the development of Intelligent Transportation Systems (ITS), which seek to make the current transportation network more effective by applying advanced technology to transportation. Information is becoming increasingly crucial to the transportation process, whether it is used by commuters to save time on their daily trips to work, traffic managers to handle accidents effectively, or freight logistics planners to move goods efficiently.

The intersection between the ITS and NII networks creates major challenges of coordination and integration, especially in the area of standards. This chapter will discuss the issues and current standards-setting work in both the NII and ITS forums, concluding with a set of suggestions for next steps in this area.

The Relationship between ITS and NII

In an ideal world of transparent communications, a truly seamless information network would include everything from simple email to complex financial or medical transactions. This network would be accessible at all times, whether the user were at home, in the office, or in a vehicle traveling to a business or leisure destination. Allowing "anywhere, anytime" access, however, is a complicated problem. The ITS goal of integrating communications and transportation can offer an important part of the solution by providing the mobile outlet for the NII information network.

Adding a mobile capability to the NII enables a host of applications. The consumer in motion could be more productive by using time spent in the car or on mass transit working electronically with direct and transparent connections to the office LAN or the World Wide Web. Public safety applications such as ambulance services could be enhanced by the transmission of medical records en route to the hospital. Almost every NII application, from Education to Entertainment, would be accessed by the mobile user.

Interaction between ITS and NII benefits both networks in other ways as well. The market for information and services could be dramatically expanded, for example, if more people could be given access to use these services more of the time. In the same way, economies of scale on hardware and software may help to drive down costs and increase the size of the market for both ITS and NII.

Technological development will also benefit from synergies between the two networks. The increased demand for integrated solutions will fuel research, and the transfer of solutions from one community to another can have favorable results for both. ITS work on an in-vehicle LAN, for example, may be an ideal platform for general NII communications and computing technologies. Similarly, NII work to integrate multimedia communications networks could provide a basic backbone for ITS communications.

ITS as a terminus for the NII does impose some basic requirements. Mobile communication is the most crucial; all mobile applications must use wireless technology, and the accompanying protocols and internetworking will need to be compatible with both wireless and wireline networks. ITS also requires a suite of universal abilities, such as prioritization, security levels, and addressing that may be expanded and extended to support all of the new users. In addition, national and international roaming may be demanded by the user groups for many of the applications. Such international compatibility may bring improvement in economies of scale.

Practical implementation of such systems will require intensive standardization work at all levels. Coordination between NII and ITS standardizers is crucial to avoiding misfits and redundancy between the two networks.

Standards Issues

Standards are key to the deployment of networked, interoperable systems. Without such standards, systems simply cannot communicate, or will require extensive customization work at every junction. In either case, the instant, the easy information access that is the end goal of the NII may not be possible.

Such standards are important not only for interoperability, but also for international competitiveness. Products and systems must be compatible, but they must also be usable in the global technology market. Products that are incompatible or require extensive modifications for use will inevitably give way to those that can interact successfully. For example, the European GSM cellular system, which in addition to air interface capabilities allows interworking with data, charging, and paging networks, has been well-accepted worldwide, in contrast to other alternative cellular standards.

Standardization of cutting-edge technology and techniques is inherently difficult because of the pace of change in today's information industry. Products are outdated almost before they are released. Instant obsolescence is an accepted fact. The traditional method of setting standards, which usually has been a multi-year process, simply does not work in such a dynamic environment. It is necessary to develop new, or at least dramatically accelerated, procedures.

Institutions at all levels, from the International Standards Organization (ISO) and International Telecommunication Union (ITU) to the U.S.-based Telecommunications Industry Association (TIA) and the government, are working to meet this challenge.[1] The ITU's work on communications standards for ITS, for example, is being handled under a special arrangement that encourages international coordination throughout the year on a joint standards contribution (a cooperatively written document which contributes to work on the final standard). Traditionally, individual countries develop separate contributions to a given standard, and these contributions are reconciled once a year during a two-week special session. Joint work allows more time for negotiations and encourages cooperative rather than country-specific solutions. Similarly, a recent change in the ISO Directives has mandated more rapid completion of standards by all ISO Technical Committees, and sets aggressive limits on the amount of time allowed for the development of committee drafts and full draft standards.

Standards-making is complicated by the fact that it is an intensely political business. It is often said that writing a good technical standard is the easy part; getting all the parties to agree to it is the difficulty. Companies that participate in industry standards often have a great deal at stake: If an adverse decision is made in the standards process, their products may suddenly become unmarketable, and valuable time may be lost in reengineering them. Countries involved in standards negotiations may have concerns about economic development—for instance, whether they will lose or gain jobs or industry. This competitive aspect makes it much harder to write standards, and can create immense delays.

Another institutional issue that arises in standards development is responsibility. Decisions must be made about who should develop and maintain standards. Ongoing maintenance is especially important in high tech fields, as standards, or portions of them, can become outmoded very quickly. This is an expensive process, however, and requires an extended, continuous effort that is very difficult for both governments and private standards organizations to maintain.

In spite of these obstacles, standards for cutting-edge technology are set and implemented constantly. The Internet is a key example of standards that worked, and its evolution offers lessons for developers in both the NII and ITS. The Internet incorporates sufficient hooks (code that will recognize certain generic data types for functions not specified in the original programs) and evolutionary practices so that different applications, networks, and devices can communicate without prohibitive configurations and barriers.

The Internet as a Model for Standards

The Internet, per se, does not exist as an entity. It is no more than its name implies: a set of protocols connecting computer networks to one another. Indeed, it is sometimes described as "a network of networks." The Internet basically consists of just two sets of protocols, or computer algorithms, that handle transmission and interconnection over disparate and noisy channels of any type. Together, these protocols are known as TCP/IP, or "Transmission Control Protocol/Internet Protocol." The Internet Protocol (IP) sets up a *virtual* connection between machines, determines the path for the connection, and handles the address details, including address translations—the so-called IP address. The Transmission Control Protocol (TCP) controls the actual traffic flow, providing both the human user and client machines with what appears to them to be a robust and error-free path for streaming bits, even over paths that contain inherently poor circuits.

Up to now, the maintenance of the protocols, addressing tables, etc., have been handled by volunteer organizations consisting primarily of the user community; This is changing with the commercialization of interconnection, backbones, Internet Service Providers, and other operational features. Just how the Internet will evolve is an open question.

The Internet follows a store-and-forward, packet data communications architecture, whose form is different than that of the switched telephone network. High-speed packet switching can minimize packet delays so that they are imperceptible for most applications. Alternatively, this delay can be exploited to guarantee delivery whether or not the recipient device is connected to the Internet at the time the data is generated. While this system has less first-order efficiency compared to networks optimized for one application (say, duplex, real-time voice, or broadcast media), this relative lack of efficiency must be balanced against the high level of robustness built into the two basic protocols and the incredible gain in trunk-route (or backbone) efficiency by maximizing circuit sharing. The Internet protocols accomplish this via sufficient intelligence in the control process, making it flexible enough to handle a range of uses from electronic mail to telephony and different types of video. These protocols are constantly being modified, and the next generation is expected to have stronger priority controls making interactive services, such as full-scale voice telephony, feasible. Furthermore, efforts are underway to create direct interfaces between the Internet's control system and protocols and those of the public switched telephone network, perhaps migrating eventually to a transparent or seamless set of data and telephone systems.

The important points to remember about the Internet as a concept are:

• The Internet is not a physical or unitary *thing* (not yet, at least). It is what its name implies: internetworked computer appliances. There are many "internets": Many interconnected networks use the underlying Internet protocols (TCP/IP) for connectivity, but may not be directly connected with the Internet.

• The Internet is delineated by its interface protocols. It has not been delineated by its corporate structure (it has none, so far), its tariffs (currently determined by cost of access to network access points), physical routes (it uses whatever is available, public or private, selected by a mix of customers, carriers, and other vendors), or boundaries (whatever device or application connects, using the Net's accepted protocols, becomes immediately part of the Internet—for that slice of connect time).

• Internetting is primarily software-driven. The software for connecting, routing, and controlling data flow is embedded in the operating systems of the connected computers.

Why Does the Internet Work?

The Internet approach has been successful both because of the technical strength of its protocols, which are flexible enough to accommodate both existing and emerging systems, and because of key institutional strategies.

• *Media independence.* The TCP/IP protocols have been designed to facilitate error-free data connections over virtually any kind of physical communications network—dial-up telephone, private digital and analog broadband circuits, satellites, radio, etc.

• *Interoperability with other protocols.* TCP functions within other protocols, such as ATM (Asynchronous Transfer Mode) fibers and wire pairs, Ethernet and LocalTalk/AppleTalk LANs, and also over the public switched telephone network (PSTN) with the use of optimized dial-up synchronous protocols such as SLIP, PPP, and AppleTalk Remote Access. Operating entities are now offering IP/ Signaling System Seven interfaces, which permit the Internet to directly dial up PSTN numbers and vice versa. Some industry watchers are predicting that Internet traffic will exceed PSTN voice traffic by the year 2000; in any case, it is likely that the Internet and the telephone network will merge, but just how this will happen is anyone's guess right now.

Similarly, IP can carry other low-level transmission protocols or be embedded in them. (It is expected that IP will eventually map or merge into other digital communications systems, such as ATM. IP interconnects almost any bitstream with anything, over anything, unlike dedicated interconnection mechanisms like television signaling, which only connects TV transmitters to TV sets.

• *Technical robustness.* IP by itself is a very unstable, unreliable connection architecture, but with TCP it can interconnect almost anything. With TCP, the user appliance perceives IP as super-robust, and therefore one can easily build in ultra-reliability with a suitable congestion mechanism (pricing, for example). TCP provides this robustness via its built-in redundant features: automatic alternate routing, multiple simultaneous connections, scaleable bitstreaming, content independence, and flexible use of IP addresses. No test data is available (i.e., no one has yet compared TCP/IP to PSTN and published verifiable results), but in principle, TCP/IP should be more robust than the PSTN, though this is a complex question with complex answers.

• *No cost to the user.* A key consideration in the implementation of any standard is cost. These interface protocols have been bundled free of charge into Unix, the operating system used on most hosts, since the mid 1980s. Microsoft has bundled the protocols into Windows 95 for client/server systems, and Apple's MacOS already has public-domain software for this purpose.

• *User-driven.* The Internet protocols were developed in response to user needs and are flexible enough to develop in concert with emerging user requirements.

The Internet approach does not have all the answers. Addressing is still a difficult question for the next-generation IP (IPng). Interfacing address schemes for interworking with global PSTN numbering plans is a potentially great financial opportunity. However, it is also a major bone of contention in telephony because the money made will be diverted from the telephone companies. IPng will also have provisions for priority transmission and other components that may hasten the acceptance of the Internet as a basic transmission mode. Yet another open question is how the Internet access points and backbones will be financed.

The Internet approach does demonstrate the crucial role of interface standards. Robust, flexible, and accessible interface standards that render intersystem connections transparent to the user are basic to the successful development of "networks of networks" such as NII and ITS.

ITS and NII Standards

Communications standardization for both NII and ITS also involve another major challenge: multi-industry coordination. The computing, communications (both wireline and wireless), electronics, entertainment, and transportation industries are all involved, and this makes discussions very difficult. Each industry speaks its own language, and has its own sets of concerns and areas of expertise. Arranging for industries to work together is a formidable project, yet if they fail to coordinate, it will not be possible to develop standards that take all of their needs into account.

One of the primary barriers to such coordination is the disparity of knowledge areas. Computer engineers rarely study the mechanics of wireless data transmission, and transportation engineers— outside of the railroad industry—have previously not needed to understand the complexities of communications protocols. The resulting Tower of Babel can cause endless delays and confusions, as both sides struggle to learn enough to communicate with each other. (It may be of interest that railroad engineers worldwide understand a common language surrounding signaling and communications, despite different implementations on almost every railroad system. There is a great deal to be learned from that effort, since many complex problems of safely controlling, communicating and interfacing with moving vehicles have been solved with extremely sophisticated and robust systems during the century and a half of rail transport design.)

Similarly, both ITS and NII cover broad ranges of applications. NII has seven major application areas: Health Care, Manufacturing, Education, Entertainment, Electronic Commerce, Environmental Monitoring, Governmental Information and Services, and Libraries. ITS has even more: ITS America has identified 29 user services, and ISO TC 204 has formed 16 Working Groups (see Table 1) that handle everything from electronic toll collection and digital map databases, to traffic management and advanced vehicle control systems. Yet most of the applications for both NII and ITS will coexist on the same communications networks and require common schemes for security, priority, addressing, and the like.

The problems of creating emergency service applications highlight this issue. Calls for help, whether they go out over cellular, wired phone, satellite, PCS, or any other medium, must be universally recognized as priority calls and routed to the appropriate responding agency. Similarly, commonly agreed-upon levels of security will be necessary to safeguard confidential communica-

Table 1 ISO TC 204 Working Groups

WG 1	System Architecture
WG 2	Quality & Reliability
WG 3	Database Requirements
WG 4	Automated Vehicle Identification
WG 5	Fee & Toll Collection
WG 6	General Fleet Management
WG 7	Commercial Freight
WG 8	Public Transport/Emergency
WG 9	Transport Information Management & Control
WG 10	Traveler Information
WG 11	Route Guidance & Navigation
WG 12	Parking Management
WG 13	Man Machine Interface
WG 14	Vehicle Road Warning & Control
WG 15	Dedicated Short Range Communications
WG 16	Wide Area Communications

tions regarding the location of police officers or the details of a patient's medical record. In each of these cases, standards must be system-wide.

The NII, with its vision of universally interlinked communications, could be the ideal forum for such standardization—but only if planners recognize the multimedia scope of the future system, which includes wireline and wireless networks around the globe.

Current ITS and NII Standards Efforts

Standards efforts are well underway in both the NII and ITS communities, although there are no standards development efforts that are explicitly organized to bridge the gap between the two. For a certain set of standards, this is not a problem. If the communications community successfully develops internetworking standards for selected media, for example, the ITS community benefits because better communications become available, without the need for further interaction. There are areas, however, in which it is vital that there is interaction so that the requirements of both communities are taken into account. A wireless communications standard developed without the ability to prioritize messages, for instance, is of limited usefulness to developers of advanced ITS emergency applications.

Although formalized integration is largely absent at this point, information technology and transportation standards are quietly coming closer together in a number of fora. ISO TC 204 is a good example of this situation. TC 204, as mentioned above, was created in order to develop international standards for ITS, and its standards in progress cover the spectrum from system architecture to advanced collision warning systems.

TC 204 also covers a variety of topics not traditionally considered transportation standards, such as wide-area and short range communications systems. WG 16 (Wide Area Communications) is working toward the development of a protocol header that will act as an interface between the communications medium and the ITS application that uses it. Common priority, security, and addressing options will be provided such that ITS applications can choose an option and be sure that it will be valid no matter what media their information travels over. WG 15 is going even farther and developing standards for an entirely new form of communication: the short-range vehicle-to-roadside beacon.

WG 3's work with digital map databases is another good example of a transportation-related information technology standard. WG 3 is developing standards for data transfer, location referencing, update publishing, and physical storage of these large and complex databases. The resulting standards will impact the databases, the means of accessing and manipulating the data, and any service provider who adds to or builds on these databases. They may also serve as a model for the handling of other massive databases being developed to support the NII's function as librarian and information provider to the nation.

These standards efforts, and others like them, are an important step towards creating the standards required to enable the mobile component of the NII. They are, however, part of another problem: that of coordinating existing standards work. There are hundreds of committees working at national and international levels around the world, as well as industry consortia and other less formal groups (see Figure 1). Failure to organize around a clear set of needed standards results in wasted efforts and conflicting standards that may not take all of the stakeholders into account.

There are a variety of efforts underway to solve the problem of coordination of standards bodies. These efforts include the U.S. DOT Federal Highway Administration (FHWA)'s ITS Architecture and the ANSI Information Infrastructure Standards Panel (IISP) project on Standards Needs. The FHWA Architecture is intended to provide a framework for the collection of ITS systems which are being implemented in the U.S. The Architecture will make it possible to pinpoint interfaces where standards are necessary. Standards development organizations will then write standards to meet the identified requirements in a coordinated fashion overseen by the FHWA and ITS America. Applicable standards will be contributed to the international standards process.

The ANSI IISP project also involves the identification and coordinated development of standards, but uses a request-driven system to collect the standards needs rather than an overall architecture. User groups and other participants in the IISP process submit needs statements, which are sent out to the standards development organizations for review. Where there are no existing standards which meet the stated need, new ones will be developed.

There are pros and cons to both of these approaches, and the real world result may not be as perfect as the stated plans of either group. Both efforts, however, demonstrate awareness of the need for coordinated efforts across standards bodies, and make an attempt to resolve this issue.

Required Standards

In order to create a truly "anytime, anywhere" communications network and the applications that accompany it, an incredible variety of standards are necessary, covering everything from individual media to overall interfaces. As in the case of the Internet, however, there are a few basic interface standards that can enable the entire system. In the case of ITS and NII, these may include:

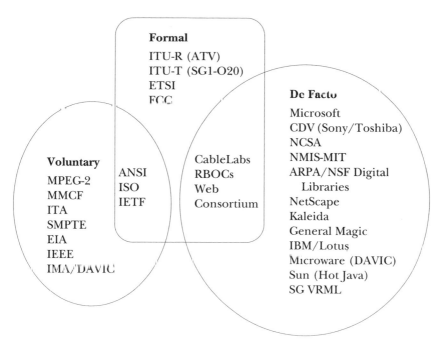

Figure 1 Proliferation of Multimedia Standards Developing Organizations (Developed with the assistance of Lee McKnight & Suzanne Neil, Research Program on Communications Policy, MIT.)

• *Universal security scheme.* While it is impossible to develop one security program that will solve the entire network security problem, it is possible and important to agree on levels of security for the entire network. These levels may be implemented in any number of different ways, but information and applications will be handled in a consistent way throughout the system.

• *Universal priority scheme.* Similarly, many different priority implementations may exist, but it is important to agree on basic levels of priority throughout the network.

• *Universal addressing mechanism.* Addressing, as mentioned in the section on the Internet, is a very complex problem. The addition of millions of roaming mobile units complicates it still further. This problem must be solved for both mobile and non-mobile users.

• *Universal header.* All of the above mentioned requirements might be handled by a universal header, which could present the most basic information about the data string it accompanies in a consistent format.

• *Mobile interfaces.* Many of the networks under discussion as the backbone of the NII are land-line (e.g., cable and telephone). Standards for mobile interface with NII applications must be set.

• *Latency standards.* There must be some way of setting consistent, end-to-end transmission times through the NII. Transportation data is particularly sensitive to this requirement. Traffic information, for example, is only valid for a short time—if it takes too long to move through the system, it is not useful.

Suggestions for Creating ITS/NII Standards

If standards for NII and ITS are to be developed successfully, there are a number of key actions and decisions that must be taken. The role of government is important here, especially considering the global competitiveness issues involved. This section will first outline suggested actions for creating communications standards, then focus specifically on governmental roles in implementing them.

• *Coordinate NII and ITS committee efforts.* As mentioned above, there is an immense proliferation of committees in both programs, covering a very broad range of often overlapping topics. Current ITS efforts, for example, are taking place at ASTM, CEN, IEEE, ISO, ITU, NEMA, SAE, and TIA. Work on communications requirements should be coordinated to prevent duplication of effort and disconnects. This last is particularly important, in view of the current NII focus on wireline communications and the ITS requirement for wireless communications.

• *Take advantage of existing work.* The communications field is developing very rapidly, and new standards are being released constantly. It is very important to identify and understand applicable existing and emerging standards and use them whenever possible. Cross-pollination is key here—wireless networking and architecture standards may be the solutions to wireline problems. Such mixing and matching is not easy, but it is crucial to efficient standards-making.

• *Focus on a core set of universal standards.* Issues such as security, priority, and addressing are basic to all communications, and complex networks require them to be handled in a standardized way. These standards requirements are most important at interfaces between systems and networks; therefore, it is key to identify and examine such interfaces. Approaches might be as simple as a common header format that references specific standards and thus identifies itself to another device, or as complicated as universal usage of a single comprehensive standard for each one of these requirements.

Governmental Roles

The role of government in the standards development process is evolving, much like the standards process itself. The government can be an important resource, but its participation also has fundamental limitations. The best model seems to be for government and industry to work together, with each filling in the gaps left by the other. While this cooperation can be very difficult to achieve because it can add another layer to the competitiveness and bureaucracy of standards-making committees, the byproducts of working towards such a goal have great potential.

In some cases, this cooperation occurs in a stimulus/response fashion. The government has the regulatory power to mandate standards, and industry is often willing to collaborate internally in order to influence such mandates or react to emerging rules. The recent FCC ruling on location information for cellular 911 calls is a good example of this. A Notice of Proposed Rule-Making (NPRM) that called for location information of increasing accuracy to be provided over the next five years sparked intense industry activity towards a workable, common solution. In this case, the government did not seek to set technical standards but instead set a requirement that encouraged technology and standards development.

Government also controls key resources, which makes it a central player in some standards decisions. Radio spectrum is one of these; spectrum allocations, whether by auction or ruling, impact both national and international technical standards for radio equipment. Private-sector standards development must coordinate with governmental actors in this area or face technical obsolescence due to changes in radio regulations. National cooperation is equally important for international negotiations: Private industry may be working in the ITU to set a global standard that is dependent on a certain frequency, at the same time that government is changing U.S. allocations because of pressure from another source. This may adversely affect the international competitiveness of American products.

Government could also be proactive about ensuring spectrum for key projects, as well as coordinating among industries. ITS efforts, for example, could be more closely coupled with FCC endeavors in reallocating underused UHF TV spectrum to new, digital uses, and parallel efforts in PCS and other cellular radio work. Similarly, a truly portable and cost-effective communications system would help extend ITS applications to the user; a vast amount of information would then become available to optimize transport. The best mechanism for achieving this interoperability would be to coordinate the unique characteristics of transport interfaces with those of telecommunication standards.

Another governmental resource is monetary and personnel support of standards work. Overseas governments leverage this capability by funding standards development teams, which then submit their work to both national and international fora, and by offering administrative support for standards work. In the U.S., private industry usually shoulders this burden, which often results in disproportionate influence from well-funded companies and haphazard support for standards activities due to a dependence on volunteer efforts. This problem is exacerbated in international standards work, which often necessitates expensive travel or video conferencing, as political negotiations are still best done face to face. Government is in a position to support U.S. work in this area by contributing funds and personnel to key efforts. A recent example of such support is the U.S. FHWA's contribution of $16 million towards the development of standards for ITS.

A major concern in the area of government support, however, is consistency. Political climates change frequently, and the budget ax can eliminate entire governmental departments overnight. It is very difficult to maintain an effective presence in the standards arena without a consistent effort over time.

Another problem with government involvement in standards is the speed of technical change. Private industry is on the cutting edge of research in today's accelerated markets, and it can be difficult for outsiders to stay abreast of fast-moving developments in the laboratory. Internet standards can be developed and implemented in a single week! In this case, private industry can be better qualified to contribute to standards development, although the key experts are often too valuable to their companies to be released for such work.

In spite of these difficulties, government/industry collaboration can yield major benefits. The government has an important role to play as a catalyst for standards development and coordinator of national policy. Effective public-/private-sector cooperation will strengthen the American position in global product and job markets.

Conclusion

Standards development is a complicated and difficult process at best. Creating standards for compound networks such as NII and ITS is even more challenging. Coordination among the myriad national and international standards-developers and vested interests in the various affected industries is a daunting task and there are no guarantees of success.

Successful standards bring a host of benefits, from enabling applications to reducing costs to consumers and product developers. The Internet demonstrates the value of establishing basic standards that are responsive to user requirements. These standards have served as a foundation for the development of revolutionary applications with major societal implications in a very short time. The Internet paradigm for standards development also serves as a possible model for NII/ITS standards.

Failure to create fundamental standards that address issues such as mobile security, priority, and addressing for both the NII and ITS will inevitably slow the expansion of both systems and will prohibit the development of beneficial applications in both arenas. It is crucial to take advantage of the considerable momentum in these industries to work towards underlying, mutually enabling standards. Serious, long-term efforts will be necessary to develop effective standards for the NII, with its focus on communications and information services, and ITS, which depends on effective mobile connections. It is important to begin discussion at all levels of both communities on methods for realizing this goal.

Note

1. ITU and ISO are separate international standards organizations. ITU is a UN treaty organization which gives it legal status in member countries. Final ITU documents are officially treaty-level agreements between countries, although countries may choose to except themselves from any given agreement. ISO, on the other hand, is based on voluntary compliance from its member countries. Some countries mandate compliance with ISO rules, while others do not.

Geospatial Data for ITS

Stephen J. Bespalko, John H. Ganter, and Marsha D. Van Meter

Introduction

In his chapter, "Common Policy Concerns," Stephen Lukasik points out:

Thus, while *traffic* and *vehicles* are a central concern of ITS, *information* is the central concern of the NII. The overlap of ITS and NII arises because traffic, in and of itself, constitutes a form of information, and information of a wide variety is needed by travelers. As its name implies, ITS is a set of transportation *systems*, whereas the NII refers to an information system *infrastructure* within which those transportation systems operate.

To take this idea a step further, ITS systems as well as systems designers require a wide variety of information to make their projects powerful and effective. This chapter begins by discussing specific examples of how the current information components of transportation systems are insufficient for advanced applications, such as ITS. The projects discussed in this chapter demonstrate that transportation technology can be hampered by lack of adequate spatial data.

Spatial data is an essential component of transportation infrastructure. Currently, however, it falls outside the scope of either the NII or the ITS. Given that all of the systems examined here are either impossible to deploy without better spatial data, or have been designed to compensate for a lack of spatial data, it is clear that the designers are doing the best they can with the technology and information at their disposal. If ITS goals are to be achieved, there is a need for a strong federal role in developing a national system for gathering and maintaining up-to-date geospatial data.

Overview

Transportation research and development at Sandia National Laboratories has been primarily technical in nature, involving computation, high-volume spatial data management, and communications as applied to the management of vehicle fleets carrying special cargoes. Recently, it has included a project to design and prototype a "next-generation" Geographic Information System (GIS) that can manage both historical and new data sources and forms. The intent of this project is to provide the information technology needed to support the spatial data infrastructure that advanced transportation projects require.

Briefly, a Geographic Information System is a relational database manager specialized for handling spatial data. In a Relational Database Management System (RDBMS), information is stored in tables that are linked in an intuitive way. GIS products tend to be an additional layer "on top" of a commercial RDBMS. The GIS then provides applications programmers with operations useful for analysis on the spatial data stored in the underlying RDBMS. One example would be the ability to define basic graphic entities common in spatial analysis and to manage the storage and retrieval of these entities, which are referred to as points, lines, and polygons. Another example would be the ability to compute the areas of geographic features stored as polygons.

Two issues presented here are the need for vastly improved digital maps, or "representations" of the surface transportation infrastructure, and the relative abilities of public and private entities to create and maintain such representations. These issues are illustrated with examples of current and anticipated advanced transportation projects that would benefit from, or clearly require, considerably better data than is currently available from public entities, which are usually state departments of transportation.

Defining "improved data" is central to the arguments presented here. The current body of spatial data used for transportation applications is for the most part, digitized (or computerized) two-dimensional maps. At typical scales, buildings are represented by dots, squares, or occasionally groups of lines. Roads are typically represented by a single line or possibly polygons. The roads are then differentiated with various attributes such as state or federal designations, direction, or road type. From these data, simple maps can be generated that display the attributes with symbology such as color, shape, and pattern.

Sandia's work to implement a prototype of the next-generation computer system to manage spatial information indicates that this two-dimensional digital map metaphor is inadequate for many applications. More specifically, applications, including those defined by the ITS program, could be greatly improved with a three-dimensional, object-oriented model.

Because today's GIS systems grew from attempts at automating maps, current GIS data models begin with one or more two-dimensional coordinates. Abstract map elements like buildings or roads are constructed by adding descriptive attributes such as color or line thickness to sets coordinates. Programming these systems is awkward and error-prone because users are primarily interested in manipulating these abstract entities. The ability to define abstract objects such as roads would benefit the programs by permitting them to manipulate complex geographic features, thus making the programs more robust and easier to write.

For example, transportation applications programmers would benefit greatly from the ability to define an object called a "road." This object could include many properties useful to transportation systems designers. One of these properties is how the road is rendered on a two-dimensional map at a particular scale; another includes the detailed path the road follows on the surface of the earth. Most of the advantages of Sandia's intended design follow from either the inclusion of the third dimension of data, or from the object orientation of the software we will use to program the system.

Three-dimensional data models represent driveable areas as thin articulated surfaces. Such linear surfaces would be coaxial and branching. For instance, two side-by-side "ribbons" would represent two lanes, and at some point additional lane(s) or ribbons would branch off. Other ribbons would run above or below to represent bridges, underpasses, etc. So by "three-dimensional object-oriented representation" we mean a representation that is neither a single surface nor a volume, but one that is suited to the unique geometries (shapes) and topologies (connections) of transportation infrastructure.

Who will design, construct, and maintain these new data representations? Many of the state Departments of Transportation (DOTs) and regional organizations (county and city governments, metropolitan planning organizations [MPOs]) are far behind other organizations (both public and private) with respect to being part of the "information revolution." Paradoxically, entities that build and maintain infrastructure for their constituents are the logical "owners" of representations, but often the least able to take on this responsibility due to fiscal limitations and short-term political pressures. Bringing these organizations into the ITS realm as both promoters and users of this advanced technology is therefore critical to the overall success of the advanced transportation program in general.

This raises important policy issues. Foremost, whose interest is being served by investing in technology (e.g., increasingly elaborate spatial referencing schemes) that will clearly be suboptimal in the near future? Too often, transportation systems designers go out of their way to use low-accuracy data because it is easy and cheap to acquire. Instead, it is possible to build ITS and other advanced transportation systems with the same basic CAD data used for designing the roads.

The remainder of this chapter will be divided into four sections. The first section will cover some of the background of how the spatial data evolved into the current technology. The second section will explain the data requirements of the typical state DOT in more detail; this will be the basis of subsequent discussion of the alternatives for promoting the state DOT participation in advanced transportation initiatives. We will also describe the recent Pooled Fund Study, which was the method used by the states to create a common technical strategy for adopting the federally mandated ISTEA systems. Although considerably less ambitious than the advanced transportation projects described in this chapter, the

Pooled Fund Study is a good example of how federal transportation policy can be used to stimulate significant technological change at the state level. Third, we will describe several advanced transportation projects, paying particular attention to data requirements. The last section discusses the implications of these new technologies for the advanced transportation projects. We will conclude by considering the opportunities for federal policy intervention to influence the introduction of new ITS technologies.

Background: Transportation Geospatial Data at Local and State Levels

Geographic Information Systems for Transportation (GIS-T)

State DOTs have varied histories, which helps to explain the very different spatial information systems that have evolved in each. Because information systems (IS) is a relatively new discipline with few formal methods, particular systems almost always reflect the personalities of those who have founded and developed them. Thus, state DOTs and similar regional organizations have different hardware, software, data formats, data structures, spatial references, etc., sometimes within the same agencies.

Nonetheless, most state agencies utilize data management systems specialized for managing spatial data, a technology known as "geographic information systems for transportation" (GIS-T). GIS-T supports specific applications such as corridor planning, property valuation and condemnation, environmental impact analysis, and a variety of permitting. GIS-T systems are also used for regional transportation planning, where census data are used to develop growth projections and predictions of commuter traffic.

To understand the flow of information within a typical state agency (and ultimately why the states will have a difficult time supplying the data needed for advanced transportation systems), let us consider the information used to design and build a road. First, planners use GIS-T to determine the rough outline of the road corridor. Next, they use it to supply rough outlines to computer-aided design (CAD) systems in the engineer's office. CAD then creates detailed, multidimensional models in which volumes of cut-and-fill, pitches of drains to carry off rainwater, and similar minutiae are designed and tested before any concrete is poured.

At this point the "flow" of data and information begins to divide and disintegrate as drawings and plans are lost or rendered useless; this is because deviations from these plans are mandated by information discovered during construction. The GIS-T and CAD systems are now used to produce large paper plans that are carried into the trailers where construction is overseen. When construction begins, plans are marked up and modified. Later, "as-built" drawings, which are themselves often lost as they become construction afterthoughts, are created to capture the final configuration for future maintenance efforts. The roadway goes into operation with a loose or non-existent connection to its past design (where underground utility lines run, what concrete batches went where) and its future (traffic volume counts for lanes).

GIS-T thus tends to be employed as a short-term operational tool, rather than a long-term, cradle-to-grave management system. It is typically comprised of data of varying scales, collection methods, and lineages. "Metadata" (data describing data) that quantify and track the collection over time seldom exist. The highway begins to age like a car whose owner's manual and service log have been discarded. Just as unfortunate, the very information that is lost would enable many of the advanced transportation projects discussed later in this chapter.

Engineers use high-quality data to design highways. However, most subsequent business applications tend to use the least amount of data possible (and often degrade existing data) to achieve short-term goals. When viewed from a global or enterprise perspective, or from the standpoint of implementing ITS, this is clearly a costly and technically unnecessary approach.

Linear Referencing

The maintenance and operational groups in state DOTs have become adept at using the low-resolution, and usually inaccurate, data that are made available to them. In fact, most if not all of the state DOTs have developed methods that reduce their information requirements to one-dimensional data. This is done through a method called linear referencing.

In linear referencing, the locations of features are established in "odometer space" relative to some starting point. An example would be: "The lane extends from 8.2 miles to 8.7 miles west along Rt. 7, based on a starting point at Rt. 7 and Rt. 4." As this example suggests, an intersection is a typical starting point, but problems can arise with consistency and ambiguity; e.g. which side of an intersection is the starting point, determining consistent names for intersections, etc. Even if milepost or other markers are installed, a change in the highway can invalidate the system.

Linear referencing alone will not serve more sophisticated transportation systems such as those defined for ITS. In addition, individual states probably will not benefit fully, at least in the short term, from more powerful location referencing systems (such as GPS) if they continue to focus on linear referencing. Therefore, it is doubtful that the states will see much immediate direct benefit from the introduction of new representational and transportation technologics. They will have to want to adopt more sophisticated methods and technologies for other reasons.

In some cases individual departments in state DOT operations groups have developed referencing systems to suit their purposes. For example, the Florida state DOT has a project underway to combine its current 14 linear referencing methods into a single generalized method. Although this project will definitely improve this DOT's ability to share data between the various groups in the department, it will do very little to prepare it for the requirements of advanced transportation projects. Other technologies such as GPS will, in the very near future, be capable of providing the same information derived from linear referencing systems but at less cost and with significantly greater accuracy. Further, since GPS data is part of a global coordinate system—that is, the locations are in relation to distance from the center of the earth—the data from one locality can easily be combined with GPS data from another.

Examples of Advanced Transportation Projects

Below are several examples of advanced transportation projects. In each case, the two-dimensional data currently being used is suboptimal, and better designs can be achieved through use of three-dimensional data.

Analyzing projects destined for the short term (1–2 years out), medium term (5–10 years), and long term (20–30 years out) will dispel the perception that the introduction of high-resolution, three-dimensional data is only advantageous for projects planned for deployment in future decades. In each example the application of three-dimensional data improves or enables the respective technology.

Short Term: The GIS-T/ISTEA Pooled Fund Study

The Intermodal Surface Transportation Efficiency Act of 1991 (ISTEA) is the most recent response to the challenges of providing efficient, safe, and environmentally sensitive transportation. Among its many new initiatives, the ISTEA emphasizes the need for intermodal connectivity, establishes new requirements for cooperative transportation planning decision making, and explicitly recognizes the need for formal systems to manage pavements, bridges, highway congestion, highway safety, public transportation facilities and equipment, intermodal facilities, and to monitor highway traffic. These new policies define the requirements for a new generation of information technologies supporting transportation management decision making. The Congress and the U.S. Department of Transportation intend that these technologies are integrated, synergistic, and comprehensive.

The Pooled Fund Study represents the first national cooperative effort in the transportation industry to address the management and monitoring systems as well as the statewide and metropolitan transportation planning requirements of the Intermodal Surface Transportation Efficiency Act of 1991 (ISTEA). The Study was initiated in November 1993 through the Alliance for Transportation Research and under the leadership of the New Mexico State Highway and Transportation Department. Sandia National Laboratories, an Alliance partner, and Geographic Paradigm Computing, Inc., are providing technical leadership for the project. This Study demonstrates how the federal government can promote the assimilation of new technology into the fifty separate state DOTs (although its future is in question given the current thinking on unfunded federal mandates).

A principal goal of the Pooled Fund Study's design team is an integrated information and systems structure. The design is also intended to be extensible as new requirements are identified, and could engender a new mode of state DOT organization and efficiency. If achieved, it would be a radical departure from current practices, including the institution of a cradle-to-grave approach to infrastructure and the associated information management.

A key component of the integrated systems design is the inclusion of a general linear referencing system intended to serve as a *de facto* standard. If adopted, the system would enable all state DOTs to maintain one set of linearly referenced data with a formal method of "transforming" one system into another. The methodology is to maintain an underlying "reference system", or method of maintaining spatial coordinate data representing the location of all elements in the transportation infrastructure, that is of sufficient generality and spatial resolution to "map" one coordinate system to another.

While the study has been successful in demonstrating coordinated information management and integration, the two-dimensional data to which these processes have been applied is insufficient to achieve the studies technical objectives. Without going into the mathematical details here, the goal of arbitrary transformation between coordinate systems is, in general, impossible using two-dimensional data. Although the transformations are possible within reasonable approximation in most cases, the errors introduced into the data by ignoring elevation are not always negligible.

With current two-dimensional systems, the error can be accommodated to a certain degree by using techniques that "adjust" the data where errors are judged to be too large. An alternative is to simply store the data needed to provide the ability to maintain an arbitrary level of accuracy or precision with calculations involving spatial data. Analysis underway at Sandia indicates that only a minimal amount of data is required to analytically eliminate errors created by coordinate transformation. The modern relational database management systems (RDBMSs) and even more current object-oriented databases (OODBMSs) appear capable of dealing with the additional data needed to solve this problem.

A second area where three-dimensional data will help achieve the goals of the Pooled Fund Study is in providing cradle-to-grave transportation management. As stated earlier, the information flow required for a road's design, construction, and maintenance currently goes through several transformations. The engineers already utilize highly detailed three-dimensional data in CAD systems, which are then discarded when the construction phase is completed. Given the emerging transportation applications where these data would be useful, it would be highly appropriate for the data to be stored and maintained in the system. Various applications could view this data in an appropriate format. In this way the degradation of road design information described above would be reduced or eliminated.

The problem with maintaining this data in a three-dimensional format is that virtually none of the state DOT business applications (at least those in areas other than engineering) are capable of benefiting from it in the short term. The consumers of the data largely will be outside of the state DOTs, and in some cases clients will not exist for years or even decades. Because data are so expensive to re-collect, it is unlikely that data will be collected in the first place unless an immediate requirement for it is identified. Unless the state DOTs shift to longer-term thinking, it is unlikely that the data will ever be available for potential advanced transportation projects.

Medium Term: Initial ITS

Intelligent Transportation Systems will use technology to reengineer our transportation infrastructure into one that maximizes safety and efficiency and minimizes harmful environmental effects. There are 29 ITS user services defining the six main systems in advanced transportation: Advanced Traffic Management Systems (ATMS); Advanced Traveler Information Systems (ATIS); Advanced Vehicle Control Systems (AVCS); Commercial Vehicle Operations (CVO); Automatic Vehicle Location (AVL); and Automatic Vehicle Identification (AVI). These 29 ITS user services will monitor and control traffic on highways and streets, giving travelers specific routes to follow, supplementing drivers with autopiloting, improving the efficiency of commercial vehicle deliveries, and eliminating the need for weigh stations and toll collectors. Several of the these systems' components are dependent upon geospatial data. For instance, route guidance, vision enhancement, and automated vehicle operation are some of the user services in which current two-dimensional geospatial data is clearly inadequate for the design and deployment of safe, robust technology. Each example is described in more detail below.

Route Guidance. Route guidance will provide users of private and commercial vehicles, as well as pedestrians, with real-time transportation information. The service will display a suggested route to help a user reach a specific destination, taking into account traffic conditions such as congestion and road closures. Information about roadway networks and transit schedules will be available in the early implementation stages.

Current route guidance applications use planar technology, which is unable to identify changes in elevation. This is sometimes a problem, especially near bridges and complex intersections like cloverleaves where the computer interprets the coincident road segments as being on one plane (i.e., having connections where none exist). For example, the current GIS technology may mislead the user by asserting that the bridge and the road beneath it are, in fact, an intersection. It is possible to manually circumvent this problem, but it is not always effective with more complex bridges and intersections or with large urban areas. By using the third dimension, the data model now incorporates an elevation coordinate and is able to discriminate between the non-planar or overlapping road segments. This system will distinguish the bridge and road as two separate objects.

Route guidance technology also will benefit from spatial data that are organized in an object-oriented manner. Current GIS programs have great difficulty when encountering different modes of transportation. Because all elements of the transportation system are represented by the same points, lines, and polygons it is very difficult to represent the difference between modes like railroad tracks, streets, bicycle paths, and subway routes. A route guidance system, like current planning models based on GIS data, frequently makes the error of routing a car onto a railroad track and pedestrians down a subway route. Today, this is corrected by manually tagging the different modes with database attributes that can be translated into humanly readable symbology such as color, line width, and graphical patterns. With object-oriented technology it is much easier and significantly less error-prone to identify the routes as being strictly for trains, people, etc.

Vision Enhancement. Vision enhancement, or the projection of information on vehicle speed, direction, proximity of other vehicles, and roadside information, would be a desirable service during adverse weather conditions, and possibly while driving on congested urban freeways. Current prototypes of vision enhancement systems utilize low-power radar and object-recognition technology to provide information to the driver. The drawback of these designs, however, is that the quality of the information available to the driver is likely dependent on the traffic conditions. For example, because all of the information is deduced in real-time by the object-recognition system, if there are too many vehicles around the driver's car the information about the vehicle path will be questionable.

A potentially stronger vision enhancement technology would incorporate a three-dimensional model of the road. Assuming that the currently expensive technologies for sensing vehicle orientation could be fused with this road model, the vision enhancement could become independent of the traffic conditions. In this new scheme there would be a constant projection of the road on the windshield (a "heads-up display"). This projection would let the driver view the road and other important information such as road signs that are difficult to see in the best of circumstances on busy freeways. In addition, this new technology could aid a driver to accurately distinguish turns and elevation differences.

Long Term: Advanced ITS

Automatic Piloting. Various alternatives exist for automatic piloting of vehicles. The less ambitious plans call for "platooning," or coordinated driving of cars to increase throughput on urban freeways, while the long-term goal of complete autopiloting is probably attainable in the 30–40-year horizon. Ultimately, a rider could simply indicate a desired location and the vehicle would drive there. In either case, however, there are benefits derived from the availability of the high-resolution geospatial data described here.

Current designs call for the auto-piloted or platooned vehicles to have dedicated highway lanes strictly for their use. These vehicles would then be controlled by magnetic nails implanted into the pavement about every 100 feet. The vehicle would turn a specific direction when polarity, as detected from the nails, changed.

Control systems based on this design reduce the piloting problem to two components: a two-dimensional lateral control problem, and a one-dimensional longitudinal speed-control system problem. Further, current designs also depend on the assumption that the special lanes would only be used on divided highways like interstates, where the designer can make many simplifying assumptions about the topography that will be encountered. The interstate systems have well-specified and standardized designs for most characteristics of the road, including maximum pavement grades, lane widths, and turn radii. The advantage of this construction from an ITS designer's point of view is simplicity. In practice, it is unclear how well these systems will work.

The magnetic nails give only approximate information about what to expect in the way of directional changes in the road. The main problem is that the telemetry derived from the nails is discrete; information is only available several times per second. Humans, by comparison, are able to use a continuous stream of information to judge when and how much to change the direction of the vehicle. At best, systems based on the magnetic nail designs will be reliable, but probably are not going to be able to achieve the smoothness of a human driver.

Here again, a three-dimensional data source would lead to a much stronger design. The magnetic nails can be used to determine speed with a very high degree of accuracy, and location with a fair degree of accuracy. The three-dimensional model would be used for refining the location data and for very precise preview calculations—in other words, to predict when changes in the road direction will occur. A system with these components would be able to achieve the smoothness of a human driver. Further, with the three-dimensional spatial data, it may be possible to operate these vehicles on more complex roads, rather than just interstate highways.

Robust geospatial representations, based on three-dimensional data and unconstrained by linear referencing systems, would be enabling for many applications in the transportation arena. Cradle-to-grave management systems that collect and preserve data throughout the lifespan of physical infrastructure could be created. User services like those discussed above, which depend on an omniscient view of locations, destinations, and moving objects, would become possible.

The Federal Role and the Future of ITS

The alternative to the largely unregulated ITS, which is focused on the surface mode of transportation, is the highly regulated aviation industry. The agency responsible for oversight of commercial aviation is the Federal Aviation Administration (FAA). The FAA has long been heralded for the unprecedented safety of the nation's air transportation system. On the other hand, the FAA has also been widely criticized for being a cumbersome bureaucracy. The most recent example of this criticism comes from the FAA's being perhaps a decade behind in updating the air traffic control (ATC) computers. This complaint is well-justified. No commercial enterprise would survive a decade of delay in upgrading its fundamental information technology. In fact, most of the calls for privatization stem from the FAA's inability or unwillingness to upgrade its computer system.

In spite of the FAA's inefficiency, however, the advantage of its highly centralized authority is that Americans' trust in the commercial aviation carriers is extremely high. The rules and regulations established by the FAA covering aviation technology and airline operations are clearly in the best interest of the flying public. While only a tiny fraction of the traveling public understands the complex operations of a modern jetliner, most Americans never give a second thought to boarding a plane operated by a commercial carrier.

Thus, while it is true that certain parts of the FAA's own operations could likely be better operated by private companies—the administration of the air traffic control system is the most visible example of this—the balance between public and private interests is the key to maintaining safety while achieving efficiency. It is unlikely that the oversight function, which is the keystone of the public's trust, could be relinquished without serious degradation of public confidence in the system.

Two areas for expanded federal activity in ITS are coordinating state activities, and defining and measuring program success. A key weakness in the overall structure of both the NII and the ITS is the lack of measurable technical goals. Without quantified targets it will be difficult to allocate resources to either project. Although there are fairly concrete and specific goals for protocols, software, and hardware interfaces, there is a lack of direction with respect to measuring the public benefit derived from these complicated and expensive systems. Thus, the possibility exists for the project to be a technical success but not publicly accepted—or worse yet, a commercial success but missing obvious opportunities to serve the public good. Even if all of the other technical issues are surmounted, how will it be possible to bring individual states, who are often happy using out-of-date technologies such as linear referencing, into the information revolution? It may well be impossible to implement many of the more advanced ITS features until a time when there is a federal legislative mechanism for propagating a common set of technologies to the states.

The 10 "stakeholder implications" (see Table 1)—the design goals that were used to gain approval for the program—from the early IVHS documents (e.g., U.S. Department of Transportation and IVHS America, 1994) need to be continually re-examined. Are these goals being met? Although it may be difficult to clearly quantify the degree that ITS serves the public good in such areas as equity, institutional empowerment, and privacy, the effort still needs to be made. The public interest must be protected by establishing a technical direction, then periodically assessing the results to assure that we are equitably benefiting from our investment.

One cause of uncertainty about the goals of both the NII and the ITS is an apprehension about mandating a strong federal role in either project. This uncertainty is a major threat to both projects. Federal authorities have a broader vision than essentially all of the

Table 1 IVHS Stakeholder Implications

Deployment:	Impact on the rate of IVHS deployment
Equity:	Effect on the distribution of benefits and costs
Financing:	Impact on financing deployment, operations and maintenance
Institutions:	Impact on institutions and organizations
Market:	Effect on the development of an IVHS market
Operations & Maintenance:	Impact of operating and maintaining IVHS
Policy & Regulation:	Effect on implementing current and setting future policies and regulations
Privacy:	Effect on the privacy of individuals and organizations
Safety:	Impact on transportation system safety
Standards:	Effect on current and future standardization efforts.

Source: U.S. Department of Transportation and IVHS America (1994).

participants in these high-technology projects, and certainly the need for substantially improved spatial data is one example of where vision is needed to provide this missing component of the transportation infrastructure. It is vitally important that the federal agencies involved in high-tech initiatives do not rescind their roles as visionaries. Would we have an interstate, or more accurately, a *national*, highway system if our government had not taken a lead role in the 1950s? Similarly, government participation will likely determine the ultimate success of both the ITS and the NII, as well as other high-technology initiatives that are yet to come.

Suitable policy must be implemented to ensure that the goals of the ITS do not, in the long run, hinder advances that are currently infeasible but well within the realm of possibility; these technologies include Route Guidance, vision enhancement, and automatic piloting. There will be considerable pressure, not from the public, but from private investors, to limit investment (or R&D) to get products to market in as short a period as possible. This will clearly limit the complexity and power of products and services coming from the ITS community. In addition, care should be taken to ensure that the consensus designs that emerge for the ITS standards do not preclude the introduction of future ITS applications. Treating three-dimensional spatial data as part of the transportation infrastructure and the importance of a third party to establish the safety and effectiveness of transportation technology were presented as two examples of the need for strong federal leadership in the development of advanced transportation projects. Although the technical advances in NII and ITS are impressive, they still require a careful, wise, and comprehensive design and planning process if society is to benefit from them. In order for our ultimate goals—a safe, efficient, and environmentally sound transportation system—to be attained, it is essential that policy lead technology rather than the other way around.

Acknowledgments

This work was supported by the United States Department of Energy under Contract DE-AC04-94AL85000. We also acknowledge Ray Byrnes for his insights on ITS technologies.

Bibliography

"Coming in for a Landing." *Scientific American*, April 1995.

"Catching that Wave." *Scientific American*, April 1995.

"Mortal Combat." *The Wall Street Journal*, May 5, 1995, p. 1.

Bauman Foundation. *Agenda for Access: Public Access to Federal Information for Sustainability through the Information Highway*. Washington, D.C.: The Bauman Foundation, January 1995.

Byrne, Raymond H. *Robust Lateral Control of Highway Vehicles*. Ph.D. Thesis, University of New Mexico, 1995.

Burkholder, Earl F. "Using GPS Results in True 3-D Coordinate Systems." *Journal of Surveying Engineering*, Vol. 119, No. 1.

Carpenter, E. J. "Intelligent Transportation Systems (ITS) User Services: A Discussion of Information Service Content." Harvard University (Center for Science and International Affairs), Preliminary Draft, 1995, pp. 5–6, 31–33.

Fenton, Robert E. "IVHS/AHS: Driving into the Future." *Control Systems*, Vol. 14, No. 6, December 1995, pp. 14.

Fletcher, David R., Thomas E. Henderson, and John Espinoza Jr. "The GIS-T/ ISTEA Pooled Fund Study: An Integrated Approach to Transportation Planning." Proceedings of the Fifteenth Environmental Systems Research Institute [ESRI] User Conference, May 1995. Published on CD-ROM and World Wide Web: *http://www.esri.com/resources/userconf/proc95/to200/p166.html.*

Hendrick, J. K., et al. "Control Issues in Automated Highway Systems."

Control Systems, Vol. 14, No. 6, December 1995, pp. 21

U.S. Department of Transportation and IVHS America. *IVHS Architecture Development Program: Interim Status Report.* April 1994.

Public and Private Roles

Shared Resources Policies and Highway Rights of Way

Thomas A. Horan and Susan Jakubiak

A common requirement for both Intelligent Transportation Systems (ITS) and the National Information Infrastructure (NII) is the provision of adequate wireline communications capacity to allow for transmission of information. In particular, an important point of intersection between ITS and NII communications deployment is in the laying and utilization of fiber-optic cable along highway rights of way (ROW). This paper reviews issues associated with "shared resource" projects that aim to utilize both public- and private sector resources in the procurement and operation of fiber-optic capacity along highway ROW.

We start with an overview of ITS systems architecture that will provide a rationale for understanding the physical architecture expectations for ITS wireline communications and highlight the institutional dynamics that help explain how state departments of transportation (DOTs) have become involved in this aspect of telecommunications provision. We then examine different forms of shared resource projects and show how methods of valuation can inform public- and private-sector decisions to pursue such projects. We conclude with a discussion of the relationship between shared resource project objectives and larger ITS and NII goals.

ITS National Systems Architecture

The ITS National Systems Architecture initiative provides a useful point of departure for considering the role of shared resources in achieving ITS/NII goals. This effort, undertaken by the U.S. Department of Transportation (USDOT), will provide an overarching logical and physical architecture for ITS user services as well as deployment guidance for various public and private providers.[1] While the final architecture is still being refined, its major components have been established and have direct bearing on both the deployment of ITS and its expected impact on related NII deployment.

By way of introducing these architecture attributes, Figure 1 distinguishes three layers of architecture design: transportation, communications, and institutions.[2] There are several implications to this conceptual approach, most of which also relate to principles of the NII.[3] First and foremost, by including an institutional layer in the national ITS architecture, we give explicit attention to how ITS adheres to existing institutional relationships. While these relationships can be fairly complex, it is necessary to understand the extent to which institutional arrangements in the transportation sector affect the deployment of ITS communication systems. As authorized in Title 23 of the U.S.C. and related acts, transportation policy involves a collaborative relationship among the USDOT, state DOTs, metropolitan planning organizations (MPOs), and a host of other transit and transportation properties. In particular, state transportation agencies typically play a central role in planning, programming, and operating the nation's highways, streets, and transit systems.

The most recent reauthorization of this legislation—the Intermodal Surface Transportation Act of 1991—reinforced the importance of having the state DOTs conduct comprehensive transportation planning as a precondition to the use of federal and related transportation funds. Within major metropolitan areas, the legislation also called for MPOs to play a pivotal role in deciding the best use of transportation funds for their respective regions. While the nature and range of these legislative requirements are beyond the scope of this paper, they do underscore an important point: The current funding and regulatory framework in surface transportation encourages state DOTs—and to some extent MPOs—to take a strong role in ITS and related technological deployments. This point is key when considering the institutional dynamics surrounding ITS/NII shared resource projects.

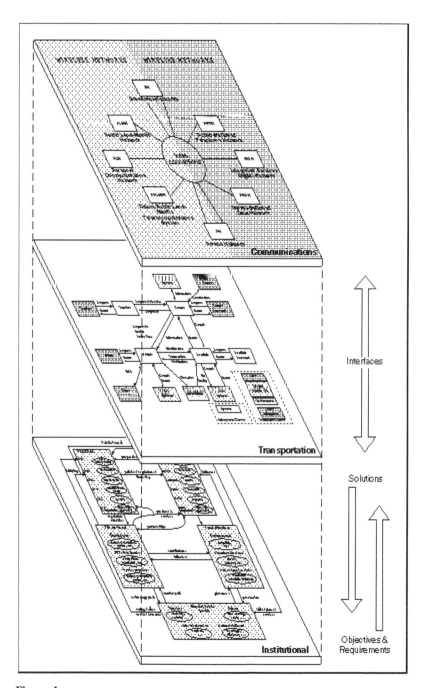

Figure 1

The existence of an institutional layer in the ITS national system architecture also highlights the roles played by the private sector. As has been delineated in various ITS plans and reports, the private sector is expected to lead the development of ITS products and services. For example, the ITS Strategic Plan notes that 80% of the total program costs are expected to be borne by the private sector.[4] And in this sense, the national ITS architecture can be seen as reinforcing the expected role to be played by the private sector, including the provision of communications infrastructure.

While the institutional layer provides vital parameters for understanding how ITS technologies can be deployed, the core analytical product of the National Architecture effort is the logical and physical architecture for ITS. Figure 2 contains a prototype (for Texas) of the physical architecture that is emerging as the national ITS architecture analysis. The figure highlights 17 subsystems across four subsystem locations: center(s), roadside, vehicle, and traveler/remote access. The "center" subsystems pertain to the various traffic and transportation management centers that will compile, integrate, and disseminate information. These centers are expected to rely mostly (though not exclusively) on wireline communications to link themselves to data sources in the roadside (e.g., traffic video and sensors). Wide-area wireless is expected to provide the communications backbone between the vehicle and the center subsystems.

While the physical architecture partitions ITS user services into subsystem centers, it does not fully convey how these systems are expected to unfold over time. Consequently, the third major aspect of the ITS/NII architecture is an implementation strategy. This will lay out a plan for incremental implementation of core ITS features, and provide guidance for various levels of government on how ITS funds should or could be invested. Thus, choices made on "core" ITS infrastructures can have implications for related NII communications needs and capacities.

While the details of this plan are still being refined, it is clear that a fundamental component will be utilizing knowledge of institutional dynamics to ensure timely early deployment of key systems and services.[4] This suggests the need to (1) understand the roles of public-sector agencies and private-sector companies in providing

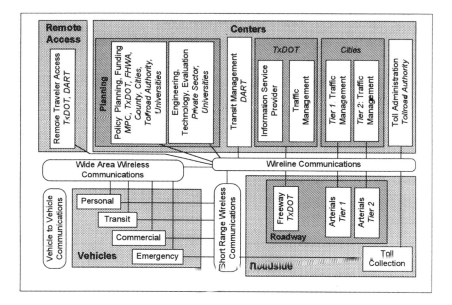

Figure 2

and maintaining a communications infrastructure and (2) use that knowledge to promote private involvement, thus leveraging public financial assets.

In many ways, early shared resource projects exemplify the types of deployments that would be consistent with the emerging national ITS architecture while also having implications for NII deployments. The balance of this chapter reviews such shared resource projects in order to increase understanding of how localities have come to value and enter into public/private ventures. Special attention is given to how different projects' objectives can affect larger ITS/NII goals.

Shared Resource Projects

For the purposes of this chapter, and as generally used by transportation and telecommunications professionals, the term "shared resource projects" refers to sharing public highway ROW, previously viewed as entirely within the public domain, with private telecommunications companies for the installation of telecommunications hardware. Although initially conceived as a way to foster ITS deployment, shared resource projects can support several compatible objectives:

• providing telecommunications infrastructure and/or services for ITS with minimum public-sector expenditure

• providing telecommunications infrastructure and/or services at minimum cost for a broader range of public-sector services (including non-transportation needs)

• expanding overall telecommunications capacity to support NII and generally stimulate economic development

• generating revenues that can be used for public-sector needs

These objectives are not mutually exclusive. Additionally, shared resource projects undertaken for broadly oriented goals such as NII and economic development can also support more narrowly defined objectives such as telecommunications for ITS. Project objectives, however, will shape any given shared resource project; that is, project objectives will influence participants' project choices. These choices may be between an exclusive partner and many partners (the latter presumably being more conducive to NII and general economic development), or a relative emphasis on in-kind compensation versus monetary compensation (the latter being generally less efficient in achieving the first three objectives in the above list).

Traditional and Shared Resource Arrangements

There are four "templates" for sharing the public ROW for telecommunications services. Two of these can be considered "traditional" arrangements:

• *Public-sector utility.* The public agency installs and owns telecommunications facilities in the public ROW and provides private parties with capacity on the system to in exchange for periodic fee or lease payments.

• *Conventional utility.* The public agency allows the telecommunications company access to highway ROW without direct compensation of any kind. The private vendor sells or leases telecommunications capacity to the public sector for ITS and other telecommunications services.

Two can be considered shared resource arrangements:

• *Barter arrangement.* Private party installs telecommunications capacity (conduits, fiber optic lines, and/or electronic equipment), receiving access to the ROW or conduits in return for providing telecommunications infrastructure to public ROW owner.

• *Cash arrangement.* Private party installs telecommunications system for own use, receiving access to the ROW or conduit(s) in return for monetary compensation to public ROW owner.

Strictly speaking, a pure public utility—the first template—is not a shared resource project because there is no partnership per se. However, a hybrid public utility in which private provision of telecommunications infrastructure is exchanged for discounted private rates on the public system or private marketing franchise for system capacity would be considered a shared resource arrangement. Similarly, template two (conventional utility) is not generally considered a shared resource arrangement because no compensation is given to the ROW owner.

Templates three and four (barter and cash arrangements) are shared resource arrangements, as are hybrids of these basic formats; that is, they are partnerships involving private cash payments in addition to provision of telecommunications capacity (barter plus cash). More precisely, a shared resource project is a specific form of public/private partnering that is characterized by:

• Private longitudinal access to public roadway ROW (or public-sector conduits in the ROW).

• Installation of telecommunications hardware (principally fiber-optic lines but also including cellular towers).

• Some sort of compensation to the ROW owner over and above administrative costs.

Shared resource projects can be initiated for a number of reasons. As will be discussed below, they can often spring from a transportation-sector need to obtain ITS services at favorable rates. However, they can also arise from broader public-sector interests in obtaining a range of telecommunications services (for example, distance-education communication requirements). And, at the most general level, they can come from states' desires to encourage communications deployment.

Issues and Examples of Shared Resource Projects

Recent shared resource projects involving state DOTs, special-purpose public authorities, and/or municipalities have been undertaken in Missouri, Maryland, California, New York and Florida; general policies have been articulated and/or exploratory steps are underway in other states such as Massachusetts and New Jersey. The formats differ according to the legal and statutory constraints applicable in each jurisdiction and according to public and private partner preferences. The partners have addressed the following issues in different ways:

Resource shared—the ROW itself or telecommunications infrastructure within the ROW.

Type of compensation—barter, cash payments, or a combination.

Exclusivity—single private partner or several partners.

Responsibility—for relocation, system modification, and legal liability.

Table 1 contrasts five recent examples of shared resource projects.[5] Two projects that have received a high level of national attention are the Missouri and Maryland initiatives. In terms of *resources shared,* both transportation agencies have granted private telecommunications firms access to the ROW for installation of fiber-optic conduits and lines. In return, the agencies are compensated in kind; that is, they receive their own fiber-optic lines and telecommunications equipment to "light" the fiber for public-sector needs. Missouri receives, in addition, maintenance services for the duration of the partnership.

While shared resources and compensation in Missouri and Maryland are quite similar, the motivation and usage of the shared resource projects are quite different. In the case of Missouri, the bartered communication service is specifically geared to the state's backbone ITS requirements. In contrast, the communications

Table 1 Comparison of Shared Resource Project Characteristics

Case	Resource "Shared"	Mode of Compensation	Exclusivity	Responsibility for: Relocation	Repairs
Maryland DOT	75 miles along I-95 selected by bidders	Barter only	No	Shared	Party responsible for damage
Missouri Highway Department	1,300+ mile inter-city backbone defined by state	Barter only	Yes	Public partner	Party responsible for damage
Ohio Turnpike	Bidder-defined segments	Cash with option for in-kind (services)	No	Private lessee	Party responsible for damage
Bay Area Rapid Transit (CA)	Full 100 miles of BART system	Cash (Caltrans receives barter and cash)	Yes (for marketing)	Shared	Private partner
Leesburg, FL	32-mile fiber optics backbone	Cash	Yes (for marketing)	Probably city (not addressed)	Party responsible for maintenance

services available to Maryland are being more broadly construed for their potential application to a host of transportation and non-transportation uses.

In other cases, the resource shared is the conduit as opposed to the ROW. This is the case for both California's Bay Area Rapid Transit (BART) project and the Leesburg, Florida, initiative. In the former case, a private company served as an exclusive broker (to telecommunications companies) for leasing space in a conduit owned by BART. In the latter case, the city acts as a public utility, leasing space within its own conduit.

As suggested by the Missouri and Maryland projects, barter is often the preferred mode of compensation; in both cases no cash payments are involved. DOTs characteristically cannot earmark cash receipts for the projects they nominate for funding. Indeed, at a recent focus group of state transportation representatives, compensation was raised as a key complication in potential shared resource projects.[6] Barter arrangements can also be an appropriate strategy for those localities that have identified specific service objectives (e.g., ITS/NII deployment) that can be furthered through such non-cash agreements. An exception to this is the Iowa shared resource project. Iowa revised its accommodations policy to permit private companies to access freeway ROW for a cash occupancy fee. Since 1990, three private firms have taken advantage of this to install fiber; Iowa does not receive any in-kind compensation and is, in fact, installing its telecommunications network at its own expense.

In contrast, special-purpose agencies such as turnpike and thru-way authorities and municipal utilities are set up with cash revenues in mind. The Ohio Turnpike leases access to its ROW for cash lease payments at an established rate per mile. The BART arrangement and the Leesburg, Florida, municipal utility entered shared resource arrangements; those arrangements involve cash payments based on a proportion of gross revenues received for private telecommunication firms' use of the publicly owned conduits in the ROW. (Both agencies invested their own funds in, and own, the conduits; private firms access the conduits rather than the ROW.)

A third dimension of shared resource arrangement is the extent to which *exclusivity* is offered. The State of Maryland already has two partners in the project; one is providing the state DOT with "dark" fibers along an interstate route and the other is providing equipment to light those plus additional fibers. The Ohio Turnpike stands willing to lease to all interested parties so long as there is space to accommodate the planned fiber-optic lines. In contrast, Missouri has one private-sector partner, which has the exclusive right to use and/or market telecommunications capacity in the fiber it controls. Like Missouri, both BART and Leesburg granted exclusive marketing rights to a single private firm, but in practice competition has been sustained because other telecommunications providers have access to the infrastructure through leases from the broker/partner.

Massachusetts DOT explicitly encourages non-exclusivity but stipulates that the interested private partners join together in a consortium with an appointed lead company that serves as point of contact for the DOT. Like the Ohio Turnpike, the number of private firms accessing the ROW on Massachusetts DOT roadways depends only the number of firms interested and the ROW capacity for repeated trenching.

Finally, allocation of financial responsibility for relocation and repairs can vary. If telecommunications infrastructure (fiber-optic lines and conduits) must be moved to accommodate roadway expansion or upgrading, the private partner may bear the full cost (Ohio Turnpike); the public sector may shoulder the burden for both the public and private (Missouri); or the public and private partners may share the cost (Maryland). Liability for repair of damages to the telecommunications infrastructure generally resides with the party responsible for the damage, though Leesburg assigns repair costs to whoever is responsible for system maintenance. Overall, both partners accept their own consequential damages (that is, the economic costs of a malfunctioning or out-of-order system) without compensation from the other or responsible party.

Methods for Estimating Shared Resource Value

Shared-resource projects are market-driven. Private-sector interest in any type of ROW is derived from market demand for telecommunications and the company's capacity to satisfy it. While the public agency typically does not have specialized knowledge of this market demand, an adequate accounting of the asset can assist it in anticipating the private-sector response to SRP initiatives. Thus, there are two parties (at least) involved in determining compensation: the "buyer"/lessee and the "seller"/ROW owner or lessor. Effective negotiation is predicated on both partners having a clear idea of the value of the resource exchanged.

While the private sector (e.g., railroad companies) has been valuing their ROW-related assets for some time, public-sector agencies have only recently focused on determining the value of shared resource assets. This section reviews six methods that can be used to determine ROW value:

• valuation of adjacent land
• cost of the next-best alternative

- historical experience
- market research
- needs-based compensation
- competitive auction

Aside from competitive auction, which may or may not elicit bids at "full market value," no single approach will yield fully accurate ROW value for a proposed partnership. Several approaches used simultaneously, however, will better pinpoint the range within which market value falls. This range of value can be further refined based on the policy objectives driving public-sector involvement in shared resource projects. And even if the public policy objective is to promote economic development (as opposed to maximizing direct return), the methods can be used to help forecast expected interest and participation by the private service providers.

Valuation of Adjacent Land

Highway ROW derives part of its value from the same factors that determine the value of adjacent property. Proximate real estate values therefore are used as a guide to highway ROW values. For example, Union Pacific Railroad has developed an extensive database of real estate values that it uses (along with other factors) to determine compensation for access to its ROW. It is misleading, however, simply to equate highway ROW value with the real estate cost of easements on adjacent land because this ignores cost differentials in installing telecommunications infrastructure in alternative locations. This issue will be addressed in the next section.

Using adjacent real estate values directly also overlooks the real advantages of dealing with one agent rather than a number of individual landowners, which can boost right-of-way values above the price of land "at the fence." Santa Fe Railroad explicitly incorporates this factor in its computation of lease rates, which are based on the value of (adjacent) real estate. More specifically, the railroad company computes annual lease rate per ROW mile as:

[fair market value of land required] * [target rate of return * tax * continuity factor]

Target rate of return is affected by tax liability on the income and also by a "continuity factor," which is the added premium for the railroad's ability to provide a continuous corridor for telecommunications infrastructure. These two factors together total about 20 percent of the ROW value (on average).

Cost of the Next-Best Alternative

Highway ROW is a more recent locale for longitudinal installation of telecommunications infrastructure; other alternatives have been used in the past and continue to be used today. Alternative sites compete with highway ROW and, in so doing, set the upper boundary on highway ROW values. Cost of access to the next-best location provides a benchmark for evaluating highway ROW access. This cost is not sufficient as a guide to highway ROW values, however, because other factors intervene, such as (1) costs of installation, which will differ among alternatives and within the highway ROW itself; and (2) timing or immediate availability, which can supersede other factors.

Timing and ease of negotiation aside, the total cost of infrastructure installed in highway ROW generally cannot exceed the cost of the same infrastructure installed in the next-best alternative location when all costs—including access payments and the value placed on less tangible factors such as security—are taken into account. Thus, as a rule of thumb, the maximum value for highway ROW is equal to:

(1) *total cost of infrastructure located along the next-best ROW*—including payment for access as well as installation and equipment costs, transaction fees for land purchases, and discounted maintenance costs

minus

(2) *total cost of installing that same infrastructure along highway ROW*—excluding access payments but *including* transactions fees and discounted maintenance costs

plus

(3) *value of (non-monetized) advantages of highway location* (e.g., those related to security or ease of negotiation).

The next-best alternative can be ROW assembled from privately held parcels, installation along ROW owned by local public utilities (gas, electric) or in a DOT-defined utility corridor, installation along railroad ROW, or a route combining several of these options. Railroad ROW is a highly competitive alternative for highway ROW on inter-regional[7] routes (for example, as an alternative to I-95 through Maryland). This is evidenced by telecommunications company use of such access. In intra-regional markets, however, railroad ROW generally offers less competition, particularly where it flows to older industrial areas and telecommunications expansion is to newer commercial business areas. For example, in Missouri's shared-resource project, telecommunication vendors expressed high interest in a St. Louis quadrant not accessed by railroad lines; hence, company interest in roadway ROW access. In this case, next-best alternative might be assembly of easements from privately held parcels or access to already crowded utility corridors.

Historical Experience

Historical precedent, where data are available, may provide a clearer example of valuation than bottom-up cost comparisons. On the other hand, data taken from completed shared resource arrangements may understate lessees' willingness to pay; that is, the terms of completed agreements only indicate that private lessees were willing to pay *at least* this level, but the compensation paid may be below what they were prepared to pay. Nonetheless, historical experience is a better guide than none at all and certainly provides a starting point for negotiations.

Since documented compensation rates vary among situations according to objective factors and the needs and expectations of the parties involved, historical analysis should include information on ROW and lessee characteristics as well. Conrail developed a systematic approach to valuation based on historical data, which the company drew from its own ROW leases. It assembled information from past contracts on lease payment and six associated factors:

- ROW location (rural/urban, whether or not it connects two major centers, whether it is vital to the lessee's system)
- lessee's business (wholesale, retail, or non-communications business, etc.)
- purpose of telecommunications line (inter-LATA[8] or intra-LATA)
- number of miles leased
- competing ROW options
- number of fibers to be installed

Conrail evaluated the characteristics associated with past agreements using a scale of +1 to +10 for the first four factors (+10 indicating high lease value), a scale of -10 to +10 for competing ROW options, and a scale that extended from +1 to beyond +10 for number of fibers. Based on the observed relationships between negotiated lease rates and the point value of the factors associated with each lease, Conrail worked backward to an estimated dollar value for each factor-point. Conrail uses this historically based matrix of values, which is pegged to the Consumer Price Index to keep pace with inflation, to set annual lease rates for new contracts.

Consulting firm Arthur D. Little used historical precedent to support two estimates of the value of Massachusetts Turnpike Authority's under-harbor tunnels.[9] Referring to the $5.50-per-foot-per-year fee charged by the Massachusetts Bay Transportation Authority (MBTA) for comparable ROW along its rail routes, Little determined a comparable price to the other estimates and recommended that the Turnpike charge the same rate as the MBTA for tunnel ROW. If they were priced at this rate, the 10,722-foot-long tunnels would garner over $58,000 per year in rental fees.

Market Research

Ultimately, ROW value is based on lessees' willingness to pay for longitudinal access. The approaches to valuation described above are attempts to (1) infer lessees' willingness to pay by analyzing the same factors they use in evaluating ROW (for example, costs of next-best alternative) or using information that reveals lessees' willingness to pay in other circumstances (historical evidence); or (2) force prospective lessees to reveal their current willingness to pay through competitive bids. Direct contact with potential lessees through market research may also provide information on willingness to pay as well as identify contract conditions and other factors that shape potential demand for ROW.

Palmer Bellevue[10] used market research as a significant portion of the market feasibility study it performed for the New York Thruway Authority. The consultants surveyed 24 private-sector telecommunications and cable companies; they also contacted 12 non-telecommunications entities, including various public-sector agencies that use telecommunications services. Palmer Bellevue queried respondents about the level and type of interest in Authority-provided facilities and the type of facilities desired. The company's initial survey was followed-up by a Request for Information (RFI) from potential "customers" to better determine specific demand characteristics such as routes, special requirements, time frame, and willingness to pay.

Such market research, though certainly useful, can also be incomplete or misleading for two reasons: First, respondents are asked about *anticipated* rather than historical behavior, and their reactions may change when the proposed situation actually comes into being. Second, because respondents may eventually become lessees, there is a strong incentive for them to understate their willingness to pay. Considered strategically, a savvy potential lessee would respond to the survey with a willingness to pay that is just high enough to ensure the Authority's continued pursuit of ROW partnerships, but not as high as the respondent's maximum willingness to pay.

Thus, in most instances, market research by itself is not likely to provide sufficient information on ROW value. Palmer Bellevue acknowledged these shortcomings and, in fact, pursued other approaches such as case studies of other highway and railroad lease arrangements (that is, historical evidence).

Needs-Based Compensation

Some ROW owners set target levels of compensation based on estimated needs, particularly in barter arrangements. This will be sufficient if objectives are limited to telecommunications capacity for public-sector use (ITS, or broader needs) *and* there are institutional/statutory limitations on cash compensation. ROW owners will know that they target too high if no potential lessees express an interest or if potential lessees come back with lower offers. On the other hand, they will not know if they target too low. If needs are underestimated or ROW owners are reluctant to bargain for all their telecommunications needs, lessors using needs-based compensation may receive less than if they had used another approach to valuation. However, needs-based barter arrangements may be more easily effected in a short time and, when the window of opportunity is limited, speed can make the difference between a deal and no deal.

One of the advantages of barter arrangements based on needs is the wide spread between cost to lessee and value to lessor of in-kind compensation. That is, the ROW owner receives more in value than the lessee pays, which is not true for cash arrangements, where a dollar is worth a dollar to both parties. In other words, the lessor's desire to avoid the cost of telecommunications infrastructure is significantly greater than the actual cost to the lessee of adding fiber-optic capacity in a conduit that they were already installing for their own use.

The disadvantage of strict needs-based valuation is the chance of the lessor's settling for less than the lessee is willing to pay for access to the ROW. On the other hand, it may be useless to bargain for compensation beyond public-sector capacity needs in many shared resource arrangements. If regulatory restrictions facing state agencies prohibit their leasing telecommunications services or even excess conduit/fiber-optic capacity, there is no incentive to push in-kind compensation beyond public-sector needs. By default, therefore, compensation is based on public-sector telecommunications needs rather than an estimate of market value.

Competitive Auction

If the number of potential buyers/lessees exceeds the number of contracts to be awarded, bidding in a competitive auction can be used to select lessees and to establish compensation levels. This would be analogous to recent FCC auctions of available spectrum. In its inverted format, auction-style bidding is used by public agencies to select low-bid contractors for specified projects. However, shared resources projects differ significantly from other auction situations because it is conceivable that more than one lessee can be accommodated in the same ROW (depending on the exclusivity arrangement).

The Missouri DOT provides an example of auction-based valuation. Having determined its fiber-optic needs, the DOT invited bidders to submit their best offers for a DOT-specified fiber optics backbone geared to ITS needs. The opening bid had to provide at least six dark fibers along stated routes (bidders could not cherry-pick segments of the specified system but had to install fiber for DOT along all selected routes). The winning contractor would be the firm offering the best terms over and above this threshold requirement. In return for providing the state with telecommunications capacity, the winning bidder also would be granted exclusive longitudinal access for its own telecommunications infrastructure alongside DOT's fiber optics backbone system.

In the Missouri case, while over 20 companies expressed an interest in the project, there was only one successful bid (out of two preliminary bids). This result highlights a major limitation of the competitive auction approach, namely, that an auction is premised on there being fewer "awards" than bidders. For example, Little[11] felt that the market for Massachusetts Turnpike ROW in 1990 was too weak to support an auction approach for the project.

Relationship to Shared Resource Objectives

While the valuation of ROW assets can assist negotiators regardless of the shared resource policy objectives, knowing these objectives can crystallize the types of analysis conducted. For example, methods such as cost of next-best alternative, historical experience, and market research can be used by agencies that seek maximum monetary value for their asset and want some indication of what the market will bear. However, to the extent that the agency's policy objectives are to further ITS/NII deployment, they may be incomplete in the extent to which they incorporate the value of in-kind or bartered services. Methods such as needs-based compensation and competitive auction can provide a broader valuation of these possibilities.

In terms of specific valuation estimates, when the shared resource project objective is cash flow, estimated value is presented as (annualized) lease value or capital purchase costs. When the project objective is ITS or public-sector telecommunications capacity, estimated value can be translated from dollars into infrastructure equivalency. That is, an estimate of ROW lease value of $\$N$ per year would be capitalized (translated into a one-time investment value) and then divided by equipment costs (using private-sector out-of-pocket costs rather than public-sector avoided costs) to yield an estimate of the number of fiber-optic cables, supporting equipment, maintenance support, etc., that might be supplied by a private-sector partner for ROW that was estimated to be worth $\$N$ per year in lease fees.

Discussion: Shared Resources and ITS/NII Objectives

The case of shared resource projects represents but one example of how meeting infrastructure communication requirements for ITS can contribute to (and, in fact, benefit from) related needs for NII. Each domain grapples with services, protocol, and policies that should govern both deployments. Many of the other chapters in this volume describe these technical and non-technical challenges. The goal of this chapter has been to examine how shared resources can serve both the ITS architecture requirement for wireline communications and NII desires for private-sector leadership in infrastructure development. And within shared resources, the issue of valuation (which has been featured here) provides both the public and private sector with concepts and tools for structuring negotiations and partnerships in line with policy and market objectives.

Finally, viewed from the perspective of ITS architecture deployment, the shared resources examples reviewed confirm the major role played by departments of transportation in providing and/or arranging for wireline communication. This is understandable for a variety of reasons, including but not limited to the fact that it is typically these agencies that (1) would have to finance ITS communications and (2) have ROW assets that could be used to offset potential costs. The projects we have discussed demonstrate how the public sector, particularly departments of transportation, can overcome ITS deployment cost constraints by using the ROW assets to leverage in-kind or related services from the private sector. In cases such as Missouri, this has saved the state upwards to $50 million in fiber-optic costs.[12]

Of course, the role of transportation departments in leading these shared resources projects raises the issue of how broader NII considerations are incorporated into such initiatives. To date, there are instances where shared resource projects have been viewed broadly to include more services than just ITS. In Maryland, for example, the public sector is organizing to provide a variety of NII-related services (e.g., tele-education). However, these relationships can also be controversial, especially to the extent that the public sector is perceived (rightly or wrongly) as providing services in lieu of the private sector.

Ultimately, the case of shared-resource projects raises the broader issue of telecommunications planning. That is, while the transportation sector can be seen as rightly advancing its preferred method for obtaining ITS-related services, there are broader public-sector NII objectives that may transcend ITS. As the examples demonstrate, these can include: providing telecommunications infrastructure and/or services at minimum cost for a broader range of public-sector services (that is, including non-transportation needs); expanding telecommunications capacity overall to support NII and generally stimulate economic development; and generating cash revenues that can be used for other public-sector needs.

State- and/or metropolitan-level telecommunications planning should consider transportation needs and assets as an aspect of overall public-sector NII needs. This would require the involvement of other agencies. While bureaucratic delays in achieving this coordination could dampen the near-term viability of such an approach, the economies of scale that could be achieved by moving in this direction suggest that it is a policy worth considering.

Nonetheless, partnerships between the public and private sectors developed through shared resources and related projects could be seen as furthering *or* thwarting desired telecommunication partnerships; however, such a determination begs the issue of having a strategic public/private telecommunications approach. And as the examples and methods in this chapter suggest, this approach should consider the full range of options, from pure private-sector provision to public-sector procurement, with shared resources being but one promising avenue.

Notes

1. U.S. Department of Transportation. *National Systems Architecture Summary.* Washington, DC, 1994.

2. Rockwell International. *National Systems Architecture, Phase I Report: Evolutionary Deployment Strategy.* Prepared for Federal Highway Administration, Anaheim, CA, October 1994.

3. See D. Whitney and T. Mottl, "Assessing Federal Roles," in this volume, for a fuller explication of the policy connections between NII and ITS.

4. See Rockwell International, 1994.

5. For a more detailed examination of these cases and the issues they raise, see Apogee Research, 1995,

6. Ibid.

7. Standard Metropolitan Area is a U.S. Census-defined region including a city and its surrounding jurisdictions or other grouping of political jurisdictions that effectively function as a single economic center.

8. Local Access Transfer Area.

9. Little, Inc., 1990.

10. Palmer Bellevue/Coopers & Lybrand, 1994.

11. See Little, Inc., 1990.

12. See Apogee Research, 1995.

References

Apogee Research. *Shared Resources: Identification, Review and Analysis of Legal and Institutional Issues, Task A Report: Literature Review, Project Survey, and Identification of Issues.* Prepared for Federal Highway Administration, Bethesda, MD, November 1994.

Apogee Research. *Shared Resources: Identification, Review and Analysis of Legal and Institutional Issues, Task C Report: Selected Issues and Case Studies.* Prepared for Federal Highway Administration, Bethesda, MD, May 1995.

Arthur D. Little, Inc. *Final Report: Massachusetts Turnpike Authority, Appraisal of ROW for Fiber Optic Occupation.* Cambridge, MA: March 1990.

ITS America. *Strategic Plan for Intelligent Transportation Systems in the United States,* Washington, DC: ITS America, 1992.

Palmer Bellevue/Coopers & Lybrand (Mark C. Ciolek, J. Cale Case, and Michael R. Press). *Analysis of the Market Potential of the Thruway/Canal Rights-of-Way for Use as Fiber Optic Cable "Electronic Highways."* Chicago, IL: August 1994.

Rockwell International. *National Systems Architecture, Phase I Report: Evolutionary Deployment Strategy.* Prepared for Federal Highway Administration, Anaheim, CA, Rockwell International, October 1994.

U.S. Department of Transportation. *National Systems Architecture Summary.* Washington, DC: 1994.

Whitney, D. and Mottl, T., "Federal Policies at the Intersection of the Information Superhighway and Intelligent Transportation Systems." Paper presented at Intelligent Transportation Systems and National Information Infrastructure Conference, Kennedy School of Government, Harvard University, Cambridge, MA, July 1995.

Public and Private Roles in Delivering Traveler Information: Two Case Studies

Randolph W. Hall and Y. B. Yim

Background

One of the critical issues in the development of the National Information Infrastructure (NII) is the division of responsibilities between the public and private sectors. Experience gained from advanced traveler information systems (ATIS), such as systems providing real-time traffic information, can provide insight into how this issue can be resolved for information services that draw on government-collected data.

Though ATIS is largely a commercial product, its quality is enhanced through access to transportation data provided by state and local agencies. Likewise, government has an interest in collaborating with the private sector. Various studies have shown that the performance of the transportation system is improved when travelers are provided with better (i.e., more accurate, comprehensive, and current) information on travel conditions [8], though the magnitude of the benefit is debatable [2]. For instance, when travelers are provided with information on traffic incidents, driver migration to alternate routes reduces the overall average travel time.

Assuming that both the public and private sectors should play some role in the dissemination of traveler information, the question remains: What is the precise responsibility of each sector and, more specifically, how far should government go in collecting, processing, and disseminating traveler information? As some companies fear, it is quite possible for the public sector to cross the threshold from product support to product competition as it finances and manages ATIS user services. It is also possible for the public sector to be so passive that no one enjoys access to critical transportation information that only government can collect.

From these issues should come public policies aimed at ensuring that:

• Individuals have easy and timely access to information that will improve travel for themselves and for the entire transportation system.

• Traveler information systems are developed rapidly and at low cost.

• The cost of creating the information system is largely borne by the beneficiaries.

• The private sector is offered reasonable opportunity to develop innovative and profitable products and services.

This paper identifies strategies for the formation of public/private partnerships in the delivery of information services. This was accomplished through a detailed examination of two major ATIS field operations tests (FOTs) conducted in California. Each of these tests experiments with new means of delivering traveler information to the public, and each is undergoing a structured evaluation.

TravInfo is a public/private partnership aimed at enabling widespread dissemination of real-time information on transportation conditions and travel options throughout the San Francisco Bay Area. A fundamental premise of the TravInfo project is that a public surveillance and database system, designed to open-architecture standards, will be an effective stimulus for private sector innovations in Advanced Traveler Information System (ATIS) technologies. *SmartTraveler* is a multimodal information system already deployed within the Los Angeles region. SmartTraveler provides automated access to information on highway congestion, bus schedules, and carpool matches via kiosks, touch-tone telephone, and personal computers/modems.

After describing the components of a traveler information system and prior research on public/private partnerships in ITS, this paper will discuss interim evaluation results from the TravInfo and SmartTraveler FOTs and summarize the lessons learned.

Information System Components

To understand private and public responsibilities in the ITS realm, one must first understand the components of a traveler information system: surveillance and data collection, data processing, data storage, communication, and displays and interfaces. While the development and manufacture of traveler information technologies is invariably a private-sector activity, the management and financing of their deployment often falls within the public sector. We will discuss these components below.

Surveillance and Data Collection

Both static and dynamic data are important for ITS. Static information includes maps and schedules; this is the most mature part of the traveler information industry, with the most clearly defined roles. In the case of mapping, the federal government, through the U.S. Geological Survey (USGS), has a long history of serving both governmental needs and niche consumer markets (e.g., hiking maps), though the USGS is currently under challenge in Congress. Private companies have repackaged these maps to serve wider consumer markets, most recently in the form of map databases. To date, there has been little commercial market for repackaged transit maps and schedules, whose paper forms are usually available free of charge from transit agencies. Airline schedules, on the other hand, while proprietary, have been accessible in printed form for decades and are increasingly accessible to consumers in electronic form through a variety of commercial services.

There exists no uniform strategy for dynamic data collection. For example, highway and street departments are recognized as the only source of data on highway speeds, by virtue of traffic sensors placed in roadways. In addition, police departments possess valuable information on traffic incidents, and maintenance departments hold important data on construction schedules and weather-related road conditions. While the private sector has many tools at its command to supplement these data sources (e.g., traffic observers in aircraft), much of the public data cannot be replicated by private sources. Access to these unique data sources is one of the principal motivations for public/private partnerships in ITS. For instance, one of the major issues in surveillance is the applicability of "probe vehicles" (i.e., vehicles that collect data on roadway speeds) as traffic sensors, as well as institutional responsibility for equipping vehicles and processing data.

Data Processing

Data processing entails conversion of surveillance and other types of raw data into a form that is meaningful to the traveler. This process may include estimating travel times and other performance measures for alternate paths, identifying optimal paths, or planning complex multiple-stop trips. Processing will almost surely take place at several locations between the data source and the traveler, and will very likely require both public and private responsibilities. At one end, the public sector must process sensor data to produce estimates of traffic speeds and volumes along highway segments. On the other, the private sector must customize the data to help travelers find the best routes for their individual needs. The choice of the amount of processing in each location affects the cost of transmitting and storing the data, the ability of the user to execute functions, and the ability of private companies to create unique and proprietary services.

Data Storage

The critical issue in this area is selecting which data are accessible to external agencies and organizations and in what form. Other issues include the distribution and centralization of data and the effects of this distribution on data processing and communication requirements.

Data Communication

Data communication includes a mixture of landline and wireless links between both stationary and mobile sources. Some transportation data may be sent on dedicated landline links, while in other cases public networks may be utilized.

The three main communication paths are: (1) surveillance sites to operations centers; (2) operations centers to external entities (private companies and other public agencies); and (3) operations centers to consumers. Critical issues include the extent to which dedicated networks are installed and determining who is responsible for operating and funding each component of the communication infrastructure (especially wireless).

Displays and Interfaces

Interfaces may be classified as broadcast or interactive, mobile or stationary, and special-purpose (SP) or general-purpose (GP). Print media constitute a separate classification. Examples of these classifications are presented below:

Broadcast/mobile: highway advisory radio (GP)

Broadcast/stationary: changeable message signs (SP); TV traffic services (GP)

Interactive/mobile: route guidance devices (SP); cellular phone/ pager (GP)

Interactive/stationary: automated kiosk (SP); PC software (GP)

Print media: maps and schedules (SP); newspaper (GP)

The public sector already plays a major role in broadcasting information through stationary sources (e.g., through changeable message signs), and has also experimented in other areas (such as highway advisory radio). The private sector plays major roles in several general purpose interfaces, and more recently is leading the development of special-purpose interactive interfaces.

Research on Public/Private Partnerships in ITS

Public/private partnerships will be needed to work effectively towards unified ITS goals, but the United States has been generally less effective at establishing public/private ventures than Europe or Japan [3]. In a public/private partnership, the public sector must facilitate development of the infrastructure and allow for contribution from the private sector. The private sector offers experience with large-scale projects, technological expertise, cross-fertilization of concepts, political neutrality, and expanded funding. Other motivations for partnerships are efficiency, faster service, shifting risk, and market responsiveness [10].

The United States DOT has identified five models for delivery of Advanced Traveler Information [11]:

• Functional division of responsibilities. This model is based on the weather information system, in which the public sector collects the information and sells it to private firms.

• Franchised operations. There are two variations of this model: exclusive and nonexclusive franchise. In exclusive franchises the public sector collects the data and sells the information to private firms for dissemination through exclusive agreements. In nonexclusive franchises, the public sector may retain some rights to the information and/or sell the information to more than one firm.

• Completely private system. The system is privately owned and operated. This model is not likely to be acceptable to the public sector.

• Publicly owned, privately operated system. In this case, the public sector would finance and deploy the ATIS system and designate standards. The private contractor would provide the equipment and operate it, allowing the public to benefit from the superior technology that the private sector could provide.

• Unified public/private partnership. Both parties would collect the information and funnel it through a traveler information center for dissemination to clients, using both public and private facilities.

Each model is applicable, in varying degrees, to each element of the total information system. As one approach, the division of responsibilities might be purely functional, with the public sector assuming its traditional highway role as infrastructure provider, with the private sector being the product provider. However, highway departments have little experience in building communication networks (especially wireless) or in software engineering. Furthermore, scale economies are not nearly so pervasive in communication as they are in transportation, making governmental involvement less necessary.

In another approach, the public sector might take a much more limited role in the industry, akin to its role in radio and television broadcasting. An unregulated manufacturing industry would develop information products, and a regulated or franchised communication industry would provide information services. The public sector might even choose to stay out of the industry completely, with the exception of providing access to some of its databases.

Finally, the public sector might go to the other extreme and become engaged in all aspects of information delivery, including mobile interactive interfaces, as it has done in the Advance (Chicago) and TravTek (Orlando, FL) projects. Such an approach is analogous to how phone systems operate in many countries, which may be evidence enough for the public sector to take a back seat in information delivery.

Public/private ventures encounter many barriers, including the public sector's unwillingness to share traffic management responsibilities with the private sector, jurisdictional fragmentation, legal constraints regarding the use of public right of way, procurement and contracting regulations, and uncertainty about the market for intelligent transportation system (ITS) technology. Turning this around, the Volpe Center [10] has identified the following ingredients for a successful partnership:

• Establish clear goals for the project and clear roles for the partners.

• Obtain a strong, experienced, and committed leader.

• Limit the size of the partnership.

• Communicate through formal and informal channels at all times.

• Implement a flexible public-sector infrastructure to support the partnership.

• Negotiate and assign liability and intellectual property rights.

• Anticipate negative public reaction with positive public relations.

• Anticipate and reduce commercial risk.

These issues will be discussed in the following section within the context of the TravInfo FOT.

TravInfo FOT

TravInfo is a field operational test (FOT) funded by the Federal Highway Administration (FHWA) to be deployed in the San Francisco Bay Area. A unique aspect of TravInfo will be its open-access database, which will allow companies to retrieve the data and repackage it for ultimate dissemination to travelers via both broadcast and products developed by value-added resellers (VARs). Hence, TravInfo's objective is not only to provide benefits to Bay Area travelers but also to stimulate the deployment of privately offered traveler information products and services.

TravInfo was a joint public/private effort from its inception in 1991. An ad hoc proposal committee was formed by a group of Bay Area individuals who were already active in IVHS (now ITS) America. These participants represented such organizations as the California Department of Transportation (Caltrans), Etak, MTC (Metropolitan Transportation Commission), Navtech, PATH (Partners for Advanced Transit and Highways), SRI, and Trimble Navigation. The committee's goal was to build an open-access database that would enable companies to develop ATIS products that draw on real-time data. Because of the collection of ATIS talents in the Bay Area and MTC experience in coordinating projects, there appeared to be a high probability of attracting federal funding through the Field Operational Test program (then only described as the "congested corridors" program).

The formation of the ad hoc committee was preceded by PATH's efforts to develop an ATIS research testbed for the Bay Area. Stimulated by California State Assembly Bill 1239, PATH completed its ATIS testbed plan in 1992 [9]. The plan provided the framework for an ATIS testbed in which researchers, practitioners, and technology developers would cooperate in conducting real-life experiments to test the feasibility of ATIS technologies, assess traveler response to ATIS, and evaluate the effects of ATIS on network performance. This could be accomplished through various demonstration projects that would fit within the framework of a real-life ATIS testbed.

The ATIS testbed concept was incorporated into the TravInfo FOT proposal when it was submitted to the FHWA in October 1992. Also incorporated were the concepts of an open-access database and a public/private partnership, raising the importance of an institutional evaluation as part of the FOT. The proposal was accepted, and TravInfo officially began in July 1993.

TravInfo's organizational structure emphasizes partnership between the public and private sectors. The effort is directed by a Management Board (MB) composed of three public agencies: the Metropolitan Transportation Commission, Caltrans District 4, and the California Highway Patrol. Several other public agencies serve as *ex-officio* members of the Management Board, which is the policy-setting body for all TravInfo test activities, including reviewing and approving procedures for the conduct of tests and setting access restrictions on databases.

The Management Board has created a TravInfo Advisory Committee (AC) with membership open to any firm or agency that wishes to participate. Within the Advisory Committee, the Steering Committee (SC) was formed with fifteen individuals selected by the Management Board. The majority of the Steering Committee's members come from the private sector, but nonprofits and the public sector are also represented. Within the Steering Committee, Working Groups are created to study various components of the TravInfo system. Working Group leaders are selected from the Steering Committee, but anyone can join one.

The Advisory and Steering Committees have no direct authority but advise the Management Board on all issues. Under the policy direction of the MB, a full-time project manager is responsible for the day-to-day activities of the project, including supervision of consultants, serving as liaison to the Advisory Committee, and delivering progress reports to the MB. The project manager is also responsible for directing technology installations and operations, including the deployment of surveillance, computation, communication, and database systems.

TravInfo Evaluation

TravInfo's success will depend on the effectiveness of the partnership, including its ability to guide a large and complex project and fairly resolve interorganizational conflicts. Hence, specific objectives of the institutional evaluation are to:

• Assess the effectiveness of the organizational structure and the management approach in meeting project goals and schedules.

• Measure the extent to which the TravInfo organizational structure facilitates active involvement and cooperation among public agencies and between public and private institutions.

• Document the effects of TravInfo on the ATIS industry, including new business opportunities, changes in organizational philosophy, and ability to develop products along common interface standards.

To gain independent and candid feedback from project participants regarding a range of institutional issues, semi-structured interviews were conducted with two groups, representing project "insiders" and "outsiders":

1. Key project participants, including members of the Management Board and Steering Committee, and key staff members at ESL, MTC, and SRI (these interviews were referred to as the "MB/SC" study). These perspectives represent the "insiders" who have been active in the TravInfo project.

2. Peripheral project participants belonging to the advisory committee but not to the Management Board or Steering Committee (these interviews were referred to as the "AC" study). These perspectives are more representative of "outsiders."

The interviews were administered during the summer of 1994, roughly one year after the formal start of the project but over two years after it was conceived. Follow-up interviews were scheduled for the summers of 1995 and 1996 to assess annual progress. In addition, value-added resellers (VARs) were interviewed in the summer of 1995, and were to be contacted again in 1996. Because TravInfo will not be operational until late 1995, the results should be viewed as preliminary. (Study details can be found in [7].)

For the MB/SC interviews, questions were divided into six sections: (1) TravInfo goals; (2) organizational structure; (3) performance and responsibilities of partners; (4) roles of the public and private sectors; (5) institutional, technical and legal barriers; and

(6) perception of TravInfo. A total of 24 people were contacted, of whom 21 participated. These 21 participants represented 19 of the 23 organizations active in TravInfo. The interviews were administered by the authors of this chapter, usually in person at the interviewee's place of business, but occasionally by phone. Interviews typically lasted one to one and-a-half hours.

The interview format for the AC study was somewhat more structured, but still largely consisted of open-ended questions. The interview was condensed, and only covered: (1) organizational structure; (2) roles of the public and private sectors in implementation and operation; (3) institutional, technical, and legal barriers; and (4) the interviewee's perception of TravInfo. In addition, interviewees were screened to exclude persons who were unfamiliar with the project or had not attended any project meetings. Attempts were made to contact 40 people (covering all AC members who were not on the MB or SC), of whom 30 were reached. Of these, four were screened out. Of the remaining 26 persons, 22 (or 85 percent) agreed to participate. Interviews were conducted by telephone and typically lasted 30 minutes.

Findings

There was generally strong support for the project and the TravInfo organization. The criticisms made could be viewed as expressing needs for refinements; however, these refinements may prove critical to meeting project schedules and retaining members. Responses to the AC interviews were largely consistent with those from the MB/SC interviews, though the interviewees tended to be less informed about the subject matter. Perhaps the most significant divergence in responses were AC members' higher level of criticism about the conduct of meetings and a higher level of frustration with the pace of progress. Also, while the MB/SC members were largely content with outreach efforts, a mild level of dissatisfaction was expressed in AC interviews. Overall, however, responses were sufficiently similar among the MB/SC and AC groups that they are not separated (for more detail, see [7]).

TravInfo Goals

No one disagreed with TravInfo's stated goals (provide a centralized database, stimulate deployment of ATIS, and evaluate effectiveness). However, there was some difference in emphasis among individuals.

Evaluation vs. Deployment. Deployment tends to be a much more significant objective than evaluation. Clearly, many participants do not look at this project as just a test but rather as the first step toward a major ATIS implementation.

Transportation vs. Economic Impacts. Some differences in priority also exist over the relative importance of transportation vs. economic goals, including job growth and the vitality of participating companies. The economic objective appears to be the stronger force at this time, and it has been a prominent factor in resolving public/private disagreements.

Consensus and Definition. Several interviewees mentioned that the project has been successful because participants have accepted a common goal set. This largely appears to be the case at a conceptual level, but conflicts certainly exist when TravInfo has defined the boundaries between "public" and "private" (as will be discussed below). Furthermore, some felt that the project had failed to clearly articulate its goals.

Organizational Structure

Interviewees felt that the TravInfo organization was effective largely because of the roles defined for the Management Board and the Steering Committee, and because of the strength of the individuals involved in running the organization. Specific strengths included:

• Responsiveness of the Management Board to the Steering Committee, including MB members' attendance at Steering Committee meetings. Interviewees clearly saw a sense of partnership.

• Sincerity of MTC in guarding the public interest in the project, as well as in building partnership with the private sector.

• Ability of the Steering Committee chair to facilitate involvement from the private sector through personal leadership and business contacts.

• Broad-based private-sector participation in the project.

• Expertise of the Steering Committee members and the quality of the advice provided. (This is one area where TravInfo might not be replicable elsewhere, because the Bay Area is home to many ATIS firms.)

• Overall openness of the project.

The most widely cited weaknesses were the inefficiency of Steering Committee meetings and the slowness in making decisions. Interviewees were nearly unanimous that meetings were too long and that issues should be settled more quickly. To a degree, this is a by-product of the Steering Committee's openness. Yet at the same time, concerns were voiced that the Steering Committee needs a stronger direction and more discipline in managing meetings. According to interviewees, the problems have both delayed the project and caused excess work for the project consultant. Some also felt that the Steering Committee's reliance on volunteers presents problems with respect to continuity and getting people up to speed.

Interviewees felt that the organization had strongly encouraged a public/private partnership and that the public sector was highly responsive to private-sector needs. On the other hand, the interviewees felt that public/public cooperation already existed and that TravInfo was not unique in this regard.

Key Institutional Issues

Public/private issues were brought to the Steering Committee at the earliest stage of the FOT. A "Public/Private" working group was formed to identify the most appropriate roles for the public and private sectors, to discuss these issues with the Steering Committee, and to solicit additional input from the Advisory Committee as a whole. Issues included:

• The existence and form of a wireless broadcasting system for communicating data to ATIS devices.

• The degree to which TravInfo should process data prior to dissemination (e.g., whether TravInfo should suggest alternate routes based on real-time conditions).

• Individuals' ability to directly access TravInfo via modem.

• Whether open access to the TravInfo database alone would provide a strong enough incentive for VARs to participate fully in TravInfo.

• TravInfo's provision of end products and services that might compete with private companies such as Metro Traffic and Shadow Traffic.

• The operating responsibility for the Transportation Information Center (TIC), location of the TravInfo database, and responsibility for the control of data collection.

• The collection of fees from private companies that access TravInfo, with revenue to be used for the project's on-going operation following the FOT.

In September 1993, while these issues were being debated, the MB retained a Bay Area consulting firm, TRW/ESL, to develop and define TravInfo's system architecture. In December 1993, the Steering Committee held a special meeting to discuss the responsibilities of the public and private sectors in providing a TravInfo database and its associated products and services. The main concerns were still the potential conflicts between public and private sector interests, specifically in the transit telephone information system, audiotext traffic information system, landline computer access, and wireless data broadcast.

A memorandum prepared by the SC chair suggested that the private-sector view of public/private partnership issues differed significantly from that of the public sector. The public sector believed that because the TravInfo database would be acquired at public expense, it should be available for public use at no charge. The private-sector view is reflected in the following quote:

Effective and widespread dissemination of TravInfo data will require its integration with other 'value added' information and services to be provided by the private sector. Government dissemination of TravInfo data in free and open forms might compete with commercial services, degrade commercial markets, and deter firms from developing TravInfo products and services. Since TravInfo depends on an effective public/ private partnership, these issues should be dealt with in a cooperative, open-minded, and constructive spirit by all participants in order to find 'win-win-win' solutions for TravInfo's government agencies, commercial firms, and ultimate end users. (Memorandum by Chair of SC, December 1993)

The wireless data broadcast system raised the most controversial issue: whether TravInfo should provide its own subcarrier signal or whether it should rely on the existing private FM subcarriers. The TravInfo concept as stated in the proposal to FHWA was to provide free broadcasts of travel information, including traffic conditions and transit services, via FM or TV subcarriers or similar media. This would allow developers to use such data in wireless products and services without having to provide their own dissemination means. Presently, three FM subcarrier data service companies potentially could use the TravInfo database in conjunction with other services such as paging and differential GPS (global positioning system) corrections. TravInfo would compete with these companies if it established an entirely new FM subcarrier dissemination service free of charge.

The debate centered on the use of existing subcarriers versus establishing an entirely new service. If TravInfo were to provide its own subcarrier signals, stations would be needed to carry them. TravInfo would have its own protocols, formats, and standards. It would also need to provide and operate transmitter modulation equipment and find commercial firms to provide receivers, products, and services to support the TravInfo signals.

In all of these cases, the issues have largely been resolved through a consensus-building process within the Steering Committee (the Management Board has accepted the Steering Committee's recommendations across the board). It appears that this resolution has depended on excluding elements from TravInfo that directly compete with private-sector interests. To a lesser degree, budgetary limitations have also played a role. Some interviewees felt that TravInfo had gone too far in accommodating the private sector, and that these issues merited re-investigation (specifically, to provide modem access without relying on private-sector intermediaries). Several people also expressed concern that the public interest was not being adequately heard through the Steering Committee.

In general, though TravInfo has attained considerable progress, public and private participants have not arrived at a complete understanding of each other's objectives.

Public Sector Concerns

The biggest issues involving the public sector have been:

• Defining the path by which CHP data on incidents would be transmitted to TravInfo (specifically, whether it would pass through Caltrans' transportation management centers, or TMC).

• Ensuring that the Caltrans TMC keeps on schedule.

• Selecting a common map database for TravInfo and the Caltrans TMC.

The Management Board has resolved these issues through consensus-building. However, delays in achieving the TMC schedule is a continuing source of friction, and some feel they may jeopardize the project.

Performance and Responsibilities of Partners

Interviewees were nearly unanimous in stating that the Advisory Committee's mission is purely information exchange and that it should have no specific duties. Hence, according to the interviewees, the AC currently has no real authority, and it should have no authority in the future.

Interviewees agreed that the Steering Committee's mission is to advise the Management Board on matters related to private-sector and user interests and on technical issues related to architecture and design. A third part of the mission, not stated by everyone, is to facilitate private-sector involvement in the project's deployment.

Differences of opinion exist on the details of the Steering Committee's role, including the following:

• Whether TravInfo relies too much on the Steering Committee for technical advice. An alternative would be to form a paid technical review committee whose members would be selected according to specific expertise.

• The role of the Steering Committee relative to the paid technical advisor. Because the Steering Committee has been so active in providing technical advice, there was some worry that it was unnecessarily duplicating work done by TravInfo's Technical Advisor.

• The scope and purpose of Working Groups. Some felt that too many Working Groups had been created without realistic or even stated objectives. In particular, some respondents believed that the Steering Committee and its Working Groups should only review and advise, rather than producing original work.

• The degree to which the Management Board should look to the Steering Committee for advice versus resolution. In this regard, some felt that the Steering Committee had too much power. One interviewee felt that some members had the misconception that the Steering Committee's role was to manage the project. However, most felt that its level of authority, while large, was appropriate.

In combination, these issues have likely contributed to the perception that the Steering Committee is inefficient.

The mission of the Management Board was variously stated as "resolving differences," assuming "legal responsibility," or "administering and assuming oversight." Everyone agreed that the Management Board was the ultimate authority for the project, though differences of opinion existed over when it should exert its authority. Some people felt that the Management Board should step in more quickly to bring resolution to some of the debates within the Steering Committee. Others felt that the Board's current approach, which allows resolution in the Steering Committee, was more appropriate and helped maintain private-sector support. Somewhat surprisingly, many of the Steering Committee members were not aware of how the Management Board functions.

Overall, interviewees felt that the Management Board was responsive, though perhaps too passive.

Roles of the Public and Private Sectors

The interviewees agreed unanimously that the public sector's role in this project is to collect and store information, and that the private sectors role is to disseminate information and to contract to develop and perhaps operate TravInfo's traveler information center (TIC). There was also consensus that the public sector should provide a minimum level of direct public access to the information. Disagreements existed on the following:

• The degree to which the public sector should process data before dissemination.

• The quality of information provided through "minimal public access."

• Whether TravInfo should have the capability to transmit information over data communication channels to individual homes and vehicles.

In general, interviewees agreed that the public sector should not be in competition with the private sector. On the other hand, many were concerned about the equity of spending public funds on a system that was not widely accessible to the public. There was near-unanimous support for charging access fees to help finance TravInfo, but only to cover incremental costs, not to pay for data that would be collected anyway. Most felt that additional public subsidies would be needed.

Overall, interviewees felt that TravInfo had been successful in resolving the disagreements and that the current roles were appropriate. While some people may not be totally happy with the outcomes, the openness of the process has ensured that participants remain involved.

Institutional, Technical and Legal Barriers

The barriers cited varied considerably from interviewee to interviewee. Almost everyone identified one or more significant concerns, including the following:

• The short-term status of the FOT, which was preventing the private sector from developing products

• Lack of transit participation

• Major schedule delays on deployment of the Caltrans TMC

• Lack of products designed to access TravInfo data

• No means to collect information on arterials

• Insufficient funding to support operations (especially data entry)

• Products being rendered obsolete by outdated technology, thereby discouraging investment by the private sector

• Insufficient attention to user needs, because the project is technology-driven

Many interviewees from the private sector were concerned that TravInfo's lack of clear technical direction would discourage enterprises from developing products for the project, because companies would not be able to foresee technological direction. Many private-sector interviewees said their companies were hesitant to put forth any new products for both this reason and because the future of TravInfo beyond its brief trial period is unknown. Hence, from a private-sector perspective, providing a clearer vision of post-FOT TravInfo would be an incentive to developing ATIS products. By contrast, there was little support for financial incentives to encourage development of end-user products.

Perception of TravInfo

On the whole, interviewees believed that TravInfo would provide important system benefits, mostly in reductions in non-recurrent congestion and related reductions in fuel consumption, emissions, and accidents. While they felt that increasing public transit usage was an important objective, many were skeptical that TravInfo would have this effect. Few felt there would be an effect on recurrent congestion.

Interviewees were most divided as to whether TravInfo would have an effect on the development of new products. Many felt the effect would be strong, while others felt that the products would be developed independently of TravInfo (though TravInfo might affect product features). Other discussed impacts included improved working relationships, development of nationwide standards, and economic effects on the Bay Area. However, interviewees were nearly unanimous in stating that TravInfo would not change their own organization significantly.

Assessment of Findings

Returning to the Volpe guidelines for successful partnerships, TravInfo has been quite successful in several areas. Its steering committee has a strong and highly committed leader, communication has been excellent, and liability and intellectual property rights were resolved early on. Unfortunately, in its first year TravInfo suffered by not sufficiently addressing the most fundamental issue: "establishing clear roles for the partners." This deficiency is most evident in defining specific areas in which the Steering Committee should provide advice, and creating clear procedures for resolving disagreements. A consequence of this non-specificity has been long meetings and slow progress in developing the system design. Nevertheless, by allowing the Steering Committee to set its own agenda, TravInfo has retained strong private-sector support, which may ultimately be the ingredient for its success.

California SmartTraveler

California SmartTraveler, like TravInfo, aims to improve the dissemination of traveler information, which entails the integration of multiple information sources. However, the means by which this goal will be accomplished is quite different than TravInfo's. SmartTraveler can be viewed as a limited public/public partnership largely under the direction of a single agency, Caltrans. The private-sector role in SmartTraveler is limited to that of vendor, for the development and production of hardware and software. The management and specification of SmartTraveler products are entirely a public-sector responsibility. Hence, SmartTraveler does not aim to stimulate product development through VARs. Instead, it is intended to provide information services directly to the public, perhaps even in competition with private-sector products. SmartTraveler is not governed by boards and committees but simply by a project manager within Caltrans, who is responsible for gaining cooperation from other public agencies.

SmartTraveler includes three user interfaces: (1) PC/modem software; (2) touch-tone telephone; and (3) automated kiosks (in 77 locations).

Kiosks

The SmartTraveler kiosks are a multimedia PC-based system for accessing information on bus routes, car pools, and freeway congestion and for viewing videos on various transportation topics. The kiosks access their information via an IBM 3090 computer at the California Health and Welfare Data Center, in Sacramento. This computer in turn accesses databases at Caltrans; the Commuter Transportation Services (CTS), the regional ride-share agency; and the Metropolitan Transportation Authority (MTA), the regional transit agency. Each kiosk operates off an IBM PS/2 personal computer connected to a Pioneer LDV-8000 laser disk player via an in-motion video adapter. Videos are stored on a laser disk, and bus-route, car-pool, and freeway-congestion databases are accessed via modem. The computer interface, for both input and output, is an IBM 8516 touch-screen monitor. Displays are in textual form, with the exception of freeway congestion, which is displayed on a map.

PC Software

Users with their own computer and modem can assess the Caltrans freeway congestion map, which classifies highway speeds by location throughout the Los Angeles region. The software was originally intended to include carpool and bus schedule information as well, but only provides freeway data at present. The PC software operates through the MTA computer, although this was not originally intended to be a permanent solution.

Automated Ridematching Service (ARMS)

The automated ridematching provides direct access to CTS via Pacific Bell. This is a feature within Caltrans' toll-free "1-800-COMMUTE" line and is intended to facilitate *one-time* ride-matches (also called "flexpool"). Users must be preregistered with the ride-share agency and must enter a preassigned identification number to gain access.

ARMS is menu-driven through a touch-tone telephone interface. Two options are available for identifying ride-matches. The manual option allows the user to listen to the names and phone numbers of potential matches through a synthesized voice. The user must then individually phone the people on the list to locate matches. Alternatively, the user can select an automated messaging feature. He or she then records a message (speaking into the phone), which is automatically relayed through automated dialing to persons on the ride-match list.

Discussion of Roles and Responsibilities

In TravInfo, organizational design has been an explicit aspect of the "test" from day one. This has not been the case for SmartTraveler. Rather, roles and responsibilities have evolved in a way that reflects expediency more so than underlying principles. Quite logically, CTS has been the source of rideshare data, Caltrans the source of traffic data, and MTA the source of bus schedule data. Not-so-logically, however, MTA became the developer and port for PC/modem software, even though the software only accesses freeway congestion data. Also not-so-logically, the State's Health and Welfare agency became the central node for the entire system, even though it has no active role in transportation. Nevertheless, the SmartTraveler organization was able to deploy a functioning multimedia information system within a short time frame. It established clear roles for the partners, obtained a strong leader, limited the number of participants, and implemented an enormously flexible partnership as well. The process for implementing the system took less time than was required to create the TravInfo design. For instance, the issue of modem access for the general public, which was controversial in TravInfo, was resolved quickly in SmartTraveler. Unfortunately, achieving this level of organizational success did not guarantee cost-effective results, as will be discussed in the following sections.

SmartTraveler Evaluation

The SmartTraveler evaluation is complete [4]. It consisted of three elements: (1) functional characteristics; (2) surveys and site visits; and (3) financial characteristics. Due to the organization's relative simplicity, the evaluation did not include an institutional element. Evaluation findings are summarized below:

• The kiosk system was both easy and fun to use, and users were satisfied with its performance. The primary drawbacks were the slowness of the kiosk's multimedia elements (i.e., video clips), and the awkwardness of the interface for entering street addresses. In addition, the kiosks suffered from low usage levels (22.6 users per kiosk per day), and it appears that the kiosks were not positioned to serve serious users.

• The ARMS system had numerous problems. It functioned inconsistently up until the end of the test. Users did not believe it was effective at its intended purpose—finding one-time ride matches. The automated messaging feature was especially problematic. Based on experimental results, users would have less than a one-in-10 chance of finding a ride-match with automated messaging.

• The PC/modem software functioned well, but never fulfilled its potential. Intended ride-share and transit features were never implemented. Software distribution was limited and somewhat random.

The biggest weakness of the project, however, was revealed in the financial evaluation of the kiosk and flexpool elements. User satisfaction (high in the case of the kiosks) cannot overcome system costs.

Kiosk and flexpool costs were estimated on an annual and a per-use basis as a function of the system lifetime. Analysis was performed for two kiosk lifetimes: one year and five years. Five years is the standard depreciation period for computer equipment, as allowed by the Internal Revenue Service. We believe that it is a reasonable maximum lifetime for the Smart Traveler kiosks. The one-year lifetime is based on the possibility that kiosks will be removed one year after installation (due to expiration of funding). Installation costs were annualized in uniform amounts over the kiosk lifetime on the basis of a discount rate of seven percent per year.

Cost estimates were produced under the favorable assumption that all installation expenses (kiosk purchase, installation, software development, etc.) are incurred only once over the kiosk's lifetime.

Internal costs at Caltrans and other participating agencies were conservatively estimated at five percent of total project cost, accounting for project management, accounting, contracting, and costs incurred internally in accessing databases. All costs were assumed to be proportional to the number of kiosks installed, with the exception of software development costs, which were assumed to be a fixed cost, independent of the number of kiosks installed. Inflation was not considered in the analysis because some of the cost elements are subject to deflation (e.g., computer hardware purchases) while others are subject to inflation (e.g., maintenance). Annual costs were converted to a cost per use by assuming that the current average of 22.6 users per day per kiosk will not change.

For the existing installation base of 77 kiosks, the cost per use is estimated at $4.64 for a one-year lifetime and $1.99 for a five-year lifetime. Cost per use declines only slightly (to $4.16 and $1.88) as the installation base increases to 200, indicating that Smart Traveler is of sufficient size to nearly exhaust scale economies. Cost per use increases significantly as the installation base decreases to 10 (to $9.86 and $3.18), indicating that a smaller kiosk network would have considerably higher cost per use. For 77 kiosks with a five-year lifetime, installation is the number-one expense, accounting for 38 percent of the costs. Other major expenses, in decreasing order, are phone charges (27 percent), kiosk maintenance (15 percent), and software maintenance (seven percent).

For the ARMS system, analysis was performed for five flexpool lifetimes, ranging from one to five years. Cost estimates were produced under the favorable assumption that all installation costs are incurred only once over the system's lifetime. This assumption ignores the possibility that software will have to be upgraded to remain compatible with the CTS database; more importantly, it ignores the need to continue promoting the service throughout its lifetime. Internal costs at Caltrans and other participating agencies were estimated at five percent of total project cost, accounting for project management, accounting, contracting, and costs incurred internally in accessing databases. Inflation was not considered in the analysis.

The cost per use, at the current level of usage (27.4 calls per week), is approximately $110, assuming a one-year lifetime, and

$25, assuming a five-year lifetime. Clearly, the level of usage is far too low to gain significant scale economies. At a usage of 1,500 calls per week, cost would drop to $1.78 based on a five-year lifetime.

Assessment of Findings

In some aspects, SmartTraveler might be viewed as a public sector success story. It proved that a purely public partnership (relying on private-sector contractors) could deliver a working, user-friendly traveler information system within a short time frame. In addition, all of the system's elements—surveillance, database, data processing, communication, and interfaces—fall under public sector control, and for the most part they function reliably and as intended.

But SmartTraveler has not been a financial success. Neither kiosks nor ARMS have attracted sufficient usage to justify fixed annual and development costs. So while SmartTraveler demonstrates that the public sector can manage the development and installation of a sophisticated interactive information system, it does not demonstrate that it is able to deliver products that cost-effectively serve the traveler information market.

Lessons Learned

It is far too early to judge the success of TravInfo, which has yet to begin operation, and the SmartTraveler FOT, while completed, might not be representative of how public systems would perform elsewhere. Nevertheless, these two FOTs already provide important lessons that should be considered in future projects, both in transportation and in other areas. Most importantly, the purely public SmartTraveler project suffered because it was not market-responsive, and the TravInfo public/private partnership suffered from delays and wasted effort. Though TravInfo could still deliver on its promise of stimulating private sector innovations, this prospect has become more doubtful because of the delays in its implementation.

Given both the rapid progress in information technologies and the delays that are inherent to partnerships, there is some question whether a centralized, publicly managed database is the proper goal for ATIS or similar services. Put another way, it is quite possible that the creation of new organizations, with their reliance on committees, have the effect of slowing the entrepreneurial spirit in the development of information services. By delaying the product development cycle, it is more difficult for companies to respond to the marketplace.

As an alternative strategy, minimal public sector involvement is looking increasingly attractive. This strategy would involve creating a policy of open access to relevant public sector databases (at a reasonable fee) through standardized interfaces. Private companies could then process, fuse, and format the data to their liking in order to serve their customers. For example, one group of private companies could create the communication infrastructure and another would develop the products purchased by consumers (similar to how the radio and television broadcast industries evolved).

The downside of minimal public-sector involvement is that companies will have to invest in the processing and communication of information or pay other companies to do so; this could create a substantial barrier to entry, especially for smaller companies. This strategy could also necessitate subscription fees, slowing technology adoption and reducing transportation benefits. Nevertheless, given the rapid pace at which private companies introduce new products, and the slow pace at which partnerships are created, minimal involvement appears to be the most attractive path.

In closing, just because public agencies have information and data that are useful does not mean that they should jump to centralizing, processing, and widely disseminating it. Government must also be careful about investing in the development of domain-specific communication systems (such as wireless traffic data broadcasts) to support traveler information devices. The public sector's most important contribution has been more simple: providing access to pertinent data through defined interfaces. Once these interfaces are established, private companies have the means to provide value-added data-processing and dissemination of travel information to end users through a variety of communication media. Such an approach allows the information consumer to pull the information that he or she needs and desires through the private marketplace. A pull-based strategy may well be more effective than pushing information onto an ambivalent public.

Acknowledgments

Our research was supported by the California Department of Transportation (Caltrans) New Technology Division, and Partners for Advanced Transit and Highways. Our appreciation goes to the project staffs of TravInfo and SmartTraveler, who were extremely helpful in providing information. Appreciation also goes to the Management Board, Steering Committee, and Advisory Committee of TravInfo for participating in interviews and to the TravInfo Evaluation Oversight Team for providing helpful comments.

References

1. Abdel-Aty, M.A., Vaughn, K.M., Kitamura, R., and Jovanis, P.P. "Impact of ATIS on Drivers' Decisions and Route Choice: A Literature Review." PATH Research Report 93-11, 1993.

2. Arnott, R., de Palma, A., and Lindsey, R. "Does Information to Drivers Reduce Traffic Congestion?" *Transportation Research*, 1991, V. 25A, pp. 309–318.

3. DeBlasio, Allan J. "IVHS Institutional Issues: Monitoring Program Framework." Federal Highway Administration, Transportation Studies Division, PM-42-93-AD3, 1993.

4. Giuliano, G., Golob, J., and Hall, R. "SmartTraveler Evaluation," PATH Research Report (draft), 1995.

5. Hall, R.W. "Non-Recurrent Congestion: How Big is the Problem? Are Traveler Information Systems the Solution?" *Transportation Research*, V. 1C, pp. 89–103, 1993.

6. Hall, R.W., Lo, H.K. and Minge, E. "Organizing for ITS: Computer Integrated Transportation, Phase 1—Results for Arterial and Highway Transportation Management Centers," PATH Research Report 94-24, 1994.

7. Hall, R.W., Yim, Y.B., Khattak, A., Miller, M., and Weissenberger, S. "TravInfo Field Operational Test Evaluation Plan." PATH Working Paper 95-4, 1995.

8. Khattak, A. J., Al-Deek, H.M., and Hall, R.W. "Concept of an Advanced Traveler Information System Testbed for the Bay Area: Research Issues." *IVHS Journal*, V. 2, pp. 45–71, 1994.

9. Khattak, A., Al-Deek, H., Yim, Y.B., and Hall, R.W. "Bay Area ATIS Testbed Plan." PATH Research Report, UCB-ITS-PRR-92-1, 1992.

10. Klick, Kent and Allen, Inc. "Partnerships in the Implementation of ITS." Prepared for the Federal Highway Administration, contract DTFH61-94-C-00116, 1995.

11. U.S. Department of Transportation. "Public and Private Sector Roles in Intelligent Vehicle-Highway Systems (IVHS) Deployment," "Searching for Solutions, A Policy Discussion Series." Federal Highway Administration, Number 3, 1992.

Market Deployment of Transportation Information Infrastructure: Siemens' European Strategy

Hans K. Klein and Joseph M. Sussman

Introduction

What form will ITS deployment take? Will ITS be deployed like other transportation infrastructures, funded by the government and operated by agencies and firms traditionally active in road construction? Or will it assume a form more associated with information technology deployment, with private financing and leadership by computer and communications firms? These are basic questions facing ITS developers today.

This chapter sheds light on these issues by examining the experiences and strategy of Siemens Corporation as it deploys ITS in Germany. Siemens' ITS technology is Euro-Scout, an advanced traveler-information system for vehicle–roadside communications that offers both individual route guidance and area-wide traffic control. Euro-Scout is being deployed by the COPILOT Corporation, an ITS operating company created by Siemens and other German ITS corporations in 1994.

Siemens' Euro-Scout deployment is noteworthy for two reasons. First, the technology is being pioneered by an electronics and communications firm more commonly associated with information infrastructure than road-building. Second, Euro-Scout's infrastructure is being privately financed by the pooled capital of leading German ITS firms. This market-financed, electronics-based approach may define an "NII model" for deployment that could inform other ITS deployments.

The discussion that follows is structured in four parts. The first part identifies some of the general issues that arise in any ITS deployment. The second part examines Siemens' experiences as it confronted these issues in its Euro-Scout development program. Following this, the institutional design of COPILOT is analyzed as the solution to the problems Siemens confronted in deploying Euro-Scout. Finally, some lessons from these experiences are offered.

General Issues in Deployment

Each ITS deployment consists of a unique interaction between new technology and an existing social context. Despite this uniqueness, however, a number of general issues arise in each deployment. These general issues are:

- technology
- functionality
- finance
- politics.

With respect to *technology*, there exists a relationship between technology design and the need for cooperation in deployment. Technology design affects the need for cooperation because deployment of each component requires participation by a corresponding organization. Integration of the components then requires cooperation among those organizations. For example, many in-vehicle units can only be deployed by auto makers, while many traffic sensors can only be deployed by public agencies; a technology design integrating these components would require cooperation by both auto makers and public agencies. Ultimately, the deployment of any system requires cooperation by all the parties that figure in its technical design.

This need for cooperation in turn affects deployment and design. In some cases the fewer organizations needed to cooperate, the easier the deployment. In other cases, the need for cooperation between public and private organizations may increase the difficulty of deployment. Because technology designers possess some latitude in their choice of components, they can use those components that minimize the difficulties of cooperation. With the relationship between technology and deployment in mind, designers can create systems to realize ITS functionality and facilitate cooperation in deployment.

The second general issue in deployment is *functionality*. If a system is to be successfully deployed, its functions must provide benefits valued by users. Deployment strategies should build on the benefits that have been proven through field tests; however, those benefits may in fact be quite different from those originally anticipated.

Most ITS development programs have sought to create traffic control functions in order to improve traffic flows. However, as in other development programs, user needs and system benefits emerged during ITS field tests. For example, although technologists predicted that most user benefits would derive from increased traffic efficiency, field tests revealed that larger benefits in fact would come from environmental protection or commercial services.

Relative to the third general issue, *finance*, the needed capital must be assembled to pay for installation and ongoing operation. Involved in this are decisions about public and private financing. Traditional transportation infrastructure deployment is financed publicly by taxes. Private-sector market deployment is financed from the sale of goods and services to consumers. The choice between public and private financing depends on many factors, and in large part on whether ITS provides public benefits (e.g. reduced overall congestion) or private benefits (e.g. the ability to reserve a parking place in advance.) The choice also depends on the availability of mechanisms for charging those individuals who derive benefits.

Different financing schemes also imply different arrangements of cooperation and competition. A publicly financed system might be deployed by a single agency, while privately financed systems might be deployed by multiple competing firms.

Finally, deployment must take into account some *political* considerations. First, operation of infrastructure should be based on legitimate public authority. To the extent that ITS serves as an instrument of public policies for traffic control, system operators must be vested with legitimate authority to exercise such control.

In a private-sector deployment, this could require special arrangements for oversight by public authorities. Second, deployment must respect the reality of political influence. ITS affects the interests of private firms, public agencies, environmental groups, and other stakeholders, many of whom possess the power to block deployment. Successful deployment requires achieving consensus among these groups.

Technology, functionality, finance, and politics must all be taken into account if ITS is to be successfully deployed.

The Siemens Experience

In the approximately 15 years it spent developing Euro-Scout, Siemens confronted all four of these issues. Today's Euro-Scout is the third generation of a technology dating back to the 1970s. The first generation, "AUTO-SCOUT," was tested through the early 1980s, and the second generation, "ALI-SCOUT," was tested from 1989 to 1991 in the LISB field test in Berlin (Leit- und InformationsSystem Berlin). In developing Euro-Scout Siemens received some financial support from the German Ministry of Research and Technology (BMFT) and from the European Union. Most development costs were born by the firm itself, however.

The design of Euro-Scout consists of three parts: a traffic control center wired to intersections throughout a city; bidirectional, infrared communication beacons for vehicle–roadside communication; and in-vehicle units that can download route guidance instructions and upload travel times on the road network. The current Euro-Scout provides individual drivers with route-guidance assistance, and provides public authorities with traffic management capabilities [1, 2].

During development Siemens learned lessons that shaped its later institutional design. First, from the beginning it designed the Euro-Scout technology to minimize the need for cooperation with other organizations. The system design manifests this strategy. By using equipped vehicles as probes to report travel times, Siemens minimizes the need to cooperate with transport authorities—the system can gather traffic data independently of public agencies. Similarly, by using infrared beacons that communicate through windshields without physically penetrating the vehicle body, Siemens minimizes the need to cooperate with auto makers—in-vehicle units can be installed independently of auto makers.

Where Euro-Scout's technical design does require collaboration, however, is in the installation of roadside beacons and in the use of cables to a traffic control center. This infrastructure is the responsibility of the transport authorities that operate the existing traffic signal systems. However, in Germany most traffic systems have been installed by Siemens, so a collaborative relationship with these public entities already exists. Thus, the technical design does require some cooperation with public authorities, but in this case Siemens already has a well-established relationship with them.

The second general issue in deployment is functionality. Euro-Scout's functionality reflects what Siemens has learned about users' conception of "benefits." Like most ITS developers, Siemens originally thought that the primary public benefits of the technology would lie in increasing the efficiency of roads. As it learned during development, however, many city governments were critical of any system that increased vehicle use in cities. At the local level, environmental protection, not traffic efficiency, was the top priority.

Only after Euro-Scout was modified to incorporate environmental "green" functionality did it offer real benefits for local government. Route-guidance information was expanded to encourage modal switches from automobiles to mass transit, and traffic control centers were given the possibility of managing traffic according to criteria of air quality. These modifications made Euro-Scout useful in the eyes of the public authorities that would use the system. Without such sensitivity to the needs of local authorities, Siemens might have encountered indifference or opposition to deployment.

Siemens also learned difficult lessons about the financing of its new infrastructure. Private, not public, funds would have to finance Euro-Scout deployment. Although Siemens had received public financial support for its LISB field test, the fall of the Berlin Wall in 1989 and the subsequent reunification of Germany made impossible any further public financing by the federal government. Public funds would now be used for essential infrastructure in the former East Germany rather than for new initiatives in the West. The financial resources needed for deployment would have to come from the private sector, and perhaps be supplemented by local public funding.

Development taught lessons about politics as well. Even privately developed infrastructure is subject to democratic norms. Public funding for the LISB field test was awarded in 1985 on the condition that the project be opened to other firms besides Siemens. National ministries feared that providing public assistance to just one firm would be unfair to its competitors. Furthermore, rival firms had a strong interest in participating in LISB, in order to keep abreast of Siemens. Bosch was able to win a place in the LISB field test. A similar dynamic could be expected at deployment: deployment would not be politically feasible without winning the support of rival firms.

Thus Siemens faced the following parameters for ITS deployment: deployment would have to unite all the groups that figured in its technical design; it would have to provide benefits such as environmental protection; it would have to be financed privately; and it would have to allow for participation by other firms.

The Institutional Design of COPILOT

Institutional design unites strategy and structure. It translates technical, functional, economic, and political parameters into an organization that formalizes the roles of the parties deploying ITS. COPILOT's different design features respond to the different issues in its deployment.

Incorporated in 1994, COPILOT is an operating company ("Betriebergesellschaft") that plans, installs, finances, and operates ITS infrastructure. The three essential design features of COPILOT are its ownership structure, its product, and its relationship to public authorities.

By far the most important design feature of COPILOT is its ownership structure. The company is a private corporation jointly owned by the leading firms in the German ITS industry. The three main shareholders are Siemens, Bosch, and Daimler-Benz's ITF Intertraffic. Two auto makers, Volkswagen and Mercedes-Benz, also participate. These five firms contribute capital and share control over the company.

This ownership structure addresses many deployment issues. First, joint ownership largely solves the financial problem of cost. Early cost estimates for the deployment of 20,000 infrared beacons throughout Germany ranged from DM 500 million to DM 1 billion ($328 million to $656 million) [3, 4]. With public financing not feasible, COPILOT pools the private capital of several large firms. In this way it marshals sufficient resources for deployment.

Second, this joint ownership arrangement satisfies the interests of public authorities and rival firms. Having learned from LISB that a go-it-alone strategy was not feasible, Siemens opened COPILOT to other firms. This decision satisfied public authorities' interest in fairness because they can allow private deployment without favoring one firm over others. It also satisfied Siemens' industry rivals by allowing them to participate in the new market for ITS.

Joint ownership also lessens the risk of inter-organizational dependence and control. With COPILOT deploying ITS, public authorities avoid depending on a single supplier. Because expertise in planning, installing, and operating ITS resides in many firms, no one firm gains strategic advantage. Furthermore, ownership of COPILOT is structured so that no single partner can control it. Ownership is divided equally among the three major partners; thus, no one firm can act without support from another partner.

A second important design feature of COPILOT is its sale of services rather than of technical devices. COPILOT earns its revenue by collecting, processing, and selling information. Its information services include dynamic route guidance, parking assistance, and warnings about hazardous driving conditions caused by fog and ice. Future services will include fleet management and access control.

This arrangement allows for the reconciliation of cooperation and competition among COPILOT's partners. Services will be available over various hardware systems sold by competing firms. Although COPILOT will install Euro-Scout's beacon infrastructure, it will also install systems produced by Siemens' partners and rivals. Thus, at the software level (information services) the partners cooperate, while they compete at the hardware level (especially in-vehicle units). The conflicting imperatives for cooperation and competition are therefore realized.

The interoperability of rival systems for Euro-Scout required agreement on technical standards. Achieving such agreement was facilitated by the fact that only Siemens was ready for the service's deployment.

In marketing Euro-Scout Siemens faced a completely new market with no historical demand curve by which to select a price. Lacking a precedent in ITS, Siemens sought a comparable technology by which to orient its market strategy. Significantly, it chose television, an information technology, rather than a traditional transportation technology. COPILOT's initial pricing of Euro-Scout matched the fee structure the German government charged to consumers for television ownership. The firm felt that consumers would make purchasing decisions about ITS in the context of another NII-related product.

The third feature of COPILOT's institutional design is the operating company's relationship with public authorities. Although COPILOT does seek financial participation from local governments, it does not assume that there will be backing from the German federal government. Most financing comes from COPILOT itself.

Local governments only give a license to COPILOT to install and operate infrastructure. In exchange, COPILOT provides local governments with environmental protection functions, such as driver information that is designed to facilitate modal switches from vehicles to mass transit. Furthermore, although privately operated, authority for traffic management functions remains with the local government. This ensures that public functions are subject to legitimate control.

In summary, the design of COPILOT responds to the many requirements of deployment. Joint ownership addresses both the issues of finance and the interests of public authorities and private stakeholders. The sale of services defines an area of cooperation separate from market competition for hardware devices. And COPILOT's relationship with public authorities avoids the need for public financing while still respecting public authority.

Conclusions

The experiences of Siemens and the design of COPILOT may offer useful lessons for other programs. First and foremost, successful deployment of ITS must reconcile a broad array of interrelated requirements. Technical, functional, financial, and political issues all figure in deployment, and an awareness of the web of interrelations is a prerequisite for devising an effective deployment strategy [5].

Second, the development and deployment of ITS require flexibility and a willingness to compromise. In response to the concerns of city governments Siemens modified the functionality of Euro-Scout. More significantly, in order to build consensus with its rivals Siemens relaxed its commitment to its own Euro-Scout technology by agreeing that COPILOT's information services would be supported by different firms' hardware. Only through such willingness to compromise on basic interests could Siemens achieve cooperation with local governments and other firms.

Third, ITS may be more valuable to local governments as a technology for environmental protection than for traffic efficiency. Most existing top-down, technology-push development programs have assumed that gains in traffic efficiency would justify deployment. Yet local governments may have a greater need for environmental functionality that leads to fewer, not more, cars on their roads. ITS programs may find that deployment requires modifying systems to address local governments' need for environmental functionality.

Fourth, COPILOT is strong evidence that private deployment of ITS is possible. The small amount of public support in both its development and deployment is noteworthy. Although receiving some public assistance in LISB and later field tests, Siemens mostly used its own capital in development. More importantly, deployment will be privately funded by Siemens, Bosch, ITF Intertraffic, and others. Other countries with limited public funds can take heart that private capital may be able to fund ITS deployment.

COPILOT does offer one potentially negative lesson, however. COPILOT is still a German, and not yet a fully European, institution. The consensus that Siemens built among ITS firms extended only to Germany's borders. Whether France, Italy, or the United Kingdom will grant deployment licenses to a German firm for infrastructure deployment remains to be seen. This may pose a risk to the deployment of compatible technology throughout Europe. With its national roots, COPILOT does not yet fully address the need for pan-European compatibility in deployment.

Siemens' deployment of Euro-Scout in COPILOT may offer a model of ITS deployment that is more similar to the NII than to traditional transportation infrastructure. Although hardly an outsider to the transportation sector, Siemens is first and foremost an electronics firm. Its success with COPILOT has shown that an electronics firm can pioneer ITS deployment. In pricing ITS according to the existing costs of television, however, Siemens bargained that consumers will conceptualize driver information services more as an NII technology than a transport technology. Furthermore, COPILOT's market-based approach differs from the traditional public financing of transport infrastructure. By pooling private capital and balancing cooperation and competition, it has shown that private firms can deploy ITS.

How does COPILOT compare with other ITS development programs? Siemens' approaches to development and deployment may be more similar to those used in Japan than to those in the U.S. In Japan, ITS development was supported early on by the Ministry of International Trade and Industry (MITI), whose mission to promote commercial technology development resembles that of Germany's Ministry of Research and Technology (BMFT). Subsequent to that early public support, most development has been funded by industry. This roughly parallels the pattern seen in Germany.

In the U.S., however, ITS development has ridden on a wave of post-Interstate public funding. In contrast to the tens of millions of dollars of public funding in Germany and Japan, U.S. public funding has been on the order of one billion dollars. Given such decisive public-sector influence, continued governmental leadership in deployment seems the likely final outcome. However, through its participation in the U.S. program, particularly in the Michigan-based Fast-Trac field test, Siemens may yet bring its NII model of deployment to the U.S.

References

1. Von Tomkewitsch, Romuald. "Dynamic Route Guidance and Interactive Transport Management with ALI-SCOUT." *IEEE Transactions on Vehicular Technology*, Vol. 40, No. 1, February 1991, pp. 45–50.

2. Hoffman, Günter, Sparmann, Jürg, von Tomkewitsch, Romuald, Zechnall, Wolf. *Schlußbericht, Forschungsprojekt Leit- und Informationssystem Berlin.* Berlin, July 1991.

3. "Siemens Operating Company Announcement Expected Soon." *Inside IVHS*, 14 September 1992, pp. 1–3.

4. "Siemens Expects Firms to Sign Operating Co. Pact in Six Months." *Inside IVHS*, 18 January 1993, pp. 7–8.

5. Hughes, Thomas P. "The Seamless Web: Technology, Science, Et Cetera, Et Cetera." *The Social Study of Science*, 1986, Vol. 16, pp. 281–292.

Afterword (added in proof, April 1996)

In January 1996, twenty months after its inception, COPILOT Corporation ceased operations. The high cost of installing roadside beacons was the reason given for the closure. However, the Euro-Scout system will continue development in field tests announced by Siemens and Daimler-Benz for Berlin, and COPILOT may be relaunched using a different technology for vehicle roadside communication [6]. Although this experience raises doubts about the ability of industry to finance ITS deployment, COPILOT's lessons concerning the interrelation of diverse requirements and the need for flexibility in deployment remain valid.

Additional Reference

6. "COPILOT Failure Triggers Euro-Scout Rethink as Siemens Looks at GSM." *The Intelligent Highway: European Transport Telematics Update*, 22 February 1996, pp. 1–3.

ITS Implementation Issues

Institutional Issues in Local Implementation

Douglas C. Melcher and Daniel Roos

Introduction

This paper explores the institutional issues associated with the deployment and use of fiber-optic backbone communication networks for Intelligent Transportation Systems. Several case studies are described and broader public-private issues in the deployment of communications infrastructure for ITS are identified.

Backbone communications systems that support broadband networking are an integral part of the future of ITS, as demonstrated by the proposed national ITS architectures developed by Loral Federal Systems and Rockwell International and by numerous ongoing ITS deployments. The communications backbone interconnects traffic management control centers with devices such as closed circuit television (CCTV) cameras, variable message signs, roadside beacons, and vehicle detectors. Many of the applications supported by these devices, such as video surveillance, require broadband, real-time communications to realize their full potential.

Compared with alternative transmission media such as wireless, twisted pair copper wire, or coaxial cable, fiber is often a technically superior option for broadband land-line communications because it is reliable, cost effective, and easy to maintain. Fiber is insensitive to electromagnetic interference, provides network security, and can transmit information over long distances without intermediate repeaters. Accordingly, transportation agencies are increasingly selecting fiber-optic networking technology to meet the backbone communications needs of ITS.

In obtaining fiber-optic communications capacity, transportation agencies must decide whether to lease capacity, build their own communications network, or leverage right-of-way to obtain communications capacity. Several key decision factors are involved, including cost, reliability, accountability, operations and maintenance, resource availability, timing, and upgrades and reserve capacity:

• *Cost.* Transportation agencies must consider the total cost of deployment for owned infrastructure, including initial and ongoing costs, versus the costs for leasing comparable communications capacity from the private sector.

• *Reliability.* The reliability of leased and owned systems can vary considerably, depending upon the network architecture and the quality of operations and maintenance. Transportation agencies that require high levels of reliability for "mission critical" applications such as emergency services will make reliability a priority.

• *Accountability.* From a political and managerial perspective, accountability for network failures is an important decision factor, since transportation officials may be held accountable for the performance of ITS.

• *Operations and maintenance.* Telecommunications networks must be operated and maintained by highly skilled technicians and engineers. Officials at transportation agencies must carefully consider whether top-quality staff can be attracted and retained.

• *Resource availability.* The viability of leasing may depend upon the availability of private sector infrastructure in strategic locations.

• *Timing.* The need for rapid project implementation may limit the options for obtaining telecommunications capacity. Also, the opportunities available for obtaining communications infrastructure may change over time.

• *Upgrades and reserve capacity.* Transportation agencies must also consider the future potential needs of the transportation system and therefore the need for an upgradeable and extensible communications system.

Many variations on the development of leased and owned systems are demonstrated by the six case studies presented in this paper; Table 1 summarizes the general differences between the cases. The Connecticut Department of Transportation (ConnDOT), which is now deploying an incident management system along a segment of the I-95 corridor, chose to own its network. The Massachusetts Highway Department (MHD) and the Texas Department of Transportation (TxDOT) in San Antonio are deploying government owned fiber-optic networks for ITS that they will eventually operate and maintain. The City of San Jose Department of Streets and Parks (SJDSP) is also deploying an owned fiber-optic network to support traffic management and is already handling operations and maintenance using in-house staff.

Several transportation agencies have leveraged right-of-way access to develop public-private partnerships for ITS. These "shared resources" arrangements offer the opportunity for transportation agencies to obtain new services and for private sector companies to expand networks. The experiences of Bay Area Rapid Transit (BART) and the Missouri Highway and Transportation Department (MHTD) are described in the case studies. BART will wholly own and operate its system, while the MHTD approach is effectively a leased capacity arrangement where ongoing costs are met with right-of-way access charges.

This chapter explores several lessons learned from the case studies and identifies some of the disincentives and incentives for pubic-private collaboration. The authors will discuss the institutional frameworks that will be needed to support the deployment, operations, and maintenance of ITS, and will conclude that transportation agencies need to more fully justify the public-private relationships selected for the deployment of communications infrastructure for ITS. Better information-sharing between the public and private sectors could benefit both transportation agencies, as they seek to deploy fiber-optic networks, and private telecommunications service providers, as they seek new business opportunities. New institutional frameworks may be appropriate to ensure that the full potential of ITS is realized.

Table 1 Summary of Cases*

Jurisdiction	Leased Service	Owned System (in-house operations and maintenance)	Owned System (outsourced operations and maintenance)	Shared Resource
ConnDOT			•	
MHD		•		
TxDOT		•		
San Jose DSP		•		
BART		•		•
MHTD	•			•

* There is some uncertainty regarding whether ConnDOT will outsource or use in-house staff for operations and maintenance in the future. The distinction between in-house- operations and maintenance and outsourced operations and maintenance is somewhat blurred because in several cases transportation agencies initially plan to outsource but may switch depending upon future costs and benefits. ConnDOT and MHD each explicitly required that operations and maintenance be initially handled by the contractors responsible for system installation to ensure that the contractor would have an incentive to develop a system with low cost operations and maintenance requirements. However, MHD indicated that operations and maintenance would most likely be handled in-house after the contract period expires. ConnDOT plans to assess the costs and benefits of various alternatives in the future. The table entries are based upon likely outcomes after the communications systems are deployed and operating.

Cases

The cases presented here include (1) the Connecticut Department of Transportation (ConnDOT) incident management system; (2) the Massachusetts Highway Department (MHD) Central Artery/Tunnel (CA/T) project; (3) the Texas Department of Transportation (TxDOT) San Antonio District Advanced Traffic Management System; (4) the City of San Jose Department of Streets and Parks (SJDSP) Traffic Signal Management Project and Motorist Information Systems Project; (5) the Bay Area Rapid Transit (BART) Telesystem; and (6) the Missouri Highway and Transportation Department (MHTD) statewide ITS deployment.

Each study was prepared in consultation with staff at the Volpe National Transportation Systems Center. Gary Ritter of the Volpe Center was particularly helpful, providing valuable directions and criticism. Phone interviews with representatives of various transportation agencies, conducted during March and April of 1995, provided the primary basis for the case studies. The cases were originally presented at a unique day-long meeting of officials from public transportation agencies and private telecommunications service providers at the Intelligent Transportation Systems Infrastructure Forum hosted by the Volpe Center in Cambridge, MA on April 27, 1995.

Connecticut Case Study: I-95 Incident Management System

The Connecticut Department of Transportation (ConnDOT) is presently deploying an incident management system along the I-95 corridor from the New York State border east through Branford, CT. The corridor has above-average congestion problems, which are caused in part by highway incidents and can be reduced using incident management techniques. The primary goal of the system is to reduce the time required to detect, verify, and respond to an accident. High-resolution video surveillance cameras will allow incidents to be monitored from an operations center, which will then provide traveler information, such as alternate route recommendations, to motorists.

Construction of the incident management system began in October 1993 and is nearing completion. The system will eventually include 91 cameras and 217 radar detectors, which will service 56 miles of roadway. A fiber network was installed along I-95 and additional fiber loops are in place for future expansion.

Parsons Brinckerhoff Quade & Douglas, Inc., of Glastonbury, CT, was hired in 1992 to research and design the incident management system, taking into consideration the technical tradeoffs of various communications system designs. Based upon their recommendation, ConnDOT decided to deploy a fiber network because of its immunity to electromagnetic interference, broadband and real-time service capabilities for video surveillance applications, and relatively small cable diameter, which conserves conduit space.

A Request For Proposal (RFP) for the system was released in late 1992/early 1993 that provided for individual contractors to install conduit for each of three contiguous sections of I-95. ConnDOT believed that a single contractor would not be capable of deploying the conduit quickly enough to meet the Department's goals. The contract for the middle portion of highway included pulling the fiber and installing the electronics for the full 56-mile deployment. Rizo Electric was awarded the contract to install the middle section of conduit and ITS components, including the communications system. Ducci Electric and Semec handled the remaining conduit installation contracts. The full cost of the deployment, including conduit, is about $26 million, of which 80 percent is funded by the US Department of Transportation (U.S. DOT) Federal Highway Administration (FHWA).

The conduit is presently in place and Rizo Electric is nearing completion of the incident management system.[1] The first two years of operations and maintenance will be handled by Rizo Electric, after which time ConnDOT will consider continuing outsourcing operations and maintenance. SmartRoutes, Inc. is under a two year contract to operate the traffic control center.[2]

The decision to own the fiber communications system rather than lease capacity was made within ConnDOT and was supported by the Department's Commissioner. No study was performed to determine the cost-effectiveness of each option, and the decision factors were not complicated or sophisticated. Officials at ConnDOT simply wanted an owned system because the Department's "philosophy" is to own the infrastructure required to carry out its mission. The one decision factor identified was that there was some concern that obtaining services through a leasing contract would take longer to arrange and could delay implementation of the incident management system. ConnDOT did not investigate the extent to which Southern New England Telephone (SNET) or another telecommunications service provider could have offered sufficient communications capacity. No reliability study was performed to ascertain whether leasing, owning, or outsourcing would be the most effective strategy. A decision simply was made to have an outside contractor handle operations and maintenance.

Massachusetts Case Study: Central Artery/Tunnel Project

The Central Artery/Tunnel (CA/T) is a multi-billion-dollar project to replace Boston's elevated Central Artery (I-93) with a subsurface expressway and to construct a third harbor tunnel to Logan

International Airport accessible from the Massachusetts Turnpike (I-90). The CA/T comprises 7.5 miles of roadway, most of which will be covered or submerged. The project is currently administered by CA/T management under the Massachusetts Highway Department (MHD). However, the state is considering transferring control of the CA/T system to the Massachusetts Turnpike Authority (MTA) to allow the project to be funded with toll revenues.[3]

The CA/T project includes the deployment of a fiber-optic network to support monitoring and control of speed-limit and lane-change signs, variable message signs, closed circuit television (CCTV) cameras, and other ITS components.

Essential characteristics for the communications system were identified in a 1990 concept report prepared by Bechtel/Parsons Brinckerhoff, including the need for highly reliable voice, video, and data communications.[4] The report concluded that the communications system should rely upon a fiber-optic backbone and that the state should adopt a policy "on the selling or leasing of publicly funded spare conduit space and spare cable capacity to private revenue producing companies."[5] The Bechtel/Parsons Brinckerhoff report was reviewed and endorsed by at least three entities: CA/T management, the Massachusetts Highway Department (MHD), and the U.S. Department of Transportation (U.S. DOT). This process involved the design managers and project directors for the state and within CA/T management. The state decided to build and maintain its own fiber-optic network. At this time MHD has no plans to lease reserve communications capacity to the private sector.

The project planners wanted to minimize potential disturbances to the communication system induced by electromagnetic interference and other physical and environmental phenomena. There was a clear recognition that standardized signal transmission technologies should be adopted to ensure network compatibility, extensibility, and reliability. These functional needs led to the selection of a fiber-optic system for the communications backbone. Alternatives, including microwave, twisted pair copper wire, and coaxial cable, were also considered. Each medium was rated on the basis of coordination, integration, compatibility, flexibility, and maintenance/service ability. In each category, fiber was determined to be superior. Specifically, fiber does not require intermediate repeaters and is less susceptible to electromagnetic interference than alternative media. Moreover, the relatively small cable diameter conserves conduit space, which is limited and may be required for future applications. Fiber is also capable of supporting a wide range of delivery needs, including voice, video, and data transmissions.

In September 1993 an RFP was issued for the third harbor tunnel portion of the communications system, which would be owned and eventually operated by MHD. The RFP required the contractor to have initial responsibility for operating the system. A single RFP was utilized to keep costs down and focus accountability. The RFP covered monitoring and controlling speed-limit and lane-change signs, variable message signs, emergency telephones, a closed-circuit television system, heat detection and fire alarms, and the control system for ventilation fans. NYNEX, the regional telephone company, did not bid in this phase of the project, presumably because the scope was significantly broader than its established line of business.[6]

Perini-Powell was selected in January 1994 as the general contractor for the communications system development. The contract required Perini-Powell to utilize off-the-shelf equipment to satisfy all of the system's requirements in order to avoid unforeseen problems, such as technical incompatibilities. The contractor will receive $8.6 million for installing the multi- and single-mode fiber network.[7] A second RFP will be issued in 1998 for the remaining portion of the communications system; the fiber backbone for the second phase is expected to cost about $11 million. When completed in 2001, the total CA/T single-mode backbone will be approximately 7.2 miles long and will have cost about $20 million.[8] The CA/T fiber network is based upon the Synchronous Optical Network (SONET) standard to ensure ease of future upgrades and system maintenance. Network capacity is OC-3 or 155 Mbps. Perini-Powell is using AT&T as the system vendor for the project.

Project planners are confident that the system can easily be upgraded using off-the-shelf components; the equipment vendor will be responsible for ensuring that its products provide sufficient interoperability and extensibility. CA/T management expressed confidence that the equipment selected by Perini-Powell is high quality and meets all of the project specifications. Life-cycle cost data suggests that Perini-Powell will succeed in making a profit from the project.

The key factors influencing the state's decision to buy rather than lease a fiber-optic network were cost, reliability, and availability of leased infrastructure; planners also considered operations and maintenance issues. According to project planners, there was no cost alternative to procurement in 1990 and there probably is not one today. Video applications for the network require broadband transmission capacity, which is typically very expensive to lease. Cost analyses carried out by technical and estimating staff showed that procurement was the only viable alternative for the state, since leasing could have been about five times more expensive.[9] Aggregate operations and maintenance costs for the entire CA/T project were repeatedly reviewed by the Project Director and will continue to be reviewed on a periodic basis. The RFP for the communications system included life-cycle costs for the first five years of system operation and maintenance to encourage Perini-Powell to consider operations and maintenance costs in designing the communications system.

System reliability was also a critical decision factor. The 1990 concept report clearly states the need for a highly reliable communications system. In an interview, project planners expressed doubts about the ability of the private sector to ensure sufficient reliability using the public switched network because communications service providers have multiple customers and therefore may not prioritize CA/T communications. Moreover, public switched network upgrades unrelated to the CA/T system could cause network failures that would otherwise not occur if the system were wholly owned and operated by the state. Although service contracts can be arranged with system reliability clauses designed to assure the buyer that network failure will not occur, state planners suggested that these clauses may be useless in preventing outages. In an interview, project engineers suggested that the required mean-time-before-failure of the system needs to be five years or greater, but that in the public switched network it is typically less than one year.[10] According to project planners, when the concept report was prepared in 1990 private companies were just getting started with fiber deployments in the area and may not have been well positioned to meet the communications needs of the CA/T system.[11]

The 1990 concept report specifically recommends that the state adopt a policy regarding leasing reserve capacity. Although the overall report was endorsed by the project managers involved in the deployment, no formal policy was adopted. It is standard engineering practice to build as much as 50 percent extra capacity for potential future needs, but no plan exists to systematically lease reserve telecommunications capacity for the CA/T system.

A policy was established to reserve conduit capacity for future needs. The Boston Transportation Department has expressed an interest in using conduit capacity in the third harbor tunnel. However, according to state planners, much of the right-of-way for the rest of the CA/T system may not be marketable because it is 70 to 100 feet below the earth's surface and therefore not easily interconnected to surface-level telecommunications customers.[12]

It should be noted that the Commonwealth is actively working to exchange right-of-way access for fiber along the state's highways.[13] For example, the MTA obtained fiber under a contract with four telecommunications companies that paid an estimated $25 million to deploy fiber along the Massachusetts Turnpike (I-90) and will pay about $50 million over 30 years to access the Turnpike's right-of-way.[14] The MTA paid an estimated $5.5 million and received twelve fibers as part of the deal.[15] The MTA agreed to allow the Commonwealth of Massachusetts to use four of the twelve fiber-optic lines that it controls. The state plans to continue to pursue similar arrangements for the purpose of developing its telecommunications infrastructure. The MTA's fiber network will eventually be integrated into the CA/T communications system.

Texas Case Study: San Antonio

The San Antonio District of the Texas Department of Transportation (TxDOT) is developing an Advanced Traffic Management System (ATMS) that will provide transportation and law enforcement officials with real-time information about accidents and incidents on the San Antonio highway system.[16] The traffic management system includes variable message signs, CCTV cameras, vehicle detectors, and signaling for intersections and lane control. The deployment will eventually service 191 miles of highway, the initial 26 miles of which are nearing completion. The San Antonio project includes the development of a fiber-based communications network to support the ATMS. The backbone will utilize the SONET standard and will run at OC3 (155 Mbps) speeds. The network is fully redundant and uses single-mode fiber.

Five aerospace companies bid to construct the initial 26 miles of the ATMS. The Request For Proposal (RFP) identified the complete design and scale of the system and bundled construction of the communications system with other ITS components. No consultants were involved in the design process. The $32 million contract was awarded to the low bidder, AlliedSignal Technical Services, which will install the ATMS, including the operations control center and the communications system. The 26-mile stretch will include 50 variable message signs, 59 CCTV cameras, 359 lane change signals, 800 loop detectors, and 15 signalized intersections. RFPs will be issued for remaining portions of the ATMS, which will eventually service 191 miles of highway with about 500 CCTV cameras and 300 variable message signs.[17] The overall cost for the ITS deployment is estimated at $151 million.

The decision to develop an owned infrastructure was made in-house by staff at the TxDOT San Antonio District office. The district staff is centrally responsible for setting deployment priorities and designing systems, and does not need permission from TxDOT in Austin to deploy new infrastructure. However, approval from the Federal Highway Administration (FHWA) was necessary because 80 percent of the funding for the deployment is being provided by the federal government. Outside consultants did not contribute to the decision to own rather than lease the communications system.

A formal study of lease/own tradeoffs was not completed because telecommunications capacity was clearly not available and the cost disadvantages of leasing were "obvious" according to a project manager. Southwestern Bell, the regional telephone company, did not have the necessary infrastructure in place to support broadband communication, which typically requires at least DS3 (45

Mbps) capacity.[18] Moreover, even if DS3 lines were in place, the leasing option could have been rejected on the basis of cost alone, because broadband capacity is typically very expensive to lease. Reliability was not a decision factor; leased services would probably have been sufficiently reliable to support transportation applications. Although it was noted that not all transportation district offices are equally capable of handling operations and maintenance for complex ATMS, staff within the San Antonio District expressed confidence that they have the personnel needed to ensure system reliability.

Many public- and private-sector organizations have tried to gain access to the fiber capacity being installed by the TxDOT San Antonio District. The system is designed with sufficient communications capacity for future ITS needs, but no extra capacity is being built. The present policy is not to lease capacity, though the District may re-examine this issue in the future.

The San Antonio District is considering leveraging its right-of-way for future deployments. The utilities use the right-of-way now, but preferred access could be offered. If future cost advantages may be obtained by leasing capacity from a private carrier, the District will consider this option for future deployments as well.[19]

Thus far, the District is satisfied with the deployment, and no technical problems have arisen. The system will become part of a regional traffic management system that will be operated out of the San Antonio control center. Eventually the system could extend across a 50,000 square mile region.[20]

California Case Study: City of San Jose

The City of San Jose is working on a Traffic Signal Management Project (TSMP) and a Motorist Information Systems Project (MISP) as part of its ongoing efforts to deploy ITS. The deployment involves applications such as changeable message signs, CCTV, and traffic-light control. The system includes CCTV cameras, message signs, and intersections with communications capabilities. By June of 1996, 550 of San Jose's 650 intersections will be connected to the control system.

An ITS deployment options report was provided to the City Council by DKS Associates and the City of San Jose Department of

Streets and Parks (SJDSP). The report was finalized in 1990, initial deployment began in 1991, and completion of the TSMP is anticipated in June 1996. Total funding for the ITS deployment is $26.8 million, of which $7.9 million is from the city and $18.9 million is from grants. The cost for the fiber component of the system is not available because of cost accounting difficulties involving the conduit, which is shared for twisted pair and fiber infrastructure. Construction of the communications system as well as operations and maintenance is handled by the SJDSP.

Twisted pair is being used for interconnecting traffic intersections, which are equipped with 1200-baud modems. The communications at each intersection supports alarm monitoring and remote traffic signal adjustment.[21] Loop detectors measure traffic flow, providing data that is used to create a schematic representation of the traffic flow at the traffic control center. About half of the twisted pair lines are leased and the remaining are owned by the city.

Fiber is being installed to support full motion video with the intention of potentially developing segments of the system into a communications backbone. The system is compatible with the Fiber Distributed Data Interface (FDDI) standard and may be upgraded to the SONET standard if a backbone is installed. The system is configured using a hub topology, with one fiber dedicated to interconnecting each CCTV camera to the central traffic control center. At this time there are no multiplexers in the system.

System planning considered the total budget of the project with the objective of maximizing both the total amount of city owned infrastructure and the overall capabilities of the ITS system. Owned infrastructure was considered superior because the SJDSP wanted to avoid the uncertainty of leasing costs and felt that the city would be much more likely to prioritize maintenance than a private-sector service provider. The City Council was made aware that higher-end ITS deployment options would require a larger funding commitment for operations and maintenance. The City Council agreed to provide necessary funding to support staffing requirements, but grant money obviated the need to request full funding.

At this time the city does not lease capacity to public or private entities because it is reserved for future ITS requirements. However, the City of San Jose Telecommunications Working Group, which is comprised of city management and directors, is developing a leasing policy. Private telecommunications service providers have not expressed any concerns with the city's deployment of telecommunications infrastructure to support the TSMP.

A new water distribution system being built in San Jose to satisfy EPA regulations will require much of the city's right-of-way to be opened for construction. The city may use this opportunity, and its ability to leverage right-of-way, to develop a fiber-optic backbone to support ITS. At this time there is considerable private-sector interest in using this opportunity to access the right-of-way and deploy fiber.

Some problems with the Department's installation work have arisen due to the staff's lack of familiarity with large-scale systems implementation. However, staff expressed confidence that as their familiarity with the technology grows, system operations and maintenance should function smoothly. No major problems are anticipated.

California Case Study: Bay Area Rapid Transit

Bay Area Rapid Transit (BART) operates a major rapid transit system in the San Francisco Bay region and is presently deploying ITS through a joint development project with MFS Network Technologies (MFSNT). The deployment consists of two separate but related projects. First, MFSNT will build and maintain a conduit system in the BART-owned right-of-way, which will provide revenue to both BART and MFSNT. Second, MFSNT will deploy a new fiber-optic and wireless telecommunications system, called the BART Telesystem, that will be wholly owned and operated by the transit system. Conduit will be installed along 71 to 86 miles of track with space reserved for a sheath of 48 fiber strands dedicated to transportation applications. The total cost of the fiber system including controllers is about $7 million. Kingston Cole Associates provided consulting advice for the joint conduit development and suggested that the conduit could pay for itself and provide enough revenue to pay for the BART Telesystem. The Telesystem was designed in-house by BART staff. MFSNT and BART finalized the agreement in December 1994.

The ITS system will eventually include high-resolution video surveillance systems, video monitors to provide traveler information, train control and monitoring, and destination sign and announcement control. Many of these systems are already operational; however, applications such as video surveillance will not be available until broadband infrastructure is in place. The Telesystem will support all of BART's needs, including communications for police and maintenance workers.

In the spring of 1993 BART issued a Request For Proposal (RFP) that provided several options for bidders. The first option was to bid on installing conduit in a joint development project with BART that would involve sharing profits from conduit tenants. The second option involved bidding on both the conduit joint development and the Telesystem as a package deal. The third option provided the opportunity to bid on obtaining right-of-way for cellular sites that would allow a cellular carrier to provide its customers service within the transit system. MFSNT was selected in August 1994 as the top candidate because of its willingness to bid on both the conduit joint development and the Telesystem. The only other bidder willing to handle multiple portions of the project was a California-based company called Info Systems Inc.; however, the company was not considered as a serious contender because the size of the job was too large for the relatively small company.

The joint development for the conduit system provides for the installation and maintenance of a four-inch conduit with an inner duct reserved for the exclusive use of BART. MFSNT will market the remaining capacity to telecommunications service providers and will split the revenue with BART, which will receive a 91% share[22] MFSNT will invest about $3 million to build the conduit system.

MFSNT will build the Telesystem and provide training to BART employees, who will then be responsible for operating and maintaining the system. The Telesystem includes both wireless and fiber technology, which, along with offering versatility, provides system redundancy. Wireless will primarily be used for police and maintenance communications, and the fiber will support applications such as video surveillance. Fiber was selected because it provides security and broadband capacity and is not susceptible to electromagnetic interference.[22] The total cost of the BART Telesystem, including both fiber and wireless components, is about $44.6 million, which is being financed by Pitney-Bowes Credit Corporation (PBCC).

All the fiber being installed is single mode and will initially run at OC-3 speeds (155 Mbps). The California Department of Transportation (Caltrans) will receive control of four fibers for its Traffic Operations System (TOS) because some of the conduit will utilize right-of-way that is jointly controlled by Caltrans and BART. The decision to procure a fiber network was made primarily within BART, although Caltrans was also involved because of the shared right-of-way.

It was felt that the Telesystem should be wholly owned and operated by BART in part because relying upon a third party in an emergency was considered highly undesirable. A strong belief was expressed that leasing capacity would undermine the quality of the transit system. There was a strong interest in maintaining full control of the system and it was described as the "philosophy" of BART to do so. It was also noted that the transit system has unique needs that are not comparable to fiber deployments that support highway-oriented ITS applications because much of the system is subsurface and includes unique operations such as vehicle control. Leasing capacity from a private company to provide system redundancy was considered, but the provider would have required access to the right-of-way controlled by BART. This seemed inappropriate because BART would then effectively be paying a private company to use its right-of-way rather than leveraging the right-of-way to create a revenue source.[23]

Another consideration in choosing to own rather than lease was that the BART Telesystem is an expensive project. It was noted that in the absence of a large amount of public funding, the joint development approach was the only feasible option for system development. Many public agencies are undergoing financial pressures that cannot be alleviated by raising taxes. The arrangement with MFSNT was considered highly compelling because it may create revenue for BART, which, according to the cost analysis performed by Kingston Cole Associates, will not only cover the debt incurred by the project but also provide excess revenue. At this time the exact revenue potential is uncertain because leasing arrangements will be negotiated on an ad hoc basis.

BART and MFS are presently looking to establish a first tenant for the conduit system. A Fortune 500 company has signed a contract with MFSNT; however, as of April 1995 the details were not publicly available because BART had yet to sign the agreement.

The Telesystem is dedicated for the needs of BART and does not provide any reserve capacity for third parties. The planners considered building and owning a telecommunications system that could offer leased capacity, but this would have required certification of BART as a public utility, which was deemed undesirable. The Telesystem is expected to have enough reserve capacity to satisfy the transit system's communications needs for the next 20 years.

So far there have not been any problems with the work done by MFSNT. It is expected that if there are problems with the project it will not be with the joint development but rather with the Telesystem because integrating the wireless and fiber communications technology will be challenging.

Missouri Case Study: DTI Deployment

The Missouri Highway and Transportation Department (MHTD) is deploying ITS statewide to support the needs of metropolitan St. Louis, metropolitan Kansas City, and rural Missouri. The state's goals for ITS deployment include increased vehicle speeds, improved air quality, reduced energy consumption, and improved safety. The services that will be made available are principally in the areas of rural and urban highway traffic management and traveler information. MHTD will utilize a fiber-optic communications network to support new applications.

Missouri's future ITS system will include components such as variable message signs, detector stations, ramp meters, and real-time video surveillance cameras, as well as computers and workstations for a central traffic operations and information center. The estimated total cost of deployment of ITS in the St. Louis metropolitan region is expected to be about $95 million. Statewide costs are not yet available. Missouri's strategy is to deploy incrementally and build support for ITS with early successes.

According to reports prepared by Edwards and Kelcey Inc., a fiber backbone was the only sensible option to support the communications needs of a regional ITS deployment.[24] Planning documents note that of the various transmission media available, only coaxial cable, microwave, and fiber are capable of supporting broadband services. Planners quickly ruled out coax and microwave, noting that fiber is more reliable and can be upgraded to higher capacity. In addition, microwave is not particularly desirable because antennas at each site would be aesthetically unacceptable and would be difficult to locate since they must be in line of sight of one another.

When planning studies by Edwards and Kelcey reported that the cost for the fiber system in the St. Louis metropolitan area alone would be an estimated $22 million, MHTD immediately began looking for alternatives to direct fiber network procurement. Planners noted that leasing costs were astronomical and that there was a fear that leasing costs would increase.[25] However, it was generally believed that system reliability could best be ensured by using a privately owned network, because the state does not have the expertise to perform operations and maintenance and because the private sector has a financial interest in ensuring the viability of the network based upon the revenue potential of the system.

In 1993 MHTD began exploring the possibility of leveraging its right-of-way to obtain communications capacity. The MHTD decision to leverage right-of-way for communications capacity was in part spurred by the national interest in fiber-optic network deployment at the time. Planners believed that the private sector was moving rapidly and that the state should act quickly while there was substantial demand for access to the state's right-of-way. Many private sector businesses expressed an interest in accessing the right-of-way. In the fall of 1993, 22 cable and telephone companies attended a pre-bid conference for a Request For Proposal (RFP) that the state was drafting to select an appropriate contractor. Top management at MHTD, the State Highway Commission, and the US Department of Transportation (U.S. DOT) approved the RFP; approval from U.S. DOT was required because ordinarily utilities are not allowed to access interstate right-of-way. The RFP was for provision of fiber communications capacity throughout the St. Louis metropolitan region, but allowed bidders to propose broader deployments including Kansas City and rural portions of the state. Early in the spring of 1994 proposals were submitted, and Digital Teleport Incorporated (DTI) was selected.

In exchange for access to the state's right-of-way, DTI is deploying fiber along 1,250 miles of state right-of-way and will provide MHTD with three T1 (1.5 Mbps) lines at each of 300–400 network nodes throughout Missouri.[26] The state will pay nothing for access to the system. DTI will be fully responsible for all operations and maintenance, while MHTD will be responsible for building and maintaining all system components that it interconnects to each network node. MHTD is confident that the system will provide sufficient communications capacity for ITS needs.[27] The total cost to DTI, including controllers, is estimated to be about $45 million statewide, of which about $22 million will be spent on the communications system in the St. Louis metropolitan area.

The project is divided into three phases. The St. Louis and Kansas City metropolitan areas will be completed by 1996 and 1997 respectively, and the rural interstate portion will be completed by 1998. Work on the telecommunications system will probably be completed one year ahead of schedule in 1997 because DTI is accelerating deployment to meet paying customer demand.

DTI's network is based upon the SONET standard to ensure that systems operated by other agencies in the region can be interconnected.[28] The fiber network will have a main backbone with OC-12 capacity (622 Mbps). OC-1, OC-3, T1, and T3 streams can be multiplexed onto the system. DTI is using a Japanese company as the system vendor for the project.[29] The contract with DTI grants exclusive rights and privileges that prevent the MHTD from providing preferential right-of-way access for alternative fiber-optic deployments or utilizing the MHTD's capacity for non-ITS applications. The Missouri Public Services Commission refused to allow the state to obtain communications capacity under a more lenient arrangement for regulatory reasons.

MHTD briefly considered building a network to serve the broader communication needs of government, but soon rejected the idea because of (1) potential opposition by telecommunications companies; (2) the Public Services Commission's opposition to having a state agency effectively become a utility; and (3) the belief that waiting for sufficiently broad consensus to form for such an ambitious project might allow the brief window of opportunity to leverage state right-of-way to be missed.

Lessons Learned

The case studies revealed a wide range of incentives and disincentives for collaboration between transportation agencies and private telecommunications service providers. These incentives and disincentives are discussed in this section within the context of the seven key decision factors introduced earlier. Table 2 summarizes the key issues.

Cost

Transportation agencies identified cost as the single most important decision factor influencing the selection of deployment strategies. Several agencies characterized the decision to own rather than lease as "obvious" because broadband capacity is typically very expensive to lease. A cost analysis prepared by Kimley-Horn Associates, a private consulting company, supports the assessment that owning can be more cost effective than leasing.[30] The analysis demonstrated that under certain conditions an owned fiber system will pay for itself after just a few years of operation. However, leased services may be justified in circumstances where wide-area network links or temporary service is required.

Rising leasing costs are also an important factor. Transportation agencies such as San Jose's Department of Streets and Parks are actively developing owned systems to avoid the uncertainty of future leasing costs. Generally, each agency in the case studies seemed to argue that simply leasing the needed capacity was not a viable option because the costs were prohibitive without special funding sources such as right-of-way access revenue.

Shared resource arrangements are an important mechanism for transportation agencies to raise needed revenue for ITS communi-

Table 2 Summary of Ownership Models*

Ownership Model	Incentives	Disincentives
Joint development project (e.g., BART)	•Reduced or no initial costs for public sector •Partnership augments operations and maintenance expertise and resources of public sector •Private sector can gain access to strategic right-of-way	•May take a long time to develop a partnership agreement •Sometimes transportation agencies cannot keep revenue from right-of-way transactions •Public and private sector organizations may not have past relationships to build upon •Private agencies may believe that working with public agencies is risky because public commitment may be erratic due to political changes
Wholly owned and operated by a commercial service provider that leases capacity (e.g., MHTD)	•No initial costs for public sector •Operations and maintenance ensured by private sector, which may provide more reliable service	•High/rising leasing costs are prohibitive to transportation agencies without funding •Transportation agencies often have a "philosophical" preference to own •Accountability and contract enforcement problems •Private sector may lack necessary infrastructure and may not be able to provide new services on a timely basis
Wholly owned by the government with operations and/or maintenance outsourced (e.g., ConnDOT)	•Potential cost savings over leasing alternative for public sector •Government controls physical network and can protect against damage that could threaten public safety •Public sector is assisted with operations and maintenance	•Large initial cost to transportation agencies •Infrastructure may be perceived as a potential competitive threat by private telecommunications service providers •Transportation agencies often have a "philosophical" preference to handle operations and maintenance

Table 2 (continued)

Ownership Model	Incentives	Disincentives
Wholly owned, operated, and maintained by the government (e.g., SJDSP)	•Potential cost savings over leasing alternative for public sector •Government controls physical network and can protect against damage that could threaten public safety •Government can prioritize operations and maintenance	•Public sector may face operations and maintenance problems and large initial costs •Infrastructure may be perceived as a potential competitive threat by private telecommunications service providers

*This table is not a comprehensive summary of all the potential ownership models that exist.

cations infrastructure deployment. Deployment of large-scale land-line networks requires access to right-of-way for cable placement. Transportation agencies are uniquely endowed in this regard because they typically control right-of-way that spans wide geographic regions; therefore they are well-suited to deploy owned infrastructure or to provide access for private telecommunications networks. As demonstrated by the BART and MHTD case studies, transportation agencies can leverage right-of-way access to obtain leasing revenue or communications capacity from the private sector.

The legal framework within jurisdictions can influence the viability of public-private shared resource arrangements. For example, if a transportation agency develops a partnership that provides a revenue stream, it may not be able to keep that money because it is legally required to return the revenue to the state or municipal general fund (in part because having the money go into the general fund can promote the bond rating of the jurisdiction). Other key issues that arise in shared resource projects include valuation of public resources, exclusivity of right-of-way, tax implications, relocation fees for future construction, and liability.[31]

In the opinion of the authors, some of the agencies discussed in the cases may not have fully reviewed the potential for developing public-private partnerships to mitigate costs. Furthermore, most of the cases showed that the cost-effectiveness of various options for obtaining communications capacity was not formally studied, as demonstrated by the fact that cost comparison reports were not available. It's not clear to the authors that transportation agencies are considering the full breadth of cost issues.

Reliability

Officials from several transportation agencies expressed concerns about the reliability of private-sector telecommunications services and noted that this was an important decision factor. For example, MHD expressed a strong belief that the private sector is not capable of providing the level of reliability required for the CA/T infrastructure. However, not all transportation agencies are convinced that they are better-positioned to ensure system reliability than the private sector. For example, the MHTD noted that system reliability could best be ensured by using services offered by the private sector because the state does not have the expertise to perform operations and maintenance. Arguably, the telecommunications industry already handles many mission-critical applications, such as telemedicine, and is therefore quite capable of ensuring network reliability. Agencies with subsurface transportation systems seemed more likely to emphasize the importance of reliability (MHD, BART) and accordingly were more adamant about using owned systems.

The authors believe that a clearer understanding of the relative reliability of owned networks and leased capacity might inform the decision making process as transportation agencies consider leasing or owning their systems. Decisions based upon reliability concerns should be backed up by evidence provided from formal engineering analysis.

Accountability

At the most fundamental level, public agencies may have a predisposition to rely upon owned infrastructure. Both ConnDOT and BART staff explicitly argued that it is the "philosophy" of their agencies to own rather than lease infrastructure, in large part because they perceive that it is their responsibility to directly ensure infrastructure viability. Fundamentally, this is an accountability issue. Transportation agencies believe that they will be held accountable for the success or failure of transportation systems and accordingly want to maintain control over the infrastructure. For example, BART chose to deploy an owned telecommunications network in part because relying upon a third party in an emergency was considered highly undesirable. A strong belief was expressed that for the health, safety, and welfare of the transit system, owning would be the best alternative.

The authors conclude that simply developing owned infrastructure because it is consistent with the "philosophy" of an organization seems totally inappropriate. However, from a political and managerial perspective, this may be an inescapable dilemma facing public agencies.

Operations and Maintenance

The cases discussed above seem to demonstrate that the private sector may be able to assist the public sector with operations and maintenance. Transportation agencies may be ill equipped to handle these issues alone because their traditional role has been to address civil, not electrical, engineering issues.[32] Clearly, the telecommunications industry has a vast pool of skilled employees that can provide assistance with deployment, operations, and maintenance of fiber-optic networks for ITS.

Resource Availability

Another important factor is resource availability. In many jurisdictions, the need for bandwidth for ITS is ahead of private-sector deployment. For example, officials with the MHD noted that NYNEX simply could not provide the level of service required for Boston's CA/T project. And TxDOT officials argued that the system capacity was simply not available from the private sector to support the needs of ITS in San Antonio.

Collaboration between the public and private sectors may be promoted by providing the public sector with a greater awareness of how changes in the telecommunications industry may influence resource availability and future prices for telecommunications services. Changes in the national telecommunications regulatory structure due to judicial and congressional action will promote competition in the telecommunications services market. In certain jurisdictions, emerging competition may be an important factor leading to more services and lower costs. Transportation agencies may be better off waiting for these changes to occur, because competition may alter the cost effectiveness of lease and own options.

Timing

Another critical decision factor is timing. The opportunities available for obtaining communications infrastructure may change over time. For example, the MHTD argued that private-sector demand for right-of-way was at a peak when the decision to leverage the state's right-of-way was made. However, the authors speculate that transportation agencies are in many cases rushing too quickly to deploy new systems, because the private sector will soon be able to meet the broadband communications needs of ITS with cost-effective alternatives as a consequence of the changing regulatory structure.

Upgrades and Reserve Capacity

Transportation agencies must also consider the future potential requirements for communications infrastructure. The cases seem to suggest that this decision factor is not being strongly considered. For example, transportation agencies may be underestimating the potential for upgrade problems associated with new technology.

The issue of reserve capacity was raised repeatedly in the cases discussed and is an important conflict of interest between the public and private sectors. Transportation agencies typically build reserve capacity to support future ITS communications requirements. Telecommunications companies are concerned that ITS deployments will generate vast reserve capacity that will ultimately be turned over to third parties, who will then forego private sector services.

However, none of the cases revealed any examples of transportation agencies leasing capacity. Officials with the MHD explicitly argued that their agency is not interested in serving the broader telecommunications needs of the state. Similarly, an official with TxDOT noted that although several public and private organizations have tried to gain access to the new fiber capacity, the agency does not lease reserve capacity.

None of the cases demonstrated an attempt by the private sector to obstruct the development of public fiber-optic networks. However, an official with the MHTD noted that the potential for private sector opposition diminished interest in developing a state network to serve the broader needs of government rather than just ITS.

Organizational Implications

The ITS case studies described in this paper focus on the delivery of specific services that are provided in limited geographic areas. As ITS develops within a metropolitan area, it is reasonable to expect that both the range of services provided and the geographic coverage area will expand. In that expanded context, the choice of an organization to operate or coordinate the services is a particularly critical decision, especially given the complexity of communications infrastructure.

The Intelligent Transportation Systems described in this paper are operated under the auspices of existing transportation agencies. Most transportation agencies have limited responsibilities within a metropolitan area, focusing on a specific mode or a particular geographic area. A primary objective of ITS is coordination of separate transportation service components and the development of an overall multimodal transportation system. Therefore, coordination of ITS by an existing agency responsible for part of the system could be sub-optimal.

ITS implementation can be a catalyst for organizational change. A single organization within a metropolitan area could provide more efficient overall ITS coordination than separate ITS services operated by existing organizations. One option would be the creation of a new organization that is not constrained by the legacy of previous missions and has a professional staff with the capabilities required to support ITS. That organization could reflect the electronic and information orientation of ITS rather than the mechanical and construction orientation of many existing transportation agencies. A metropolitan area-wide coordinating organization could be responsible for more than transportation services. Many municipal functions such as police, fire, and ambulance services could benefit from ITS-like technology and services, such as emergency communications. Clearly, an appropriate balance should be achieved between the benefits of coordination and the inefficiencies of a large bureaucracy. A coordinating agency need not (and probably should not) directly provide services; the responsibility for operation can remain with existing agencies.

It is premature at this time to determine precisely what organizational structure should coordinate ITS. The authors suspect the choices will vary considerably depending on many factors. The point the authors want to convey is that ITS involves not only the choice of the proper technologies but also the selection of an institutional setting to ensure successful evaluation, implementation, and operation of ITS services.

Conclusion

The cases suggest that transportation agencies need to do a more effective job of justifying the institutional frameworks selected for deploying ITS. Better information sharing could promote public-private collaboration that would be beneficial to both transportation agencies and private telecommunications service providers. Transportation agencies should seek to develop win-win relationships with the private sector whenever possible. As demonstrated by the BART and MHTD case studies, public-private partnerships can be in the interests of both the public and private sectors.

Many state and local transportation agencies are skeptical about the services that the private sector can offer. Traditionally, the "philosophy" of transportation agencies is to own, operate, and maintain transportation infrastructure rather than to lease or outsource services. Providing more information to public agencies about private sector resources may encourage collaboration. For example, private providers point out that even if owned systems are deployed, leased services can provide network redundancy to enhance system reliability. Simply arguing that leasing capacity is incompatible with the "philosophy" of a transportation agency is clearly insufficient justification for deploying expensive owned systems.

Increasing the awareness of the private sector about the issues and concerns of transportation agencies may also encourage collaboration. For example, private companies are often not used to interacting with state and local agencies and may not understand the needs and interests influencing the decision making process. Furthermore, private businesses may not be aware of the opportunities for partnerships. For example, the MHD adopted a policy of negotiating broader access to strategic right-of-way in return for leasing revenue, but many private sector businesses were simply not aware that state's right-of-way policy had been modified.

An institutional framework that adequately provides for the deployment, operations, and maintenance of ITS is needed. The authors speculate that new institutional frameworks that coordinate ITS services in a metropolitan area may be appropriate to ensure that ITS is properly deployed and utilized. As demonstrated by the BART and MHTD case studies, public-private partnerships are an important institutional innovation for developing transportation infrastructure.

Notes

1. According to ConnDOT staff, as of April 1995 the system was roughly 75% complete, with work remaining on the system's software.

2. Note that ConnDOT staff are in the operations center monitoring the work.

3. The MTA operates and maintains the Massachusetts Turnpike and other facilities. Pending legislation in the Massachusetts legislature would give the MTA authority over the CA/T system (see LeHigh and Phillips, 1995).

4. Bechtel/Parsons Brinckerhoff, 1990.

5. Ibid., pp. 9–10.

6. However, NYNEX could have worked as a subcontractor to the general contractor, Perini-Powell. To the knowledge of the authors, no telecommunications company has called into question the CA/T communications system project.

7. According to a press release from Perini-Powell, "The Perini/Powell joint venture will design and install a fully-integrated traffic control system that will

maintain the surveillance of traffic along Boston's Central Artery and Third Harbor Tunnel by means of a sophisticated computer system. The system will monitor and control 118 speed limit and lane change signs and 39 variable message signs providing current traffic information. In addition, the division will also furnish and install an emergency assistance radio system, an emergency telephone system, a closed circuit television system, a heat detection and fire alarm system, and the control system for high-capacity ventilation fans. Work on the project will begin immediately with completion scheduled for June 1998" ("Perini Division Awarded Three New Construction Contracts"). The total contract award is for $52 million.

8. Cost includes controller equipment, single mode fiber, and multimode fiber. The multimode fiber is used to connect system components such as video cameras to the main backbone.

9. However, in an interview, project planners were unable to identify a formal project report in which system costs were identified for various options.

10. In this context, mean time before failure refers to critical, system-wide failure where the network does not recover within a specified period of time.

11. NYNEX, MFS, and Teleport are major telecommunications service providers in the Boston area. NYNEX is the main local access provider in Massachusetts; MFS and Teleport are competitive access providers (CAPs) that compete with NYNEX in the region.

12. This suggests that the state may not have been well positioned to leverage right-of-way access to obtain communications capacity for the CA/T project.

13. The MHD's policy is described in "Wiring Massachusetts." The position paper specifically states "In exchange for the rights to the highway Right-of-Way and other property, the MHD will receive system capacity. For optical fiber conduit systems, the MHD will receive exclusive use of the 'Commonwealth Component,' defined as, three 1.5 inch diameter conduits, lateral branching, manholes and handholes where ever a participant requires the same, and lateral branching for the MHD's Intelligent Transportation System equipment. For tower facilities, the MHD will receive exclusive use of reserved tower space including all tower connections and structural support and electrical power supply required for the Commonwealth's equipment. The Commonwealth Component shall be deemed to be a shared cost among all participants in the Telecommunications Facility and shall be constructed and maintained by the Lead Company. Thereafter, and upon completion of construction, title to all improvements on the premises shall vest in the Commonwealth, excluding any participant's Personal Property. As this initiative currently anticipates optical fiber cable and wireless tower facilities, other Telecommunication Facilities will require separate negotiation."

14. The Massachusetts Turnpike Authority has an explicit policy not to lease reserve telecommunications capacity but does lease conduit capacity and exchange conduit capacity for communications capacity.

15. Palmer, 1994.

16. Note that the Texas Department of Transportation has 25 districts.

17. In mid-April 1995, the District was planning to issue a second RFP for another segment of the 191 mile highway system.

18. DS0 (64 Kbps) and DS1 (1.5 Mbps) are not fast enough to support full-motion video.

19. Note that in Houston a CCTV system that includes a fiber communications backbone is being leased from a private-sector service provider.

20. The region is comparable to the size of Pennsylvania, which covers 45,000 square miles.

21. An alarm indicates when a signaling device has failed.

22. Presently a T1 carrier is being used to support some of BART's telecommunications needs. However, T1 capacity is insufficient to support broadband applications.

23. It should also be noted that the BART Telesystem includes a redundant fiber network and the wireless system also provides for additional redundancy.

24. Edwards and Kelcey Inc., 1993, 1994.

25. In an interview with a project worker, past increases in leasing costs for twisted pair were cited.

26. The contract formally states that MHTD will receive six fibers but according to MHTD staff, DTI will provide T1 connections as described.

27. The April 1994 *Final Report* states that "The type of media used for communication from the nodes to the field equipment can vary, depending upon the specific situation requirements. For instance, the media could be fiber optic, copper twisted wire pair, spread spectrum radio, microwave, or other appropriate technology. The media could even be the re-use of existing interconnect cable from an existing signal system. The recommended communications media for connection of field equipment is fiber optic cable." (section 4, p.31)

28. This is particularly important for the St. Louis metropolitan area, which includes areas of both Missouri and Illinois.

29. There was some difficulty obtaining the vendor name from DTI.

30. Presentation by Bruce Abernathy during the "Intelligent Transportation Systems Telecommunications Forum" at the Volpe National Transportation Systems Center in Cambridge, MA on April 27, 1995.

31. Apogee Research (Bethesda, MD) is preparing a report on shared resources that addresses these considerations in detail.

32. See Hyman, 1993.

References

Bechtel/Parsons Brinckerhoff. "Central Artery (I-93)/Tunnel (I-90) Project: Communications Systems." Concept Report No. 2AB10, October 1990.

Court, T., S. Prosi, A. Alonzi, and W. Stoeckert. "Using Freeway Incident Management to Reduce Congestion." *Public Works*, 125:9, August 1994.

De Zutter, Mary. "Omaha's MFS Wins Contract." *Omaha World Herald*, October 12, 1994, p. 20.

Edwards and Kelcey Inc. *Technical Memoranda, Bi-State St. Louis Area IVHS Planning Study.* 1993.

Edwards and Kelcey Inc. *Final Report, Bi-state St. Louis Area Intelligent Vehicle Highway System Planning Study.* April 1994.

Hyman, William. "IVHS Staffing and Educational Needs." Proceedings of the IVHS America Annual Meeting, *Surface Transportation: Mobility, Technology, and Society.* Washington, DC: April 14–17, 1993, pp. 613–620.

Lehigh and Phillips. "Weld would remove some Pike tolls." *Boston Globe,* March 31, 1995, p. 45

Intelligent Transportation Systems Telecommunications Infrastructure Forum. Cambridge, MA: Volpe National Transportation Systems Center, April 27, 1995

Palmer, Thomas. "State will get lanes on 'Information Turnpike'." *Boston Globe,* December 3, 1994.

"Perini Division Awarded Three New Construction Contracts." News Release. Framingham, MA: Perini Corporation, March 22, 1994.

Pictrzyk and Yettaw. "Finding The Right IVHS Partnership on a Local Level." *Proceedings of the IVHS America 1994 Annual Meeting, Moving Toward Deployment.* Atlanta, GA, April 17–20, 1994, Vol. 2, pp. 625–629.

Stark and Mattenson. "Communications Deployment Alternatives for IVHS." *IVHS Review,* Summer 1994, pp. 55–60.

Strategic Plan for Intelligent Vehicle-Highway Systems in the United States. Washington, DC: IVHS America, May 20, 1992.

Sussman, Joseph. "Intelligent Vehicle Highway Systems." *OR/MS Today*, December 1992.

Weld, W., A. Cellucci, J. Kerasiotes, and L. Bedingfield. "Wiring Massachusetts: An Agenda for Public/Private Cooperation to Facilitate Deployment of Telecommunications Systems Along Massachusetts Highways." Executive Office of Transportation and Construction, Massachusetts Highway Department (No date).

Why Driver Privacy Must Be a Part of ITS

Simson L. Garfinkel

Introduction

ITS will be a failure if nobody uses it. Of what use are smart roads that nobody drives on? I will argue that privacy will be a key factor in making ITS work. Moreover, due to the potential breadth and depth of the monitoring and surveillance components of ITS, the active government role in ITS development, and the immediacy of ITS planning, ITS could serve as a proving ground for the development of standards and guidelines for the public and private sector treatment of personal information.

Consider the case of Hong Kong's ITS system. In the mid 1980s, the government built a sophisticated system for electronic road pricing. The goal of the system was to reduce congestion and pollution; but shortly after the system was deployed, questions were raised about its ability to track people. Drivers began receiving statements showing where and when they had traveled. The citizens of Hong Kong soon became worried that this tracking could be used for political purposes, especially after 1997. As a result of their protests, the system was turned off, never to be used again.[1]

The same thing could happen in the United States. If ITS systems are developed and deployed which do not respect the privacy of the American driver, there is a good chance that Americans will demand that the systems be shut off. Without strong privacy provisions, ITS may not succeed.

Many ITS systems today are being designed and deployed which have few or no provisions for driver privacy. In places such as New

York, Florida, and Los Angeles, ITS systems have been deployed which keep detailed records of driver movement. The purpose of these records is to allow for drivers to pay road tolls from a pre-established account; drivers are then sent a monthly bill detailing their toll crossings. These are exactly the type of reports that caused an unacceptable level of concern in Hong Kong. The information they represent is of high value to third parties, for whom there is no agreement on acceptable use. Fortunately, the goals of ITS can be accomplished without creating such invasive records.

Privacy is a key concern to the DOT ITS Joint Program Office. But privacy has not been a priority for some state and local ITS planners. Many of the systems that have been deployed to date have addressed privacy concerns only as an afterthought, or not at all. Indeed, plans are now underway for dual-use systems that would make the information obtained from ITS available for use by law enforcement agencies, advertising agencies and marketing firms. Already, many state departments of motor vehicles reap substantial revenue from the sale of driver records. For example, the R. L. Polk company, in Detroit, Michigan, is a major purchaser of motor vehicle and driver records throughout the county; this information is used to assist marketing firms and to build directories. It is possible that fiscally strained states will see ITS records as a similar source of revenue. Ironically, this is at a time when states are trying to tighten up restrictions on the public release of driver-related information, in order to protect the privacy of their citizens.[2]

Many of the privacy issues associated with ITS are similar to other consumer information systems, such as credit databanks and records of financial transactions. A reasonable rule for implementing fair information practices is that information obtained for one purpose should never be used for another purpose without the consent of the customer or consumer. Like credit-card companies that market their mailing lists to junk mail firms, plans for dual-use of ITS information[3] plainly violates this principle of consumer privacy.

ITS has unique privacy problems, largely due to the fact that the information being collected may contain detailed records of a person's movements. These records give insight into a person's private life that are potentially far more detailed than a his or her credit history or spending patterns. As ITS systems become ubiquitous, drivers who chose to "opt out" of these systems will be increasingly penalized with slower commutes (due to delays at toll plazas) or the inability to travel on certain roads where the use of ITS is mandatory.

Most ITS systems will be deployed by federal, state, and local governments. As such, ITS planners have a responsibility to set a standard for the highest level of privacy protection. The simplest, most effective, and cheapest way to do this is by the adoption of ITS technologies based on anonymity, such as anonymous payment schemes. Any per-driver or per-vehicle records that are created should be kept with the driver in the vehicle, and not in a centrally operated database. Proliferation of such anonymous systems may also be in the interest of commercial ITS systems developers. In most areas, privacy is more strongly protected by law in Canada and Europe, than in the United States, and to reach these markets, the ITS products of U.S. companies will need to comply with this stringency.

Rightly or wrongly, many Americans have an expectation of privacy—especially with new information technologies. It is true that this expectation is often misplaced. For example, many believe that electronic mail is as secure and private as paper mail, even though it is not. Nevertheless, if the data collected for ITS is used for purposes other than those directly related to traffic management, such as law enforcement, collecting demographics for marketing, or as a way to directly advertise to consumers, it may only contribute to political discontent. There are, of course, desirable applications, such as in the event of a car theft or kidnapping, but enabling these applications by their nature creates the opportunity for privacy. This abuse can be addressed through sound, prospectively developed guidelines and controls, but such systems can not avoid a privacy trade-off.

The "Non-Issue"

Many Americans got their first taste of ITS during the summer of 1995, the first year that drivers could pay highway and bridge tolls using Electronic Toll and Traffic Management (ETTM) systems. These systems are now in use in many states, including New York, Florida, and California. They allow drivers to pay tolls for bridges and highways automatically, without the need to slow down, using a small radio transponder that is mounted on the vehicle.

For others, 1995 marked the first time that they used real-time, or at least semi-real-time, traffic information systems. One such system, SmartRoute System's SmarTraveler, can now be used by anybody in the Boston metropolitan area from their cellular telephone by dialing "*1." Signs for SmarTraveler are prominently visible on Boston's Southeast Expressway. As the radio advertisement says, "It's a free call"[4]—even at the times that other cell phone traffic and weather reports cost 50 cents per minute or more. Even Americans who could not benefit directly from ITS in 1995 read about it in newspapers and watched it on the evening news broadcasts.

As ITS has become more visible, much of the dialogue concerns itself solely with questions of system cost, compatibility between ITS systems in adjacent states, and ease of use. Privacy issues are often not addressed, except to say that drivers who don't want to pay with credit cards can avoid this problem by denying themselves the benefits of ITS.

The preoccupation with technical standards and implementation details is not surprising: for many in the ITS field, these are the primary ITS issues that need to be addressed over the next few years. They say that it will be difficult enough to make ITS systems work within a single administrative domain; their dream is to make ITS work between geographical areas, so that a driver can use a single tag to pay tolls from California to New York. Making ITS work and informing the public how it works is a hard job. It is easy to get lost in the details and ignore issues that appear to be secondary to the primary, technical goal. As a result, some planners are ignoring the issue of driver privacy.

During the spring and summer of 1995, I wrote a series of articles about ITS.[5] In conducting the interviews for those articles, not a single ITS planner or equipment vendor ever raised the issue of driver privacy. When I raised the issue with John Judge, Director of Operations of the Massachusetts Turnpike Authority, I was told that "privacy is a non-issue."[6] I pressed Judge, and asked him if the Turnpike Authority was paying special attention to privacy issues. He responded:

"Actually, no. I think that is the experience nationwide, at least as it relates to electronic toll collection. Privacy has not been an issue that has emerged nationally. I think that [is] principally because it is a voluntary system. If you are of a mind where you might be concerned about privacy issues, you just don't have to join the program, and can use the traditional toll collection methods. I don't think that it is any more an issue than credit cards."

Judge is not alone in his thinking. Many other ITS planners say that there are so many threats to privacy today, it doesn't really matter if ITS invades peoples' privacy a little more.[7] The belief is that toll-crossing information is not really that important, with respect to personal privacy, particularly since systems are *voluntary*. Anybody who doesn't like the privacy implications can either pay with cash, or not use the systems at all.

There are indications that the driving public may think otherwise. According to a 1995 survey by Equifax, one of the nation's leading credit reporting agencies, and Lou Harris, the national polling organization, 82 percent of Americans are very concerned or somewhat concerned about privacy.[8] Eighty percent believe they have lost all control over personal information. As a result, 90 percent of Americans now favor legislation to protect them from businesses that invade their privacy, according to a recent survey by the Yankelovich Group.

Not using ITS is an unfair and unnecessary solution. Forsaking ITS benefits, may mean spending an extra 10 minutes in toll collection lines. This penalizes those citizens who want to protect their privacy, by preventing them from enjoying the benefits of ITS. With anonymous systems it is possible to achieve the goals of ITS, without forcing drivers to opt out in order to preserve their privacy.

Anonymous Technology Is the Key to Secure ITS

It is possible to design an ITS system that both respects personal privacy and accomplishes many goals set forth by ITS planners. The trick is to design in privacy from the beginning, rather than adding it as an afterthought. ITS does not have to identify individuals in order to offer individualized service. Indeed, many applications that have been proposed for ITS can be implemented in a manner that provides for the complete anonymity of the user. Already, such a system has been developed by Massachusetts-based AT/Comm, and deployed in Illinois.

Electronic toll payment can be implemented with smart cards or other kinds of digital cash, so that named accounts do not need to be maintained. When a toll is crossed, the value is automatically deducted from the smart card. The card can be recharged with new toll-crossing credits by driving through a special toll lane. Alternatively, new cards can be purchased with cash or by credit card; drivers could even subscribe to smart-card renewal services.

The typical smart card can have a few kilobytes or more of on-card storage, which can be used to store the record of hundreds of toll-crossings. Thus, a user of this pro-privacy smart-card-based system can still obtain a detailed record of toll-crossings for their own personal use (such as for reimbursement by an employer.) The cards can even generate a random trip sequence number, allowing the anonymous tracking of cars through the highway system in order to learn trip times. The key difference between this approach and others is that the transit authority does not amass a database containing detailed driving records for every driver.

A smart-card-based system can fulfill other ITS features as well, such as incident management. For example, the system can be equipped with some kinds of information that is only released in the event of an emergency, but not at other times. For example, smart cards may have input concerning your vehicle's license plate, make, model and color of car. This information would be stored in an encrypted format. In the event of a crash or theft, the information would be decrypted and transmitted by the car's two-way radio system.

Anonymous systems also overcome the FOIA-related problems that have haunted some ITS projects. There is no chance that the press or a marketing firm will obtain a copy of the database through a FOIA lawsuit, and there is no need for special legislation exempting the database from FOIA actions, because these anonymous systems have no database of personal information. Similarly, the use of digital cash significantly reduces accounting and computer security burdens.

Systems that rely on anonymity for protecting personal privacy also avoid the problem of insiders misusing their privileged access to sensitive databanks. In his classic book *The Rise of the Computer State*, journalist David Burnham discusses how a reporter at *The New York Times* had been surreptitiously tracked all over the United States by an agent at an Avis counter in Atlanta with whom he had become romantically involved. She had tracked his movements by using his car rental records.[9] The Avis case illustrates that there are many opportunities for these sorts of records to be misused and to fall into unapproved hands. They can be stolen or photocopied by an employee at the turnpike authority, stolen from a driver's mailbox, or intercepted by an angry or suspicious spouse. Furthermore, the records that are used to create the statements do not go away—they may be safe today, but could become a problem in the future. Digital cash avoids these problems.

ITS Data Is Privacy-Sensitive

Intelligent Transportation Systems give state and local governments unprecedented ability to monitor the flow of traffic. This is, after all, why these systems are being built. The best way to assure that ITS information will not be abused is to avoid recording information that can be identified with individuals or groups of individuals. Without the use of anonymous technologies, ITS planners are presented with the challenge of designing systems which collect massive amounts of personal information and somehow prevent that information from being disclosed or otherwise misused.

Consider the information that might be collected by a typical ITS system:

• A detailed record of all toll crossings.

• The location of every car on the road at all times of the day and night. (ITS tags used for automatic toll collection could easily be used for this purpose.)

• The speed of each car. (By calculating the distance moved during a certain amount of time.)

• Photographs of the car's passengers. (Video surveillance.)

This could represent many gigabytes of raw data being generated every day. Many ITS proposals now aim to find sensible ways to reduce the bulk of this raw data by using higher-level representations. It is the higher-level representations that would then travel over the network to a data center and be archived for later use. Ideally, these representations would be stripped of all personal identifiers before they were stored, eliminating the danger to personal privacy. Archiving is a likely component of ITS systems, providing data for traffic planning purposes, testing new applications, and as a back-up in the event of system failure. The existence of such archives makes the case for keeping ITS data anonymous even stronger. However, those archives could be reduced to statistical form, and the original data erased. This would preserve privacy without loss of value in the applications suggested. It would also reduce the cost of data archiving.

Even without data reduction and personal information stripping, raw ITS information for medium-sized metropolitan area could easily fit in a shirt pocket. Today, a tape drive that can store six gigabytes of information on a single 4mm digital audio tape (DAT) the size of a matchbox costs less $1,000; the DAT tape itself has a retail cost of less than $10. The location, speed, weight, and number of passengers in a car can be encoded in less than 16 bytes of information, and a color can easily be compressed to less than 30 kbytes. Thus, a single $10 DAT tape could easily store the record of an entire day's commute in a major metropolitan area, including 10 million hour-long trips, recording every car's position every second (a total of 576 million bytes) and a photograph of every car every five minutes (a total of 3.6 gigabytes).

Storing ITS data is cheap and easy, and can offer open up an array of new applications. For example, the following are plausible opportunities for ITS:

• Instituting road-pricing schemes that would double or triple the number of people that can travel a highway by encouraging people to car-pool.

• Facilitating the building plans for new highways.

• Analyzing people's driving habits and matching up people who would make good car-pooling companions.

• Cutting the number of lights installed on routes that were rarely traveled at night, lighting certain routes only on certain days or at certain times of the night, or even turn the street lights on and off on demand.

• Retroactively charging people for traveling in an HOV lane with only a single occupant.

• Automatically issuing traffic citations for such violations as speeding, driving through red lights, running stop signs, or making a left-hand turn from the right-hand lane.

• Sending drivers friendly warnings if they tend to follow other cars too closely, or recommending driving schools best suited to their particular faults.

• Automatically issuing driving and parking tickets.

All of these applications require raw ITS data. Some of them require retroactive raw data. By not discarding raw data, new applications can be brought online faster and with fewer problems.

Unfortunately, raw ITS data lends itself to abuse. There is demand among commercial firms for ITS data, and these markets could be an important source of revenue. Many organizations and companies might be interested in purchasing the databank of ITS information, just as organizations eagerly purchase DMV databases today. For example:

• A cellular telephone company could use this information to determine where new towers should be built.

• A billboard company could use it to determine the optimal placement for advertisements along the highway. These locations could even be correlated with average driver income and ethnicity.

• An auto maker could use the information for advertising, market research, or even new product development. For instance, recorded images of cars driving down the highway could be used to determine the percentage of drivers who use sunroofs and convertibles.

There are also many ways that such a databank could be misused:

• A private investigator could use ITS information to determine if an errant husband is actually working late in the office, or if he is secretly visiting that blond woman who lives up near exit 4, on the other side of the bridge.

• An insurance company could use frequent travel to the beach during skipped work days as way of disqualifying worker's compensation payments.

• Another insurance company could offer discounts for drivers who did not take their cars into dangerous neighborhoods.

The distinction between secondary markets that are benign from a privacy perspective, and those that may be threatening is that the former can rely on statistical data, either aggregated, or from anonymous systems, while the later require raw data with personal identifiers. The only way to virtually eliminate the opportunity for abuse through anonymous systems which do not gather personal data in the first place.

ITS Monitoring Is Happening Now

In Florida, the Orlando–Orange County Expressway Authority has a system called E-PASS which lets drivers pay their tolls on the East–West Expressway and certain parts of the Central Florida GreeneWay. Billing is accomplished through the use of a windshield tag, which causes a predetermined amount of money to be subtracted from the driver's account each time a toll is crossed. A sample statement from the Florida system clearly states the exact time, down to the nearest second, of each toll crossing.

In March 1995, the California Department of Motor Vehicles conducted a series of surveillance operations along Interstate Route 5. The state took photographs of cars driving down the highway, located the car's license plates, matched the license plates to registration records, and sent the following letter to some drivers:

Dear Motorist:

The California Department of Transportation (Caltrans) is studying potential transportation improvements in the Sacramento–Stockton region. We would greatly appreciate your assistance with this effort.

On Sunday, March 5, 1995, Caltrans observed traffic on Interstate 5 between Sacramento and Stockton. On this day we believe we observed a vehicle registered to this address traveling southbound.

Please have the vehicle driver take a few minutes to fill out and return the entire survey below. This response is anonymous; no personal information about you will ever be revealed. All records of names, addresses, and data sources connected with this survey will be destroyed. Postage is pre-paid.

If you should have questions regarding the survey or the study please call (916) 327-4577. Thank you for your contribution to this important study.

Sincerely,

Cindy McKim
Deputy Director

If the vehicle license number appearing on the front of this survey was recorded in error, please check here [box] and return this form.[10]

Phil Agre, a professor at the University of California at San Diego who has written extensively about ITS privacy issues, noted in his article describing the survey, "this kind of routine surveillance is probably not now illegal under U.S. law. For example, the Supreme Court, in U.S. v. Knotts, 460 U.S. 276 (1982), has asserted that, so far as the Constitution is concerned, "[a] person traveling in an automobile on public thoroughfares has no reasonable expectation of privacy in his movements from one place to another.

But that doesn't make it right. Agre explains, "This clearly sets a very poor precedent for citizens' ability to drive on public roads without fear of surveillance....It is far from clear that the advantages to the public of creating these additional statistics in this manner outweigh the danger of chilling the fundamentally important freedom of association upon which democracy is based."

State and federal highway organizations are in a unique position with respect to the deployment of ITS technology: These agencies hold a monopoly on public roads. A consumer who does not like Citibank's policies regarding consumer financial records is free to obtain a credit card from Bank of America, American Express, or even EuroCard. They can pay by check, or even with cash. But someone who wishes to drive from New Jersey to Manhattan has little choice but to travel a roadway operated by the Port Authority. If the Port Authority chooses to install video cameras and record license plates there is no avoiding it.

ITS America's Non-Privacy Principles

Many ITS planners do know that privacy is in fact an issue in the deployment and use of their systems. Indeed, the federal advisory group ITS America has been working to develop a set of privacy principles. During the first half of 1995, ITS America published its "draft final privacy principles" approved by the ITS America Coordinating Council and Executive Committee. While the stated intent of these principles is privacy protection, they accept as given an unnecessary level of intrusion, and seek to establish legitimate criteria for the use of personal information, rather than exclude it.

The "Draft Final" principles do not take any position on issues such as driver anonymity, or the belief that data collected for one purpose should not be used for another. The principles do suggest offering individuals a means of opting out of the use of their personal data for secondary purposes, but this makes privacy the exception, rather than the norm.

Draft Final
Intelligent Transportation Systems
Fair Information and Privacy Principles

These fair information and privacy principles were prepared in recognition of the importance of protecting individual privacy in implementing Intelligent Transportation Systems. They have been adopted by ITS America in draft final form. The Privacy Task Group of the Legal Issues Committee will present these principles for review and comment to organizations and groups interested in privacy and ITS outside of ITS America during 1995. They will then be submitted for final adoption to the ITS America Legal Issues Committee, Coordinating Council, and Board of Directors.

The principles represent values and are designed to be flexible and durable to accommodate a broad scope of technological, social, and cultural change. ITS America may, however, need to revisit them periodically to assure their applicability and effectiveness.

These principles are advisory, intended to educate and guide transportation professionals, policy makers, and the public as they develop fair information and privacy guidelines for specific intelligent transportation projects. Initiators of ITS projects are urged to publish the fair information privacy principles that they intend to follow. Parties to ITS projects are urged to include enforceable provisions for safeguarding privacy in their contracts and agreements.

1. INDIVIDUAL CENTERED. Intelligent Transportation Systems (ITS) must recognize and respect the individual's interests in privacy and information use.

ITS systems create value for both individuals and society as a whole. Central to the ITS vision is the creation of ITS systems that will fulfill our national goals. The primary focus of information use is to improve travelers' safety and security, reduce travel times, enhance individuals' ability to deal with highway disruptions and improve air quality. Traveler information is collected from many sources, some from the infrastructure and some from vehicles, while other information may come from the transactions like electronic toll collection that involve interaction between the infrastructure and vehicle. That information may have value in both ITS and non-ITS applications. The individual's expectation of privacy must be respected. This requires disclosure and the opportunity for individuals to express choice.

2. VISIBLE. Intelligent transportation information systems will be built in a manner visible to individuals.

ITS may create data on individuals. Individuals should have a means of discovering how the data flows operate. Visible means to disclose to the public the type of data collected, how it is collected, what its uses are, and how it will be distributed. The concept of visibility is one of central concern to the public, and consequently this principle requires assigning responsibility for disclosure.

3. COMPLY. Intelligent Transportation Systems will comply with state and federal laws governing privacy and information use.
4. SECURE. Intelligent Transportation Systems will be secure.

ITS data bases may contain information on where travelers go, the routes they use, and when they travel, and therefore must be secure. All ITS information systems will make use of data security technology and audit procedures appropriate to the sensitivity of the information.

5. LAW ENFORCEMENT. Intelligent Transportation Systems will have an appropriate role in enhancing travelers' safety and security inter-ests, but absent consent, government authority, or appropriate legal process, information identifying individuals will not be disclosed to law enforcement.

ITS has the potential to make it possible for traffic management agencies to know where individuals travel, what routes they take, and travel duration. Therefore, ITS can increase the efficiency of traffic law enforcement by providing aggregate information necessary to target resources. States may legislate conditions under which ITS information will be made available. Absent government authority, however, ITS systems should not be used as a surveillance means for enforcing traffic laws. Although individuals are concerned about public safety, persons who voluntarily participate in ITS programs or purchase ITS products have a reasonable expectation that they will not be "ambushed" by information they are providing.

6. RELEVANT. Intelligent Transportation Systems will only collect personal information that is relevant for ITS purposes.

ITS, respectful of the individual's interest in privacy, will only collect information that contain individual identifiers which are needed for the ITS service functions. Furthermore, ITS information systems will include protocols that call for the purging of individual identifier information that is no longer needed to meet ITS needs.

7. SECONDARY USE. Intelligent Transportation Systems information coupled with appropriate individual privacy protection may be used for non-ITS applications.

American consumers want information used to create economic choice and value, but also want their interest in privacy preserved. ITS information is predictive of the types of goods and services that interest consumers, for example the right location for stores, hospitals, and other facilities. However, that same information might also be used to disadvantage and harm a consumer. Therefore, the following practices should be followed.

ITS information absent personal identifiers may be used for ITS and other purposes.

Other unrelated uses of ITS information with personal identifiers may be permissible if individuals receive effective disclosure and have a user friendly means of opting out.

Data collectors will only provide personal information to private organizations that agree to abide by these privacy principles.

8. FOIA. Federal and State Freedom of Information Act (FOIA) obligations require disclosure of information from government

maintained databases. Database arrangements should balance the individual's interest in privacy and the public's right to know.

In determining whether to disclose ITS information, governments should, where possible, balance the individuals right to privacy against the preservation of the basic purpose of the Freedom of Information laws to open agency action to the light of public scrutiny. ITS travelers should be presumed to have reasonable expectations of privacy for personal identifying information. Pursuant to the individual's interest in privacy, the public/private frameworks of organizations collecting data should be structured to resolve problems of access created by FOIA.

The ITS America guidelines may appear to be good on first reading, but they are flawed. The guidelines say that ITS information may be used for secondary purposes with its personal identifiers intact as long as individuals have a "friendly" means of opting out. A document that is supposed to be pro-privacy should not allow personal information to be shared unless the individual takes a specific action to prevent the free flow of data. Instead, it should adopt a stronger stance—for example, forbidding the carriage of personal information unless explicitly authorized by the individuals in question. It would be possible to offer this choice at the time of driver's license or registration application or renewal. The guidelines also do not recognize the option of anonymous systems.

Providing the option to opt out is not a complete solution. The practice of allowing people to "opt out" of marketing programs has not always proven succesful. Further what standards will be applied to determine whether there is an acceptable degree of ease in opting out, and what measures should be taken to ensure that drivers are aware of the option?

Another concern about the guidelines is that they allow virtually unlimited use of individual driving records, provided that personal identifiers are stripped out, but do not address what is stripped and what is not. Even if all potential identifiers are removed, the nature of driving records is that they are personal; the stripped personal information might therefore be recreated from the remaining information in the files. Drivers could be identified by their start and stop locations, the times of their travel, the performance of their car, and their driving habits.

The ITS America guidelines violate a central tenet of the American privacy doctrine. Information collected for one purpose should never be used for another purpose without the express consent of the person providing the information. This tenet was voiced in a 1973 report by the U.S. Department of Health, Education and Welfare,[11] and the principles are embodied in the 1971 Fair Credit Reporting Act. It has been understood by both privacy activists and legislators for more than 20 years.

ITS America is working on a new set of privacy principles. The new principles will reportedly minimize the resale of information for non-ITS purposes. But two questions remain: the role of law enforcement and the use of technologies such as digital cash that provide for true anonymity. ITS gives local, state, and federal authorities unprecedented abilities to follow the movements of the public. Unlike wiretaps, which technically require a court order before they can be used, the U.S. Constitution gives citizens no right to anonymous travel, and many law enforcement agencies are interested in using ITS in the fight against crime.

The problem is that ITS has been designed and sold to the public as a system for improving transportation, and not as a system that will make it easier to enforce the nation's laws or control unruly segments of our population. Simply because ITS *can* be used for law enforcement does not mean that it *should* be used for law enforcement. Before public funds are applied to the development of ITS systems, questions about the uses to which ITS data will be applied should be broadly aired, and citizens should understand that there are solutions, such as anonymous systems, that do not gather personal information.

Conclusion

ITS may free us from highway congestion, ease air pollution, and eliminate the need of a new generation of highway-building. But ITS also has the potential to be one of the most invasive technologies to date.

ITS need not be a Faustian bargain. The technology exists today to deploy systems that both preserve privacy and allow the realization of many ITS goals. Whether and how this technology is adopted nationwide should be a matter of public debate. The choice should not be made void of public opinion, or based purely on cost or revenue considerations. Nor should it be decided by the desire to maintain compatibility with the anti-privacy systems that have already been installed.

Notes

1. *Transportation Infostructures*, The Diebold Institute for Public Policy Studies, Inc. 1995.

2. The Driver's Privacy and Protection Act passed in mandates that by the end of 1997, states wishing to make use driver's license and registration information available for marketing purposes must give individuals the ability to opt out.

3. ITS America Draft Privacy Principles, 1995.

4. Advertisement, WGBH Radio, Boston, November 30, 1995.

5. "The Road Watches You: 'Smart' highway systems may know too much," *The New York Times*, March 3, 1995.

6. John Judge, Director of Operations, Massachusetts Turnpike Authority. Personal Communication. 1995.

7. Personal interviews, March 1995.

8. Equifax-Harris Mid-Decade Consumer Privacy Survey, Equifax, Inc., Atlanta, Georgia 30309.

9. Burnham, David. *The Rise of the Computer State.* New York: Random House, 1980 (Vintage edition 1984), p. 40.

10. Agre, Phil. "Highway Surveillance." In *PRIVACY Forum Digest*, September 1, 1995, 04:19.

11. *Records, Computers, and the Rights of Citizens.* Secretary's Advisory Committee on Automated Personal Data Systems, U.S. Department of Health, Education and Welfare, July 1973. Also published by MIT Press.

Problems of Success:
Privacy, Property, and Transactions

Marcus Wigan

Remember that accumulated knowledge, like accumulated capital, increases at compound interest: but it differs from the accumulation of capital in this: that the increase of knowledge produces a more rapid rate of progress, whilst the accumulation of capital leads to a lower rate of interest. Capital thus checks its own accumulation: knowledge thus accelerates its own advance.—Charles Babbage[1]

Babbage's point is well taken in the discussion of the convergence of the National Information Infrastructure (NII) and Intelligent Transportation Systems (ITS). These electronic infrastructures, now being developed and deployed, have the potential to generate massive quantities of data that will create huge information systems—with societal, legal, and commercial effects that will be welcomed by some, but not by all.

The rapid deployment of ITS and NII initiatives is forcing social, legal, and organizational transformation to take place at least at the same pace as technology changes. This process parallels the recent acceleration of manufacturing strategies,[2] in which multiple generations of products, and their corresponding marketing strategies, are now being developed simultaneously. In communications and transport policy, the equivalent approach would be to concurrently design infrastructure, services, deployment policy, and social evaluation.

Problems of Failure and Problems of Success

Two types of problems develop in the deployment of any new initiative: problems of failure and problems of success. Problems of failure occur in the course of implementation, keeping a project from reaching its primary goals. In the case of ITS/NII initiatives, problems of failure might take the form of purely technical issues of communications and control,[3] an inability to make internet-working operate effectively, inadequate organizational responses, unresolved issues of public or organizational liability for information management or enforcement action (or the lack of it) on the basis of the information flows, or loss of public credibility in key areas such as the safety and reliability levels of active ITS systems. Any of these problems might be a potential barrier to ITS deployment.

Problems of success, the focus of this chapter, occur when a project has successfully met its objectives, but then encounters the effects of its new market or societal presence. In the case of ITS and NII joint initiatives, the problems of success might take the form of differential (and possibly also inequitable) access to information systems on the NII, discrimination due to inability to purchase NII and ITS access, the appearance of natural monopolies and monopsonies, the loss of privacy due to surveillance and monitoring functions, public and organizational liability, and new bases for trade transactions.

With the NII and ITS, the problems of success are heightened due to the potentially seamless nature of data flows which are inherent. Consider the operation of commercial ITS services over an NII infrastructure. Transactions in such an electronic framework must meet a number of basic criteria:

• They must be known by both the host and the client to be received

• They must not be replicated if they represent a cash transfer

• They require positive and enforceable verification of the identity of both the receiver and the sender

• They require a verification process that is either redundant (as in cash transfers) or is an intrinsic requirement.

If the ITS service is simple—for instance, providing timetables for bus connections—most of these requirements are unnecessary. This example is one of passive coordination that depends on the customer being provided with information, then relying on him or her choosing to make use of it. It requires no action on the part of the user, and is not a sensitive type of transaction.

Once active participation by the customer occurs, however, a charge may be levied, and a second layer of requirements is evoked. Auditing, tracing, verification, and government regulation of access to the information all become pertinent. This combination of auditability and monitoring is frequently demanded by government regulations or required by the data provider's internal financial monitoring procedures, and has always involved some degree of surveillance and loss of personal privacy. It is likely that both auditability and privacy loss will be necessary in any practical ITS/NII system.

If the requested ITS information has been developed by a government agency or an entity supported by public funds, it is likely that at least part of the information must be made accessible to the general public at marginal cost. If the information has been developed by a private or commercial entity, it may be regarded as commercially valuable and a resalable asset. Further, privately generated information is far less regulated with respect to its use, and issues of privacy may be largely ignored by its owner. Currently, privacy regulation in the U.S. applies almost exclusively to information in the public sector. The ITS/NII infrastructure may already be deployed before pressures to create a different balance between information availability and personal privacy take effect. On the other hand, privacy issues have dogged ITS for so long that deployment may create a demand for their resolution. Some have suggested that anonymous smart cards be used for ITS transactions at both vehicle and individual levels, but in many cases these cards cannot protect the privacy of their users.

One problem is that smart cards are just that: smart. They can accept programming for active functions and can easily be updated with information invisible to the user. For example, a smart-vehicle identity card installed in a car may receive a message via a monitoring system beacon when the vehicle has been detected in a speeding violation. The card is tagged with this information; the violation can now be picked up via beacon by another monitoring station and recorded. This smart, updatable system can easily be used for very different functions than was originally devised—and operate these functions entirely invisibly to the user.

Smart cards with public-key encryption provide a promising ITS support technology that may avoid at least a measure of the public resistance to such activities as electronic road pricing.[4,5] However, smart-card technology promoted to car owners as a car maintenance aid is already being used to gather extensive information on vehicle usage and behavior for the manufacturer—without the full knowledge of the car owner. This example simply illustrates the potential for a smart card promoted for one purpose but used simultaneously for another. If this occurred, or even was widely suspected to have occurred, it would severely erode public confidence in this valuable technology. Any lack of trust in smart cards could slow down a range of NII and ITS initiatives that depend on anonymity but still require verified transactions. Therefore, policy measures to ensure transparency of smart-card capabilities are highly desirable. For example, lack of trust associated with the potential misuse of ITS was largely responsible for the failure of the otherwise technically "successful" Hong Kong road pricing experiment,[6] which used inductive loops on car identification and tolling units. And if these systems are not designed to operate without detailed surveillance in the U.S. and elsewhere, then an auditing process will be necessary to maintain acceptable personal privacy standards.

Information Issues

Information flows are intrinsic to both NII and ITS, but the systems differ in their ownership of and responsibility for the information traveling within these flows. ITS is a subset of the NII, but differs because it embraces a narrower (but still open-ended) set of applications, largely within a specified set of facilities (highways and vehicles), and at its core is a public service. As the number of ITS initiatives expands, the need grows for both a common infrastructure for different ITS subsystems and a communications standard to link them. The NII and ITS have similar problems building these infrastructures and communications standards. Both require an alliance between business and government in order to be successful, and regulatory bodies play a key role. Both organizations must deal with questions of intellectual property, privacy, and the effective dissemination and use of the information created.

U.S. government policy emphasizes private investment to fund ITS initiatives. Government support is largely limited to the development and coordination of standards, demonstration projects, and sustained efforts to ensure consensus. Governmental, organizational, and regulatory efforts can also publicize the issues of data and information access, to help in the process of reaching a balanced policy between the commercial benefits and societal costs of using the information created. However, the commercial trade in ITS transport information and its close relative, spatial information developed by the U.S. Office of the Census, is already creating concern because of the very limited constraints on commercial database matching in the U.S.[7] Substantial market power will be experienced by enterprises created to trade in information flow capture and control, with sure effects on clients, transactions, goods, and consumers. Should this market power be subject to government controls or regulations?

In Australia, EDI has created a glaring example of monopsony power. This situation arose as an unexpected side effect of several major organizations progressively building up practical experience with EDI prior to the emergence of a complete legal framework for electronic commerce. Now, Australian retail trade is dominated by a single, huge retail trading group with massive buying power, a group in a position to demand that EDI be used by all its suppliers—and on its own terms. The wielding of market power by a single group has also occurred in the automotive industries of many countries.

The changes in information flow that ITS will bring, in conjunction with the system operators' increased potential ability to control and monitor, will have as profound an effect on organizational structures and power relationships as did the 1980's revolution in traffic automation.[8] This revolution stimulated widespread restructuring of safety, road management, and road construction organizations as the information flows changed—largely in response to technical innovations in area traffic control and centralization of safety and management information. ITS projects will consolidate and accelerate this trend.

Surveillance

Surveillance—a combination of real-time and retrospective data integration—is a feature that integrates the NII's high bandwidth and distributed power and the services, data capture, and storage capabilities of an ITS system.

Using surveillance techniques, a retrospective search on the vehicle or person of interest can be implemented and the subject checked for potentially overlooked past violations. A database may also provide a detailed movement and timing pattern that could be useful for other purposes unrelated to transport issues, such as tracking stolen vehicles and identifying the types of services and locations visited.

This retrospectivity raises the question of who owns the retrospective data, which is simply an automatically collected factual database. Who may have access to this data? If the government owns it, does the public have a right to access or copy it for searches and investigations—or even to purchase a real-time selective feed from it? If a commercial body owns the data, would the situation be any different? What forms of regulation, if any, would be appropriate for such information? These are not questions that can be answered easily.

The issue of surveillance and access to the resulting data has been confronted in the trucking and freight-forwarding industries. Few people object to the identification of a package of goods or freight. Both tracking number systems and container and railway rolling stock identification systems are widely recognized as valuable to the efficient operation of the transport system. However, the individuals who drive trucks, taxis, and transit vehicles, as well as emergency and police staff, are also part of the transport operating system in this same sense, and their terms of employment reasonably expect them to use immediate location and monitoring systems.

Real-Time and Retrospective Access

Real-time access to transport information available through ITS services is a lively interest of enforcement agencies. How better to enforce transport regulations than by having real-time monitoring of the actions of identified and precisely located vehicles and individuals? The very efficiency of the projected NII infrastructure ensures that real-time access to ITS services will be technically possible. But how long will it be before that access is mandated?

Retrospective transport data captured through ITS services are as important as real-time data. Once a particular behavior or event occurs, even one that is not necessarily a violation, the combination of NII and ITS allows it to be recorded and reported automatically to a monitoring or enforcement body. The ability to examine collections of data in retrospect for events and patterns of behavior is a powerful tool. At first it may be intended just for surveillance, but subsequently be used for exception detection and targeted group monitoring. This progression has been observed in at least one country (Australia) regarding automatic speed detection and vehicle identification technologies.

Identification issues

Real-time ITS monitoring is another small step towards widespread ITS systems. The extensive location and communication systems now common in trucks (including satellite links and GPS systems for high-value vehicles and cargoes in Australia) seem to be a simple extension of an established management practice: automated workplace surveillance. This is an area of acute sensitivity for many people, one expected to be exacerbated by the rise of telecommuting and other communications-dependent modes of work.

The ITS location and identification system is a small but significant step in the move from passive anonymous systems of customer information to interactive systems that require positive participation. Activating a rideshare or pickup request, destination requirement, or collection time creates an active record that uniquely identifies the customer (in space at least). System designers should be aware of the commercial and surveillance opportunities and privacy threats created by data built up from such active participation.

Other user demands on a transport system may be routing or parking guidance requirements, or even requests for priority for an emergency journey. Are these examples of vehicle- or user-based intelligent transportation systems? If vehicle-based, then the use of telemetry and real-time monitoring of vehicles is entirely sensible and obvious; however users are likely to be discomfited by recorded evidence of their precise location and driving behavior. On the other hand, container and railway rolling stock identification and monitoring systems usually do not affect individuals at all.

The steady trend toward longer, unique "personal" telephone numbers, combined with the growth in mobile telephone use, provides convenient methods of individual identification and location, and undermine the argument that people who use ITS systems must be prepared for a loss of privacy. There are already ITS performance detection and response systems that operate without any option on the part of the user. These include some automatic speed and vehicle-load detection systems.

Capturing such information also means that all private transport users become subject to the same basic terms of travel as a truck driver. In other words, users become potentially subject to continuous monitoring and to retrospective analysis of behaviors, origins, destinations, and trip times.

This scenario presents a rich haul for the legal system in all sorts of ways. Data like the kind described above is carefully collected under privacy and confidentiality provisions in transport surveys. Linking this information to individuals offers a continuous automatic travel survey, yet no framework has been set up for access to such data, or for rights of access to it. Consider the issues of legal defense of individuals, or their prosecution, where such data could be material evidence on either side.

A distinction therefore needs to be drawn between a system that has high integrity and security for validating transactions, and one that can be used to match transactions by the same individual at different times or between different systems. The need for a high-security, high-quality, and secure identified transaction system underpins the future of electronic commerce. If this requirement can be implemented in such a way as to prevent "dataveillance," then many of the potential problems with ITS information flows and storage can be avoided.

Many conflicting views exist on the balance of interests between privacy and the surveillance required to gather data (see other chapters in this book). What cannot be disputed is that capacity exists to attain an unacceptably high level of intrusiveness into the lives of private individuals. The public may not yet be aware of this, but the commercial possibilities for exploiting this personal information are clear—and government policies are still needed to define the ground rules for balancing emerging public, private, and commercial interests. Copyright/data issues are among the most critical issues surrounding ITS/GIS, because they largely determine the commercial potential of exploiting these information flows.

Generating Wealth from Networked ITS Information

Tradeoffs between privacy and commercialization will determine what ITS and NII services can be provided, and the potential for new products and services that offer a compromise between the two is substantial. This is especially apparent in the area of freight and goods movement, where many of the more successful ITS developments are occurring first.[9] Freight and transport logistics both depend on communications, and automatic vehicle location and monitoring is of real value to logistics operators. The information generated by operating these ITS systems is itself is an asset, and gives rise to such issues as information-driven competitive advantage, as well as monopoly power in information provision. The economics of information suggest that distributing such information at marginal cost the maximum level of system-wide benefit,[10] but this must be balanced by ensuring value-added investment and returns. This means rationing the information supply by price, or providing a tiered market of goods with different levels of quality or segments.

In the U.S., this practice is widely accepted. Indeed, copyright is not available for government documents. In addition, the U.S. has long provided a substantial subsidy to commercial enterprises, by making government paid for information collection or software production available to the wider community for the transfer costs alone. This practice helps to lower barriers to new enterprise, adds value, and enhances the range of products and services available in the marketplace. As an example, the U.S. Office of the Census develops detailed spatial information, such as road networks, address ranges, detailed street and highway maps, and other spatial data, for census purposes and publishes it as the Tiger files. CD-ROM Tiger files are readily available covering each state and allow anyone to build detailed Geographical Information Systems (GIS) models of cities, small regions, or entire states for the minimal cost of $250 US per state. Availability of this data has spawned many small companies, such as ETAK (vehicle navigation products) and Caliper (GIS transportation software). Moreover, combining GIS system data with the detailed locational search capabilities of ITS creates huge opportunities in the area of targeted marketing alone.

Telecommunications Issues

A major issue of communications services providers is the content of data they carry. Should NII services as carriers for ITS services be concerned about the content traveling their corridors? Should they ignore the content of ITS data (as is normally the case for a common carrier service), or take some responsibility for it? It is not clear at this point which approach will be applied.

Content monitoring may yet become necessary if censoring of information carried by NII services becomes a legal requirement, and could make NII carriers the holders and potential purveyors of identification and flow pattern data. Should there be a requirement for certain forms of traffic to be recorded for legal auditing and compliance purposes? Alternatively, should recording of such data be explicitly forbidden? Neither situation is clear-cut nor unconditionally desirable.

Ownership of Data

Intellectual property in the networked, multimedia environment is becoming a critical issue. The discrepancies between moral and usage rights among Western and non-Western traditions led to major problems in the GATT TRIPS protocols and will continue to be a source of conflict in the new World Trade Organization. These discrepancies will not easily be reconciled, and ownership of automatically collected personal and vehicular ITS images could also be affected by these disagreements.

The rapid and continuing growth in the collection of location, movement, and transaction data has a cumulative potential. The three major features are the ability to: (1) access massive data flows, (2) match and correlate different forms and sources of data, and (3) to pick out individual items in real time as a result of previous history or special conditions of current interest.

It is not at all obvious who owns these mass assemblies of data. Until fairly recently, the level of originality required to assemble and structure the raw information necessary to ensure ownership rights for a database or collection of facts was fairly low. However, the recent Feist case[11] has shaken the basis for assuming ownership rights; the Court's decision has made the originality tests for copyright considerably more stringent, raising doubts about the ability to establish ownership for automatic data collations. This decision also affects GIS data that has such power when combined with ITS data.[12,13]

The NII and ITS each have significant potential for data-based services or enterprises, if the ownership status of data collected can be confirmed. Under U.S. law, facts cannot be copyrighted, but the organization and structure of the facts (data) can be. The tradeoffs between ownership, privacy, and data registration need examination to ensure that a good market emerges without the development of either natural monopolies or the barriers created by market power. The questions of ownership of such data are therefore far from trivial, such linkages between location, time, identity, and other records give rise to great business opportunities. If individuals willingly give up some privacy for conveniences they may gain, such information becomes of real value, and will be in demand not only for commercial use, but also for use in legal defense and prosecution. Our society must decide if this is a burden we wish to accept.

The question of "information ownership" has been transformed from the commercial plane to the moral plane of an individual's access to and control over—or at least knowledge of—the details of microscopic examination of his or her life style and behavior. There are precedents in a person's control over the use made of his or her portrait; the European Union pressed for these and other moral rights and principles in the TRIPS negotiations on intellectual property, but without great success. This may now be an area of policy requiring revisiting.

Summary

In England we have come to rely upon a comfortable time lag of fifty years or a century intervening between the perception that something ought to be done and a serious attempt to do it.--H.G. Wells[14]

Wells's comment seems as if it were written in the Middle Ages rather than only half a century ago. With the acceleration in information production and dissemination, the pace of information technology's growth is accelerating so rapidly that time lags are now measured in months, weeks, or even hours, rather than half-centuries. The world's social, legal, and organizational systems are under almost as much pressure to adapt to the NII/ITS technology[15] as those organizations working to meet the technical demands of these two large-scale and complex initiatives. Policy and project now must always be developed in tandem, and each must affect the other on a continuing basis.

Rich new opportunities are arising from the data flows inherent in ITS and carried by NII. However, the barriers to realizing these potentials are many; social pressures and tradeoffs, information access equity, and surveillance issues are all beginning to arise as ITS and NII initiatives develop. An effective, secure, and acceptable identity system linked to monetary transactions but not to surveillance capacity will serve both ITS and NII better than any other single development. But considerable technical and political effort and skill will be needed to realize and implement such a system. This could be costly to achieve.

Some mechanisms for gaining full advantage of NII/ITS integration from both commercial and community standpoints have been discussed; suggested approaches have involved developing policy on some immediate problems. For example, in the U.S., the natural, localized GIS information monopolies that will affect ITS areas have been weakened by the public access to the Tiger spatial data files. A similar public-access initiative is appropriate for some aspects of ITS/NII travel and transport data. This data can vary in quality (like the Tiger files); however, there would be plenty of room for added-value enterprises to improve and enhance this basic data.

It remains to be seen to whom such data will be dispensed—and whether it will be provided as real-time or retrospective collections, or a combination of both. Either way, a new data-mining industry is set to grow from the synergy of NII and ITS. This industry will need some governmental oversight. The low level of privacy protection in the U.S. commercial domain will demand reexamination as a result of availability of new levels of detailed personal data.

These are problems created by a successful NII/ITS infrastructure deployment. Polices should be developed to avoid these problems and to maximize the economic and social gains available in these infrastructures. Indeed, many of these issues will only arise if the substantial technical and political difficulties in achieving consistent and standards linkages between NII/ITS systems are overcome and the two infrastructures are successfully deployed.

The information resources created by any link between NII and ITS are of major potential value to business and enforcement bodies, as well as to individuals. However, the questions of ownership of, access to, and exploitation of this information are matters of real policy concern.

The NII and ITS initiatives provide an excellent opportunity to work out many surveillance, privacy, data exploitation, and access issues in direct conjunction with the implementation of the systems for which they are needed. Policy development should run in parallel with and develop with the timetable for standards, roll-out, and coordination of ITS services and NII infrastructure agreements and regulatory frameworks. If this is not done, it may not be possible to realize many of the benefits of these major and highly significant infrastructure programs.

Notes

1. Babbage, C. *The Exposition of 1851*. London: Murray, 1851.

2. Anonymous. "What Makes Yoshio Invent." *The Economist*. 318 (7869), 1991, p. 61.

3. Schopp, B.J. White Paper on Intelligent Vehicle Highway Systems (IVHS) and the National Information Infrastructure. MITRE Corporation Working Note WN 93W0000062. Federal Highway Administration, July 1994.

4. Stoelhorst, H.J. and Zandbergen, A.J. "The Development of a Road Pricing System in the Netherlands." *Traffic Engineering and Control*, 31 (2), 1990.

5. Agre, P.E. and Harbs, C.A. "Social Choice about Privacy: Intelligent Vehicle Highway Systems in the United States." *Information Technology and People*, 7 (1), 1995, pp. 63–90.

6. Luk, J.Y.K. Report on an OECD Seminar in Tokyo and Electronic Road Pricing in Hong Kong. Internal Report AIR 395-4. Australian Road Research Board, Vermont, Victoria. 1985.

7. Onsrud, H.J. *Law, Information Policy and Spatial Databases*. NCGIA Initiative 16. U.S. National Center for Geographic Information and Analysis. April 1993.

8. Wigan, M.R. "When the Dust Settles." In *The Traffic Engineering Revolution: Information Technology in Traffic Engineering*. Melbourne, Victoria: Institution of Engineers Australia and the Institution of Traffic Engineers, 1986.

9. Giannopoulos, G.A. and Moller, K. "Applications for Freight and Fleet Management in the Advanced Transport Telematics Programme (Area 6)." Report. European Union Advanced Transport Telematics Program, 1994.

10. Oniki, H. Mathematical Appendix. In *The Economics of Intellectual Property in a World Without Frontiers: A Study of Computer Software*. M. Jussawalla, Ed. New York: Greenwood Press, 1992, pp. 115–135.

11. Feist Publications v. Rural Telephone Service, 111 S.Ct. 1282, 113 L.Ed. 2d 358 (1991).

12. Dando, L.P. "Open Records Law, GIS and Copyright Protection: Life After Feist." In *URISA*, San Francisco: URISA, 1991.

13. Miller, P.H. "Life After Feist: Facts, the First Amendment and the Copyright Status of Automated Databases." *Fordham Law Review*. 60 (3), 1991, pp. 507–539

14. Wells, H.G. *The Work Wealth and Happiness of Mankind*. London: Heinneman, 1934.

15. Department of Transportation. *Nontechnical Constraints and Barriers to Implementation of Intelligent Vehicle–Highway Systems*. Report to Congress, June 1994.

Conclusion: Opportunities for Policy Convergence

Lewis M. Branscomb and James H. Keller

The minimal engagement between ITS planners and the much wider audience participating in the public debate about the NII has perhaps been surprising, given the similarity of these initiatives. Both the NII and ITS are based on rapidly evolving innovations in information services. Both programs represent a new type of public/private initiative in which the federal role is one of enabler/ facilitator, rather than investor/builder/manager (although in the case of ITS many state investments will be supported with federal funds). Major ITS and NII development initiatives remain with the private sector, and in both cases the progress of deployment depends critically on clarification on the nature and size of markets, the demand for which is limited by lack of public experience with the new services. Finally, if government fails in its enabling role, neither development is likely to be optimally rapid or effective in both economic and social terms.

Given the common programmatic themes between ITS and the NII—decentralized environment, information systems orientation, and reliance on the private sector—potential synergies exist across a wide spectrum. They range from loosely coupled activities such as information sharing, to tightly coupled joint program and policy activities. On the loosely coupled side of the spectrum are mutual opportunities to benefit from experiences gained in closely related policy environments. In standards policy, ITS planners may benefit from understanding the reasons behind the success of prior standards development efforts for the NII, such as the Internet protocols (as explained by Shuman and Solomon, in "Global Interoperability for the NII and ITS") and the failure of efforts such as the OSI protocols and Ada to dominate the architecture of open networks.

More importantly, opportunities exist for first-order interactions, where policy is jointly developed and designed to serve both domains. These occur primarily in the area of telecommunications policy, but also in the area of standards development, and in strategies for reliance on private-sector innovation to support ITS applications that do not require real-time support or represent public responsibilities for safety.

Telecommunications policy decisions are being made within the FCC and Congress that will shape the availability of communications services over the next decade. Wireless spectrum allocations may be a defining event for ITS, impacting the economics of service deployment and availability. Similarly, if passed, the new telecommunications reform legislation will directly and indirectly affect the environment for ITS communications services. RBOC lobbyists have argued for restrictions on the use of federal funding to build ITS networks. Whether it is the ITS bandwidth requirements themselves or the potential for excess capacity that drove this concern, these key stakeholders clearly anticipate the impact of ITS on the telecommunications marketplace.

From the perspective of the NII, ITS might be considered as one among many sets of advanced applications in which both public and private investment decisions depend on clarification about the value and timing of returns. However, it may well be one of the earlier applications to engage the participation of a broad segment of the U.S. population and stimulate a further acceleration of commercial information services. The ITS community, for its part, tends to see the NII as the nation's underlying telecommunications infrastructure, without adequate appreciation of the significance of the new services and business models the Internet is demonstrating. Indeed, the fact that the Internet has, in effect, erased geographic definitions of communities of interest may well force municipalities organizing ITS services to think about the scale economies that can come from software and data sharing across every major U.S. city.

Focal Points for Interaction

From a public-sector perspective, NII/ITS relationships can be roughly broken down into four categories:

1. Opportunities for shared physical communications infrastructure, including both wired and wireless networks.

2. Shared resources and processes for standards and technology development.

3. Communications and information policy issues in which ITS and the NII have a common stake.

4. Coordinating federal, state, and private sector initiatives.

Clearly there is some overlap across these categories, but this breakdown offers some structure around which to think about the connections between ITS and the NII.

Opportunities for Shared Physical Infrastructure

While several states are pursuing shared resources policies, as discussed in Horan and Jakubiak's "The Key Role For Shared Resources in Highway Rights of Way," the vast majority are building dedicated ITS networks. Though further research is required in this area, it appears that preference is one element of municipalities' decisions to construct dedicated ITS networks.[1] In their examination of state decision-making, "Institutional Issues in Local Implementation," Melcher and Roos found that states' analyses were typically incomplete, and did not offer thorough justification based on costs or technology requirements. Thorough analysis of this choice needs to involve not only understanding the direct cost implications, but also the larger, long-term market implications. For example, a proliferation of state-owned ITS networks raises the question of what will be done with excess network capacity. The importance of this question is heightened by the speculative nature of bandwidth demand for ITS. This uncertainty is a function of both market uncertainty and questions about which technologies will best support ITS applications.

ITS planners are not acting irrationally in choosing dedicated networks, although they do seem to be taking a short-term view. At both the state and federal levels, the environment for spending transportation dollars supports capital expenditures over recurring costs. Local transportation officials typically fund new initiatives through a combination of federal Highway Trust Fund (HTF) allocations and monies secured through the state budget process. Although current HTF requirements do not explicitly restrict funds from being spent on things other than capital, there is a perceived restriction. While states are permitted to outsource, doing so typically requires a request for federal concurrence. This is often a minor hurdle, but as a non-standard procedure, it can be perceived as a deterrent.[2] Federal funding requires not only that state implementers have the appropriate level of flexibility in applying federal funds, but also that this flexibility is easily understood and accessible.

Similarly, in contending for state funds, transportation officials have stated that it is easier to go to the legislature and secure a large one-time allocation than to depend on the yearly allocations required by outsourcing. The incentives to build are also bolstered by the fact that state officials are operating within the current regulated local exchange carriage regime, and are offered formal tariffs from the carriers. The costs presented to the states in response to initial cost inquiries are often far in excess of what they might obtain once the states and Congress complete their deregulation of local telecommunications services, or what they may be able to negotiate in the current environment.

In analyzing lease–build decisions, it is very high ITS bandwidth requirements that have tipped the scales towards building state-owned networks. These high-bandwidth forecasts are driven by anticipated video requirements. Video is estimated to account for 40 percent of the cost of building an Advanced Traffic Management System (ATMS).[3] but it is not clear that video is the best technology for ITS monitoring—and even if it is, it may not require the level of bandwidth that has been forecast. For example, as Chen anticipates in "Intelligent Agents and ITS," intelligent agent software may reduce the need for propagating video images across ITS networks. Or, non-video sensors may prove equivalent or even superior in providing analyzable data. In either case, the highly video-dependent ITS bandwidth forecasts may prove excessive.

While it may prove wise to put video capabilities in place, well-managed use may only require transmission of video images when an incident is detected through other monitoring technology. What would public agencies likely do with excess communications capacity—use it to support the requirements of non-transportation government services? Resell it? Let it lie idle? Many municipal and state governments have not developed an internally consistent policy on network service acquisition for all the public functions of state and local government. The general trend, however, is that while ITS planners are looking to construction of dedicated networks, other branches of government—policy, education, public information services—are relying on the rapidly improving and increasingly price-competitive public offerings by the telecommunications and information service industries.

Whether these commitments to dedicated networks are wise or questionable, they certainly are not in the spirit of the prevailing view of both the Clinton Administration and the Congress that private sector development of the NII will result in the most rapid innovation and the lowest costs for most applications. If states are building their own ITS networks, it should be done with a clearly articulated policy about what the network will and will not be used for, in order to not inadvertently deter private investment.

If ITS implementers are to be expected to behave differently, the incentive structure that drives their behavior must be changed. Legislative changes to the HTF allocation guidelines may be one route to addressing this, better communication of options available under the current guidelines may be another. By structuring the fund so that state O&M (versus capital) dollars can be leveraged with trust fund allocations, state legislatures may be more sympathetic to ITS budgets.

A degree of market coordination might also further the use of general-purpose infrastructure for ITS purposes. State DOTs and service providers are currently far apart in many of their views about providing ITS communications services. States are building their own systems, and RBOC lobbying efforts have sought to restrict ITS funding. At the federal level, buying of telecommunications services has been consolidated through the General Services Administration (GSA) and a very deep discount has been negotiated for the entire federal government. The GSA is a very large consumer of telecommunications services and was able to apply this buying leverage to achieve the FTS 2000 agreement. By aggregating their buying power, the states may be able to reach a similar agreement. A difficult element of this, however, is determining the optimal level of aggregation—regional, statewide, interstate, or national—and what user groups should be included. The answer to this question will be a function of the particular geography, set of applications, and budget relevant to each potential participant.

Standards and Technology Development

Interoperability across different applications and the networks that provide data for them is an important goal of both NII and ITS architectures. Standards development to achieve functional compatibility and scale economies is critical for ITS. This is one area in which ITS planners may benefit from the work and experience of NII and Internet developers. In most cases the key will not be to standardize processes themselves, but rather to standardize how they interface with other ITS and NII elements. Achieving interoperability in the presence of diversity, heterogeneity, and rapid change calls for the widespread adoption of common standards that allow independently developed (and possibly managed) pieces of the system to interoperate. This requires timely identification and articulation of the issues the standards need to address—and a process through which they are to be realized.

In the case of the NII, the government has no intention, or indeed capability, of imposing a system-level architecture. The TCP/IP protocol standard that facilitates internetworking and makes both communications and applications innovation possible is critical to the NII, but market forces are thought to be sufficient to retain the interoperability of Internet services. Standards are expected to evolve from the experimentation, competition, and market acceptance of services, many of which are yet to be conceived and tested. Governmentally mandated standards are likely to be restricted to issues such as security (encryption, authentication) and efficient spectrum use. At the same time, traditional standards development procedures and institutions that ensure producer and user consensus about how mature technologies should be specified, have not fit well with the rapid development of digital information technology. Ratification by international standards development organizations has been important for physical telecom facilities development, but is clearly not a prerequisite for rapid deployment of the NII.

Three distinct models for standards development converge in the NII: the competitive, market-driven model of computer software and applications; the collaborative, flexible, and innovation-based model of the Internet; and the more traditional and formal practices in the telecommunications industry, now pressed by deregulation and the prospect of intense competition. These three models—applications, internetworking, and telecommunications—circumscribe the principal issues in the standards landscape. All increasingly confront a complex and rapidly changing environment in which an array of strategic elements must be evaluated and balanced by a growing and unstable mix of stakeholders. All face the paradox that standards are critical to market development but, once accepted, standards may threaten innovation, inhibit change, and retard the development of new markets. These factors require standards processes to be future-oriented.

Progress is being made in the timely identification and articulation of the issues that ITS standards need to address. The American National Standards Institute (ANSI) established the Information Infrastructure Standards Panel (IISP) to provide a mechanism for coordinating NII standards requirements across industries. The IISP has broad industry participation, including ITS America, and appears to be succeeding in identifying and consolidating key interoperability requirements. However, this effort may come up short in its continued reliance on traditional standards-setting organizations for standards development. These organizations continue to move slowly, and there is no reason to think that they will be able to meet the pace required by technology and market development for information and communications systems. DOT has allocated $15 million to ITS standards development to accelerate this usually voluntary process. This is a positive step, but the process must still contend with the structural and political bottlenecks of traditional standards development organizations.

Another avenue for integrating ITS requirements into NII standards development, currently being explored by the ITS Joint Program Office, is the Cross Industry Working Team (XIWT). XIWT is a multi-industry coalition formed by the Corporation for National Research Initiatives to identify key technical requirements for the NII. This type of broad-based approach is critical, but, similar to the IISP it will be challenged by the need to reconcile a diverse set of requirements.

In most areas of ITS, the critical interoperability points will be network, appliance, and application interfaces. In some areas, however, it will be key to seek standardization of the processes themselves, as well as their interface with other elements. For example, the software development and integration elements of ITS are expected to be very costly in the aggregate, particularly since much of the computer code will have to meet very high reliability requirements, necessitating extensive testing. States will require heavy and ongoing investment in ITS system software to support the management of ITS data. Currently, states appear to be independently pursuing software development efforts. By coordinating some aspects of system requirements and interfaces, states and ITS users may benefit from more rapid commercialization and market aggregation, amortizing development and testing costs across multiple projects. This coordination may also contribute to development of common data structures across separate ITS systems, lowering the development costs of private value-added traffic information services.

The creation of a national market for ITS services and data management can allow ITS to participate in the most striking change in the institutional arrangements for standardization in the information industry: the emergence of a large number of consortia assembled, principally by vendors, to address issues of compatibility and interoperability that impede the aggregation and growth of markets. Some consortia consist of only a few companies, and might be more properly described as ad hoc alliances. At the other extreme, the Object Management Group (OMG) has some 500 members, 40% of which are headquartered outside the U.S.

The debate around critical interfaces in the NII reveals the growing tension between the push for widely implemented standards to support interoperability and the desire to retain incentives for proprietary investment. This is not a simple matter, and no doubt similar tensions will appear in the industries supporting ITS. There are complex strategic issues on the standards side, and unresolved and controversial issues of both substantive law and policy and administrative process on the intellectual property side. Continuing uncertainty also exists about the extent to which interface specifications can be controlled by either patents or copyright—if not directly, then by patents on underlying functionality or copyright on implementations that have resulted in de facto standards. These intellectual property issues will also have to be sorted out to balance investment incentives with openness and competition.

Common Information and Communications Policy Concerns

ITS and the NII offer federal policymakers a similarly structured set of problems, tools, and environmental factors. In each case, the challenge is to stimulate a loosely coupled set of third parties to invest heavily in the development and implementation of an advanced information infrastructure that encompasses communications, information, and services. The federal role in both initiatives addresses not only capabilities, but also public-access and competitiveness issues. ITS and the NII are not only parallel policy environments, but also overlapping, mutually dependent domains. In many areas, the infrastructure supporting transportation will be a virtual component of the NII, and many regulatory and information policy issues and decisions will have cross-cutting impact.

The mobility inherent in transportation systems will make wireless services a particularly critical component. The wireless market, while not yet mature, does appear to be at a development threshold. Cellular services are still analog, but digital cellular is beginning to move out, and the FCC is considering spectrum allocation decisions for a more robust set of wireless technologies. The FCC has already allocated 26 MHz of spectrum (902–928 MHz) for "Transportation Infrastructure Radio Service," but additional spectrum will be required.

While not highlighted in early NII policy discussions, wireless technology is a key enabling component of advanced services. Spectrum is a finite resource for which there is active competition, as demonstrated by the FCC auctions. Even in those areas where ITS-specific spectrum allocations will not be required, it will be critical to ITS service development that appropriate and adequate allocations are made. The wireless requirements for ITS services are probably best understood in the private sector. DOT and the ITS community should actively respond to relevant FCC dockets, and convene prospective service providers in articulating an ITS spectrum requirements statement that can inform FCC decision-making.

Other areas of common policy concern include liability, privacy, authentication, and intellectual property. New media are stretching existing legal and institutional structures in each of these areas. In each, policy development and dialogue are progressing. The ITS community must participate vigorously in these activities to ensure that they are consistent with ITS objectives.

Personal privacy is highlighted by several authors as an issue warranting particular attention due to the potentially extensive monitoring and data warehousing aspects of ITS. As Garfinkel points out, the universality of travel and the immediacy of ITS implementation position ITS as a proving ground for privacy issues in other NII domains. Fortunately, there are technological solutions, utilizing anonymous or key-encrypted systems, which can minimize privacy concerns without compromising ITS objectives. Of course, issues will still arise concerning the appropriate use of ITS data. The key for policy makers is to determine whether this should be dealt with proactively, by promulgating principles and guidelines, and perhaps legal solutions regarding the appropriate use of personal information. Clearly defining the rules up front will hopefully reduce system deployment delays and costly litigation. One such solution may be amending the "Driver's Privacy and Protection Act" to include ITS data.

Coordinating Federal, State, and Private-Sector Initiatives

As with the NII, the federal role in ITS will be an indirect one, despite the fact that substantial funding for the states flows through the Highway Trust Fund. In the past, product and technology development for large agency mission programs was guided by federal dollars. From a transactions perspective, the sale was often made before the product was built, minimizing the risk on the part of the private technology provider. Government was the market maker. In the case of both ITS and the NII, however, businesses will have to expose themselves to more risk than in previous federal technology initiatives. In each case, federal dollars are subsidizing some of the development costs. The HPCC initiative supports the NII, and the ITS architecture program supports directions for ITS. Market coordination for both will be complex relative to traditional federally funded initiatives.

One difference between ITS and the NII is that in the case of ITS, the states act as market intermediaries between end-users and private technology and service developers for some parts of the transportation information infrastructure. It is safe to assume that these state investments will be at least partially subsidized by federal highway dollars. The degree to which markets for ITS network elements mature quickly will be in part a function of the degree to which the states adopt common interface standards and architecture principles. Applying indirect leverage to coordinate state and local ITS initiatives around such standards and principles will be one of the biggest challenges in fostering national ITS services. But so far, federal efforts have had little impact in coordinating ITS implementations, despite the fact that ongoing system costs can be better controlled by being shared across states. Each state—indeed each municipality—is proceeding at its own pace, and to a great extent in its own way.

The Highway Trust Fund presents one opportunity for influencing state activities. Broad guidelines for spending HTF allocations are set in the ISTEA legislation. Within these broad guidelines, implementation standards are recommended each year by the states and ratified by DOT to achieve continuity across trust-fund-sponsored development initiatives. Conformance to these standards is criteria for states to receive Trust Fund allocations. By coordinating state development of HTF implementation standards to focus more on ITS standards, and fostering greater understanding of the opportunities for applying Trust Fund allocations, the HTF can be structured as a powerful mechanism to support and align state ITS activities.

As federal infrastructure initiatives are increasingly dependent on the states for implementation, it is critical that formal mechanisms be put in place to link state programs and federal policy efforts. Within the ITS America discussions, state interests are loosely coupled with federal activities. The ITS Architecture Program is also working to engage the states in its activities. Judging by current activities in the states, it is not apparent that these efforts are sufficient to achieve broad state-level compliance with national level architecture plans, or to induce adequate federal response to state issues. In establishing meaningful architecture guidelines, it will be vital to establish functionally based definitions of conformance and to outline a program through which these definitions can be applied to assess from a functional perspective the success of state conformance efforts. Assessment based purely on conformance to technical specifications is often not enough to ensure interoperability.

For NII policy, the disconnect between state and federal efforts has been even wider. In response, Governors Richard Celeste and Dick Thornburgh, in response to a request by Jack Gibbons, the director of the White House Office of Science and Technology Policy, launched a task force on April 25, 1995, to examine how federal–state relationships might be strengthened or restructured in the area of science and technology. Sponsored by the Carnegie Commission on Science, Technology, and Government, the National Governor's Association, and the National Council of State Legislators, the Task Force looked at a number of specific cases, including the ITS program.

The Task Force report recommends Presidential action to facilitate the participation of state governments in federal S&T programs that call for state-level participation. It also addresses the necessity for states to put their internal houses in order, and to cooperate with one another in presenting a somewhat more consistent face to their federal partners. Here both states and municipalities have quite a distance yet to travel. There are at least three semi-independent sources of state authority over matters of telecommunications and information policy: the state regulators of telecommunications and utilities, the state-level investors in telecom services for the broader functions of state governments, and the transportation authorities. Few states have the institutional mechanisms to build consistent policies across these separate functions. And at the municipal level, there is often little coordination merely within the planning of ITS services for traffic management, public transportation, ramp access management, and emergency and traveler information. In many cases, each of these areas is developing its own network solution. Smooth collaboration with federal authorities can hardly be expected until some of these discontinuities are remedied.

Conclusion

A mechanism for engaging state governments more formally in the architecture and policies of the NII and the ITS needs to emerge—either out of the States Federal Partnership Task Force, or perhaps out of the President's NII Task Force. The NII Task Force has not, however, engaged state governments in its work. The ITS project could be a good vehicle through which to build this bridge, but a federal inter-agency task force is an awkward structure for intergovernmental coordination. In addition, if this linkage should be made through the NII Task Force, the Department of Transportation, together with other departments and agencies concerned with the nation's transportation systems, would need to participate actively in the work of the Task Force. This will ensure that the interoperability, security, and other features of the NII are appropriate for the national transportation system's needs.

ITS is also dependent on the participation of the private sector. Success will require large investments on the part of automakers, technologists, and information service providers. The nature of information infrastructure, large sunk costs, dependence on standards, and a large set of autonomous and interdependent players requires unusually broad coordination across an array of industries. Previous experience with complex national systems with mixed public/private interests does not suggest that this coordination will be easily achieved. In the mid-to-late 1980s ISDN was widely regarded as a "holy grail" for communications technology. The technology for ISDN has been available since this time, and telephone companies have offered it selectively in many areas, but it has yet to fully make it in the marketplace. A successful ISDN rollout would have required market coordination between switch makers, customer equipment developers, service providers, and applications developers. This coordination did not happen. ISDN applications did not appear, because of the lack of hardware and service offerings, and vice-versa. The telecommunications industry appears to have learned from this mishap, and generational technology advances, such as frame relay, SMDS, and ATM, have been ushered in by industry groups made up of service providers, LAN and WAN vendors, and others. These fora have rapidly developed implementation agreements for technical specifications, and helped promote a more coherent marketplace.

ITS introduces new market complexity into the transportation sector, and is vulnerable to the same "chicken-and-egg" problem that affects information infrastructure generally. It is difficult to predict accurately the demand characteristics of new markets. As many NII-related investments have been postponed or canceled, it is reasonable to expect that ITS will similarly evolve in fits and starts. ITS planners must now determine how best to promote confidence amongst product and service developers. Communication is one key element of this. Public-sector service plans, technical specifications, and data structures should be articulated quickly and with as much detail as possible. Included in these announcements should be a clear policy statement on the terms of availability for ITS data, and the acceptable uses of state-owned networks. Taking leadership in this communication has been an obvious role for the DOT and for institutions it has encouraged into being, such as ITS America.

The Internet presents another model for the government role in infrastructure development. Like communication, transportation is typically not undertaken for its own sake, but to serve a larger need, such as delivering a product or getting to work. In the case of the Internet, its development was funded initially to meet defense communications needs, and later to serve the scientific research community. All the while, the Internet architecture and NSF policies kept it open as a vehicle through which anyone could develop and test new applications, through which new markets could be validated. The NSFNet, the precursor to the commercial

Internet, was funded under cooperative agreement by the National Science Foundation with the understanding that the commercial sector would not otherwise meet its requirements. Now that Internet services are no longer considered a vehicle for "pre-competitive" technology development, but have matured into a great variety of commercial and non-commercial services, NSF has withdrawn funding for production-level Internet service.[4]

Just as the Internet was as a tool to support government-funded research, advanced ITS applications could similarly be developed through funding to support a specific public-sector transportation requirement, such as the postal service, defense, public transportation, or federal procurement. So long as the ITS architecture and policies remained open to unsolicited innovations, technology and standards would mature and commercial applications could be justified on a marginal cost basis.

The true importance of this coordination role for the federal government may not become self-evident for some time, but by then the opportunities could be missed. A central focus of debate on the development of ITS systems is now on physical networks. What are the appropriate roles of states and municipalities in building ITS communications systems? Though this issue became a serious point of conflict in recent federal appropriations, it can be expected to sort itself out over the next several years, and will not, in and of itself, be a major barrier to the successful development of ITS. What may prove critical are a more subtle set of issues related to the economics of ITS application deployment, and the importance of bringing a systems view to the earliest phases of ITS planning. Systems must be affordable, modular, and scaleable— scaleable not only within jurisdictions, but also between them.

Whether through direct federal investment, or the more apparent role of facilitation and coordination, common hardware and software platforms will be critical to managing the cost and technical aspects of maintaining ITS systems. State and municipal funding for ITS may bring pressure to contract locally for systems development. While local developers can probably be found who possess the required technical expertise, there is a serious risk that some municipalities may adopt one-off solutions that could lock projects into customized upgrades and enhancements. In a decade or two large municipalities may find that they are struggling with the great difficulty and expense of transforming "legacy" software into more robust and better supported software systems from commercial firms at the national (or international) level. Indeed, too much local variation in system specifications can also delay the integration of those national markets. The key role for DOT will be in developing effective institutional mechanisms to encouraging states to undergo joint planning and development, both to achieve system interoperability and to allow reliance on common software systems. DOT's commitment in January 1996 of significant funding for standards development is a strong step in the right direction.

This type of scalability, allowing systems to coalesce at the regional and national levels, will be a prerequisite for maturing of the rich array of traffic and traveler systems that have been forecast. The potential barrier to this integration is independently planned local systems that do not rationally integrate. The issues are not necessarily complex, but do require broad acceptance of standards to avoid the type of problems that are plaguing the medical information industry, where the same data elements may have different meanings in different systems, preventing easy aggregation. To achieve this coordination, DOT must not only understand the issues, but also the set of factors that are currently driving state and local decision-making. The National Architecture Program is the right type of effort in seeking national coordination, but is challenged to better understand the local decision-making process and respond to it.

Notes

1. *ITS Bandwidth Requirements*, White Paper, John A.Volpe National Transportation Systems Center, Cambridge, MA, November 1995.

2. Ibid.

3. Diebold Institute, *Transportation Infostructures*, p. 97.

4. The NSFNet program has transitioned to fund a very high speed backbone network service, for the exclusive use of the high-end research community.

Glossary of Acronyms

AC	Advisory Committee
AHCPR	Agency for Health Care Policy Research
AHS	Automated Highway Systems
ANSI	American National Standards Institute
ARMS	Automated Ridematching Service
ARPA	Advanced Research Projects Agency
ARPANET	Advanced Research Projects Agency Network
ASTM	American Society for Testing and Materials
ATIS	Advanced Traveler Information Systems
ATM	Asynchronous Transfer Mode
ATMS	Advanced Traffic Management Systems
AVCS	Advanced Vehicle Control Systems
AVI	Automated Vehicle Identification
BART	Bay Area Rapid Transit
BMFT	German Ministry of Research and Technology
CAD	Computer-Aided Design
CA/T	Central Artery/Tunnel
CCTV	Closed-Circuit Television
CDPD	Cellular Digital Packet Data
CEN	Committee of European Normalization
CEV	Controlled-Environment Vault
CHP	California Highway Patrol
CTS	Commuter Train Systems

CVO	Commercial Vehicle Operations
DAT	Digital Audio Tape
DOC	Department of Commerce
DOD	Department of Defense
DOE	Department of Energy
DOT	Department of Transportation
EDI	Electronic Data Interchange
EMS	Emergency Management Services
EPA	Environmental Protection Agency
ETC	Entertainment, Telephone, and Cable TV
ETTM	Electronic Toll and Traffic Management
FAA	Federal Aviation Administration
FCC	Federal Communications Commission
FDDI	Fiber Distributed Data Interface
FHWA	Federal Highway Administration
FOIA	Freedom of Information Act
FOT	Field Operations Test
FRA	Federal Railroad Administration
FTA	Federal Transit Administration
FTP	File Transfer Protocol
FTS	Federal Telecommunications Service
GIS	Geographic Information System
GPS	Global Positioning System
GSA	General Services Administration
HDTV	High-Definition Television
HPCC	High-Performance Computing and Communications
HROW	Highway Right-of-Way
HTF	Highway Trust Fund
IDEA	Ideas Deserving Exploratory Analysis
IEEE	Institute of Electrical and Electronic Engineers
IISP	Information Infrastructure Standards Panel
IITA	Information Infrastructure Technology and Applications
IITF	Information Infrastructure Task Force

IP	Internet Protocol
IPng	Internet Protocol next generation
ISO	International Standards Organization
ISTEA	Intermodal Surface Transportation Efficiency Act of 1991
ITS	Intelligent Transportation Systems
ITU	International Telecommunications Union
IVHS	Intelligent Vehicle Highway Systems
JPO	Joint Program Office
LAN	Local Area Network
LISB	Leit- und Informations System Berlin
MFSNT	Metropolitan Fiber Systems Network Technologies
MHD	Massachusetts Highway Department
MHDT	Missouri Highway and Transportation Department
MISP	Motorist Information Systems Project
MITI	Ministry of International Trade and Industry
MPO	Metropolitan Planning Organization
MTC	Metropolitan Transportation Commission
NAHSC	National Automated Highway Systems Consortium
NASA	National Aeronautics and Space Administration
NEMA	National Electrical Manufacturers Association
NIH	National Institutes of Health
NII	National Information Infrastructure
NIST	National Institute of Standards and Technology
NITA	National Telecommunications and Information Administration
NOAA	National Oceanic and Atmospheric Agency
NPRM	Notice of Proposed Rule Making
NSA	National Security Agency
NSF	National Science Foundation
O&M	Operations and Maintenance
OMG	Object Management Group
OODBMS	Object-Oriented Database Management Systems
OSI	Open Systems Interconnection
PBX	Private Branch Exchange

PSTN	Public Switched Telephone Network
PTMC	Public Transit Management Center
R&D	Research and Development
RBOC	Regional Bell Operating Company
RDBMS	Relational Database Management System
RFI	Request for Information
RFP	Request for Proposal
RMTIC	Regional Multimodal Traveler Information Center
ROW	Right of Way
RSPA	Research and Special Projects Administration
SAE	Society of Automotive Engineers
SC	Steering Committee
SJDSP	San Jose Department of Streets and Parks
SMDS	Switched Multimegabit Data Service
SMTP	Simple Mail Transfer Protocol
SNET	Southern New England Telephone
SONET	Synchronous Optical Network
SRP	Shared Resources Policy
TCP	Transmission Control Protocol
TIA	Telecommunications Industries Association
TIC	Transportation Information Center
TII	Transportation Information Infrastructure
TSMP	Traffic Signal Management Project
USDOT	U.S. Department of Transportation
USGS	U.S. Geological Survey
VA	Veterans Administration
VAR	Value Added Reseller
XIWT	Cross-Industry Working Team

Contributors

Robert Arden is Senior Analyst, Intelligent Transportation Systems, at Bellcore and Chah of ITS America's Wireline Communications Working Group.

John H. Bailey (jbailey@arinc.com) is a Senior Principal Engineer with ARINC, Inc., in the Systems Division's Surface Transportation unit. He is the principal investigator for ARINC's Communications Alternatives Test and Evaluation contract with the Federal Highway Administration.

Stephen J. Bespalko (sjbespa@sandia.gov) is a Senior Member of the Technical Staff at Sandia National Laboratories, where he is working on the development of new quantitative methods for environmental and public health studies. Before coming to Sandia, he spent 17 years at Xerox Corporation.

Lewis M. Branscomb (lewisb@ksgrsch.harvard.edu) is Aetna Professor of Public Policy and Corporate Management at Harvard's Kennedy School of Government, where he directs the Science, Technology and Public Policy Program. Trained as a physicist, he has served as Director of the National Bureau of Standards, vice president and chief scientist of IBM, and chairman of the National Science Board. His most recent books are *Confessions of a Technophile* (1995), *Beyond Spinoff* (1992), and *Empowering Technology* (1993), co-authored with Harvard colleagues.

Elisabeth J. Carpenter is on the technical staff at the U.S. DOT's Center for Navigation, Volpe National Transportation Systems Center, in Cambridge, Massachusetts. She is responsible for coordinating the biennial Federal Radionavigation Plan, in addition to projects related to radionavigation and ITS.

Su-Shing Chen (schen@uncc.edu) is a Professor of Computer Science at the University of North Carolina at Charlotte. He is also a business consultant on Internet-based information systems, workflow processes, electronic commerce, and advanced manufacturing.

John H. Ganter (jganter@sandia.gov) is a Member of the Technical Staff at Sandia National Laboratories. He works in the areas of transportation risk assessment and GIS systems, with additional research interests in GIS interoperability, computer-assisted visualization, and software engineering.

Simson L. Garfinkel is a freelance journalist who covers issues relating to technology and privacy. Garfinkel is the author of five technical books on computer science, including *PGP: Pretty Good Privacy* (O'Reilly & Associates, 1994) and *Practical UNIX and Internet Security* (O'Reilly & Associates, 1996).

Randolph W. Hall (HALL@atlas.usc.edu) is Associate Professor of Industrial and Systems Engineering at the University of Southern California, and Associate Director of its Center for Advanced Transportation Technologies. He has previously worked at Advanced Transit and Highways (PATH) and on the faculty of the University of California at Berkeley.

Susan Jakubiak is a Senior Economist at Apogee Research. She has directed studies of economic impacts, regulatory and policy analysis, infrastructure and investment needs, and innovative financing for both the transportation and environment sectors.

James Keller (jkeller@harvard.edu) is a Research Associate at the Information Infrastructure Project in the Science, Technology and Public Policy Program at Harvard's Kennedy School of Government.

Hans K. Klein is on the faculty of the Institute of Public Policy at George Mason University and a Research Associate at the Information Infrastructure Project at Harvard's Kennedy School of Government.

Stephen Lukasik has been Director of the Advanced Research Projects Agency and Chief Scientist of the Federal Communications Commission. He has also held executive positions at several major corporations. He is a Trustee of Harvey Mudd College and currently serves as Advisor to the CEO of SAIC.

Douglas C. Melcher is a candidate for the Master of Science degree in Technology and Policy at the Massachusetts Institute of Technology. He has worked as an intern at the Federal Communications Commission in the last two sessions of Congress.

Thomas O. Mottl (mottl@tiac.net) is a venture advisor and consultant operating as Stratec Consulting. He was until recently Corporate Vice President and Division Director at TASC. He has also worked at Bell Labs and the University of Michigan.

Federico Peña is the Secretary of the United States Department of Transportation.

Gary Pruitt has worked in the Intelligent Transportation Systems, rail, transit, maritime, and airline segments of the transportation industry. His primary areas of technical expertise are in systems engineering, application of communications and information systems technology, and implementation of industry standards programs.

Daniel Roos (drdr@mit.edu) is Professor of Civil Engineering, Japan Steel Industry Professor, and Director of the Center for Technology, Policy, and Industrial Development at MIT.

Valerie Shuman (vshuman@sei-it.com) is a Venture Development Manager for the Technology Group division of SEI, a national software consulting organization. She is primarily responsible for SEI/TG's telecommunications standards efforts in the area of ITS, and serves on committees of ISO, ITS AMERICA, ITU, TIA, and TRB in that role.

Richard Jay Solomon (richard@rpcp.mit.edu) is Associate Director of the MIT Research Program on Communications Policy, working on social, political, and economic issues related to evolving networks. He is co-author of *The Gordian Knot: Political Gridlock on the Information Highway,* with R. Neuman and L. McKnight (MIT Press, 1996).

Padmanabhan Srinagesh (nagesh@faline.bellcore.com) is a Senior Economist with Bellcore's Information Networking Research Laboratory. His current responsibilities include developing the

Information Superhighway. Before joining Bellcore, Dr. Srinagesh was on the faculties of Williams College and the University of Illinois at Chicago.

Joseph M. Sussman, a member of the MIT faculty for 28 years, is the J.R. East Professor in the Department of Civil and Environmental Engineering. He is currently a member of the ITS America Board of Directors and the Transportation Research Board Executive Committee.

Marsha D. Van Meter is a Student Intern at Sandia National Laboratories. She recently graduated from Eldorado High School in Albuquerque, where she was 5th in a class of 396, and she is currently studying physics at the University of New Mexico.

David A. Whitney (dawhitney@tasc.com) is a Senior Principal member of the Advanced Development Staff at TASC.

Marcus Wigan (marcus.wigan@eng.monash.edu.au) is principal of Oxford Systematics, a decision analysis and strategy consulting organization in Melbourne, Australia. He has worked on freight, transport, policy, and computing issues as a senior staff member of a number of organizations and universities.

Youngbin Yim (ybyim@uclink.berkeley.edu) is a researcher at the University of California, Berkeley, Institute of Transportation Studies. Her current work includes evaluation of the San Francisco Bay Area ATIS field operational test and consumer response to automated highway technologies.

Index

Active sensing, 182
Addressing, 145
Advanced Traffic Management System (ATMS), 218
San Antonio, 302–304
video and, 358
Advanced transportation projects, 215–222
automatic piloting, 220–222
GIS-T/ISTEA Pooled Fund Study, 216–218
route guidance, 219–220
vision enhancement, 220
Advanced Traveler Information Systems (ATIS), 218, 251
FOTs, 252
models, 256
product development, 269
public-sector involvement in, 276
research testbed, 258–259
SmartTraveler, 252–253, 270–275
TravInfo, 252, 258–270
user services, 252
Advanced Vehicle Control and Safety Systems bundle, 33, 123–127
Automated Highway Systems (AHS), 126–127, 132
Intersection Collision Avoidance, 124–125
Lateral Collision Avoidance, 124

Longitudinal Collision Avoidance, 123–124
NII interface, 199
Pre-Crash Restraint Deployment, 126
Safety Readiness, 125–126
user services list, 123
Vision Enhancement for Crash Avoidance, 125
See also Bundles
Advanced Vehicle Control Systems (AVCS), 218
ALI-SCOUT, 282
American National Standards Institute (ANSI), 361
Anonymous technology, 328–330
Applications. See ITS applications
Architecture
ITS, 10–11
system-level, 360
top-down approach, 11
Asynchronous Transfer Mode (ATM), 158, 197
Automated Highway Systems (AHS) service, 126–127
NII application possibilities, 132
See also User services
Automated highways, 88
Automated Ridematching Service (ARMS), 271–272

Automated Roadside Safety Inspection service, 116
  NII application possibilities, 132
  See also User services
Automatic piloting, 220–222
  platooning plan, 220–221
  three-dimensional data source and, 221–222
Automatic Vehicle Identification (AVI), 218
Automatic Vehicle Location (AVL), 218
AUTO-SCOUT, 282

Bandwidth
  forecasts, 358
  requirements, 153–156, 356
  video requirements, 155
BART (Bay Area Rapid Transit), 237–238, 295, 306–309
  MFS Network Technologies (MFSNT), 306–307
Bundles, 129, 139
  Advanced Vehicle Control and Safety Systems, 33, 123–127
  Commercial Vehicle Operations, 33, 114–120
  defined, 30
  Electronic Payment, 33, 113–114
  Emergency Management, 33, 120–122
  Public Transportation Operations, 33, 108–113
  Travel and Transportation Management, 32, 95–104
  Travel Demand Management, 32, 104–108

Case studies, 296–312
  accountability and, 315–316
  cost and, 312–315
  lessons learned, 312–318
  operations and maintenance and, 316
  organizational implications, 318–319
  reliability and, 315

resource availability and, 316–317
  timing and, 317
  upgrades and reserve capacity and, 317–318
CA/T project. *See* Massachusetts Central Artery/Tunnel (CA/T) project
CDPD (Cellular Digital Packet Data), 143
Classifier, 184–185
Clinton-Gore Administration, NII vision, 27
Commercial fleet operators, 135
Commercial Vehicle Administration Processes service, 118
  NII application possibilities, 132
  See also User services
Commercial Vehicle Electronic Clearance service, 115–116
  NII interface, 130
  See also User services
Commercial Vehicle Operations bundle, 33, 114–120
  Automated Roadside Safety Inspection, 116
  Commercial Vehicle Electronic Clearance, 115–116
  estimated daily traffic, 139
  Freight Mobility, 119–120
  Hazardous Material Incident Response, 118–119
  NII interface, 129
  On-Board Safety Monitoring, 116–118
  user services list, 114–115
  See also Bundles
Commercial Vehicle Operations (CVO), 218
Common benefits, 54–55
Common policy concerns, 59–88
Communications
  bandwidth requirements, 153–156
  cost and efficiency, 166–167
  cost considerations, 160–162
  endpoints and characteristics, 151–153

higher-level services, 161
infrastructure, 154
ITS issues, 142–145
loading, 140–142
mobile requirements, 145
operations and support, 161–162
policy concerns, 363–364
procurement policy assessment, 169–170
security and, 159
strategic objectives, 157
theoretical analysis, 162–166
traffic characteristics, 156
transport, 160–161
traveler information system, 254–255
wireless, 182
wireline, 151–156
Commuter Transportation Services (CTS), 271, 272
Competitive auction, 245–246
Congestion, 163
ConnDOT incident management system, 297–298
Content regulation, 64, 65, 67
COPILOT, 284–286
market-based approach, 288
negative lesson, 287
See also Euro-Scout
Copyright/data issues, 349
Cost
case studies and, 312–315
communications, 160–162
Internet user, 198
kiosk, 273
networks and, 156–157
ROW next-best alternative, 241–242
SmartTraveler, 273–274
spectrum, 144–145
traffic management facilities, 82
Coverage, 153
Cross-Industry Working Team (XIWT), 47, 362
Cross-ownership, 64

Data integrity, 142
Data ownership, 64, 350–352

Data storage, 331–333
misuse of, 332–333
opportunities of, 331–332
Dataveillance, 348
Dedicated networks, 13, 15
Demand management, 69–71
Demand Management and Operations service, 107–108
NII application possibilities, 131
See also User services
Department of Transportation. See DOT
Deployment, 3, 146, 164, 179–180
application, 369
Euro-Scout, 279–280
finance and, 281
functionality and, 281
general issues in, 280–282
NII/ITS infrastructure problems, 353
political considerations, 281
private-sector, 282
rapid, 341
technology issues and, 280–281
Digital Teleport Incorporated (DTI), 311
DOT
FCC inquiries and, 86
FHWA, 41, 202
ITS Architecture Program, 34, 42
ITS role, 10, 38
Joint Program Office, 325, 362
JOT, 41
key role for, 370
state, 218
Driver advisory, 96
Driver privacy, 324–340
anonymous technology and, 328–340
issue of, 326–328
ITS data and, 330–333
ITS monitoring and, 333–335
non-privacy principles, 335–339
See also Privacy

Electronic Data Interchange (EDI), 33, 75
Electronic payment agents, 188–189

Electronic Payment bundle, 33, 113–114
estimated daily traffic, 139
NII interface, 129
See also Bundles
Electronic Payment services, 113–114
NII interface, 130
wireline communications and, 153
See also User services
Electronic Toll and Traffic Management (ETTM), 326–327
Electronic toll payment, 329
Emergency Management bundle, 33, 120–122
estimated daily traffic, 139
NII interface, 129
See also Bundles
Emergency Notification and Personal Security service, 120–121. See also User services
Emergency Vehicle Management service, 121–122. See also User services
Emergency vehicles, 135
Emissions Testing and Mitigation service, 103–104
NII application possibilities, 131
See also User services
Enabling services, 30–31
En-Route Driver Information service, 96–97
NII interface, 130
See also User services
En-Route Transit Information service, 110–111
NII interface, 130
See also User services
E-PASS, 333
Era of the Enhanced Vehicle (2010), 29
Era of Transportation Management (2000–2005), 29
Era of Travel Information and Fleet Management (1995–1999), 28–29
Euro-Scout, 279–288
ALI-SCOUT, 282
AUTO-SCOUT, 282

deployment, 279–280
development lessons, 282–283
financing, 283–284
functionality, 283
initial pricing, 286
LISB field test and, 284
parts, 282
politics and, 284
technical design, 283
See also COPILOT

Failure problems, 341–344
Federal Aviation Administration (FAA), 222
Federal Railroad Administration (FRA), 41, 42
Federal roles, 23–56
alternative models, 49–50
coordination, 369
in ITS, 41–43
ITS future and, 222–225
in NII, 39–41
in policy concerns, 363–364
private sector as role model, 50
program evolutions and, 35–38
programmatic elements, 46
in standards development, 205–207
in standards establishment, 84
today, 38–44
Federal Transit Administration (FTA), 41, 42
Fiber-optic networks, 145–146
for broadband land-line communications, 293
communications capacity, 294
First-order interactions, 356
Freight Mobility service, 119–120. See also User services
Funding
facility, 82–83
of infrastructure facilities, 82–83
NII sources, 40–41

GATT TRIPS protocols, 350
General Services Administration (GSA), 359–360

Geographic Information System (GIS)
building, 350
data models, 211
defined, 210
transportation software, 350
Geographic Information Systems for
Transportation (GIS-T), 213–214
defined, 313
information flow, 213–214
ISTEA Pooled Fund Study, 216–218
as short-term tool, 214
Geospatial data, 209–225
advanced transportation projects
and, 215
flow of, 213–214
GIS-T, 213–214
linear referencing, 214–215
at state/local levels, 213–215
See also Spatial data
Global interoperability, 191–208
Global Positioning System (GPS), 98
open standard for, 76
utilizing, 75
Government initiatives, 83–87

Hazardous Material Incident Response
service, 118–119. See also User services
High-definition television (HDTV), 73
High-Performance Computing and
Communications (HPCC), 36, 39
"National Challenges," 29–30
support, 365
Highway right-of-way (HROW), 229–
249
conduit space on, 169
defined, 168
issues, 168–169
maximum value of, 241
sharing, 168, 169
See also Right-of-way (ROW)
Highway Trust Fund (HTF), 11
allocation guidelines, 359, 365
allocations, 358
implementation standards, 365
requirements, 358

state activities and, 365

Identification issues, 347–349
Implementation
ITS issues, 48–49
NII issues, 46–48
Incident Management service, 101–103
NII application possibility, 131
wireline communications and, 152
See also User services
Information
database systems, 13
flows, 344–345
generating wealth from, 349–350
interconnected, 68
NII and, 62
open systems, 86–87
ownership of, 61, 350–359
policy concerns, 363–364
Information Infrastructure Task Force
(IITF), 18, 39–40, 361, 366
standards and, 202
Working Group, 47
Information issues, 344–350
identification, 347–349
information flows and, 344–345
real-time/retrospective access, 346–
347
surveillance, 346
wealth and, 349–350
Information service content, 93–133
Information Service Providers (ISPs)
defined, 136
roles of, 136–138
service type examples, 137
Infrastructure
communications, 154
deployment, 179–180
elements of, 5
facilities, funding of, 82–83
general-purpose communication, 15
to increase size and competitiveness,
62
integration, 5–6
ITS requirements, 12–17
physical, 30

Infrastructure (*continued*)
  shared opportunities, 17
  shared physical, 357–360
  transportation information, 32
Institutional issues, 293–320
  case studies, 296–312
  lessons learned, 313–318
Integration infrastructure
  defined, 5
  ITS, 6
Intelligent agents, 177–189
  defined, 178, 184
  electronic payment, 188–189
  information access, 185, 188
  interoperability and, 187–188
  ITS information space and, 185–186
  sensor technology and, 186–187
  software components, 184
Intelligent Transportation Systems. *See*
  ITS
Intelligent Vehicle Highway Systems
  Act (IVHS), 6, 28, 42
  stakeholder implications, 223–224
Interaction
  first-order, 356
  focal points, 357–367
  user service, 127–128
  See also Policy coordination
Interconnected information, 68
Interfaces
  devices for, 68
  driver, 123
  ITS system, 187
  mobile, 204
  NII, 129, 130
  traveler information system, 255
Intermodal Surface Transportation
  Efficiency Act (ISTEA), 28
  GIS-T Pooled Fund Study, 216–218
  transportation planning require-
    ments, 216
Intermodal transportation, 88
International Standards Organization
  (ISO), 194
  Technical Committees, 194, 201
  Working Groups, 200, 201

  See also Standards
International Telecommunications
  Union (ITU), 194
Internet
  characteristics, 196–197
  development model, 368
  as standards model, 195–200
  store-and-forward architecture, 196
  success, reasons for, 197–198
  user cost, 198
  See also TCP/IP
Internet Protocol (IP)
  defined, 195
  See also TCP/IP
Interoperability, 74–77
  across applications, 360
  global, 191–208
  intelligent agents and, 187–188
  TCP/IP, 197
Intersection Collision Avoidance service, 124–125. *See also* User services
In-vehicle signing, 96, 97
ISDN, 367–368
ITS, 4–6
  addressing, 145
  advanced, 220–222
  applications, 150
  architecture and system coherence,
    10–11
  bandwidth forecasts, 358
  bandwidth requirements, 153–156,
    356
  barriers, 18
  challenges, 182–183
  communication issues, 142–145
  communications procurement policy
    assessment, 169–170
  Congressional actions related to, 44
  coverage, 143
  data types, 330
  demand management, 69–71
  deployment, 3, 146, 164, 179–180,
    279
  development, 3
  DOT role in, 10, 38
  federal activity opportunities, 7–9

federal involvement in, 2, 41–43, 47
fiber optics and, 145–146
with fixed facilities, 2
in framework of NII, 94–95
geospatial data for, 209–225
global interoperability, 191–208
government role in, 6–10
implementation issues, 48–49, 318
information service content, 93–133
information space, 185–186
infrastructure requirements, 12–17
initial, 218–220
integration infrastructure, 6
intelligent agents and, 177–189
interoperability, 74–77
interoperable set of implementations, 8
knowledge infrastructure, 6
latency of data processing, 144
law and, 9
linkages, steering through federal action, 53–55
location and identification system, 347
management of, 7
mapping of, 180–182
market penetration, 143–144
market size, 75
milestones, 37
mission of, 4
mobile communication requirements, 145
monitoring, 333–335
national scope and, 24–25
negative views of, 80
networks, 17
NII boundaries and, 4
NII common benefits, 54–55
NII relationship with, 149–151, 192–193
as NII subset, 95
NII support for, 53
opportunities, 18, 331–332
overview of, 24–35
paradigm, 60
planners, 83

policy issues, 65–67
privacy and, 80–82, 144
privacy-sensitive data, 330–333
program evolution, 35–38
public/private partnerships in, 255–258
requirements, 182–183
secure, 328–330
service adequacy, 143–144
service reliability, 143
shared resources and, 247–249
snapshot, 26
spectrum availability/costs, 144–145
spectrum management, 71–74
standardization issues, 2
standards, 198–200
standards efforts, 200–204
success barriers, 61–63
support for NII, 54
system interfaces, 187
technical standards, 74–77
today, 44–45
traffic and, 62
universal basic service and, 66
user services, 31–33, 95–104
vehicles and, 62
vision of, 28–35
vision stages, 28–29
See also Bundles; NII
ITS America, 180, 199, 366
ITS applications, 30
areas of, 8–9
communications requirement, 12–13
deployment, 369
infrastructure elements and, 14–15
interoperability across, 360
ITS Architecture Program, 34, 202
ITS National Program Plan, 49
ITS National Systems Architecture, 229–233
design layers, 230
illustrated, 231
institutional layer, 232
physical prototype, 233
user services and, 232
ITS/NII Workshop, ix

Knowledge infrastructure, 6

Latency
 of data processing, 144
 standards, 204
Lateral Collision Avoidance service, 124
Liability, 9
Linear referencing, 214–215
Loading
 analyses, 141
 communications, 140–142
 illustrated, 141
Longitudinal Collision Avoidance service, 123–124. *See also* User services

Market
 complexity, 368
 coordination, 359
 for ITS service, 362
 penetration, 143–144
 research, 243–244
Massachusetts Central Artery/Tunnel
  (CA/T) project, 298–302
MBTA (Massachusetts Bay Transportation Authority), 243
Metropolitan communications requirements, 134–147
 communications loading observations, 140–142
 fiber-optic networks and, 145–146
 ISP roles, 136–138
 ITS communication issues, 142–145
 ITS information/data volume estimates, 138–140
 viewpoints, 134–136
 See also Communications
Metropolitan Planning Organizations
  (MPOs), 36
 information revolution and, 212
 role, 230
Metropolitan Transit Authority (MTA),
  271, 272
MHTD (Missouri Highway and Transportation Department), 295, 309–
  312
Mobile communications, 16

Mobile interfaces, 204
Mobile spectrum planning, 85–86
Monitoring, 333–335
 auditability and, 343
 examples, 333–334
Motorist Information Systems Project
  (MISP), 304–306
Multimedia standards developing or-
  ganizations, 203

National Automated Highway Systems
  Consortium (NAHSC), 29, 43
National Information Infrastructure
  Advisory Council (NIIAC), 40
*The National Information Infrastructure:
  Agenda for Action*, 149, 150
National Information Infrastructure.
  See NII
National ITS Architecture Develop-
  ment Program, 10
National Telecommunications and
  Information Administration
  (NTIA), 40
Needs-based compensation, 244–245
Networks
 communications traffic and, 156
 costs and, 156–157
 fiber-optic, 145–146, 293
 ITS, 17
 special-purpose vs. general-purpose,
  156–160
 special requirements and, 157
NII, 129
 applications, 149
 challenges, 182–183
 Clinton-Gore Administration's vision,
  27
 component functional layers, 30
 congressional actions related to, 43
 core network management services,
  31
 data and knowledge management
  services, 30
 defined, 3
 demand management, 69–71
 deployment, 179–180

distribution systems, ix
emerging technology and, 94
enabling services, 30–31
entertainment-based vision, 27
federal areas of emphasis, 47
federal involvement in, 39–41
funding sources, 40–41
global interoperability, 191–208
horizontal technology base, 36
IITA, 40
implementation issues, 46–48
information and, 62
Internet-based vision, 26–27
interoperability, 74–77
ITS as subset of, 95
ITS boundaries and, 4
ITS common benefits, 54–55
ITS relationship with, 149–151, 192–
 193
ITS support for, 54
linkages, steering through federal
 action, 53–55
milestones, 37
national scope, 24–25
organizational focus, lack of, 59–60
overview, 24–36
policy issues, 63–65
privacy and, 80–82
program evolution, 35–38
programs, 25
security/protection services, 31
shared resources and, 247–249
snapshot, 26
software interoperability and, 179
spectrum management, 71–74
spinoff, 25
standards, 198–200
standards effort, 200–204
success barriers, 51–53
support for ITS, 53
system-level architecture and, 360
Task Force, 366–367
TCP/IP and, 360
technical standards, 74–77
today, 44–45
translation/interchange services, 31

travel, view of, 61
universal basic service and, 63–64
user service interaction, 127–128
vision of, 5, 25–27
See also ITS
Non-privacy principles, 335–339
Notice of Proposal Rule-Making
 (NPRM), 205
NSFNet, 368–369

Object Management Group (OMG),
 362
Object-Oriented Database Manage-
 ment Systems (OODBMSs), 217
On-board components, 14
On-Board Safety Monitoring service,
 116–117
NII application possibilities, 132
See also User services
Open information system, 86–87
Ownership
 data, 64, 350–352
 models, 313–314
 rights, 68

Palmer Bellevue, 244
Personal communication systems
 (PCSs), 144
Personal privacy, 9
Personalized Public Transit service,
 111–112
NII application possibilities, 132
See also User services
Physical infrastructure, 30
Policy concerns, 59–88
 authentication, 364
 common, 68–83
 communications, 363–364
 demand management, 69–71
 facility funding, 82–83
 information, 363–364
 intellectual property, 364
 interoperability, 74–77
 liability, 364
 privacy, 80–81, 364
 spectrum management, 71–74

Policy concerns (*continued*)
technical standards, 74–77
universal basic service, 77–79
Policy coordination, 355–370
first-order interactions, 356
information/communications policy
concerns, 363–364
private-sector, 364–367
shared physical infrastructure, 357–
360
standards development, 360–363
technology development, 360–363
Policy issues
ITS, 65–67
NII, 63–65
Pre-Crash Restraint Deployment service, 126
Pre-Trip Travel Information service,
105
NII interface, 130
See also User services
Privacy, 57, 144, 364
DOT Joint Program Office and, 325
"Draft Final" principles, 335–338
driver, 324–340
expectation of, 326
information use and, 339
ITS and, 80–82, 325
ITS problems, 325–326
monitoring and, 333–335
NII and, 80–81
non-privacy principles and, 335–339
personal, 9
policy concerns and, 80–81, 364
rights of, 64, 68
tradeoffs, 349
voluntary systems and, 328
See also Security
Private-sector initiatives, 364–367
Private vehicles, 134
Public goods, 163–164
Public switched telephone network
(PSTN), 197–198
Public Transit Management Center
(PTMC), 153

Public Transportation Management
service, 109–110
wireline communications and, 152–
153
See also User services
Public Transportation Operations
bundle, 33, 108–113
En-Route Transit Information, 110–
111
estimated daily traffic, 139
NII interface, 129
Personalized Public Transit, 111–112
Public Transportation Management,
109–110
Public Travel Security, 112–113
user service list, 108
See also Bundles
Public Travel Security service, 112–113
wireline communications and, 153
See also User services
Public/private partnerships, 255–258
sector roles, 267–268
Volpe guidelines and, 270

Rate regulation, 65
Real-time access, 346–347
Regional Multimodal Traveler Infor-
mation Center (RMTIC), 151–152
Regulation
content, 64, 65, 67
rate, 65
of tele-activities, 85
Relational Database Management Sys-
tem (RDBMS), 210, 217
Research and Special Projects Admin-
istration (RSPA), 41–42
Retrospective access, 347
Retrospective data, 346
Ride Matching and Reservation ser-
vice, 106–107
NII interface, 130
See also User services
Right-of-way (ROW)
assets, 246, 248
highway, 234, 242

leases, 242–243
owners, 235, 245
public roadway, 235
railroad, 242
trenching capacity, 239
value of, 239–247, 341
See also Highway Right-of-Way
    (HROW)
Rights
    ownership, 68
    privacy, 64, 68
Roadside element deployment, 13
Route guidance, 219–220
    planar technology and, 219
    spatial data and, 219–220
Route Guidance service, 97–98
    NII application possibilities, 131
    See also User services

Safety Readiness service, 125–126. See
    also User services
San Antonio ATMS, 302–304
San Jose TSMP and MISP, 304–306
Scalability, 370
Security
    communications and, 159
    universal scheme, 203
    See also Privacy
Sensors, intelligent agents and, 186–
    187
Services
    adequacy of, 143–144
    deployment of, 16
    development of, 16
    enabling, 30
    NII and ITS overlapping of, 30–31
    points of, 13
    reliability of, 143
    See also User services
Shared physical infrastructure, 357–
    360
Shared resources
    in highway rights of way, 229–249
    ITS/NII objectives and, 247–249
    objectives, relationship to, 246–247
    projects involving, 233–239

revenue and, 314
values, estimating methods, 239–247
Siemens. See Euro-Scout
Smart cards, 329
    problems with, 343
    with public-key encryption, 344
SmarTraveler, 327
SmartTraveler, 252–253, 270–275
    Automated Ridematching Service
        (ARMS), 271–272, 274
    evaluation, 272–275
    lessons learned, 275–277
    user interfaces, 270
    See also TravInfo FOT
Software components, 178, 184–185.
    See also Intelligent agents
SONET, 161
Spatial data, 209
    route guidance and, 219–220
    for transportation applications, 210–
        211
    See also Geospatial data
Spectrum
    allocation, 73
    availability, 144–145
    cost, 144–145
    efficient use of, 360
    management, 71–74
    planning, mobile, 85–86
    radio, 205
    resource management, 64, 65, 66
Standards, 193–195
    ANSI, 361
    creating, 204–205
    cutting-edge technology, 194
    development, 360–363
    evolution of, 360
    government role in development of,
        205–207
    IISP and, 202
    international organizations, 361
    Internet as model for, 195–200
    ITS, 198–200
    ITS/NII efforts, 200–204
    latency, 204
    models, 361

Standards (*continued*)
  multimedia organizations, 203
  NII, 198–200
  required, 202–204
  successful, 207
  universal, 205
  See also International Standards Organization (ISO)
Success
  barriers, 51–53
  Internet, 197–198
  problems, 341–353
Surveillance, 346
System interfaces, 187

Tariffs, 166
TCP/IP, 195–198
  defined, 195
  NII and, 360
  See also Internet
Technical standards, 74–77
Tele-activity regulation, 85
Telecommunications
  infrastructure, 5
  issues, 350
  policy decisions, 356
Telecommunications Industry Association (TIA), 194
Tiger files, 350
TII, 56
  development of, 34
  information space, 185–186
  requirements, 180
  scope of, 178
  supported elements, 178
  See also ITS; NII
Traffic
  capacity, 61
  congestion, 69
  daily, estimated, 139
  ITS and, 62
  management, facilities cost, 82
  real-time control of, 181
  See also Traffic data
Traffic and Freeway Management Centers (T&FMCs), 152–153

communication bandwidth requirements and, 153–156
  function of, 152
  PTMC and, 153
  video monitor, 153
Traffic Control service, 100–101
  wireline communications and, 151–152
  See also User services
Traffic data
  historical, 84–85
  models, 84–85
  public real-time, 83–84
  See also Traffic
Traffic management center (TMC), 136
Traffic Signal Management Project (TSMP), 304–306
Transit vehicles, 135
Transmission Control Protocol (TCP)
  defined, 195
  See also TCP/IP
Transportation Information Infrastructure. *See* TII
Travel and Transportation Management bundle, 32, 95–104
  Emissions Testing and Mitigation, 103–104
  En-Route Driver Information, 96–97
  estimated daily traffic, 139
  Incident Management, 101–103
  NII interface and, 129
  Route Guidance, 97–98
  Traffic Control, 100–101
  Traveler Services Information, 98–100
  user services list, 95–96
  See also Bundles
Travel Demand Management bundle, 32, 104–108
  Demand Management and Operations, 107–108
  estimated daily traffic, 139
  NII interface and, 129
  Pre-Trip Travel Information, 105

Ride Matching and Reservation, 106–107
See also Bundles
Traveler information systems, 251–257
lessons learned, 275–277
SmartTraveler, 252–253, 270–275
TravInfo, 252, 258–270
Traveler Services Information service, 98–100
NII interface, 130
See also User services
TravInfo FOT, 252, 258–270
Advisory Committee (AC), 259
ATIS testbed concept, 259
defined, 258, 262
disagreement resolution, 268
end products and services, 264
evaluation, 259–261
fee collection, 264
goals, 262
institutional issues, 263–266
lessons learned, 275–277
Management Board (MB), 259, 267
organizational structure, 262–263
partner performance and responsibility, 266–267
public/private sector roles, 267–268
Steering Committees (SC), 259, 263, 265, 266–267
transportation vs. economic impacts, 262
Working Groups, 267
See also SmartTraveler
Travel Information Center (TIC), 264, 268

Universal basic service, 65, 77–79
defined, 63–64
ITS and, 66
likelihood of, 79
NII and, 63
See also User services
Universal connectivity and interoperability, 63, 64, 66
User rate regulation, 64, 66

User service bundles. *See* Bundles; User services
User services, 30, 95–133
ATIS, 252
Automated Highway System (AHS), 126–127
Automated Roadside Safety Inspection, 116
Commercial Vehicle Administrative Processes, 118
Commercial Vehicle Electronic Clearance, 115–116
definition of, 93–94
Demand Management and Operations, 107–108
Electronic Payment, 113–114
Emergency Notification and Personal Security, 120–121
Emergency Vehicle Management, 121–122
Emissions Testing and Mitigation, 103–104
En Route Driver Information, 96–97
En-Route Transit Information, 110–111
Freight Mobility, 119–120
groups of, 94
Hazardous Material Incident Response, 118–119
Incident Management, 101–103
Intersection Collision Avoidance, 124–125
ITS, 31–33
Lateral Collision Avoidance, 124
Longitudinal Collision Avoidance, 123–124
NII interaction, 127–128
On-Board Safety Monitoring, 116–117
Personalized Public Transit, 111–112
Pre-Crash Restraint Deployment, 126
Pre-Trip Travel Information, 105
Public Transportation Management, 109–110
Public Travel Security, 112–113

User services (*continued*)
  Ride Matching and Reservation, 106–
    107
  Route Guidance, 97–98
  Safety Readiness, 125–126
  security and privacy issues, 188
  in subsystem centers, 232
  Traffic Control, 100–101
  Travel and Transportation Manage-
    ment, 95–96
  Traveler Services Information, 98–
    100
  Vision Enhancement for Crash Avoid-
    ance, 125
  See also Bundles
User-level views, 135

Vehicles
  emergency, 135
  ITS and, 62
  private, 134
  transit, 135
  views, 134–135
Video bandwidth requirements, 155
Views, 134–136
  traffic management center, 136
  user-level, 135
  vehicle, 134–135
Vision enhancement, 220
Vision Enhancement for Crash Avoidance service, 125
Volpe guidelines, 270

Wireless communications, 182
Wireline communications, 151–156
  communication bandwidth require-
    ments, 153–156
  Electronic Payment and, 153
  Incident Management and, 152
  Public Transportation Management
    and, 152–153
  Public Travel Safety and, 153
  Traffic Control and, 151–152
  See also Communications